To Aunt Joy

Best wishes

HAPPY Baking

Roland Mesnier

P9-BYK-085

BY ROLAND MESNIER

WITH LAUREN CHATTMAN

PHOTOGRAPHER: MAREN CARUSO

ILLUSTRATOR: JOHN BURGOYNE

DESSERT
UNIVERSITY

More Than 300 Spectacular Recipes

and Essential Lessons from

White House Pastry Chef

Roland Mesnier

SIMON & SCHUSTER
New York   London   Toronto   Sydney

SIMON & SCHUSTER
Rockefeller Center
1230 Avenue of the Americas
New York, NY 10020

Copyright © 2004 by Roland Mesnier and Lauren Chattman
Illustrations copyright © 2004 by John Burgoyne
Photographs copyright © 2004 by Maren Caruso
All rights reserved,
including the right of reproduction
in whole or in part in any form.

SIMON & SCHUSTER and colophon are registered trademarks
of Simon & Schuster, Inc.

For information about special discounts for bulk purchases,
please contact Simon & Schuster Special Sales:
1-800-456-6798 or business@simonandschuster.com

Designed by Katy Riegel

Manufactured in the United States of America

10   9   8   7   6   5   4   3   2   1

Library of Congress Cataloging-in-Publication Data

Mesnier, Roland.
    Dessert university : more than 300 spectacular recipes and essential lessons from White
House pastry chef Roland Mesnier / by Roland Mesnier with Lauren Chattman.
        p.   cm.
    Includes index.
    1. Desserts.   I. Chattman, Lauren.   II. Title.

TX773. M465   2004
641.8'6—dc22   2003067335

ISBN 0-7432-2317-9

Photography: Maren Caruso
Food Styling: Kim Konecny
Prop Styling: Kim Konecny and Erin Quon
Photo Assistant: Faiza Ali

I WORKED FOR many great chefs before I took the helm at the White House pastry kitchen. This book is dedicated to them, for teaching me so much about creating fine desserts and for inspiring me to strive for excellence every day in my work.

ACKNOWLEDGMENTS

I would like to thank the following people for their help and encouragement during the course of my career and as I wrote this book:

My wife, Martha, for her patience during my long absences from home due to time spent on the job, and also for typing and proofing the many pages of this book. Also my son, George, for his support.

My brother, Jean Mesnier, who introduced me to the pastry world. All my other brothers and sisters for their support: Gabriel Mesnier, Lucien Mesnier, Geneviève Guyez, Bernard Mesnier, Serge Mesnier, René Mesnier, and Marie Thérèse Mesnier.

Sydny Miner, who helped me to get started and introduced me to my wise and knowledgeable agent, Angela Miller.

Lauren Chattman, my writer, who does beautiful work.

Maren Caruso, the supremely talented photographer who took the gorgeous pictures for this book.

Faiza Ali, for ably assisting Maren.

Kim Konecny, the food stylist who did such a wonderful job preparing the desserts to be photographed, and who, with Erin Quon, handled the prop styling.

John Burgoyne, for his precise and elegant illustrations.

Katherine Ness, for eagle-eyed copy editing.

At Simon & Schuster, Laura Holmes in editorial; Jackie Seow in the art department;

Jonathon Brodman in copy editing; Katy Riegel in design; and Elizabeth Hayes in publicity.

Ted Conklin and the staff of the American Hotel in Sag Harbor, New York. A place for great inspiration!

Jack Bishop, for his advice as I was writing.

For inspiring me to always strive higher and higher, a special thank-you to First Ladies Rosalynn Carter, Nancy Reagan, Barbara Bush, Hillary Rodham Clinton, and Laura Bush.

I would like to thank all the executive chefs who have influenced my career so greatly: Pierre Chambrin, Hans Rafert, Henry Haller (The White House); Albert Schnarwyler (The Homestead, Hot Springs, Virginia); Eddie Gurrett (The Princess Hotel, Bermuda); Louis Virot (The Savoy Hotel, London); Lucien Maujean (Hôtel George V, Paris); Hermann Rusch (The Greenbrier Hotel); Kranke Konditorei (pastry shop in Hamburg, Germany); Herman Hesing (pastry shop in Hanover, Germany); and my two apprenticeship master chefs, Paul Maurivard and Raymond Ligney.

Special thanks to all my colleagues, friends, and supporters: Michel Finel for always sharing ideas; Michel Galand for his friendship and support; Michel Bus for his hospitality while in Sag Harbor; Yvon Hezard, my good friend and a very talented pastry chef; Jean Marc Raynaud, a gifted chef who is always there with words of encouragement and hospitality; Michel Gaudin for his wisdom and knowledge; Georges Carlioz, a very good friend.

A special thanks to my good friend Wolfgang Bierer.

A big thank-you to the wonderful full-time and part-time staff at the White House Pastry Shop. And special thanks to Susie Morrison, for holding down the fort while I finished the book.

My thanks to Gary Walters, Chief Usher at the White House, and to the entire Usher's Office.

Thank-you to Mr. Bodo von Alvensleben, former general manager of the Princess Hotel in Bermuda, for encouraging me and making it possible for me to exhibit at the culinary salons in New York City.

Many thanks to Johnson & Wales University for my thirty years' affiliation with them. I want to thank also the Académie de Cuisine and its owner, François Dionot, and the school's wonderful pastry chef, Mark Ramsdel.

Many thanks to Bernard DuClos, of Valrhona Chocolate, for providing outstanding chocolate, and to Brian Maynard and Justin Newby for the donations from KitchenAid.

CONTENTS

DESSERT
UNIVERSITY

INTRODUCTION

Devoted to Dessert

EVER SINCE I WAS A BOY growing up in the very small town of Bonnay in France, I have had a deep admiration for fine pastry and a curiosity about how it is made. On my way to school each morning, I would pass the local bakery, where I would peek in and see the red-hot coals of the oven. I would inhale the aroma of fresh yeast and baking bread as I walked to my classes. My family had an account at the bakery, and it was my job to bring home a loaf for lunch every day. In addition to bread, this bakery made beautiful croissants, and one day I found them irresistible. I requested one and ate it on my way home. When my mother got the bill at the end of the month, she was shocked. Money was tight, and croissants were not in the budget. But she forgave me eventually. As it turns out, sampling croissants on my way home was as much a part of my education as the lessons I learned in school.

At the age of twelve I took a summer job at a nearby pastry shop where my older brother was already well established. At fourteen I began a more formal apprenticeship that lasted for three years. From there it was a long and exciting journey to the kitchen of the White House, where I served as Executive Pastry Chef for twenty-five years. In all that time, my desire to learn and to improve my skills has not diminished. I have also become a teacher myself, passing on the lessons I have learned to a new generation of pastry chefs training in the United States.

This book is the result of those years of studying, working, and teaching. I am happy and proud to share the techniques and recipes that I have refined during the course of my career. Making wonderful desserts and serving them to kings, queens, presidents, and statesmen was a source of joy and satisfaction for me. I hope that you will derive just as much pleasure, and feel the same sense of accomplishment when you serve dessert to family and friends.

My Education in Pastry

From my very early days as a kitchen apprentice, I devoted myself entirely to learning everything I could about making desserts. My first teacher was my older brother Jean, who let me hang around and help out in his pastry shop to see if I would like the work. A formal apprenticeship in a larger town followed. The hours were long, my master was stern, and the salary was next to nothing, but at the end of three years I felt only the urge to travel the world and understand more about this fascinating art.

If I had not been truly committed to becoming a chef, I would have been discouraged by the hard life of a pastry assistant. My next job, at a very fine shop in Hanover, Germany, paid so little that I barely had enough money to cover my rent and the cost of getting to work. I had about 25 cents a day budgeted for food. On my way home at night I would stop and play the slot machine at a coffee shop. If I won, I would buy dinner. If I lost, I'd eat the apple that I had taken from the kitchen. For a year I fantasized about the cold cuts on display in the window of a delicatessen nearby. When I received a small bonus at the end of my time at the shop, my first thought was, "Watch out, Cold Meat Platter, here I come!" But I left with extreme gratitude toward the chef because he was the one who really taught me the foundations of good pastry. It was by his side that I learned how to bake all kinds of basic cakes and cookies. Here, also, I learned how to work with chocolate to make a variety of classic candies and glossy decorations.

I moved to Hamburg next, to a family-owned pastry shop and tearoom famous for its marzipan. At Christmastime the shop looked like a fabulous fairyland, decorated with every kind of marzipan figurine imaginable. I loved working with marzipan, copying the traditional pieces and experimenting with new shapes. The shop became like home to me, so it was with great sadness that I forced myself to leave. But I knew that there was more to learn before I could ever run a kitchen of my own.

I arrived at the kitchen of the Savoy Hotel in London, clutching my letters of recommendation but speaking no English. This was the place where all of the really ambitious young chefs wanted to work. The quality of the food and of the service in the hotel restaurant was unbelievable, unmatched by any other establishment at the time. All desserts were made to order and assembled tableside. A Peach Melba, probably the simplest dessert on the extensive menu, became a full-scale production at the Savoy. First, a peach was carefully chosen from the storeroom, dropped in boiling water to remove its skin, and pitted so that it remained whole. It was placed in a glass bowl, and that bowl was placed on top of a silver bowl of crushed ice. A portion of ice cream was placed in another glass bowl over ice. The maître d' would carry the peach, ice cream, melba sauce, whipped cream, and almonds out to the diner on a huge silver tray lined with a white linen napkin and assemble the dessert, topping the peach with as much or as little of the melba sauce, whipped cream, and almonds as the diner desired. I carry so many lessons with me from the Savoy about choosing quality ingredients and preparing them meticulously. I also learned much about presentation and the theatricality of tableside service that made dessert truly exciting. As a result of my experience at the Savoy, my desserts absolutely must be beautiful and presented with a flourish if possible, because I like to hear "oohs and aahs" when they are brought to the table.

The head chef at the Savoy was an amazing manager who inspired a staff of about eighty chefs with his gentlemanly and calm manner. He was demanding but fair. If you made a mistake he would certainly let you know, but as soon as he was finished reprimanding you, there were no hard feelings and you got back to work. We tried hard to please him, not because we were afraid of him but because we wanted to live up to his standards and become better chefs ourselves. All these years later, if I am struggling to keep my cool in the kitchen when things are going wrong, I remember how this exemplary chef was able to focus on fixing mistakes and then move on.

After making desserts and observing the head chef at the Savoy for quite a while, I was ready to be a head pastry chef. I left London for the Princess Hotel in Bermuda and a kitchen of my own. Any sense of complacency I had about knowing it all was immediately shaken by the new climate, which made me rethink many of the tricks and techniques I had learned in Europe. Through hard work and ingenuity, I was able to produce the desserts I had promised. The experience taught me that no matter how expert I thought I was in pastry and baking, there was always more to learn. This is a lesson that I still carry with me. Knowing that I don't know it all, and wanting to learn something new every day, has made me a better cook and a better teacher.

$\mathcal{B}$ECOMING A TEACHER

Running my own kitchen made me think about how to teach my staff the things they needed to know. I discovered that I enjoyed teaching almost as much as I enjoyed making desserts. When the Greenbrier Hotel in West Virginia called to ask if I would like to lead some pastry courses for guests and apprentices during my time off from the Princess, I had my first formal opportunity to teach. When I moved to the Homestead resort in Hot Springs, Virginia, I continued to run dessert seminars for guests and kitchen apprentices. Remembering my own training, I always demanded that my students master the basics before moving on to more complicated desserts. I was very proud if they left my class able to make a perfect crème caramel or genoise.

In 1979 I was hired by Rosalynn Carter to be the Pastry Chef at the White House. I had applied for the job at the urging of some Washington-based guests of the Homestead who had enjoyed my desserts, but I really had no reason to think that I had a chance. I drove up to Washington for an interview with the First Lady, and after a brief chat, she asked me when I could start! I cannot tell you how shocked I was to realize that all of my studying and working had led to a job making desserts for the President of the United States. I had come a long way from Bonnay.

Working at the White House was a delight. Every day was something new. It was a great challenge, but also a great opportunity, to have to come up with a different dessert for each state dinner, White House function, and First Family event. I felt that my desserts were on view to the world, and I wanted them to be beautiful as well as delicious. It was at the White House that I developed a personal style, refining my ideas about decorating and garnishing until I was satisfied that my desserts were a pleasure to look at as well as to eat.

It seemed only natural to share with aspiring pastry chefs what I had learned before and what I was still learning. I had visited the new professional schools for chefs that were being established around the country and was excited by what I saw. I thought it would be wonderful to teach pastry arts to committed students at a real school, where the subject was taken seriously and there was time and space to learn without having to meet the demands of pastry shop or restaurant business.

I was quite busy at the White House, but when the director of L'Académie de Cuisine in Maryland approached me about developing a professional pastry training program, I eagerly said yes. At the time, there were only a couple of such programs in the United States.

Here was a once-in-a-lifetime chance to influence the way desserts would be made in the future. While designing the curriculum, I thought long and hard about what tomorrow's pastry chefs would need to know. In my off-hours I taught this course. It is still being taught today by a former student, and hundreds of its graduates now work in prestigious restaurant and hotel kitchens around the country.

Although I was on call at the White House twenty-four hours a day (it was not unheard of for me to be summoned to the pastry kitchen at 2 A.M. to make a last-minute cake for the President to carry onto *Air Force One* first thing in the morning), I continued to teach both professional and amateur cooking classes whenever I could. On my days off, I would show an auditorium full of future pastry chefs the tricks of covering a globe of ice cream with hot caramel to create an autumn dessert that looks like a pumpkin. Or I would demonstrate some tricks for making the perfect blueberry muffin to a group of avid weekend bakers. To be honest, teaching was not entirely selfless. Working with eager students, watching them learn, and feeling their enthusiasm often gave me the energy and inspiration I needed to do a good job at the White House.

After cooking at the White House for twenty-five years, I wanted very much to write a book for home cooks. The idea is not as odd as it might sound at first. After all, I devoted a large portion of my working life to making dessert for an American family. Even when the President and First Lady were entertaining hundreds of people, they were still doing so in their home. And a large part of my job was to make the First Family and their guests feel at home. Writing this book has allowed me to refine my ideas about desserts made at home. I have learned so much, and I hope you will too.

A FEW THINGS I HAVE LEARNED ABOUT MAKING GREAT DESSERTS

My dearest hope is to pass on the general principles of good dessert-making revealed to me by my best teachers. In brief, here are five golden rules that have guided me in the kitchen and that inform the rest of this book. They may seem obvious, but it is surprising how many times they are ignored in professional and home kitchens, with sad results.

LEARN THE BASICS AND THEN PRACTICE, PRACTICE, PRACTICE

You can't become a good dessert chef without a solid knowledge of the basics and a lot of experience with your recipes. Don't be discouraged if the first time you whip egg whites they dry out and collapse. Try again. It's a wise idea to perfect your technique before you attempt a Floating Island. Cooking is a practical art. Even if you have a good, detailed recipe to guide you, you still need hands-on experience to truly understand the way the ingredients should come together into a dessert. Perfection isn't an accident—it's the result of taking care and learning from your previous mistakes.

RESPECT THE CLASSICS

Classic recipes are the foundation of dessert-making. There is a lot to learn by making a Chocolate Petit Pot, Apple Tart, or Marjolaine. I am the first one to embrace innovation in the kitchen, but only if it is informed by the past. Take, for example, crème brûlée. I must have tried ten different variations on the basic recipe before I developed my own way of making this dessert. And only after I was satisfied with my version of Vanilla Crème Brûlée did I attempt to develop variations such as Orange Crème Brûlée and Champagne Crème Brûlée with Green Grapes. One of the reasons that I am so confident about the recipes in this book is that all are relatives (however distant) of venerable recipes, and all use time-tested techniques that really work.

VALUE ECONOMY AND SIMPLICITY

I hate to waste time, energy, and ingredients. There is no way I could have produced the number of high-quality desserts that I did at the White House, usually by myself or with just one assistant, if I had not worked with maximum efficiency. If there is a quick way to do something, I will always choose it. If I can think of a way to cut out steps in order to save time, I do so. Nothing makes me happier than figuring out a way to use one mixing bowl instead of two, to save on cleanup time.

My biggest pet peeve is a recipe loaded down with unnecessary ingredients that add nothing more than expense and effort. To me a recipe is truly successful when its ingredient list is pared down so that it contains only the ingredients that truly contribute to its success.

FOCUS ON FLAVOR

This is, after all, what dessert is about. Fresh, natural flavor is the most important quality in any dessert. I am not concerned with richness for its own sake. I prefer a tart filled with plain yogurt, fresh fruit, and a drizzle of red clover honey to one weighted down by heavy pastry cream. A terrine made with lime sorbet, vodka parfait, and frozen raspberries appeals to me more than a leaden chocolate cake. I carefully choose my ingredients and flavor combinations so that the finished dessert will refresh rather than weight you down, no matter how caloric it really is. At many points in the book, I will suggest how to choose ingredients and design your own desserts so that they are as flavorful as possible.

BE AN ARTIST: DEVELOP YOUR TALENT

With the right inspiration, anyone can be creative. Everyone has talent. Dessert is an opportunity to make something beautiful as well as delicious. This doesn't mean that you have to garnish everything with chocolate curlicues or spun sugar bows. It can mean arranging a fruit salad with contrasting colors and shapes that please the eye as well as the palate, or taking the extra step of dusting shortbread cookies with confectioners' sugar and running them under the broiler to give them a beautiful caramelized glaze.

$\mathcal{U}$SING THIS BOOK

When I am teaching in the classroom, I try very hard to stick to the essentials and not overwhelm students with unnecessary detail. If I am giving a lesson on rolling out pie dough, I don't throw out a lot of numbers about the protein content of every different kind of flour. If I am teaching a lesson on tempering chocolate, I don't discourse on the discovery of cacao plants in the 16th century. Personally, I find these subjects fascinating, but they are a distraction for most people who want to learn practical ways to make great desserts. In writing this book, I have tried to replicate my classroom teaching style, which I hope is economical and a little bit entertaining. For information on the science and history of desserts, go to one of many wonderful reference works already out there. For advice on how to make a light and silky Bavarian, on the other hand, turn to Chapter 3.

Different types of advice can be found in different parts of the book. Chapter introductions stick to the basics of making a particular kind of dessert. The introduction to meringues in Chapter 5 has information on choosing eggs, separating them, whether or not cream of tartar is necessary to a good meringue, and what kind of sugar makes the best meringue. Turn to the introduction to Chapter 6 and you will find directions for mixing crêpe batter, cooking the very lightest and most delicate crêpes, and freezing the crêpes for later use.

Throughout each chapter, there are boxes containing information relevant to nearby recipes. In the middle of a group of recipes for cookies that are piped onto baking sheets, there is a box about how to fill and use a pastry bag. In a section on layer cakes, you will find a box about choosing the right buttercream frosting.

Don't skip over the introductions to individual recipes. In writing these, I was less concerned with praising the beauty and flavor of my creation than with providing information that will help you to successfully prepare the dessert. Read the notes carefully for tips on technique, ingredients, and serving suggestions. In the headnote to Chocolate Meringue Mousse, for example, you will be advised to fold your melted chocolate into the meringue while it is still warm so that it won't seize up before it has been completely incorporated. You will also learn to fold the egg whites into the chocolate rather than vice versa, since the chocolate bowl is probably warmer than the egg white bowl, and a cold bowl may chill and harden the chocolate. As a bonus, the headnote includes quick directions for a simple, light chocolate cake made by sandwiching Chocolate Meringue Mousse between layers of Chocolate Meringue and covering the filled layers with the remaining mousse.

Finally, the recipes themselves are like mini-lessons, with specific, step-by-step instructions. Vague language has been banished in favor of precision. In the recipe for Blueberry Sauce, for example, I tell you to avoid stirring and instead to shake the pot several times during cooking to end up with a sauce that is well cooked but has lots of whole fruit. When necessary, I have included illustrations that show you what I mean. Giving puff pastry a double turn is difficult to visualize if you have never done it before. The picture adjacent to the recipe should help.

Basic Ingredients

It struck me once again as I was compiling this list how few ingredients you really need to make dessert. Many impressive and delicious recipes in this book can be made from items that you probably have in your pantry, refrigerator, and freezer right now. I am not the kind of chef who will send you scurrying to six different stores for obscure ingredients. For the most part, you will find the makings of my desserts in the supermarket, with perhaps a trip to the farmers' market for some local fruit.

When I do ask for a special ingredient, you can be sure that it is because the result is well worth the trouble. I solemnly promise that if a recipe calls for an unusual item, it is because this is absolutely the best way to make a particular dessert. Yes, it is possible to make Coconut Mousse without homemade coconut puree, but the difference between a mousse made with processed coconut and one made with fresh is vast. I am not one of those doctrinaire chefs who insists on always using fresh coconut, however. As you will see, sweetened shredded coconut and canned coconut milk are used in those recipes where I have found that it simply does not make a difference, or that in some cases the easier-to-obtain ingredient is actually better.

Here is a list of staples used regularly in desserts. Individual chapters and recipe notes will have recommendations about shopping and ingredients specific to particular recipes.

BUTTER: Nothing gives flavor to baked goods like fresh, sweet butter. All the recipes in this book were tested with **unsalted butter.** When a dessert requires salt, I prefer to add it myself. Higher-fat European butter is delicious when spread on bread but is not necessary for baking. Supermarket butter does the job beautifully. Well wrapped, butter will keep in the refrigerator for several weeks. You may buy large quantities to store in the freezer for several months. Defrost frozen butter in the refrigerator overnight. To soften butter, un-wrap it and let it stand at room temperature until pliable. To hasten softening, cut the butter into pieces. Don't soften butter in a microwave. Chances are that parts of it will melt before other parts are soft enough to use.

COCOA AND CHOCOLATE: I use either non-alkalized or Dutch process **cocoa powder** for making brownies, Chocolate Bavarian, and other desserts, depending on what I have on hand. Some people think that non-alkalized cocoa has a deeper chocolate flavor. Personally, I don't think it makes much difference. Either type will work in all of the recipes where it is called for.

When tempering chocolate for candy-making and chocolate decorations, I use **couverture chocolate** because it has a high proportion of cocoa butter, which makes it pourable and smooth (see page 431 for more on couverture chocolate).

I am also very picky about **white chocolate.** Most commercially available white choco-late barely tastes of chocolate and has an unpleasant aftertaste. It is imperative to choose a brand with the highest amount of cocoa butter possible. When cooking at home, I rely on Lindt, a high-quality brand available in many supermarkets.

When a recipe calls for **unsweetened chocolate,** I use Baker's or Hershey's baking squares, available in the baking aisle of any supermarket.

When I need **bittersweet chocolate,** I prefer a high-quality brand such as Valrhona, which has a relatively high quantity of cocoa solids and a deep chocolate flavor. But in a pinch, I am not a snob about brand-name bittersweet chocolate. What I am about to say goes against baking orthodoxy, but it comes from my own experience: I have had great success substituting **semisweet chocolate chips** for semisweet and bittersweet chocolate in all of the recipes in this book. I have read that chocolate chips have additives to prevent them from melting when baked in cookies, and that these additives make them unsuitable for melting and using as you would bittersweet chocolate. But, at least with my own recipes, this is simply not true. The chocolate flavor from chocolate chips is actually quite intense since the chips contain a relatively small amount of cocoa butter, which dulls the flavor of the cocoa solids. So if you are about to make a recipe and realize that all you have in the pantry is a bag of chocolate chips, proceed without worry.

CRÈME FRAÎCHE is heavy cream that has been thickened and given a slightly tangy taste through the addition of a lactic bacteria culture such as buttermilk or lemon juice. It is possible to make crème fraîche at home, but the process can take up to 24 hours, and the results are not uniform. I always buy it at the supermarket, for convenience and reliability.

EGGS: All of the recipes were tested with U.S. grade **large eggs.** Nutritionally and flavorwise, there is no difference between white and brown eggs. It is more important to buy eggs from a reputable grocery store where the turnover is frequent and the eggs are fresh. Keep eggs in the refrigerator until ready to use. Leftover raw egg whites and yolks will keep in airtight containers in the refrigerator for up to 2 days, and may be frozen for up to 3 months. There are several recipes in this book that call for raw eggs or egg whites. Note that raw eggs should not be used in food to be consumed by children, pregnant women, or anyone in poor health or with a compromised immune system due to salmonella.

FLOUR: Flour is categorized by its protein content, which gives baked goods their structure. **Cake flour** has the smallest amount of protein, resulting in the softest, most tender baked goods. I use it in cakes, pastries, and doughs where I want a very soft, almost crumbly texture. **All-purpose flour** works very well in most other recipes, producing tender baked goods with good shape and structure. Very occasionally I will use **bread flour** when I want to bake something with a little bit of toughness. For example, I make croissant dough with bread flour so that my croissants have crackly, well-defined layers. Store flour in an airtight container in a cool, dry place for up to 1 year. For more information on flour, see page 249.

DRIED FRUIT: I frequently use raisins and dried currants, prunes, blueberries, apricots, and pears in desserts and baked goods. They are good to have on hand and keep well when stored at room temperature in airtight containers or zipper-lock bags. Make sure to buy moist, plump fruit that hasn't been sitting on the shelf too long. To plump up overly dry fruit just before using, place it in a heatproof bowl and pour boiling water over the fruit to cover. Let it stand for 5 minutes, then drain well and pat dry.

GELATIN: Gelatin gives shape to mousses, Bavarians, and puddings. I also like to thicken fruit glazes for tarts and other desserts with gelatin. Professionals use **sheet gelatin,** which resembles brittle strips of very thin, clear plastic. It is available by mail (see page 523) and at baking supply shops. We like sheet gelatin because it is easier to dissolve and has less of an aftertaste than **powdered gelatin.** Powdered gelatin is a perfectly adequate substitute, however. All of the recipes in this book give quantities for both types of gelatin. For more on how to use gelatin, see the box on page 119.

MILK AND HEAVY CREAM: Unless otherwise directed, use **2 percent** or **whole milk** in the recipes. Organic pasteurized heavy cream has a wonderful fresh flavor and whips up very high, but ultra-pasteurized heavy cream works very well in all of the recipes.

NUTS: Nuts add wonderful richness and flavor to many desserts and are delicious in nougat and other candy. I frequently use almonds, pecans, walnuts, and hazelnuts, and I like to have them on hand for spur-of-the-moment desserts. Buy nuts from a reputable market with a high turnover. They go rancid quickly, so unless you will be using them right away, you should store them in zipper-lock bags or airtight containers in the freezer.

SALT: The selection of salt can be confusing, with the range of products that have recently become available. What do you buy—iodized salt, which is the cheapest and most common type, additive-free kosher salt, or the expensive sea salt that comes in a bewildering selection of grinds? When I am cooking dinner, I prefer kosher salt, which has a pure flavor without a high price tag. But I have found that because the amount of salt used in most baked goods is so small, **iodized salt** will not affect the flavor of the finished product, so this is what I use in baking.

SUGAR AND OTHER SWEETENERS: I am not a big fan of exotic sweeteners. Blocks of palm sugar, boxes of Sucanat, and bottles of barley malt syrup would overcrowd my already crowded pantry. If you have **granulated sugar, confectioners' sugar,** and **light brown sugar** on hand, you will have the right sweetener for 90 percent of the recipes in this book. Bottles of corn syrup, pure maple syrup, molasses, and honey will allow you to sweeten the rest.

YEAST: Yeast-risen doughs form the basis of some of the most delicious desserts in this book. **Compressed yeast** and **active dry yeast** are both available at any supermarket. I prefer compressed yeast, which comes in cakes and must be refrigerated. It has a superior aroma and gives baked goods a beautiful, yeasty flavor. Active dry yeast, which is compressed yeast that has been dehydrated so that it can be stored at room temperature, has a longer shelf life. Either one will cause your dough to rise, and quantities for both are given in the recipes that call for yeast. Just make sure that your yeast hasn't passed its expiration date and that you store it properly for successful baking. For more on yeast, see page 250.

ESSENTIAL EQUIPMENT, PLUS A FEW EXTRAS

The White House pastry kitchen is a relatively small space, with just enough room to store the equipment that is absolutely necessary for making dessert. This didn't bother me much, because I have never been interested in gadgets. For example, I don't use a double boiler at work or at home, since a heatproof bowl set over a pan of simmering water does the same job. And believe it or not, my wife and I lived without a rolling pin for the first years of our marriage. If one of us wanted to roll out dough at home, we'd improvise and use an empty wine bottle!

To this day, I'd rather figure out a convenient and cheap way to produce a dessert than invest in a costly specialty item that's hard to track down. The fancy blown sugar decorations that amazed guests at the White House weren't made with a pump marketed for that purpose. Instead of spending hundreds of taxpayer dollars, I went to the local auto supply shop and bought a brake line tube. Blowing air through the tube with my own lung power, I was able to make sugar decorations that were as good as, if not better than, decorations made with special equipment.

Here is a list of equipment used in recipes throughout this book. As you will see, there are very few expensive items and very few that you won't be able to find at your local housewares shop. Read the recipe carefully before you begin, to make sure that you are not missing some essential piece of equipment. Once you have some experience making desserts, don't be afraid to improvise if you have to. You just might discover a more convenient, cheaper, and better piece of equipment for doing the job than the one I suggest.

BAKING PANS: Look for sturdy, heavy pans that won't warp or dent. If you own two loaf pans (one large and one small), one 10-inch round pan, two 9-inch round cake pans, two 16 x 12-inch rimmed baking sheets, a 10-cup bundt pan, and a muffin tin, you are well equipped. Add an angel food cake pan with removable bottom, a mini muffin tin, an 8-inch savarin mold, and a madeleine pan, and you will have many of the baking pans called for in this book.

BISCUIT CUTTERS: A nesting set of round cutters measuring from 1½ to 3 inches in diameter comes in handy for cutting biscuits, cookies, and circles of ganache for covering chocolates.

BLENDER: One of the few electric appliances I absolutely depend on, a blender makes smooth crêpe batter, purees fruit, and can even rescue curdled custard by smoothing out the lumps.

CITRUS REAMER: This wooden implement juices lemons, limes, and oranges quickly and efficiently.

CRÊPE PAN OR 6-INCH NONSTICK SKILLET: A special crêpe pan is nice to have for making crêpes but not necessary. A small skillet, preferably nonstick, will do the job just as well.

DECORATIVE MOLDS: Some of the prettiest desserts in this book can by made by simply pouring mousse, Bavarian, or ice cream into a mold and letting the mixture set up. The same desserts can be made in a bowl, but molds are nice to own, not terribly expensive, and often go on sale at cookware shops.

ELECTRIC MIXER: I use a standing mixer that comes with both whisk and paddle attachments. A handheld mixer may be used in most of the recipes in this book, but the mixing might take a bit longer with the less powerful machine.

FOOD PROCESSOR: In general, I don't like to use a food processor to make desserts. It is just too powerful, and it will overmix doughs and batters in just a few seconds. I sometimes use a food processor fitted with the metal blade if I have to chop a large quantity of nuts, but I am very careful not to overprocess the nuts, or they will release their oil and become very greasy.

GRATER: A grater with very small holes is essential for finely grating citrus zest.

HEAT LAMP: This is very helpful in keeping your cooked sugar warm when you are making pulled or blown sugar decorations, but a special heat lamp is not necessary. Just buy a heat bulb at the hardware store and use it with any desk lamp.

ICE CREAM MACHINE: Many frozen desserts can be made without using an ice cream machine, but sorbet and ice cream must be churned in one. Buy an inexpensive hand-crank model with a canister that you can chill in your freezer. If you become a devoted ice cream maker, consider purchasing a more expensive but more efficient electric model.

ICE CREAM SCOOPS: Very handy for a variety of pastry tasks, from portioning out cookie dough to scooping out meringue for floating island desserts. I have a collection in different sizes. The numbers (#100, #70) indicate how many scoops to the quart you will get.

KNIVES: Heavy, sharp, high-quality knives make any kitchen task easier and more enjoyable. For desserts, I primarily use a paring knife, a chef's knife, and a serrated knife.

MARZIPAN SCULPTING TOOLS: You can sculpt marzipan with any number of common kitchen implements (the dull edge of a paring knife, a tiny measuring spoon, the tines of a fork), but a set of plastic sculpting tools, available at pastry supply shops and by mail (see page 524), is inexpensive and fun to work with if you are going to be doing any amount of marzipan work.

MEASURING SPOONS AND CUPS: All successful dessert recipes begin with accurate measuring. Professional pastry chefs are so determined to duplicate their results time after time that they weigh their ingredients rather than measuring them. Measuring is fine for home cooks, as long as you measure carefully. Use clear "liquid" measuring cups for liquid ingredients, "dry" measuring cups for large quantities of dry ingredients, and measuring spoons for small quantities.

MEDIUM-WEIGHT ACETATE: Plastic sheeting is useful for finely piped chocolate decorations. Medium-weight acetate is available at pastry supply shops, but the clear plastic on sale at stationery and art supply shops is just the same.

MIXING BOWLS: Mixing bowls in a variety of sizes come in handy not just for mixing but also for organizing ingredients. Glass bowls can go in the microwave. Stainless steel bowls set on top of a pot of simmering water make a good substitute for a double boiler.

PARCHMENT PAPER: I rarely bake a cake or cookies without lining the pan with parchment paper. It is available in rolls in the baking aisle of any supermarket. If you bake a lot, you might want to purchase a quantity of precut sheets through a mail-order source (see page 523).

PASTRY BAGS AND TIPS: As you will see, I don't do a lot of ornate decorating with a pastry bag. But I do use it for many other tasks, including piping cookie dough and choux paste. Disposable plastic pastry bags are convenient. Coated canvas bags are more economical, however. A very basic set of several tips is all you will need to make any of the recipes in this book.

PASTRY BRUSHES: A couple of good-quality pastry brushes are necessary for routine tasks like brushing egg wash on pie dough and brushing syrup on cake layers. Keep the pastry brushes you use for desserts separate from the ones you use to brush barbecue sauce on your spareribs!

PIE AND TART PANS: You will be able to make any of the pie and tart recipes in this book if you have a 9-inch pie pan, a 10-inch tart pan with removable bottom, and eight 3-inch nonstick tartlet pans. I prefer clear Pyrex pie pans so that I can see how the bottom crust is browning as my pie bakes.

PIE WEIGHTS: If you have to bake a tart or pie shell before filling it, you will need to weight it down during baking to keep it flat. Special pie weights are available at pastry supply shops, but several cups of dried beans work just as well and can be used over and over again.

PLASTIC WRAP: I wish I owned stock in a plastic wrap company, for all the miles of the stuff I used during my years at the White House. I rely on plastic wrap for keeping baked goods and other desserts fresh, whether they are stored at room temperature, in the refrigerator, or in the freezer.

ROASTING PAN: If you want to make a smooth, uncurdled baked custard, you will need to place it in a roasting pan and fill the pan with water before baking.

ROLLING PIN: An essential piece of pastry-making equipment (although in a pinch you may try the wine bottle trick). I prefer a straight dowel-style wooden rolling pin, although you may use whatever you already have. See the box on page 270 for more opinions and advice on choosing a rolling pin.

SAUCEPANS: Good-quality, heavy saucepans in several sizes are necessary for making stovetop custards and puddings, heating cream for ganache, cooking sugar, and performing many other pastry tasks.

SCALE: Professional pastry chefs often measure their ingredients by weight rather than volume, so in a professional kitchen a scale is a must. For the home cook, I supply volume measurements but occasionally will refer to weight, as when I measure out an amount of pastry dough to be used in a pie. For this reason, and because a scale comes in handy for many other kitchen tasks, I recommend owning one. I use an electronic scale, battery operated, which can weigh up to 10 pounds.

SILPAT PAD: This silicone pad, the size of a baking sheet, prevents any baked goods from sticking. In many cases a Silpat Pad can be used in place of parchment paper, and unlike parchment paper it is reusable. If you do a lot of baking, it is definitely worth the small investment, and you'll never have to worry about running out of parchment.

SOUFFLÉ DISHES, CERAMIC BAKING DISHES, RAMEKINS, AND CUSTARD CUPS: Ceramic bakeware is wonderful for desserts that are to be served in the containers in which they are made, including soufflés, bread puddings, petits pots, and crème brûlée.

SPATULAS: Of all the utensils that a pastry chef uses, these are probably the most important. Rubber spatulas are used for scraping down the sides of a mixing bowl and for folding ingredients together. Buy the kind made from special plastic that won't melt, so you can also use them to stir puddings and stovetop custards. Offset spatulas are used for frosting cakes, making sure that pie dough doesn't stick to a work surface, spreading tempered chocolate into thin sheets to make decorations, and many other tasks. Flexible metal spatulas are convenient for lifting hot cookies off cookie sheets and placing them on wire racks.

STRAINER: A fine-mesh strainer is essential for many tasks, including removing lumps from custard and seeds from fruit puree. A larger-gauge strainer comes in handy for rinsing fruit and also for sifting dry ingredients together if you don't have a sifter.

THERMOMETERS: A candy thermometer is good insurance when you are cooking sugar. An instant-read thermometer will give you peace of mind when tempering chocolate.

VEGETABLE PEELER: The most efficient way to remove the skin from an apple, and handy for many other common pastry tasks as well.

WIRE RACKS: Placing hot baked goods on wire racks allows air to circulate all around them, so they cool quickly and evenly. I also use a wire rack when glazing or pouring ganache over a dessert, so that the excess can drip down onto a sheet pan below.

WIRE WHISKS: Whisks in several sizes will ensure that your eggs and egg whites are well broken up, your custards are smooth, and your ganache is lump-free. They are also good for stirring dry ingredients together and for breaking up clumps of cocoa powder and cornstarch.

WOODEN SPOONS: If you are unsure whether your rubber spatula is heatproof, you can always count on a wooden spoon to stir a hot liquid without melting.

ZESTER: Sometimes you want to remove citrus zest in long, thin strands instead of grated bits. When you do, this inexpensive kitchen implement will do the job.

ONE

The Secrets of Simply Wonderful Fruit Desserts

GROWING UP IN FRANCE, I was definitely spoiled when it came to fruit. I used to spend half a day up in a cherry tree, sampling the ripe fruit. In my house and at the local pastry shops, only the most fragrant, sweetest apricots, pears, and figs were used to make pastry. I remember the wonderful aroma of fresh cherry tarts baking in my mother's kitchen.

In those days European bakers and home cooks respected fruit's freshness and seasonality. Tree-ripened fruit was carefully handled from the moment it was picked to the way it was stored and ultimately prepared. This thoughtfulness translated into the freshest-tasting fruit desserts and pastries imaginable.

During the course of my travels in the early part of my career, from London to Bermuda to Mexico, I was often disappointed by inferior imported fruit—year-old apples, tasteless melons, strawberries that were pretty to look at but not very exciting to eat. I did what I could with what was available, but I wasn't often inspired.

Until I arrived at the White House, fruit desserts were part of my repertoire, of course, but I wouldn't say that they were my passion. Once in Washington, this changed. Suddenly all of America's finest produce, as well as wonderful fruit from South America, was available to me in abundance. My time in the White House kitchen coincided with Americans' awakening interest in healthy eating, and thus the importance of fresh fruits and vegetables. Growers responded to this, and increasingly I was able to obtain the kind of flavorful fruit I remembered eating as a child.

The audience I was cooking for was a demanding and self-disciplined one. Most First

Families and their guests were counting calories. People in the limelight want to stay slim. I had never encountered so many people with the willpower to refuse a slice of chocolate cake or a superb crème brûlée! I decided that fruit was the way to tempt these guests to try dessert. The idea was to create dishes that would give people the sensation of eating fresh-picked, perfectly ripe fruit. Who could possibly feel guilty about that? I could usually get everyone to try a fruit preparation that looked light and fresh on the plate; if it tasted great, no one could resist taking a few more bites.

Rediscovering the pleasures of fruit, and introducing my large and ever-changing audience to these pleasures, has been my joy for the last twenty-five years. Many of my fruit desserts are low in fat and calories; some are not. What they all have in common, I hope, is a light touch and a respect for the beautiful aroma and flavor of fresh-picked fruit. Whatever their final calorie count, these desserts will never weight you down.

The desserts that I've gathered together in this chapter are all as natural-tasting as possible. If you have ever eaten a truly ripe pear or peach, homegrown strawberries, or a perfect cantaloupe, you know that there is not much to improve on. When creating a fruit dessert, I try to figure out the best way to highlight what is naturally wonderful about that particular fruit. I cook strawberries and blueberries on top of the stove without stirring, to bring out their sweetness without destroying their shape and texture. I poach peaches with their skins on, cooking them for only a minute, to preserve their beautiful color and firm flesh. Reverence for these gifts of nature is my mantra. When I stick to it, I cannot go wrong.

$\mathcal{B}$UYING AND STORING FRUIT

Strolling the produce aisle of an American supermarket, I am still stunned at the variety of fruits available year-round. In the Europe of my childhood, we could buy one or two beautiful fruits in season at a time. Here in Virginia, I can choose from probably a dozen varieties on any day of the year.

When I taste most of this fruit, however, I'm not grateful for its abundance and the ingenuity behind it. Growers have often responded to consumers' desire for a variety of fruits all through the year by delivering a product that sacrifices fresh, ripe flavor for shelf life. Clementines from Spain, which used to be a delightful treat available only in December and a couple of weeks in January, are now in markets from November to March. But if you've ever eaten one in March, you know that it is a tasteless distant cousin of a truly in-season clementine.

I hope that someday farmers, chefs, and home cooks will get together to solve these problems of extended growing seasons and the development of fruit that can be shipped long distances at the expense of its natural goodness. In the meantime, I just use common sense and caution when choosing fruit for my desserts.

When possible, I buy fruit at a nearby farmers' market. There is a very big difference between an apple picked yesterday a couple of miles from home and one that has been sitting in storage for six months on the other side of the country. I love to support local agriculture and to feel that my dessert is a truly local creation. As more people have recognized the need for high-quality, locally grown, often organic fruits and vegetables, these markets have proliferated. There is probably one open near you for at least part of the year.

When the farmers' market is closed or just not convenient, I pick and choose very carefully at the supermarket around the corner, where there is plenty of high-quality fruit. I use my eyes, nose, and hands to determine the quality and potential of a piece of fruit. Is that melon fragrant? Is it slightly yielding at the stem end? Can I see any mold? Really inspect fruit before you buy it. If it doesn't look and smell good enough to eat out of hand, think about choosing something else that does.

I try my utmost to work with fruit in season—raspberries in the summer, apples in the fall, rhubarb in the spring. In the winter, when imported fruit dominates the shelves, I rely on the wonderful fruit from Central and South America that travels well with little or no loss in quality—mangoes from Mexico, golden pineapples from Costa Rica. Not only does fruit in season taste best, but there is something unnatural about eating apple pie in July or strawberry soufflé in December. As divorced from the environment as we can be in this day and age, we are still human beings who live in the seasons and crave certain foods at certain times of the year.

In the best of all possible worlds, storage wouldn't be an issue; you'd buy fruit at its peak of ripeness and use it immediately. But this isn't always practical. If you are not going to use ripe fruit, store it in the refrigerator to slow down its shift into overripeness. If you've been able to buy only partially ripened fruit, keep it at room temperature out of direct sunlight. To speed up the ripening process, place fruit in a brown paper bag and store it at room temperature. Check it often, and move the ripened fruit into the refrigerator in a timely fashion.

If you aren't going to use the fruit right away, don't let it sit on a hard surface on the counter or in the refrigerator. Fruit is delicate; it should be babied. Line a baking sheet with kitchen towels and place the fruit on the towels. It's less likely to bruise while sitting on a softer surface. If you are holding it for any length of time, turning it frequently will also prevent bruising and discoloration.

THE RECIPES

Because fruits are so different from one another, I have taken an A to Z approach in this chapter, describing the different fruits I use in desserts; making suggestions about buying, storing, and handling them; and including favorite recipes for simple fruit preparations.

You'll also find instructions for preparing fruit to be used in different dessert recipes—baked sliced apples for tarts, blueberry sauce for shortcakes, cooked cranberries for sorbet.

Among the recipes for fruit desserts, some of the quickest and easiest are among my favorites: Orange Ambrosia (page 57) was a First Ladies' choice for years, and Fresh Fruit Salad (page 24) is so much more than its name indicates. Caramelized Costa Rican Pineapple (page 66) is just a simple sauté, but the technique truly enhances what is already a wonderful fruit.

Choose a dessert recipe after you've seen what fruit is available at your market and which is at peak freshness and ripeness. If you begin with the best ingredients and follow a few simple steps, you are guaranteed a delicious dessert that highlights that fruit's best attributes.

FRESH FRUIT SALAD

PREBAKED APPLE CHUNKS

PREBAKED APPLE SLICES

POACHED APPLES

POACHED APPLES IN CONFETTI WINE JELLY

WHOLE BAKED APPLES

OVEN-POACHED APRICOTS

BANANAS IN RASPBERRY CREAM

BLUEBERRY SAUCE

BLUEBERRY FOOL

COCONUT PUREE

CRANBERRY PUREE

FIGS IN PORT WINE

FRESH FIG AND APPLE CHARTREUSE

FROSTED GRAPES

GLAZED KUMQUATS

LEMON COMPOTE

ORANGE JELLY WITH LITCHIS

ORANGE COMPOTE

ORANGE AMBROSIA

POACHED PEACHES

POACHED PEACHES WITH CHESTNUT MOUSSE

POACHED PEARS

PEARS IN RED WINE

CARAMELIZED COSTA RICAN PINEAPPLE

BRANDIED PRUNES

RHUBARB COMPOTE

STRAWBERRIES AND CREAM

FRESH FRUIT SALAD

Serves 6

Fruit salad can be made with any combination of fruits and with as many types as you like. To make the freshest-tasting, prettiest salad, however, you do need to keep a few things in mind.

It goes without saying that the ripest, best-tasting, in-season fruit will make the best fruit salad. Look for locally grown fruit when possible; always choose the ripest, most fragrant fruit available.

To prevent fruit from discoloring, I like to sweeten my fruit salad with apple juice. I also usually add orange segments, which are available throughout the year, because the acid in the oranges prevents discoloration. Lemon juice is too harsh and overpowers the flavors of the fruit.

I firmly believe that fruit should be cut following its natural shape so that you can recognize what you are eating: Apples should be cut in wedges, oranges separated into segments. Fruits cut into different shapes make for a prettier, more interesting-looking salad. A bowl full of cubed fruit lacks personality and does not display any of the cook's talent!

If you are using very delicate fruit or fruit that will discolor the salad (raspberries, blueberries, or strawberries, for example), wait until just before serving to add it. Other fruit can be cut up, mixed with apple juice, and stored in the refrigerator for up to 1 day.

I also like to pile ice on top of the plastic-wrap-covered fruit until just before serving. This keeps the fruit nice and cold, just the way you want to eat it. It also lets you prepare your salad up to 2 days in advance without reducing its fresh flavor. Before serving, gather the edges of the plastic wrap together, so that the melted ice doesn't fall into the container. Stir in the syrup and any liqueur or wine that you decide to use, and enjoy.

If you are using melon or pineapple, think about using the hollowed-out shell as a container (see page 65).

A fruit salad, however simple, can be a celebratory end to a meal, especially if you stir in a little Champagne and serve the rest as an accompaniment!

4 cups mixed fresh fruit, cut into
   bite-size pieces
2 cups apple juice
½ cup Heavy Syrup (page 506),
   or ½ cup honey

¼ cup fruit-flavored liqueur such as
   Kirsch, Grand Marnier, or
   Framboise, or ¼ cup Champagne
   or sweet white wine (optional)

1. Reserving any delicate fruit or fruit that may discolor the salad, combine the remaining fruit with the apple juice in a bowl, making sure that all of the fruit is covered with the juice. Place the bowl on a rimmed baking sheet. Loosely cover the bowl with two layers of plastic wrap, making sure that at least 5 inches overhang the rim. Put a 2-inch layer of ice cubes on top of the plastic wrap. Refrigerate for up to 2 days.

2. When you are ready to serve the dessert, gather the edges of the plastic wrap together, taking care not to let the melted ice drip into the bowl, and discard. Transfer the fruit and juice to a serving bowl. Pour in the Heavy Syrup or honey, and a liqueur or wine if desired. Stir well. Gently stir in any reserved fruit, and serve immediately.

Fruit Salad Combinations

Here are a few combinations I like for fruit salad. Use them as a starting point for your own creations.

TROPICAL-ORIENTAL:
Litchis, mangoes, cherries, oranges, and strawberries

CALIFORNIA PREFERRED:
Peaches, apples, melon, kiwis, and oranges

TROPICANA:
Golden pineapple, bananas, pears, nectarines, and watermelon

$\mathcal{A}$PPLES

Apples are indispensable in my kitchen. They are extremely versatile: I bake them whole or inside pies and tarts; poach them; and make ice cream and sorbet with them. Apples are a safe choice when you're preparing dessert for a crowd because most people like them. I use apples from September through the winter and early spring, but the best months for apples are when they are being picked, from September through early November. Apples keep well in storage cellars, but there's nothing like the taste of a just-picked apple.

For eating out of hand or for fruit salad, I like Golden and Red Delicious apples. I look forward to tasting heirloom and unusual varieties when they're available at the local orchard. It seems that every autumn there are several new kinds, and I never know what I might discover. The new Honey Crisp variety, grown outside of Washington, D.C., is a recent favorite.

For baking and poaching, however, I turn to Granny Smiths. These tart, light green apples hold their shape when cooked, giving desserts great flavor and texture. They are available almost year-round in any supermarket.

Store apples in the refrigerator. If you let them sit on the counter at room temperature, they will become mealy and soft.

PREBAKED APPLE CHUNKS

Makes about 6 cups

As a rule, I prebake apples before using them in baked desserts. That way I know that the fruit will be properly softened and won't make the final dessert watery. I use Prebaked Apple Chunks for any dessert in which the apples are inside and unseen—such as French Apple Tart (page 352), Apple-Mango Charlotte (page 372), and any type of apple turnover. Apples may be baked ahead of time and frozen for up to 1 month. Freeze them in small portions in zipper-lock bags.

8 apples, peeled, cored, and cut into ¾-inch cubes

6 tablespoons unsalted butter, cut into small pieces
6 tablespoons sugar

1. Preheat the oven to 400 degrees. Arrange the apple cubes on an ungreased baking dish so that they form a well-packed 2-inch-thick layer. Dot the apples with the butter and sprinkle with the sugar.
2. Bake the apples, stirring every 3 to 5 minutes, until they just start to give when pressed with the back of a spoon, 8 to 10 minutes. Remove the dish from the oven and push the apples together in a mound. Let them cool to room temperature (they will cook further in the residual heat). Prebaked Apple Chunks may be covered and refrigerated for up to 3 days or frozen in zipper-lock bags for up to 2 months. Defrost overnight in the refrigerator before using.

PREBAKED APPLE SLICES

Makes about 8 cups

For perfect apple tarts—and any other dessert where I want to see the shape of the apple slices—I prebake apple slices to concentrate their flavor and eliminate excess moisture. Prebaked Apple Slices may be frozen and are wonderful to have on hand for making an apple tart on the spur of the moment.

Whether you are baking apples in slices or chunks, it is important to bake them until just al dente. As they cool they will reabsorb the juices and all of the great apple flavor. If you overbake the apples, they won't take back the juices and will taste bland.

8 apples, peeled, cored, and halved lengthwise	2 tablespoons unsalted butter
	6 tablespoons sugar

1. Preheat the oven to 400 degrees. Place an apple half on a cutting board, flat side down. Using a sharp paring knife, cut the apple half into very thin slices horizontally, leaving the slices slightly attached at one side. Place the apple half on an ungreased baking sheet, flat side down, and press with the palm of your hand to fan out the slices. Repeat with the remaining apple halves.
2. Put a dab of butter on each apple half. Sprinkle with the sugar. Bake until slightly soft but not fully cooked, about 10 minutes. Remove from the oven and let the apples cool on the pan. Use immediately or wrap the pan in plastic wrap and refrigerate for up to 1 day. Or transfer the cooled apples to a disposable aluminum tray, double-wrap the tray in plastic wrap, and freeze for up to 2 months.

POACHED APPLES

Makes 8 poached apples

Poached apples are used in Apple Sorbet with Caramel Sauce (page 156), applesauce, and a variety of other desserts. To prevent browning, place the apples in the acidulated water as soon as you peel them. It's also important to choose apples that aren't bruised, because bruises will turn brown as the apples poach. The timing is the trick when poaching apples: Overcook them and they will fall apart; undercook them and they will be hard and crunchy. Small, very ripe apples might need less than the suggested 2 minutes; if they are large and quite hard, they may need more. To test for doneness, push a sharp, thin skewer through one of them. The skewer should go straight through the apple easily, without breaking it into pieces.

2 large or 3 medium lemons, halved	2 quarts water
8 Granny Smith apples	4 cups sugar

1. Fill a large bowl with ice water and squeeze the juice from the lemon halves into the water. Place the squeezed halves in the water. Peel and core the apples, halving them if desired (this will depend on how you intend to use them once they are poached). Place each one in the ice water as soon as you have peeled and cored it.

2. Combine the 2 quarts water and the sugar in a pot that is wide enough to hold all of the fruit in one layer. Cut a circle of parchment paper the same size as the poaching pot. Bring the water to a boil and place the apples in the pot. Cover with the parchment, pressing down on the paper to make sure that all of the apples are submerged. Lower the heat and cook, covered, at a slow boil until just a little soft to the touch, about 2 minutes. Push a sharp, thin skewer through one of the apples. If it doesn't go through easily, cook for another 30 seconds to 1 minute, until tender.

3. Remove the pot from the heat and allow the fruit to cool completely in the syrup, making sure that the fruit is still submerged as it cools. Remove the parchment after the fruit has cooled. Covered and refrigerated, the apples will keep in the poaching liquid for up to 1 week.

POACHED APPLES IN CONFETTI WINE JELLY

Serves 8

This fun dessert absolutely sparkles when you bring it to the table. Not only beautiful, it is full of flavor and low in calories. You can always make it richer by serving whipped cream or crème fraîche with it.

Because these apples are poached in advance, you won't be able to use their peels to make the "confetti"—they will become discolored. You'll need fresh apple peel. Use the peeled apples to make Prebaked Apple Slices (page 28) or Prebaked Apple Chunks (page 27), and you'll be ready to make an apple tart or turnovers whenever the mood strikes.

2 red apples	6 tablespoons sugar
2 green apples	2 cups fruity white wine such as
1 cup water	Gewürztraminer, at room
1 envelope unflavored gelatin	temperature
(or 7 sheets; see page 12)	8 whole Poached Apples (page 29)

1. Using a vegetable peeler, remove the peel from the apples in large strips. Set the peeled apples aside for another use. Cut the strips into tiny squares (the confetti).

2. Pour 1 inch of water into a medium saucepan and bring it to a bare simmer. Place the 1 cup water in a medium heatproof bowl and sprinkle the gelatin on top. Let it stand to dissolve. Then place the bowl on top of the saucepan, without letting it touch the simmering water. Add the sugar and heat, whisking constantly, just until the gelatin has melted and the sugar has dissolved, 30 seconds to 1 minute. Remove the bowl from the heat, let it cool slightly, and then stir in the wine and the chopped apple peel.

3. Arrange the Poached Apples on a rimmed serving dish and place in the freezer until very cold but not frozen, about 30 minutes. Meanwhile, set the bowl of wine jelly into a larger bowl of ice water and let it cool, stirring occasionally, until it just begins to thicken, 25 to 30 minutes.

4. Take the apples out of the freezer and ladle some of the partially set jelly over them. The jelly should thicken more on contact with the cold apples. Return the apples to the freezer for 10 minutes. Take them out again, ladle some

more jelly over them, and freeze again for 10 minutes. Repeat this once or twice more, until the apples are well coated. Spoon any remaining jelly around the apples and refrigerate, uncovered, until completely set, at least 3 hours and up to 1 day.

WHOLE BAKED APPLES

Serves 8

Baked apples served with ice cream or whipped cream are a comforting, casual dessert. As they bake, their incredible aroma perfumes the kitchen. You can vary the dried fruit filling according to your preference and what you have on hand. Don't worry if your apples sag or collapse inward slightly during baking—it's more important that they're fully cooked than that they stay whole. Just reshape them with your hands after they have cooled for 15 minutes. For a more unusual dessert, large pears may be substituted for apples.

8 large Granny Smith or Honey Crisp apples

½ cup raisins, dried cherries, dried cranberries, or chopped dried prunes

4 tablespoons unsalted butter

½ cup sugar

3 cups sweet white wine such as Riesling or Gewürztraminer

½ cup Grand Marnier or other orange-flavored liqueur

Peel of 1 orange

Four 3-inch cinnamon sticks

2 tablespoons apricot jam

Vanilla Ice Cream (page 185) or Sweetened Whipped Cream (page 521) for serving (optional)

1. Preheat the oven to 400 degrees. Using a vegetable peeler or a sharp paring knife, remove the peel from the top third of each apple. Remove almost all of the core with a paring knife or a small melon baller, leaving the bottom of the apple intact to hold the filling.

(continued)

2. Fill the cavity of each apple with dried fruit. Place the stuffed apples in a 9 x 11-inch baking dish. Top each apple with ½ tablespoon butter, and sprinkle each with 1 tablespoon sugar. Pour the wine and Grand Marnier into the baking dish. Add the orange peel and cinnamon sticks to the baking dish.

3. Bake, basting the apples with the wine mixture every 10 minutes, until soft, about 1½ hours. Remove the apples from the oven and let them cool in the dish for 20 minutes.

4. Transfer the apples to a serving platter. If some of the apples have collapsed slightly, reshape them with your hands. Pour the liquid from the baking dish into a small saucepan and stir in the apricot jam. Bring to a boil and cook, stirring occasionally, until slightly thickened, about 2 minutes. Pour the hot sauce over the apples and serve immediately, with ice cream or whipped cream if desired.

$\mathcal{A}$PRICOTS

Apricots lend a wonderful sweet-and-sour flavor to fruit salads, cobblers, mousses, and many other desserts.

I use uncooked apricots primarily in fruit salads. For use in tarts and pastries, I prefer them cooked. Sweet-tasting apricots can become sour during dry baking, so I prefer to oven-poach them in sugar syrup. This concentrates their natural sweetness and tempers their tartness, bringing their flavors into perfect balance.

The best apricots are local. Very often when apricots are destined to be shipped long distances, they are picked too soon to ever ripen properly. Apricot season runs from June to August, depending on where you live. If you want to enjoy fresh apricots, this is the time to buy them. Choose fruit that has smooth, lushly colored orange skin. Ripe apricots should yield slightly to the touch and have a sweet but not overpowering aroma.

Because of the uneven quality of fresh apricots in this country, I often turn to canned apricots in light syrup for use in tarts, puff pastries, and Danish pastries. Just drain away the syrup and use the apricots the same way you would oven-poached fruit.

Another choice if you love apricot flavor but are unable to buy fresh is dried fruit. Dried apricots deliver a lot of flavor and are especially valuable when you want to create a low-fat, high-flavor dessert. Try to buy dried apricots with no added sulphur, which can leave an aftertaste. Plump them up by cooking them in a pot with water to cover until they are falling apart. Strain them, reserving the flavorful liquid for another use.

OVEN-POACHED APRICOTS

Makes 16 poached apricots

Even, gentle heat from the oven ensures that delicate fruits like apricots and rhubarb don't fall apart during poaching. I use Oven-Poached Apricots in Bavarians, mousses, and tarts. They can be substituted for canned fruit in any recipe if you happen to have bought some beautiful fresh apricots in season.

16 medium-size ripe apricots (about 2 pounds)	1½ quarts water
4 cups sugar	1 vanilla bean

1. Preheat the oven to 375 degrees. Halve and pit the apricots. Place the apricots in a large baking dish that is at least 2½ inches deep.
2. Combine the sugar, water, and vanilla bean in a large saucepan and bring to a boil. Pour the boiling syrup over the apricots.
3. Cut a piece of parchment paper the same size as the baking dish. Poke a few holes in the paper and place the parchment on top of the apricots, pressing down to make sure that all of the apricots are submerged. Bake until the apricots feels soft to the touch, 20 to 30 minutes. Do not overbake or the apricots will fall apart.
4. Remove the dish from the oven and allow the apricots to cool in the syrup, making sure they remain submerged as they cool. Remove the parchment after the fruit has cooled. Refrigerate in the syrup in an airtight container for up to 1 week.

BANANAS

Don't overlook this lunchbox staple when you are thinking about dessert. Bananas add a lot of flavor and texture to fruit salads and are delicious in ice cream, mousses, and Bavarians. Choose bananas with smooth, unblemished skins. Allow green bananas to ripen at room temperature until they are bright yellow. If you are not going to cook sliced bananas, be sure to sprinkle them with lemon juice, or they will quickly discolor.

BANANAS IN RASPBERRY CREAM

Serves 8

Let's face it—bananas don't usually create a lot of excitement on the dessert menu. Most diners consider them a breakfast fruit or a convenient snack food, rather than the basis of a fabulous dessert. But I love the flavor and texture of bananas, and I especially love the combination of bananas, raspberries, and cream. If you are a doubter, try this very simple but beautiful and festive dessert and see if it doesn't convert you.

I have been making this dessert since I was an assistant pastry chef at the Savoy Hotel in London many years ago. It was a special favorite of one guest in particular—Charlie Chaplin. I served it at Christmastime at the White House, garnishing it with bright green marzipan leaves. People would hunt me down to ask for the very simple recipe.

8 ripe bananas
3 tablespoons fresh lemon juice
2 cups heavy cream, chilled
1½ cups Raspberry Sauce (page 516)
1 tablespoon confectioners' sugar

1 teaspoon pure vanilla extract
3 tablespoons sliced almonds, toasted
Marzipan holly leaves (page 468, optional)

1. Cut the bananas into ¼-inch-thick rounds. Place them in a large bowl and toss with the lemon juice so they don't turn brown.

(continued)

2. Whip the heavy cream with an electric mixer until it holds stiff peaks. Place 1 cup of whipped cream in a bowl and set it aside.

3. Fold 1 cup of the Raspberry Sauce into the remaining whipped cream, being careful not to deflate the cream.

4. Reserve 16 banana slices. Arrange a third of the remaining banana slices in a serving bowl or compote dish that is approximately 8 inches in diameter and 6 to 7 inches deep. Smooth a third of the raspberry cream over the bananas. Repeat twice more with the remaining bananas and raspberry cream, so that you have three layers of each. Smooth the top with a small offset spatula.

5. Gently fold the confectioners' sugar and vanilla extract into the reserved cup of whipped cream. Spoon the sweetened whipped cream into a pastry bag fitted with a #6 rosette tip, and pipe 16 rosettes around the edge of the dish. Place a banana slice upright in each of the rosettes. Pour the remaining ½ cup Raspberry Sauce in the center of the dish so that it covers all of the raspberry cream. Sprinkle the sauce with the toasted almonds, and garnish with marzipan leaves if desired. Serve immediately or refrigerate, uncovered, for up to 8 hours before serving.

$\mathcal{B}$LUEBERRIES

Blueberries add color and flavor to fruit salads. They are loaded with pectin and thicken up nicely when baked in pies and tarts. I love them when they are cooked only with sugar so that they are coated in a thick, glossy sauce.

I very rarely use frozen blueberries—I find them watery and lacking in flavor. Dried blueberries, on the other hand, are a wonderful resource. In fact, one of my favorite recipes, Brioche Butter Pudding with Dried Blueberries and Lemon Sauce (page 89), relies on dried berries for an intense blueberry flavor without the unwanted moisture of fresh or frozen.

Domestic blueberries are available from May through July. Berries imported from South America can be purchased during the winter months, but I don't recommend them. When shopping for blueberries, look for plump fruit with silvery blue skins. Blueberries should not look green, shriveled, or dried out around the stem ends. Store them in the refrigerator until ready to use.

BLUEBERRY SAUCE

Makes 4 cups

Cooking blueberries briefly and gently with sugar and cornstarch allows them to keep their shape while sweetening and softening them. Shake the pot so the berries won't stick, but don't stir them or you will crush the fruit. The idea is to have as much whole fruit as possible while transforming them into a glossy sauce. Use this over ice cream, Cheesecake (page 390), and with Blueberry Shortcakes (page 264).

3 tablespoons cornstarch
½ cup water
2 pints fresh blueberries, picked over
   and washed

1 cup sugar
¼ cup fresh lemon juice

1. Combine the cornstarch and ¼ cup of the water in a small bowl, and whisk until smooth. Set aside.
2. Combine the blueberries, the remaining ¼ cup water, and the sugar in a small saucepan. Bring to a simmer over medium heat and cook, shaking the pot occasionally to prevent sticking, for 1 minute. Do not stir or you will break up the berries.
3. Pour the mixture into a strainer set over a bowl to separate the whole berries from the juice. Return the juice to the saucepan and stir in the lemon juice. Bring to a boil and then stir in the diluted cornstarch. Boil, stirring constantly, until the juice is thickened, 2 to 3 minutes. Remove from the heat and carefully stir in the berries. Use warm, or refrigerate for up to 3 days and rewarm slowly, without stirring, before using.

BLUEBERRY FOOL

Fools are simple desserts of fresh fruit puree folded together with whipped cream. Pureed blueberries give the cream a beautiful color, and whole berries sprinkled on top give the fool some texture.

2 pints fresh blueberries, picked over and washed	**3 tablespoons fresh lemon juice**
1 cup sugar	**2 cups heavy cream, chilled**

1. Combine 1 pint of the blueberries, the sugar, and the lemon juice in a blender or food processor. Puree until smooth. Strain into a bowl.
2. Whip the heavy cream with an electric mixer until it holds stiff peaks. Fold the blueberry puree into the cream with a rubber spatula, being careful not to deflate the cream. Spoon the fool into 8 individual dessert bowls, and sprinkle the remaining blueberries on top of each bowl. Refrigerate, uncovered, for up to 1 day.

CHERRIES

Sour cherries are wonderful in tarts, Danish pastries, strudel, and other baked goods. Canned and frozen sour cherries are good substitutes for fresh, which are rarely available. When I can buy fresh sour cherries, I always reserve some, stems and pits intact, to soak in brandy and use later in candy.

Fresh sweet Royal Anne and Bing cherries are wonderful in fruit salads, on the bottom of crème brûlée, or served with Vanilla Ice Cream (page 185) topped with Melba Sauce (page 518).

Cherry season peaks in June. Look for shiny, plump fruit with the stems still attached. Sweet cherries should have a deep, dark, even color. Sour cherries range in color from light yellow to purple, depending on the variety. Store cherries in the refrigerator until ready to use.

Both sweet and sour fresh cherries are underused in desserts, probably because they are so difficult to pit without mangling. Cherries should be pitted without showing any hole or puncture wound. Cherry pitters and olive pitters break or smash the fruit more often than not.

Back when I was an apprentice pastry cook, one of my teachers showed me how to pit cherries flawlessly using a cork and a hairpin. I have not to this day discovered a better way to do the job. Open the hairpin slightly and insert the ends into a cork. The hairpin should form a loop about 1½ to 2 inches long. Hold the cherry tightly between the thumb and index finger of your left hand (assuming you're right-handed). With your right hand, insert the rounded end of the hairpin into the stem end of the cherry and slightly to one side, bypassing the pit. Then pull the hairpin back through the hole in the stem end, pulling the pit out along with it. It takes a little practice, but cherries pitted this way look almost untouched.

COCONUT

The forbidding appearance of fresh coconut, with its rock-hard, shaggy outer shell, discourages people from attempting a fresh coconut dessert. This is too bad, since there is nothing like the flavor of fresh coconut, especially in mousses, sorbets, and Bavarians.

It's not difficult to extract the coconut meat from the shell; it just takes a little elbow grease. On one end of the coconut there are three small eyes. Use a large nail and a hammer to make an opening in each of the eyes, and pour out the coconut milk. Then just tap the coconut all over with the hammer to break up the hard shell. Bake the pieces in a preheated 375-degree oven for 10 minutes. Let them cool. Then insert a paring knife between the flesh and the shell, and use a twisting motion to pry the flesh loose. Using a sharp paring knife, remove the thin brown skin still attached to the flesh. Rinse the white flesh under cool water, pat it dry, and grate it in a food processor or with a cheese grater.

Buy a coconut that has no mildew on the outside. Shake it to make sure that it is full of milk, an indication of freshness. Coconuts are now available year-round in supermarkets but are best purchased from September to January.

COCONUT PUREE

I have never been satisfied with commercial coconut puree. This homemade version has a pure, strong coconut flavor and works as a base for several favorite sauces, cake fillings, and mousses.

5 ounces grated fresh coconut
   (from about 1 whole coconut;
   see page 41)
1 quart whole milk

2 vanilla beans, split lengthwise
1½ cups confectioners' sugar
One 15-ounce can Coco Lopez or
   other brand of cream of coconut

1. Combine the grated coconut, milk, and vanilla beans in a medium saucepan and bring to a boil. Turn the heat down and simmer uncovered until the coconut softens, about 30 minutes.
2. Remove the vanilla beans. Whisk in the confectioners' sugar and cream of coconut. Puree, in batches, in a blender. Coconut Puree can be refrigerated in an airtight container for up to 3 days or frozen for up to 2 months.

CRANBERRIES

Most people use cranberries only to sauce a turkey, but this deliciously tart fruit has many dessert possibilities.

Fresh cranberries, available from September through December, should be plump, with a bright red, even color. They will keep well in the refrigerator, stored in a plastic bag, for up to 2 months, or in the freezer for up to 6 months.

I use fresh and frozen cranberries interchangeably. Too tart to eat raw, cranberries must be cooked with sugar before being used in desserts. Pick through the berries, discarding any dried-out or unevenly colored ones. Cook them on top of the stove, stirring frequently, until you hear them "pop."

CRANBERRY PUREE

Makes 6 cups

I use this puree when making sauces, jellies, and sorbet. It is also wonderful spooned over Cheesecake (page 390), Baked Apple Soufflé (page 106), or Vanilla Ice Cream (page 185).

1 pound fresh or frozen cranberries, picked over and washed	**1½ cups sugar**
	¼ cup fresh lemon juice
1 quart water	

1. Combine the cranberries and water in a large saucepan and bring to a boil. Lower the heat and simmer until the berries are very soft and have popped, 10 to 15 minutes.
2. Push the cranberry mixture through a strainer into a bowl. Stir in the sugar and lemon juice, and let cool to room temperature. Refrigerate in an airtight container for up to 3 days, or freeze for up to 3 months.

CURRANTS

Fresh currants are very popular in Europe, where they are used in making jellies, liqueurs, and syrups. Vibrantly colored and delicately shaped, currants also make beautiful garnishes for Christmas Tree Crêpes (page 240), Orange Jelly with Litchis (page 53), or a bowl of Cherry Trifle with Port Wine (page 80).

FIGS

I look forward to fig season, which runs from July through September. The most delectable of fruits, figs barely need any preparation to become a delightful dessert.

Of the two types of fresh figs available in U.S. supermarkets, Mission and Calimyrna, I prefer Mission figs for their relatively large size and sweet flesh. Look for figs with smooth skins. They should be soft to the touch but not split open. Figs are delicate and highly perishable, and do not keep well. Use ripe figs immediately after purchase, or store them for up to 1 day in the refrigerator.

FIGS IN PORT WINE

Serves 6

Ripe, fresh figs are so delicious and special that they need very little in the way of prepa-ration in order to turn them into a dessert. Here they are sprinkled with a little ground cinnamon and marinated in Port overnight. Some chopped chestnuts and whipped cream complete the dish.

12 ripe Mission figs, wiped clean	1 cup heavy cream, chilled
1 teaspoon ground cinnamon	2 tablespoons confectioners' sugar
3 cups Port wine	6 cooked chestnuts in syrup, coarsely
½ cup strained red currant jelly	chopped

1. Prick each fig in several places with a fork. Place the figs in a nonreactive baking dish and dust lightly with the cinnamon. Whisk together the Port and currant jelly in a bowl, and pour the mixture over the figs. Cover the dish with plastic wrap and let the figs marinate overnight in the refrigerator.
2. Just before serving, whip the heavy cream with an electric mixer until it just be-gins to hold soft peaks. Add the confectioners' sugar and continue to whip until it holds stiff peaks.
3. Arrange the figs on a rimmed serving platter, and spoon some of the Port mix-ture over them. Sprinkle with the chopped chestnuts and serve, with the sweet-ened whipped cream on the side.

FRESH FIG AND APPLE CHARTREUSE

Serves 6

I developed this recipe in response to the many requests I began receiving several years ago for wheat-free desserts. It may surprise your guests that this beautiful and unusual dish requires no special technique or equipment and can be made a day in advance. On top of that, it is relatively low in fat and calories. Figs, apples, and raspberries are perfect together in early fall, when all are in season. Choose ripe, sweet fruit, because there is very little added sugar. Be careful to bake the apples until just soft; if they are allowed to brown, their flavor will be harsh rather than mellow.

24 ripe Mission figs	½ cup Raspberry Sauce (page 516)
2 cups prebaked Apple Chunks (page 27), made with 2 Granny Smith apples, cooled completely	12 fresh raspberries for garnish (optional)

1. Line six 3-ounce ramekins with plastic wrap, leaving at least 3 inches overhanging.
2. Peel the figs with a sharp paring knife, and cut them crosswise into ¼-inch-thick rounds. Place 5 fig slices in an overlapping circle at the bottom of each ramekin. Line the sides with a vertical ring of fig slices, also overlapping slightly. Fill the center of each ramekin with the cooled apple chunks, and cover the filling with the remaining figs. Keeping the overhanging plastic folded back, wrap each ramekin in plastic wrap, pressing down on the surface of the fruit, and refrigerate for at least 6 hours or up to 1 day.
3. To assemble the dessert, unwrap the ramekins. Invert a dessert plate over a ramekin, and then invert the ramekin and plate together. Gently tug on the overhanging plastic wrap while lifting the ramekin from the plate. Peel the plastic wrap away from the dessert. Repeat with the other ramekins. Spoon a little Raspberry Sauce around each dessert, and garnish with fresh raspberries if desired. Serve immediately.

$\mathcal{G}$RAPES

I use both red and white seedless grapes in fruit salad. They also make a beautiful, simple garnish when frosted.

Grapes should be plump, with smooth skins and uniform color. The produce manager might not like it, but try to sneak a taste before you buy. Store them in the refrigerator for up to 3 days, and rinse them just before using.

It sounds like a lot of work, but peeling the grapes gives them a much more delicate texture and improves any dessert in which they are used. This step is absolutely essential in a rich, sophisticated dessert like Champagne Crème Brûlée with Green Grapes (page 95).

FROSTED GRAPES

Makes ¾ cup

This is a wonderful, quick decoration, lovely when served with Pineapple Champagne Sorbet (page 158) or Chocolate Champagne Mousse Cake (page 415). For best results, make Frosted Grapes in cool, dry weather or in an air-conditioned kitchen. High humidity will prevent the egg whites and sugar from drying into a sparkling coating.

1 large egg white (see note, page 11)   **¾ cup sugar**
¾ cup red or white seedless grapes

1. Briefly whisk the egg white in a medium bowl until it is just foamy, about 10 seconds.
2. Add the grapes to the bowl and stir until each one is completely coated in egg white.
3. Spread the sugar in a thin layer on a sheet pan. Roll the grapes in the sugar until coated. Transfer the grapes to a parchment-lined sheet pan and let them dry on the counter or in a cool gas oven with the pilot light on and the door open. Frosted Grapes will keep, uncovered, for up to 3 hours, depending on the humidity.

IWIS

Kiwis are native to New Zealand but are now also cultivated in California. They are available year-round. Sweet, with a mild citrus flavor, kiwis add zest and color to fruit salad and make pretty garnishes.

A ripe kiwi will give a little when pressed; avoid mushy fruit. Harder kiwis will ripen if left out at room temperature. Store ripe kiwis in the refrigerator for up to 1 week.

Kiwis contain an enzyme that breaks down gelatin. They must be poached before being used in mousses or Bavarians, or this enzyme will prevent the dessert from setting up. Because cooked kiwis tend to lose their brilliant green color, I stir a drop or two of food coloring into cooked kiwi desserts to compensate.

UMQUATS

The kumquat is a powerful little wonder, sadly underused in desserts. If it appears at all, it's usually as a garnish, more often than not pushed aside and left ignored and uneaten. It's a wonder that kumquats haven't just refused to grow, after all the abuse they've taken.

I use kumquats to add piquancy and color to fruit salads and tarts. Their season runs from November to June, so I am happy to take advantage of them at a time when there is very little local fresh fruit to be had. Too sour to eat out of hand, they must be cooked in sugar syrup before they are used in a recipe. Once glazed in this way, they will keep in the refrigerator for several weeks, ready to serve your pastry needs.

Choose firm, bright kumquats with no brown spots.

GLAZED KUMQUATS

Makes 1 quart

It is important to strain the kumquats from the syrup after they've cooled overnight, because the syrup will be bitter and will impart a bitter flavor to the kumquats. Pureed glazed kumquats can be stirred into buttercream or pastry cream and used in tarts. One of my favorite tart combinations is kumquat-flavored pastry cream topped with cherries. I also use Glazed Kumquats in fruit salad, to give it a marvelously tangy flavor, or as a garnish for a variety of desserts.

1 quart water	2 pounds fresh kumquats, washed,
3 cups sugar	halved, and seeded
¼ cup light corn syrup	

1. Combine the water, sugar, and corn syrup in a medium saucepan and bring to a boil. Add the kumquats, cover, turn the heat down, and simmer until tender, 30 to 40 minutes. Remove the pan from the heat and let the kumquats cool in the pan, covered, overnight.
2. Strain the kumquats and discard the syrup. Glazed kumquats will keep, refrigerated in an airtight container, for up to 1 month.

ℒEMONS

Lemon is the dominant flavor in many classic desserts. It is most often used for its juice and zest. The zest may be removed with a vegetable peeler, paring knife, grater, or zester, depending on how it will be used in a recipe.

I prefer seedless organic lemons—they seem to be juicier and to have larger segments than the regular supermarket variety. But regular lemons, seeds removed, are just fine in all of the recipes in this book. It may go against fashion, but I just don't understand the big deal about Meyer lemons. They are difficult to find, and not all that different from regular lemons when used in desserts.

Whatever lemons you buy, make sure that they feel heavy for their size and have firm, unblemished skin. Store them in the refrigerator for up to 2 weeks.

LEMON COMPOTE

Serves 6 to 10 as an accompaniment

Lemon is one of the few fruits that you really can't enjoy out of hand. But I love lemon, and I was determined to figure out a way to make a dessert that used it as a fruit rather than just as a flavoring. Sugar syrup poured over the lemons makes them sweet enough to eat on their own, but I usually stir other fruit into the compote. Lemon brings out the best fruit flavor in blueberries, strawberries, raspberries, and cantaloupe chunks. Lemon Compote is also terrific with pound cake or angel food cake.

One of my favorite things to do with any extra lemon syrup is to mix it with vodka and serve it on the rocks as an aperitif or after-dinner drink. People are always amazed that I made this delicious liqueur myself!

Candying lemon zest is a little tricky. You don't want to overcook the zest, because it will toughen up. Just a couple of minutes will plump the zest sufficiently while keeping it tender.

12 large lemons, seedless if possible   ½ cup water
2 cups sugar   Yellow food coloring (optional)
2 tablespoons light corn syrup

1. Use a zester to remove the zest from the lemons, forming long thin strands. Set the zest aside.
2. Divide the lemons into segments and remove all the white path. Place the segments in a heatproof bowl so that they are piled no higher than 1 inch.
3. Combine the sugar, corn syrup, and water in a large saucepan and bring to a boil. Cook until the mixture reaches the soft ball stage (235 degrees on a candy thermometer). Pour the hot syrup over the lemons and let cool to room temperature.
4. Meanwhile, place the lemon zest in a small saucepan, cover with cold water, and bring to a boil. Boil for 2 minutes. Strain the zest, rinse it under cold water, and drain.
5. Transfer the lemon segments to a bowl with a slotted spoon, being careful not to break them up. Scrape the syrup into a medium saucepan. Add the lemon zest, and a few drops of yellow food coloring if desired. Simmer until the zest is tender, 1 to 2 minutes. Pour the zest and syrup over the lemons and let cool slightly before refrigerating overnight. The lemons in syrup will keep in an airtight container for up to 1 week in the refrigerator. Stir in a fresh fruit of your choice, if desired, just before serving.

LIMES

I use limes mainly to flavor pastry cream, Bavarians, and sorbets. Buy them using the same criteria you would use for lemons and oranges: Choose fruit that feels heavy for its size, with smooth skin and no brown or soft spots.

LITCHIS

The tough, bumpy skin of this tiny tropical fruit conceals sweet and fragrant flesh. Combined with other fruits, it holds on to its character. Fresh litchis, shipped from such far-flung locations as Hawaii and South Africa, are available from late June into early August. Canned litchis are an adequate substitute. Refrigerate ripe litchis for up to 1 week.

To prepare the litchi for serving, make an incision all the way around the fruit and slip the skin from the flesh. Cut into the flesh and squeeze out the almond-shaped pit.

ORANGE JELLY WITH LITCHIS

Serves 10

Serve this beautiful and refreshing dessert alongside Orange Sabayon Cake (page 384) or Lemon Pound Cake (page 383), with or without dollops of crème fraîche. Canned litchis are readily available in Asian groceries and most supermarkets, and are equal in quality and flavor to fresh.

¼ cup water
2 envelopes unflavored gelatin
   (or 10 sheets; see page 12)
1 quart fresh-squeezed orange juice
¼ cup fresh lemon juice
¾ cup sugar
2 cups peeled and pitted fresh or
   canned litchis

½ cup fresh raspberries
½ cup fresh blackberries
½ cup fresh blueberries, picked over
   and washed
¾ cup melon balls and ¾ cup
   strawberries (optional)

1. Place the water in a small bowl. Sprinkle the gelatin on top and let stand to dissolve.
2. Combine the orange juice and lemon juice in a medium saucepan and bring to a bare simmer. Remove the pan from the heat, and stir in the sugar and the dissolved gelatin.
3. Arrange the litchis, raspberries, blackberries, and blueberries on the bottom of an 8- to 10-inch round ring mold. Pour the orange jelly over the fruit, cover with plastic wrap, and refrigerate overnight or up to 2 days.
4. To serve, dip the bottom of the mold in a bowl of warm water for 30 seconds; wipe dry. Place a serving dish on top of the mold and invert. Carefully insert a fingertip between the jelly and the side of the mold to break the suction. Tap the mold gently against the platter to unmold. Arrange the melon balls and strawberries in the center of the mold if desired.

MANGOES

I am so thankful for this gift from the tropics! There is no better fruit to eat on its own than a ripe mango, which has the sweetness of a peach, the tartness of an apricot, and the creaminess of a banana. This is Mother Nature at her best. The mango is also wonderful in sorbet, ice cream, fruit salad, and fruit tarts. It makes a very nice dessert sauce as well.

To prepare a mango for eating or for use in a recipe, peel away the skin with a sharp paring knife. Cut the two large oval pieces of flesh away from the hard pit in the center. Cut away as much of the remaining flesh as possible, leaving behind any prickly fibers extending from the pit. You can also squeeze the pit with your hand to extract the juice. Once the flesh is cut away from the pit, it may be sliced into cubes, half-moons, or ribbons that can be formed into decorative rosettes.

Domestic mangoes, grown in Florida, are available from May through September. Mangoes grown in South and Central America are often available during the rest of the year.

Choose brightly colored mangoes with a smooth skin; they should give slightly when pressed but not be soft. Let unripened mangoes sit on the counter until ripe. Refrigerate the ripe fruit for up to 2 days.

MELONS

Cantaloupe and watermelon both have a place in my kitchen (I pass on honeydew and casaba melons, since I usually find them to be bland and watery). Both are terrific additions to fruit salad and make good sherbets, sorbets, and cold soups.

Melons are shipped from California, Florida, Georgia, Texas, and Central and South America, and can be found almost all year round. But there is nothing like locally grown melon of either variety, whenever it is in season in your area.

Melons should give off a sweet smell and yield slightly when pressed at the blossom end. Slightly unripe melons may be kept on the counter to ripen. Store ripe melons in the refrigerator for up to 1 week.

ORANGES

I choose navel oranges, which are large and seedless, when making fruit salad and other uncooked fruit desserts. For sorbet, Florida juice oranges are best.

Blood oranges have a vivid flavor to match their color. I use them whenever they are available in place of either navel or Florida juice oranges.

Oranges are available year-round but peak between November and April. Choose fruit that feels heavy for its size, with bright skin and no dark or soft spots. Oranges will keep in the refrigerator for several weeks.

ORANGE COMPOTE

Serves 8

Oranges in syrup can be served on their own or over ice cream, sherbet, or sorbet. Orange zest adds pure orange flavor to the dessert. Use a fruit zester to remove the peel, since you want very fine strips of zest with the minimum amount of bitter pith. Be sure to rinse the cooked zest under cold water to wash away any remaining bitterness.

8 navel oranges	Red food coloring (optional)
4 cups sugar	½ cup Grand Marnier or other
1 cup water	orange-flavored liqueur (optional)

1. Use a zester to remove the peel from the oranges in long narrow strips. Set the zest aside.
2. Place each orange on a cutting board, stem end down, and carefully cut away the bitter white pith with a sharp paring knife. Cut the orange in half from top to bottom, and pare away the white membranes in the center. Place the oranges and any juice from the cutting board in a heatproof bowl.
3. Combine the sugar and water in a large saucepan and bring to a boil. Cook until the mixture reaches the soft ball stage (235 degrees on a candy thermometer). Pour the hot syrup over the oranges and let stand for 1½ hours.
4. Place the orange zest in a small saucepan, cover with cold water, and bring to a boil. Boil until just tender, about 2 minutes. Strain the zest, rinse it under cold water, and drain.
5. Return the syrup to the large saucepan, leaving the oranges in the bowl. Add the zest to the saucepan. Add a couple of drops of red food coloring if desired. Simmer until the zest is tender, 1 to 2 minutes. Pour the zest and syrup over the oranges and let cool slightly before refrigerating overnight. The oranges in syrup will keep in an airtight container for up to 1 week in the refrigerator. Stir in the Grand Marnier, if desired, just before serving.

ORANGE AMBROSIA

Serves 8

This colorful fruit preparation is good on its own and even better served with slices of Lemon Pound Cake (page 383), Susie's Citrus Angel Food Cake (page 387), or plain Genoise (page 397). I like to use fresh pomegranate juice, but grenadine syrup is a good, simple substitute.

8 navel oranges
1½ cups grenadine syrup

1 cup grated fresh coconut
  (see page 41)
Crushed candied violets (optional)

1. With a sharp paring knife, peel off the rinds of the oranges, removing as much of the bitter white pith as possible. Slice the oranges into ¼-inch-thick rounds. Arrange the orange slices in a mound on a serving platter.
2. Pour the grenadine syrup around but not over the mound of orange rounds. Sprinkle the orange rounds with the coconut. Sprinkle the violets, if desired, over the coconut. Allow the Orange Ambrosia to rest in the refrigerator, uncovered, for 2 to 6 hours before serving.

PAPAYA

The papaya is a large tropical fruit with a strong, sweet flavor. Halved and seeded, papayas make nice containers for fruit salads or mousses (see Lime Mousse with Papaya, page 121).

Papayas are available year-round, peaking in May through September. Ripe papayas are fragrant, with greenish yellow skin. They yield slightly to pressure but are not soft or spotted. Unripened papayas should sit on the counter at room temperature until ripe. Ripe papayas may be stored in the refrigerator for up to 1 week.

PEACHES

There is nothing as good as a peach at peak ripeness. Peaches have it all—beautiful color, amazing fragrance, and delicate flavor. To prepare peaches for most desserts—sorbets, Bavarians, tarts—I poach them. This softens them and heightens their sweetness while preserving their texture.

I have worked with a number of delicious varieties of peaches. My absolute favorite yellow peach is a freestone peach called the O'Henry. The Red Heaven has an incredible fragrance. As for white peaches, the Snow Flame is fantastic. During the late harvest, I go out of my way to purchase Indian Blood peaches from California. Their deep red, white-veined flesh is beautiful and their fragrance unmatched.

Domestic peaches are in season from May to September; imported peaches appear in markets year-round. (Nectarines may be substituted for peaches in the recipes, since they are actually a variety of peach without the fuzz. Hardy Grown nectarines are the most reliable variety I've tried.) Look for firm but not hard fruit with a beautiful fragrance and no bruises. Underripe peaches will ripen at room temperature. Ripe peaches will keep in the refrigerator for up to 1 week.

POACHED PEACHES

Makes 8 poached peaches

I poach peaches with their skins on because I like the beautiful color that the skins give the fruit and syrup. When the peaches are cool, the skins will slip right off. For the best flavor use ripe but not mushy fruit.

4 cups sugar	8 ripe, unbruised peaches,
2 quarts water	unpeeled

1. Combine the sugar and water in a pot that is just wide enough to hold all of the fruit in one layer. Cut a circle of parchment paper the same size as the poaching pot. Bring the water to a boil and place the peaches in the pot. Cover with the parchment, pressing down on the paper to make sure that all of the peaches are submerged. Bring back to a boil and boil for 1 minute.

2. Remove the pot from the heat and allow the fruit to cool completely in the syrup, making sure that the fruit is still submerged as it cools. Remove the parchment after the fruit has cooled. The peaches can be poached several days in advance. Covered and refrigerated, they will keep in the poaching liquid for up to 1 week.

3. Remove the pit by holding a peach tightly in your left hand (assuming you're right-handed), stem entrance facing you. With your right hand, push a new clean pencil, eraser end first so it does not slip on the pit, through the pit stem end and all the way through the peach. The pit should come out the other end without breaking open the peach.

POACHED PEACHES WITH CHESTNUT MOUSSE

Serves 8

Here is an elegant but really very simple dinner party dessert, perfect for late summer, when local peaches are in season.

1 cup apricot jam
2 tablespoons water
8 whole Poached Peaches (page 59), peeled and pitted
3 cups heavy cream, chilled

2 cups sweet chestnut spread (see page 523)
Chocolate Shavings (page 436) or Chocolate Leaves (page 437) for garnish (optional)

1. Combine the apricot jam and water in a small saucepan and simmer until liquid. Place the peaches in a circle on a rimmed serving dish, and brush the warm apricot glaze over them with a pastry brush. Set aside to cool.
2. Whip the heavy cream with an electric mixer until it holds soft peaks. Gently fold in the chestnut puree.
3. Spoon the chestnut mousse into a pastry bag fitted with a #8 star tip, and pipe the mousse into the cavity of each peach. As you draw the bag out, pipe a rosette on top. Pipe the remaining mousse into the center of the platter. Refrigerate, uncovered, until serving, up to 1 day. Garnish the platter with the chocolate shavings or leaves if desired just before serving.

PEARS

Pears have the versatility of apples but with a little more mystery. The best-tasting pears have an elusive spiciness that reminds me of their origins in Asia Minor.

Today pears are grown in this country as well as in Europe and Asia. Although they are available year-round, their peak season runs between August and December. Look for slightly yielding fruit with no bruises or soft spots. I find that especially with pears, fragrance indicates ripeness. If they smell like pears, they will taste like pears.

Underripe pears can sit at room temperature until ripe. Ripe pears will keep in the refrigerator for up to 1 week.

POACHED PEARS

Makes 8 poached pears

For eating out of hand and when making sorbet, I choose juicy and flavorful Comice pears. But for poaching, I prefer Bartlett or Anjou because their flesh is very smooth, unlike the grainy flesh of other varieties. But more important than variety is ripeness. If your pears are ripe, you will not have to cook them forever to soften them, as can happen with unripe pears. Overcooking leaches the flavor from fruit, resulting in pears that taste as if they came from a can rather than from a tree. When poaching pears, I remove the pot from the heat as soon as the poaching syrup comes to a boil and let the residual heat cook the fruit. This results in fully cooked but still firm and fresh-tasting fruit. The pears can be fully or partially peeled. You may also use a zester to make decorative designs on the fruit. As with apples, keep your peeled pears in acidulated water until you are ready to poach them, to prevent discoloration.

(continued)

Pears Belle Hélène—poached pears topped with vanilla ice cream and warm choco-late sauce—is the classic pear dessert. Poached pears can also be served with Vanilla or Strawberry Bavarian (pages 129, 134) or Quick Chocolate Mousse with Crystallized Ginger (page 115).

2 large or 3 medium lemons, halved	2 quarts water
8 ripe Bartlett or Anjou pears	4 cups sugar

1. Fill a large bowl with ice water and squeeze the juice from the lemon halves into the water. Place the squeezed halves in the water. Peel and core the pears, halving them if desired (this will depend on how you intend to use them once they are poached). Place each one in the ice water as soon as you have peeled and cored it.

2. Combine the water and sugar in a pot that is just wide enough to hold all of the fruit in one layer. Cut a circle of parchment paper the same size as the poaching pot. Place the pears in the pot and cover with the parchment, pressing down on the paper to make sure that all of the pears are submerged. Bring to a boil. Then remove the pot from the heat and allow the pears to cool completely in the syrup, making sure that the fruit is still submerged as it cools. Remove the parchment after the fruit has cooled. Cover and refrigerate in the poaching liquid until needed, up to 1 week.

PEARS IN RED WINE

Makes 5 pears

These beautiful poached pears are wonderful with ice cream. For a spectacular presentation, wrap Rum Raisin Ice Cream in a crisp phyllo shell and surround it with the pear halves (page 190). Make sure you use multicolored peppercorns; they are milder than black peppercorns.

3 cups robust red wine, such
    as a Médoc
1 cup water
2¼ cups sugar
Three 3-inch cinnamon sticks,
    smashed
1 tablespoon multicolored whole
    peppercorns

8 whole cloves
Peel from 1 lemon
Peel from 1 orange
One 12-ounce bag frozen
    raspberries
5 ripe Bartlett or Anjou pears
2 tablespoons cornstarch

1. Combine the wine, water, sugar, smashed cinnamon sticks, peppercorns, cloves, lemon and orange peel, and raspberries in a medium saucepan and bring to a boil. Strain the liquid into a pot that is just wide enough to hold all of the pears in one layer.

2. Cut a circle of parchment paper the same size as the poaching pot. Peel and core the pears. Place them in the pot and cover with the parchment, pressing down on the paper to make sure that all the pears are submerged. Bring to a simmer and then remove from the heat. Cover the pot and let stand overnight to cool completely. Remove the parchment after the fruit has cooled. (The pears can be poached several days in advance. Cover and refrigerate in the poaching liquid; then bring to room temperature before serving.)

3. When you are ready to serve them, transfer the pears to a serving platter, reserving the poaching liquid. Place the cornstarch and 3 tablespoons of the poaching liquid in a small bowl and whisk to combine. Pour the remaining poaching liquid into a saucepan and bring it to a boil. Whisk in the cornstarch mixture, bring back to a boil, and remove from the heat. Pour some of the hot liquid over the pears, so that all of the fruit is covered. Serve immediately.

Poaching Fruit

Poaching is a technique that works well with other fruits besides peaches, apples, and pears. Here is a basic recipe that will allow you to poach a range of fruits to increase your dessert-making options.

BASIC POACHED FRUIT

To prevent the fruit from discoloring after it has been peeled, keep it in a bowl of ice water combined with the juice of a couple of lemons as you work. I remove the pot from the heat as soon as the poaching syrup comes to a boil and let the residual heat cook the fruit, which results in fully cooked but still firm and fresh-tasting fruit. Use very ripe fruit for the best flavor. Be aware that kiwis will lose their bright green color when poached; a few drops of green food coloring added to the poaching liquid will restore lost color.

2 quarts water
4 cups sugar

2 pineapples, peeled, cored, and sliced; 16 small plums; 16 kiwis, peeled and cut into ¼-inch-thick slices; or 1 quart cherries, pitted

Combine the water and sugar in a pot that is just wide enough to hold all the fruit in one layer. Cut a circle of parchment paper the same size as the poaching pot. Place the fruit in the pot and cover with the parchment, pressing down on the paper to make sure that all the fruit is submerged. Bring to a boil, then immediately remove the pot from the heat. Allow the fruit to cool completely in the syrup, making sure that it is still submerged as it cools. Remove the parchment after the fruit has cooled. Cover and refrigerate the fruit in the poaching liquid until needed, up to 1 week.

ℐINEAPPLES

Pineapples used to be hit-or-miss: You had to cut one open to find out if it was sweet and juicy or tasteless and woody. Since the advent of the golden pineapple imported from Costa Rica, they are a sure thing. This wonderful variety always seems to be perfectly ripe, so my advice is to look for this label.

Although they are available year-round, the best time to buy pineapples is between spring and early summer. If golden pineapples are unavailable, look for other varieties that are very yellow, fragrant, and slightly yielding. An unripe pineapple will never ripen on the counter, so it is crucial to buy one that was picked at peak ripeness and is ready to eat. Ripe pineapples should be refrigerated until ready to use; they will keep for up to 5 days.

The prickly exterior of a pineapple can be intimidating, but all you need is a long, sharp knife to get at the flesh. Place the pineapple on a cutting board. Slice off the leaves and rind from the top of the pineapple. Stick a fork into the core so you have something to hold on to while peeling. Pare away the rind in thin vertical strips, taking care to remove enough so that no tough spines remain, but also taking care not to lose too much flesh. Slice off the ends. Cut the pineapple in half and then remove the woody core by making a V-shaped cut around the center of each half.

To remove the flesh while keeping the pineapple shell for later use as a container, follow these steps: Cut off the top of the pineapple with its leaves intact, and set it aside. (You can use this as a "cap.") Insert a long, slim, flexible knife into the pineapple about ¼ inch from the rind. Rotate the pineapple while using a sawing motion with the knife to cut the flesh away from the rind, being careful not to cut through the bottom of the pineapple. Insert the knife horizontally into the pineapple, 1 inch from the bottom, making sure not to pierce through the other side. Move the knife back and forth inside the pineapple to loosen the flesh from the bottom. Insert a fork into the core of the pineapple and twist it back and forth to loosen and release the pineapple. If you will be using the pineapple rind to hold fruit salad, you can refrigerate it, unwrapped, for up to 2 days until ready to use. If you will be filling it with ice cream or sorbet, you can freeze it, unwrapped, for up to 3 weeks before using.

To cut the pineapple flesh into rings, slice the released pineapple into ½-inch-thick slices and remove the core from each piece with a small biscuit cutter.

CARAMELIZED COSTA RICAN PINEAPPLE

Serves 8

When experimenting with flavor combinations, I often pair ingredients according to their indigenous climates. Coffee and pineapple are both products of the tropics, so I wondered what would happen if I combined the two. The result was delicious. The coffee brings out a spiciness in the pineapple that balances its sweetness. This dessert will dazzle your guests and take them back to their favorite island, with the sound of calypso ringing in their ears. Keep the rum coming!

5 tablespoons unsalted butter
5 tablespoons sugar
1 Costa Rican pineapple, peeled, cored, and cut into 8 rings about ¾ inch thick
1 teaspoon instant espresso powder
¾ cup canned pineapple juice

½ cup dark rum
2 tablespoons Caramelized Almonds (page 503)
2 tablespoons grated fresh or store-bought unsweetened coconut
Vanilla Ice Cream (page 185)

1. Divide the butter and sugar between two medium-size skillets and heat over medium heat, stirring occasionally, until the sugar has dissolved and the mixture is golden.
2. Place the pineapple slices in the skillets in one layer and cook, turning once, until golden, about 2 minutes per side.
3. While the pineapple is cooking, dissolve the espresso powder in the pineapple juice. When the pineapple is cooked, add half the juice mixture to each of the skillets and bring to a boil. Boil for 2 minutes, turn the pineapple rings over, and boil for another 2 minutes.
4. Working one at a time, add half the rum to each pan and carefully light it with a long kitchen match. Tilt the pan back and forth constantly until the flame goes out. (If you are cooking on a gas stove, take extra care not to spill any of the contents of the pans onto the burner flame.) When the flame has died down, use a slotted spoon or spatula to transfer the pineapple to a serving platter. Combine the juices and boil the sauce until slightly thickened, 2 to 3 minutes. Pour the hot sauce over the pineapple and let it cool slightly, about 5 minutes. Sprinkle with the Caramelized Almonds and coconut, and serve warm with Vanilla Ice Cream.

# PLUMS

Large round plums with red flesh are delicious for eating out of hand. For baking, however, I like the smaller Italian plums, which are oval and have dark purple skins and greenish flesh.

Plums are best in August and September. This is the time to make an Italian Plum Tart with brioche dough (page 363). Look for plump, firm, but slightly yielding fruit. Ripen slightly hard plums on the counter at room temperature. Refrigerate ripe plums for up to 5 days.

An alternative to the plum, always welcome in the winter, is the prune. Although it has an unglamorous image, it has an intense, concentrated flavor that is wonderful in Danish pastries, in winter fruit salads and compotes, and in ice cream.

BRANDIED PRUNES

Makes 1 pound

Velvety Brandied Prunes are delicious served on their own and are a terrific addition to many desserts and baked goods. They keep well in the refrigerator, so I like to have them on hand for spur-of-the-moment cooking. I puree them to spread on brioche toast or to use as a filling for Danish pastries. They make a superb topping for ice cream and are wonderful stirred into rice pudding or used instead of raisins in Whole Baked Apples (page 31). If you prefer nonalcoholic prunes (which are preferable, say, when topping oatmeal for breakfast), just leave out the brandy.

1 pound pitted dried prunes
1½ cups inexpensive red wine
1 cup water
Two 3-inch cinnamon sticks
Zest of 1 lemon, removed in one wide
   strip with a vegetable peeler

Zest of 1 orange, removed in one
   wide strip with a vegetable peeler
¾ cup sugar
⅔ cup brandy

(continued)

1. Place the prunes in a medium saucepan and add the wine, water, cinnamon sticks, and citrus zest. Cook over low heat at a slow boil until the prunes float to the top, 20 to 30 minutes.

2. Remove from the heat and add the sugar and the brandy, stirring until the sugar has dissolved. Cover and let cool completely. Then transfer the prunes and the liquid to an airtight container and store in the refrigerator until ready to use. Brandied Prunes will keep in an airtight container in the refrigerator for up to 1 month.

RHUBARB

Because it looks like pink or red celery and has a reputation as a poisonous plant, rhubarb might not seem like the most promising dessert ingredient. But its tart, fresh flavor is a refreshing thing to look forward to in warmer weather.

Rhubarb is available from late winter through spring. Classically, it is combined with strawberries, but I like it on its own as well. Make sure you buy young, tender stalks. Mature rhubarb is coarse, stringy, and too acidic for use in desserts. Refrigerate rhubarb for up to 1 week. Remove the strings with a small paring knife, and trim the stalks. Stringed and trimmed rhubarb may be wrapped in plastic wrap and frozen for up to 3 months.

RHUBARB COMPOTE

Makes about 3 cups

When it is cooked on top of the stove, rhubarb falls apart before it is cooked properly. In the oven it keeps its shape while its flavors are intensified. Rhubarb compote, on its own or mixed with fresh strawberries, is good with Strawberry or Banana Bavarian (pages 134, 138) and on top of Vanilla Ice Cream (page 185). Or serve it alongside Lemon Pound Cake (page 383) or any other plain cake.

2 pounds young fresh rhubarb	1½ quarts water
4 cups sugar	1 vanilla bean

1. Preheat the oven to 375 degrees. Trim the ends from the rhubarb stalks, and cut the stalks in half lengthwise if they are thick. Peel away the outer layer of the rhubarb, removing the tough strings. Cut each stalk into 2-inch pieces. Place the rhubarb in a large baking dish that is at least 2½ inches deep.
2. Combine the sugar, water, and vanilla bean in a large saucepan and bring to a boil. Remove the vanilla bean from the pan and pour the boiling syrup over the rhubarb.
3. Cut a piece of parchment paper the same size as the baking dish. Poke a few holes in the paper and place the parchment on top of the rhubarb, pressing down to make sure that all of the rhubarb is submerged. Bake until the rhubarb feels soft to the touch, 20 to 30 minutes. Do not overbake, or the rhubarb will fall apart. Remove the dish from the oven and allow the rhubarb to cool in the syrup. Remove the parchment after the fruit has cooled. Refrigerate in an airtight container for up to 1 week.

$\mathcal{S}$TRAWBERRIES

Strawberries are grown in every state of the Union, making them a truly American fruit. At the White House I used them constantly—with ice cream, marinated with wine or other spirits, in soufflés, and in cakes.

Strawberries are available all year round but they are best early in the season, which runs from late spring to early summer. Look for berries that are red all the way up to their stems, avoiding those with white tops. Keep them in the refrigerator, unwashed, for up to 2 days.

STRAWBERRIES AND CREAM

Serves 10

I struggled for years to come up with a way to cook strawberries that would really enhance their beautiful fragrance. The solution came to me when I was preparing a state dinner for Prime Minister Tony Blair. What would be the best way, I wondered, to present that most British of combinations: strawberries and cream?

Strawberries can give off a lot of water, and I wanted to avoid a watery dessert. Cooking the berries in sugar draws out the water and releases it as steam, leaving behind only the flavorful pulp. I use pectin to thicken the mixture because unlike gelatin, it can withstand heat without breaking down. The Lemon Cream gives the whipped cream some extra flavor, adding an extra dimension when it is combined with the berry compote.

For the state dinner, I served the Strawberries and Cream in small chocolate cups. Any chocolate container will do (see page 445), or you can simply serve the Strawberries and Cream in dessert goblets or bowls.

2½ cups fresh strawberries, washed and stemmed
¼ cup water
2½ cups sugar
1 tablespoon powdered pectin, such as Sure-Jell

Red food coloring (optional)
1 cup heavy cream, chilled
1 cup Lemon Cream (page 510)
10 Chocolate Cups, molded with small balloons (page 447, optional)

1. Combine the strawberries, water, and 2 cups of the sugar in a medium saucepan. Cover, and slowly bring to a boil over low heat, shaking the saucepan every minute so the bottom does not burn. After about 10 minutes the strawberries should release a lot of water. Simmer without stirring (which would break up the fruit), shaking the pan occasionally, until the strawberries are soft but not falling apart, 5 to 6 minutes.

2. Remove about three fourths of the juice from the pan, reserving it for another use. Add the remaining ½ cup sugar and the pectin, and shake the pan to distribute. Add the food coloring if desired, and shake again. Cook on low heat, covered, for 5 minutes. Then remove the pan from the heat and allow the berries to cool in the pan. The berries should resemble a thick preserve. Gently transfer the berries to an airtight container and refrigerate overnight, or up to 2 weeks.

3. Whip the heavy cream with an electric mixer until it holds stiff peaks. Gently fold the Lemon Cream into the whipped cream. Gently fold in the strawberries. Spoon into Chocolate Cups if desired. Serve immediately, or cover with plastic wrap and refrigerate for up to 1 day before serving.

TWO

Light and Silky Puddings, Custards, and Soufflés

ALTHOUGH I OFTEN turned out many more desserts in one day than a typical restaurant pastry chef, I always approached my job at the White House not as a restaurant worker but as the chef for a private family. After all, most days my primary task was to provide dessert for every lunch and dinner that the First Family ate at home.

Restaurant chefs want to create desserts to impress and amaze diners. Family chefs want to make diners feel comfortable and at home. Over the years, I developed a repertoire of puddings, custards, and soufflés that served this purpose no matter how humble or elegant the occasion.

Puddings, custards, and soufflés are the original "comfort" desserts. Soft, often served warm, and eaten with a spoon, they make us feel pampered and even babied. Whether you are a grandchild on a sleepover or the King of Spain, this is a good way to end a home-cooked meal!

With these desserts, it's all about texture. If you don't get it right, there is no disguising the failure. Whipped cream spooned on top of leaden and gluey rice pudding will not lighten it up. A curdled crème brûlée can't be salvaged, and there is no hiding a heavy soufflé with sauces and garnishes.

But there is no reason to be fearful if you know a few simple tricks. I have developed foolproof methods and recipes for light and silky comfort desserts of all kinds. This chapter contains the lessons I have learned and the discoveries I have made about creating perfectly textured puddings, custards, and soufflés.

As with all cooking, the difference between a merely edible dish and a sublime one is in the details: To prevent baked custards from curdling, line your roasting pan with brown paper bags for the most evenly heated water bath. Remember to run your finger around the edge of the soufflé dish to ensure the highest rise. Whether you are making a simple Chocolate Petit Pot to end a weeknight family dinner or an elaborate Apricot Sunburst soufflé with a spun sugar decoration for a fancy dinner party, it's the little things that will make the difference between failure and success.

HE RECIPES

I have divided this chapter into five categories, according to the cooking methods employed in the recipes:

Simple layered puddings don't require much cooking at all. For Tiramisù, Summer Pudding, and Cherry Trifle with Port Wine, success depends on the ingredients that you choose for layering, how you handle them, and how you get them to set up into a properly textured chilled pudding.

For **baked custards,** I concentrate on tips for even cooking. A water bath is essential, but there are several other tricks for achieving a perfectly smooth oven-baked custard.

Stovetop puddings are thickened with cornstarch or eggs or both. With these recipes, I'll show you how to make them flawlessly.

I am very proud of my **crème brûlée** variations, which are also made on top of the stove. Crème brûlée should be different from a baked custard, creamier and less rubbery than the examples that we've become accustomed to. In this section I describe my method and explain why it works.

The difficulty with **soufflés** is achieving a balance between texture and flavor. You want the dessert to be as light as air, but you want it to taste like something, too. How do you add flavor without weighting your soufflé down? The recipes here will show you.

TIRAMISÙ

SUMMER PUDDING

CHERRY TRIFLE WITH PORT WINE

HONEY CUSTARD

COCONUT CUSTARD

CHOCOLATE PETITS POTS

COFFEE PETITS POTS

ORANGE PETITS POTS

BRIOCHE BUTTER PUDDING WITH DRIED BLUEBERRIES
  AND LEMON SAUCE

SILKY CHOCOLATE CREAM PIE

RICE PUDDING

VANILLA CRÈME BRÛLÉE

CHAMPAGNE CRÈME BRÛLÉE WITH GREEN GRAPES

ORANGE CRÈME BRÛLÉE

APPLE CIDER BRÛLÉE

WARM STRAWBERRY SOUFFLÉ

MANGO TROPICO SOUFFLÉ

GRAND MARNIER SOUFFLÉ WITH
  CHUNKY STRAWBERRY SAUCE

BAKED APPLE SOUFFLÉ

DRIED PEAR SOUFFLÉ

APRICOT SUNBURST

SIMPLE LAYERED PUDDINGS

The following three puddings are all wonderful combinations of dry and wet ingredients: cookies and cream, bread and fruit, genoise and cherries. When layered and chilled, they combine and become a cohesive, spoonable dessert. The trick is in the proper proportions of wet and dry: You want the wet ingredients to fully moisten the dry ones, but you don't want the finished dessert to be at all runny or soggy.

With Tiramisù and Summer Pudding, a little bit of gelatin thickens the dessert so that it will be solid enough to dish out but not too loose. Pastry cream, thick with eggs, does this job in the Cherry Trifle with Port Wine.

What is essential in achieving the proper texture is an adequate amount of time in the refrigerator. It is here that the ingredients really meld together, becoming something more than their parts. Don't skimp on the recommended refrigeration time. Taking one of these puddings out of the refrigerator too soon is like taking a cake out of the oven before it has finished baking.

TIRAMISÙ

Serves 10

Here is my version of the Italian dessert that Americans love so much. Store-bought ladyfingers are crisper than homemade cookies, and they won't disintegrate when layered with so many wet ingredients.

1¾ cups heavy cream, chilled
6 large egg yolks
1¼ cups sugar
1¼ cups mascarpone
1 tablespoon cold water
¾ envelope unflavored gelatin
   (or 4 sheets; see page 12)

1¾ cups espresso or very strong
   brewed coffee
¼ cup brandy or grappa
24 store-bought ladyfingers
2 to 3 tablespoons unsweetened
   cocoa powder

1. Whip the heavy cream with an electric mixer just until it holds stiff peaks.
2. Combine the yolks and sugar in another bowl and beat with the electric mixer on high speed until pale yellow and increased in volume, about 5 minutes. Add the mascarpone and beat until smooth.
3. Pour 1 inch of water into a small saucepan and bring to a bare simmer. Place the cold water in a small heatproof bowl and sprinkle the gelatin on top. Let stand to dissolve. Then place the bowl over the simmering water and heat, whisking constantly, just until the gelatin melts, 30 seconds to 1 minute.
4. Whisk the melted gelatin into the egg mixture, working quickly so that the gelatin doesn't have time to form rubbery strands. Fold in the whipped cream, gently but thoroughly, so that no white streaks remain.
5. Combine the espresso and brandy in a large bowl or baking pan. Place the ladyfingers in the mixture and let stand, turning once, until they are moistened but not falling apart. Arrange half of the ladyfingers on the bottom of 7 x 10-inch baking dish. Spoon half of the egg mixture over the ladyfingers, and smooth with a spatula. Arrange the remaining ladyfingers on top, and spoon the remaining egg mixture over them. Smooth with a spatula. Refrigerate, uncovered, for at least 4 hours or overnight.
6. Just before serving, sift the cocoa powder over the Tiramisù.

NOTE: Raw eggs should not be used in food to be consumed by children, pregnant women, or anyone in poor health or with a compromised immune system. Make sure you buy the freshest eggs possible.

SUMMER PUDDING

Serves 8 to 10

This is one of the recipes I rely on when fresh berries are at their peak. To maintain the individual flavor and texture of the different kinds of berries, I cook each separately and keep them separate when layering the fruit and bread.

1 cup cold water
1 envelope unflavored gelatin
　(or 6 sheets; see page 12)
½ cup fresh lemon juice
　(from 2 medium lemons)
1¼ cups sugar
1 pint fresh strawberries, washed and
　stemmed
1 pint fresh raspberries, picked over
　and washed

1 pint fresh blueberries, picked over
　and washed
1 loaf commercial white bread
　(18 to 20 slices), crusts removed
　and slices cut in half
1 cup Raspberry Sauce (page 516)
Additional berries for garnish
Mint sprigs for garnish
Crème fraîche or Vanilla Ice Cream
　(page 185)

1.　Pour 1 inch of water into a medium saucepan and bring to a bare simmer. Place the cold water in a medium-size heatproof bowl and sprinkle the gelatin on top. Let stand to dissolve. Place the bowl over the simmering water and heat, whisking constantly, just until the gelatin melts, 30 seconds to 1 minute. Stir in the lemon juice and sugar, and stir to dissolve the sugar.

2.　Combine one third of the gelatin mixture and the strawberries in a small saucepan, and bring to a boil. Turn the heat down and simmer until the berries have softened, 3 to 4 minutes. Transfer the strawberries to a bowl and repeat, using a clean pan, with the raspberries and another one third of the gelatin, and then the blueberries and the remaining gelatin. Let each bowl of berries cool to room temperature.

3.　Line a 2- to 3-quart soufflé dish or bowl with plastic wrap, making sure that the wrap is pressed against the inside surface of the dish and that there is at least 1 inch overhanging on all sides. Arrange bread slices on the bottom and extending up the sides of the dish so that they overlap each other slightly. Spoon the strawberries, with any juices, over the bread slices. Place a layer of bread slices over the strawberries. Repeat with the blueberries and bread, and then the raspberries, covered with a final layer of bread. (The dish will be very full.) Cover the dish with plastic wrap and set a baking sheet over the plastic. Weight down the baking sheet with a heavy pot to compress the pudding. Refrigerate overnight or up to 4 days.

4. Take the pudding out of the refrigerator 2 to 3 hours before you plan to serve it. Remove the pot, baking sheet, and plastic wrap. Place a serving platter upside down over the dish, invert the two together, and tug gently on the overhanging plastic wrap to unmold. Peel away the plastic wrap. Pour the Raspberry Sauce over the pudding so that it covers the top and drips down the sides. Garnish with fresh berries and mint sprigs. Spoon into dessert bowls, and serve with crème fraîche or small scoops of Vanilla Ice Cream.

CHERRY TRIFLE WITH PORT WINE

Serves 8

This is a terrific holiday dessert, perfect for Christmas or New Year's Day. It can be made well in advance of serving—a real advantage if you have a lot of other cooking to do. In fact, the flavors develop and the trifle tastes even better after it sits in the refrigerator for 2 to 3 days.

One 9-inch round layer Genoise (page 397)
½ cup seedless raspberry jam
½ cup Port wine

1 cup heavy cream, chilled
2 cups Pastry Cream (page 509)
Two 14-ounce cans sweet black pitted cherries, drained and patted dry

1. Using a sharp serrated knife, cut the genoise round horizontally into 3 equal layers, each about ⅔ inch thick. Spread ¼ cup of the jam across the top of each of two layers, and stack the three layers, placing the two jam-covered layers on the bottom so that the jam holds the cake together. Slice the cake into 1-inch cubes. Place the cubes in a bowl and sprinkle with ¼ cup of the Port, stirring several times to make sure that all the cubes have been moistened.
2. Whip the heavy cream with an electric mixer until it holds soft peaks. Stir the remaining ¼ cup Port into the Pastry Cream. Fold the whipped cream into the Pastry Cream mixture.
3. Reserve about 12 cherries for garnish. Arrange some of the genoise cubes in a single layer across the bottom of a large serving bowl or compote dish. Spoon some of the cream mixture over the cake, and smooth with a spatula. Arrange a layer of cherries over the cream. Continue to build the layers, finishing with a layer of cream. Cover with plastic wrap, making sure that the plastic does not stick to the surface of the trifle. Refrigerate for at least 3 hours or up to 3 days.
4. Garnish with the reserved cherries, and serve.

$\mathcal{B}$AKED CUSTARDS

When I decide to bake a custard, whether it be a large honey or coconut custard, individual petits pots, or a bread pudding, I do everything I can to make sure that it bakes in gentle, even heat. Otherwise there is a danger that the custard will curdle, resulting in a dessert that resembles scrambled eggs rather than silk.

A water bath is essential. Water creates a buffer between the custard mixture and the harsh heat of the oven. Use a roasting pan that's large enough to comfortably hold the baking dish or dishes. The sides of the roasting pan should be higher than the sides of the dish(es).

Water alone will not guarantee a smooth custard—sometimes even a roasting pan filled with water conducts enough heat to curdle a custard. To prevent the hot metal bottom of the roasting pan from doing any damage, place brown paper (such as a supermarket bag) on the bottom of the pan before putting the custard dish(es) in the pan. The paper will further insulate the custard from the heat of the oven.

Place the custard(s) in the roasting pan, and place the pan on the oven rack; then pour the water into the pan. (There's less of a chance of splashing water onto the custard if it is already in the pan and the pan is already in the oven.) You don't have to boil the water. Hot tap water will do.

Many people think that a little water will do the job, but I've found that the higher up the sides of the baking dish the water reaches, the less likely it is that the custard will curdle and form little holes on the surface. The water should reach at least three fourths of the way up the sides of the baking dish or dishes.

In the case of petits pots, I like to place a sheet pan on top of the roasting pan. The surface of the sheet pan should not touch the custard dishes, but should rest above them on the edges of the roasting pan. If you do this, the custard steams rather than baking, giving the finished dessert an unbelievably delicate texture. The sheet pan also prevents a skin or crust from forming on top of the custard. Skip this step for any dessert where a golden, crunchy crust is desired, such as bread pudding.

When using individual ramekins, you may find it easier to strain the hot custard into a large glass measuring cup and then divide it among the ramekins.

HONEY CUSTARD

Serves 8

When making this custard, be sure to scrape all the precious seeds from the vanilla pods and to bring the milk to a boil very slowly to get the most vanilla flavor out of the beans. I like vanilla beans from Madagascar because they have a pure, intense, irresistible aroma and flavor. For the honey, I choose clover honey for its balanced flavor and fragrance. If your honey is too strong, it may taste bitter when cooked. Covering the custard with a stainless steel sheet pan or cookie sheet during baking, so that it steams, results in an unbelievably delicate dessert. (Don't use aluminum foil, which does not conduct heat as well.) I make this dessert year-round, varying the fruit garnish according to the season. In the summer, cantaloupe, berries, and pineapple are wonderful; in the winter I'll often use Fresh Fruit Salad (page 24), or apples, dates, and walnuts.

½ cup sugar
½ cup water
6 large eggs
2 large egg yolks
1 cup honey

1 quart 2 percent milk
2 vanilla beans, split lengthwise
3 cups cut-up seasonal fruit
   (bite-size pieces)

1. Combine the sugar and ¼ cup of the water in a small saucepan. Bring to a boil and cook until the mixture turns dark amber. As soon as the syrup is uniformly amber, remove the pan from the heat. At arm's length, slowly pour the remaining ¼ cup water into the pot. Be careful—the water may splatter and the caramel will bubble up. Stir with a long-handled spoon or ladle until smooth. Pour the caramel into an 8-inch savarin mold or eight individual 6-ounce ramekins, and set aside to cool completely.
2. Preheat the oven to 375 degrees. Whisk the eggs, yolks, and honey together in a large bowl. Place the milk in a medium saucepan. Use a sharp paring knife to scrape the seeds from the inside of the split vanilla beans. Add the seeds and the beans to the milk. Very slowly bring the milk to a boil over medium-low heat. Remove the pan from the heat and let rest 5 minutes to extract all of the flavor from the vanilla pods and seeds.
3. Slowly whisk the hot milk into the egg mixture. Pour the custard through a fine-mesh strainer into the savarin mold or ramekins.

4. Line a large roasting pan that is at least 2 inches taller than the custard mold with a few sheets of brown paper. Carefully place the custard dish(es) in the pan, and place the pan on the rack in the oven. Add enough hot tap water to the pan to reach three-fourths of the way up the side of the dish(es). Place an upside-down sheet pan or cookie sheet over the roasting pan to cover it. Bake until the custard is set around the edges but still a little wobbly in the center when gently shaken, 25 to 35 minutes for a large savarin mold, 15 to 20 minutes for ramekins.

5. Pull the pan from the oven and let the custard cool in the water for 45 minutes. Then remove the dish(es) from the roasting pan. Serve slightly warm or at room temperature, or cool completely and refrigerate, uncovered, for at least 4 hours or overnight. Let come to room temperature before serving.

6. To unmold and serve: Run a sharp paring knife around the edge of the mold or ramekin. Place a serving dish upside down on top of the mold, invert the two together, and gently shake to release the custard and caramel. (If the custard won't come out of the mold, carefully lift one side of the inverted mold from the serving plate and insert a finger between the custard and the mold to break the suction. Remove your finger and gently shake again to release.) Arrange the fruit on the serving dish around the custard, and serve immediately.

COCONUT CUSTARD

Serves 12

Fresh coconut is wonderful in this custard cake and fairly easy to prepare (see page 41), but grated unsweetened coconut, available at natural foods stores, may be substituted. (In that case, omit the confectioners' sugar.) Raspberry Sauce and fresh raspberries add color to the finished cake. I also like to scatter some Pecan Galette around the custard before serving.

2 large eggs
4 large egg yolks
1½ cups sweetened condensed milk
1½ cups whole milk
7 ounces grated fresh coconut (from 1 coconut), or 3 cups store-bought grated unsweetened coconut

1 tablespoon pure vanilla extract
2 tablespoons confectioners' sugar, if using fresh coconut
1 cup Raspberry Sauce (page 516)
2 cups fresh raspberries
Pecan Galette (page 314)

1. Preheat the oven to 425 degrees. Butter and flour a 1½-quart soufflé dish or twelve 6-ounce ramekins. Whisk the eggs, yolks, and sweetened condensed milk together in a large bowl.

2. Place the milk in a medium saucepan, and very slowly bring it to a boil over medium-low heat. Slowly whisk the hot milk into the egg mixture. Whisk in the coconut and vanilla. Pour the coconut custard into the prepared soufflé dish or ramekins.

3. Line a roasting pan with a few sheets of brown paper or newspaper. Place the custard dish(es) in the roasting pan, and carefully transfer the pan to the oven. Pour enough hot tap water into the pan to reach three-fourths of the way up the sides of the dish(es). Bake until the custard is fully set, 50 minutes to 1 hour for a large soufflé dish, 25 to 30 minutes for ramekins.

4. Remove the pan from the oven and place it on a wire rack. Allow the custard to cool in the pan for 45 minutes, where it will continue to cook in the hot water. Then carefully remove the custard dish(es) from the pan and transfer to a wire rack to cool completely. Cover and refrigerate overnight.

5. To unmold and serve: Place a rack in the top third of the oven, and preheat the broiler. Dip the bottom of the custard dish(es) in hot water for 1 to 2 minutes.

Place a heatproof serving dish upside down on top of the custard dish, invert the two together, and gently shake to release the custard. Sift the confectioners' sugar over the unmolded custard. Place the custard under the broiler and broil until the sugar begins to brown, less than 1 minute. Remove from the oven, spoon the Raspberry Sauce around the custard, and garnish with fresh raspberries. Scatter the Pecan Galette around the base of the dessert if desired.

CHOCOLATE PETITS POTS

Serves 8

Conventional chocolate petit pot recipes call for stirring chopped chocolate directly into the custard. The problem with that method is that the chocolate tends to separate from the custard as the petits pots bake. I have found that making a paste with the chocolate and a little of the cream before stirring it into the custard eliminates this threat, and results in perfectly even and smooth little desserts.

6 large egg yolks, lightly beaten
¼ cup sugar
2 cups plus 6 tablespoons heavy
  cream
5 ounces semisweet or bittersweet
  chocolate, finely chopped

1 teaspoon pure vanilla extract
Sweetened Whipped Cream
  (page 521, optional)
Chocolate Shavings (page 436,
  optional)

1. Preheat the oven to 350 degrees. Whisk the egg yolks, sugar, and 2 cups plus 2 tablespoons heavy cream together in a medium bowl. Set aside.

2. Place the remaining ¼ cup heavy cream in a medium saucepan and bring to a boil. Add the chopped chocolate and whisk constantly until the mixture becomes a paste, about 2 minutes. Remove the pan from the heat and slowly whisk in the egg mixture until smooth. Stir in the vanilla extract. Pour the custard through a fine-mesh strainer into eight 6-ounce custard cups or ramekins.

3. Line a roasting pan with a few sheets of brown paper or newspaper. Place the ramekins in the pan, and carefully transfer the pan to the oven rack. Add enough hot tap water to the pan to reach three fourths of the way up the sides of the ramekins. Place an upside-down sheet pan or cookie sheet over the roasting pan to cover it. Bake until the custard is firm around the edges but still jiggly in the center, about 1 hour.

4. Remove the pan from the oven and allow the petits pots to cool in the water for 45 minutes. Then transfer the ramekins to a wire rack and let cool completely. Place the ramekins in a deep container and cover the container so that the cover does not touch the surface of the petits pots. Refrigerate overnight or up to 3 days. Serve chilled, with whipped cream and chocolate shavings if desired.

COFFEE PETITS POTS

Serves 8

I use aromatic Kona coffee from Hawaii in these petits pots. It's expensive but worth it. This is a bracing, refreshing dessert—like a very rich cup of iced coffee. Be sure to strain the infused cream several times in order to remove all the coffee grounds. These can be made several days in advance. Don't wrap the individual ramekins in plastic wrap, since it might cling to the surface of the custard and ruin the smooth, shiny top. Instead, store the petits pots in a deep container with a cover that doesn't come in contact with the desserts.

8 large egg yolks
½ cup plus 1 tablespoon sugar
3 cups heavy cream

7 tablespoons freshly ground
    coffee beans

1. Preheat the oven to 350 degrees. Whisk the egg yolks and sugar together in a large bowl. Set aside.

2. Combine the heavy cream and coffee in a medium saucepan, and bring to a boil. Remove the pan from the heat and let stand 5 minutes. Then pour the mixture through a fine-mesh strainer into a large bowl. Strain it twice more into the cleaned bowl, making sure that no grounds remain in the mixture.

3. Slowly whisk the coffee-infused cream into the egg mixture. Continue whisking until smooth. Pour the custard through a fine-mesh strainer into eight 6-ounce custard cups or ramekins.

4. Line a roasting pan with a few sheets of brown paper or newspaper. Place the ramekins in the pan, and carefully transfer the pan to the oven rack. Add enough hot tap water to the pan to reach three fourths of the way up the sides of the ramekins. Place an upside-down sheet pan or cookie sheet over the roasting pan to cover it. Bake until the custard is firm around the edges but still jiggly in the center, 1 hour.

5. Remove the pan from the oven and allow the petits pots to cool in the water for 45 minutes. Then transfer the ramekins to a wire rack and let cool completely. Place the ramekins in a deep container, and cover the container so that the cover does not touch the surface of the petits pots. Refrigerate overnight or up to 3 days. Serve chilled.

ORANGE PETITS POTS

Serves 8

For a large crowd, I will often make an assortment of chocolate, coffee, and orange petits pots and allow everyone to choose a favorite flavor. Be careful to use only the orange part of the peel and not the bitter white pith, or your custard will be bitter.

8 large egg yolks	2 large oranges
½ cup plus 1 tablespoon sugar	3 cups heavy cream

1. Preheat the oven to 350 degrees. Whisk the egg yolks and sugar together in a large bowl. Set aside.
2. Remove the zest from the oranges with a sharp vegetable peeler. Reserve the fruit for another use. Combine the heavy cream and orange zest in a medium saucepan and bring to a boil. Remove the pan from the heat and let stand 5 minutes.
3. Slowly whisk the orange-infused cream into the egg mixture. Continue whisking until smooth. Pour the custard through a fine-mesh strainer into eight 6-ounce custard cups or ramekins.
4. Line a roasting pan with a few sheets of brown paper or newspaper. Place the ramekins in the pan, and carefully transfer the pan to the oven rack. Add enough hot tap water to the pan to reach three fourths of the way up the sides of the ramekins. Place an upside-down sheet pan or cookie sheet over the roasting pan to cover it. Bake until the custard is firm around the edges but still jiggly in the center, 1 hour.
5. Remove the pan from the oven and allow the petits pots to cool in the water for 45 minutes. Then transfer the ramekins to a wire rack and let cool completely. Place the ramekins in a deep container and cover the container so that the cover does not touch the surface of the petits pots. Refrigerate overnight or up to 3 days. Serve chilled.

BRIOCHE BUTTER PUDDING WITH DRIED BLUEBERRIES AND LEMON SAUCE

Serves 10

Bread pudding is usually a humble dessert made with leftover bread and some eggs and milk that you already have in the refrigerator. But when it's made with brioche and dried blueberries and served with lemon sauce, it becomes positively exciting and definitely worthy of company. The slightly acidic dried blueberries balance the richness of the brioche and egg yolks. Fresh blueberries won't work here; their juice would make the pudding too watery.

One 8 x 4-inch Brioche Loaf
   (page 294)
4 tablespoons unsalted butter,
   softened
1½ cups dried blueberries
6 large eggs

Pinch salt
¾ cup sugar
1 quart whole milk
2 vanilla beans, split lengthwise, or
   ½ tablespoon pure vanilla extract
2 cups Light Lemon Sauce (page 515)

1. Preheat the oven to 375 degrees. Cut the ends off the brioche loaf and discard them. Slice the brioche into ten ¾-inch-thick slices. Trim the crusts from each slice and cut each slice in half. Butter one side of each piece of brioche.

2. Butter a 7 x 12-inch baking dish and arrange the blueberries in an even layer on the bottom of the dish. Arrange the brioche slices, buttered side up, overlapping them slightly, over the blueberries.

3. Whisk the eggs, salt, and sugar together in a medium bowl. Set aside.

4. Place the milk in a medium saucepan. Use a sharp paring knife to scrape the seeds from the inside of the split vanilla beans. Add the seeds and the beans (or the extract) to the milk. Very slowly bring the milk to a boil over medium-low heat. Remove the pan from the heat and let rest 5 minutes to extract all of the flavor from the vanilla pods and seeds.

5. Slowly whisk the hot milk into the egg mixture. Pour the custard through a fine-mesh strainer over the bread. Press the bread down with the back of a large spoon so that it is completely soaked.

(continued)

6. Line a roasting pan with a few sheets of brown paper or newspaper. Place the dish in the pan, and carefully transfer the pan to the oven. Add enough hot tap water to the pan to reach halfway up the sides of the dish. Bake until the custard is set around the edges but still a little wobbly in the center when gently shaken, 30 to 40 minutes.

7. Transfer the pan to a wire rack and let the brioche pudding cool in the water for 15 minutes. Then remove the baking dish from the roasting pan and let it stand another 10 to 15 minutes. Serve warm with Light Lemon Sauce.

Stovetop Puddings

The following recipes, for chocolate cream pie and rice pudding, are among the least fussy and most beloved of all the desserts I made during my time at the White House. The pie is simply a cornstarch-thickened chocolate pudding poured into a pie shell and allowed to set up in the refrigerator. The rice pudding is thickened with egg yolks and enriched with heavy cream. But just because these are one-pot desserts doesn't mean they don't deserve beautiful finishes. When covered with whipped cream and garnished with chocolate curls, the pie is fit for a king (and has been served to several). My rice pudding is so rich and flavorful that it deserves a caramelized sugar topping, just like the most elegant crème brûlée.

SILKY CHOCOLATE CREAM PIE

Serves 10

It never failed to amuse me when U.S. Presidents and heads of state went crazy for this simple chocolate pudding pie. This was a perennial favorite at casual White House affairs, and it would be right at home at a family Sunday supper.

6 tablespoons sugar
¼ cup cornstarch
8 large egg yolks
1 quart whole or 2 percent milk
8 ounces semisweet chocolate, finely chopped
4 tablespoons unsalted butter, cut into small pieces

1 prebaked 9-inch pie shell made with All-American Pie Dough (page 269)
1½ cups heavy cream, chilled
2 tablespoons confectioners' sugar
1 teaspoon pure vanilla extract
Chocolate Shavings (page 436)

1. Whisk the sugar and the cornstarch together in the bowl of an electric mixer. Add the egg yolks and beat on high speed until thick and pale, about 4 minutes.

2. Place the milk in a saucepan and bring to a boil over medium-high heat, whisking frequently to make sure the bottom isn't burning. Whisk about one third of the hot milk into the egg mixture, and return the egg mixture to the saucepan. Cook over medium-high heat, whisking constantly, until the mixture reaches a full boil, 3 to 4 minutes.

3. Remove the pan from the heat and whisk in the chocolate and butter until melted. Scrape the pudding into the pie shell and cool completely. Cover and refrigerate until completely chilled, at least 2 hours or up to 1 day.

4. Two to 3 hours before serving, place the heavy cream, confectioners' sugar, and vanilla in the bowl of an electric mixer and whip until the cream holds stiff peaks. Smooth the whipped cream over the pudding. Scatter the Chocolate Shavings over the whipped cream, and serve.

RICE PUDDING

Serves 6

I've seen recipes for rice pudding that don't call for eggs, but to me those puddings taste too starchy. Eggs added at the end of the cooking time make this rice pudding rich and custard-like, giving it an extra dimension. Take care not to overcook the eggs—just a minute on the stove will allow them to thicken the pudding sufficiently. Too long on the stove and the egg-enriched pudding will become tough and rubbery as it cools.

The addition of heavy cream at the end gives the pudding extra richness; crème fraîche adds a hint of tartness and is even better. If you like, arrange some fresh fruit in the bottom of the serving bowl before you pour the hot rice pudding in. I like strawberries, cherries, orange slices, or Prebaked Apple Slices (page 28).

1 quart whole milk	5 large egg yolks
½ cup plus 2 tablespoons long-grain rice, such as Carolina rice	¼ cup heavy cream or crème fraîche
1 vanilla bean, split lengthwise	¼ cup heavy cream, chilled, for the topping
½ cup sugar	2 tablespoons confectioners' sugar
Pinch salt	

1. Combine the milk, rice, vanilla bean, sugar, and salt in a large saucepan and bring to a boil. Turn the heat down and cook uncovered, stirring occasionally, at a bare simmer until the rice is very soft, 40 to 45 minutes.
2. Whisk the egg yolks and ¼ cup cream or crème fraîche together in a medium bowl. Whisk about ½ cup of the hot rice mixture into the bowl, a tablespoon at a time. Whisk the egg mixture back into the saucepan and bring just to a boil. Pour the rice pudding into a heatproof ceramic serving bowl. Serve warm, or let cool slightly and then cover and refrigerate until well chilled, at least 3 hours and up to 2 days.
3. Whip the ¼ cup heavy cream and the confectioners' sugar with an electric mixer; spread the whipped cream over the top of the pudding, and broil until golden, just a few seconds.

CRÈME BRÛLÉE

It has always been difficult for me to distinguish conventional crème brûlée from crème caramel. Aside from the differences in the caramel toppings—one crunchy and one liquid—the custards seem the same. Both are often stiff and even rubbery in texture, with an overwhelmingly eggy flavor.

I wanted to develop a crème brûlée that would have a more delicate flavor and texture than crème caramel, so I could taste the cream as well as the eggs. I wanted the texture to be soft. You'd really need a spoon for this ideal crème brûlée; you wouldn't be able to mold it or have to cut it with a knife!

The following recipes reflect years of experimenting to come up with a lighter, creamier dessert, a true "crème." Instead of baking the custard in the oven, I've come around to cooking it on top of the stove and then pouring it into ramekins just to chill. Stirring the custard as it cooks incorporates air into the mixture, making the finished dessert much lighter than the baked version. To this end, I also whip the egg yolks very well to give them as much volume as possible.

Adding cornstarch allows me to make the custard with fewer egg yolks than is customary, and this too contributes to the exceptionally silky and delicate texture.

The best (and in my opinion, the only) way to caramelize the sugar is with a small propane or butane torch. A torch gives you complete control over the sugar, allowing you to melt and cook it evenly. Placing the custard under the broiler, in contrast, results in an unevenly caramelized crust. Propane and butane torches are very useful, relatively inexpensive, and available in most cookware shops.

VANILLA CRÈME BRÛLÉE

Serves 10

Here is the basic recipe, simple and foolproof.

10 large egg yolks
¾ cup sugar, plus about ½ cup for
   sprinkling
3 tablespoons cornstarch
1 quart heavy cream

Pinch salt
2 vanilla beans, split lengthwise
6 tablespoons unsalted butter, cut
   into pieces

1. Combine the egg yolks, ¾ cup sugar, and cornstarch in a medium bowl and whisk until smooth and pale.

2. Place the heavy cream and salt in a medium saucepan. Use a sharp paring knife to scrape the seeds from the inside of the split vanilla beans. Add the seeds and the beans to the cream. Very slowly bring the cream to a boil over medium-low heat. Remove the pan from the heat and let rest 5 minutes to extract all of the flavor from the vanilla pods and seeds.

3. Slowly dribble one third of the hot cream into the egg yolk mixture, whisking constantly. Whisk the egg yolk mixture back into the cream and return the pan to the heat. Whisking constantly, bring the mixture back to a boil. Then remove the pan from the heat and whisk in the butter until completely melted. Pour the custard through a fine-mesh strainer into a 7 x 12-inch baking dish or ten 6-ounce ramekins. Refrigerate uncovered for at least 4 hours or up to 2 days.

4. When you are ready to serve the crème brûlée, sprinkle the custard with enough sugar to make a ⅛-inch-deep layer (this should be about ½ cup). Using a small propane torch, begin in one corner and apply the flame to the sugar using a small circular motion, moving on when the sugar has melted and caramelized. Don't be afraid to really brown the sugar—the darker it is, the crisper and more flavorful your crust will be. Move the torch in this manner over the entire surface of the custard until the sugar is completely browned. Serve immediately.

CHAMPAGNE CRÈME BRÛLÉE WITH GREEN GRAPES

Serves 10

You can actually feel and taste the Champagne bubbles in this unusual and festive version of the classic dessert. For best results, handle the Champagne very gently, being careful not to shake the bottle or to fold the wine into the custard too vigorously. Although it's not necessary, when I have the time I peel the grapes before soaking them in the Champagne. This step makes the dessert extra smooth and silky.

4 cups seedless green grapes, halved
3 cups Champagne, chilled
10 large egg yolks
1 cup sugar, plus about ½ cup for sprinkling
6 tablespoons cornstarch

1 quart heavy cream
3 vanilla beans, split lengthwise
Pinch salt
8 tablespoons unsalted butter, chilled
Frosted Grapes (page 47, optional)

1. Place the split grapes in a nonreactive bowl and pour 1 cup of the Champagne over them. Cork the Champagne tightly and refrigerate it. Cover the bowl with plastic wrap and let it stand overnight in the refrigerator.
2. Drain the grapes well and pat dry. Set them aside.
3. Combine the egg yolks, 1 cup sugar, and cornstarch in a medium bowl and whisk until smooth and pale, at least 5 minutes.
4. Place the heavy cream in a medium saucepan. Use a sharp paring knife to scrape the seeds from the inside of the split vanilla beans. Add the seeds and the beans to the cream. Add the salt. Very slowly bring the cream to a boil over medium-low heat. Remove the pan from the heat and let rest 5 minutes to extract all of the flavor from the vanilla pods and seeds.
5. Slowly dribble one third of the hot cream into the egg yolk mixture, whisking constantly. Whisk the egg yolk mixture back into the cream and return the pan to the heat. Whisking constantly, bring the mixture back to a boil. Remove from the heat.
6. Pour the custard through a fine-mesh strainer into the bowl of an electric mixer. Add the butter and mix on low speed until the custard is at room temperature.

(continued)

7. When the custard is at room temperature, very slowly pour in the remaining 2 cups Champagne with the mixer still on low speed, and mix until just combined. Do not overmix.

8. Arrange the grapes on the bottom of a 7 x 12-inch baking dish or ten 6-ounce ramekins. Pour the custard over the grapes. Refrigerate uncovered for at least 4 hours or up to 2 days.

9. When you are ready to serve the crème brûlée, sprinkle the custard with enough sugar to make a ⅛-inch-deep layer (this should be about ½ cup). Using a small propane torch, begin in one corner and apply the flame to the sugar using a small circular motion, moving on when the sugar has melted and caramelized. Don't be afraid to really brown the sugar—the darker it is, the crisper and more flavorful the crust will be. Move the torch in this manner over the entire surface of the custard until the sugar is completely browned. Garnish with Frosted Grapes if desired, and serve immediately.

ORANGE CRÈME BRÛLÉE

Serves 10

Orange zest–flavored custard hides orange segments in this wonderful variation on crème brûlée. For the best flavor, use a sharp vegetable peeler and remove only the zest of the oranges, leaving the bitter white pith behind.

6 navel oranges
2 tablespoons plus ¼ cup Grand Marnier
10 large egg yolks
1 cup sugar, plus about ½ cup for sprinkling
6 tablespoons cornstarch

1 quart heavy cream
Pinch salt
2 vanilla beans, split lengthwise
8 tablespoons (1 stick) unsalted butter
Glazed Orange Segments (page 487, optional)

1. Peel 3 of the oranges with a sharp vegetable peeler, removing just the zest. Place the zest in a small zipper-lock bag and refrigerate. Peel and segment all the oranges, removing all the white pith, and place them in a nonreactive bowl. Sprinkle the 2 tablespoons Grand Marnier over the oranges, cover with plastic wrap, and refrigerate overnight.

2. Combine the egg yolks, the 1 cup sugar, and the cornstarch in a medium bowl and whisk until smooth and pale.

3. Place the heavy cream, reserved orange zest, and salt in a medium saucepan. Use a sharp paring knife to scrape the seeds from the inside of the split vanilla beans. Add the seeds and the beans to the cream. Very slowly bring the cream to a boil over medium-low heat. Remove the pan from the heat and let rest 5 minutes to extract all of the flavor from the vanilla pods and seeds.

4. Slowly dribble one third of the hot cream into the egg yolk mixture, whisking constantly. Whisk the egg yolk mixture back into the cream and return the pan to the heat. Whisking constantly, bring the mixture back to a boil. Pour the custard through a fine-mesh strainer into a bowl. Whisk in the butter until completely melted. Then whisk in the remaining ¼ cup Grand Marnier.

5. Arrange the marinated orange segments on the bottom of a 7 x 12-inch baking dish or ten 6-ounce ramekins. Pour the hot custard over the oranges. Refrigerate uncovered for at least 4 hours or up to 2 days.

6. When you are ready to serve the crème brûlée, sprinkle the custard with enough sugar to make a ⅛-inch-deep layer (this should be about ½ cup). Using a small propane torch, begin in one corner and apply the flame to the sugar using a small circular motion, moving on when the sugar has melted and caramelized. Don't be afraid to really brown the sugar—the darker it is, the crisper and more flavorful the crust will be. Move the torch in this manner over the entire surface of the custard until the sugar is completely browned. Garnish with Glazed Orange Segments if desired, and serve immediately.

APPLE CIDER BRÛLÉE

Serves 10

The seasons inspire me. On the way to work one autumn a couple of years ago, I noticed fresh apple cider at a farm stand, and wondered if I could use it in a custard dessert. I whipped up this Apple Cider Brûlée and served it at the White House for lunch that day, where it was enjoyed for its seasonal flavor and rich texture. The recipe is based on my recipe for Vanilla Crème Brûlée, with cider standing in for the cream.

12 large egg yolks
¾ cup plus 2 tablespoons sugar, plus about ½ cup for sprinkling
6 tablespoons cornstarch
1 quart apple cider
1 teaspoon ground cinnamon
¼ teaspoon ground cloves
¼ cup fresh lemon juice
½ teaspoon grated lemon zest
8 tablespoons (1 stick) unsalted butter

5 Whole Baked Apples filled with prunes (page 31), cut into quarters
1 cup Caramelized Pumpkin Seeds (page 504, optional)
6 lady apples (optional)
¼ cup candied lemon zest (page 505, optional)

1. Combine the egg yolks, the ¾ cup plus 2 tablespoons sugar, and the cornstarch in a medium bowl and whisk until smooth.

2. Place the cider, cinnamon, cloves, lemon juice, and grated lemon zest in a medium saucepan and bring to a boil. Slowly dribble one third of the hot cider into the egg yolk mixture, whisking constantly. Whisk the egg yolk mixture back into the remaining cider and return the pan to the heat. Whisking constantly, bring the mixture back to a boil. Pour the custard through a fine-mesh strainer into a bowl. Whisk in the butter until completely melted.

3. Arrange the quartered baked apples on the bottom of a 7 x 12-inch baking dish or ten 6-ounce ramekins. Pour the hot custard over the apples. Refrigerate uncovered for at least 4 hours or up to 2 days.

4. When you are ready to serve the brûlée, sprinkle the custard with enough sugar to make a ⅛-inch-deep layer (about ½ cup). Using a small propane torch, begin in one corner and apply the flame to the sugar using a small circular motion,

moving on when the sugar has melted and caramelized. Don't be afraid to really brown the sugar—the darker it is, the crisper and more flavorful the crust will be. Move the torch in this manner over the entire surface of the custard until the sugar is completely browned. Garnish with Caramelized Pumpkin Seeds or lady apples and candied lemon zest if desired, and serve immediately.

SOUFFLÉS

I prefer minimalist soufflés—no egg yolks, no butter, no flour. It's not just that these ingredients add fat and calories to the finished dessert; they also weight down the soufflé batter and mute the fresh, natural fruit flavors that I want to come through.

The soufflé recipes here are my very favorites. Each delivers strong, pure fruit flavor and ethereal texture. The techniques for achieving this vary from recipe to recipe, tailored to the particular qualities of the fruit in question.

When I make a soufflé with strawberries, I use an Italian meringue, whipping the egg whites with a boiling sugar syrup instead of simply with granulated sugar. Italian meringue is more stable and won't break even when combined with a very liquidy fruit like strawberries.

For the Baked Apple Soufflé, I add a touch of cornstarch. Although the fruit is baked before it is stirred into the meringue, it is still quite watery. The cornstarch helps bind the batter together.

Pears contain quite a lot of water also. I have found that a soufflé made with dried pears delivers wonderful fruit flavor without the water.

Certain rules always apply:

Butter baking dishes and ramekins generously, and sprinkle them generously with sugar. If you don't, the batter will stick to the unbuttered and unsugared spots and your soufflé will rise unevenly.

Take care in whipping egg whites. Make sure your bowl and beaters are very clean, with no traces of grease. Don't allow traces of yolk to find their way into the whites. Begin to add the sugar only after the whites are already at the soft peak stage, and add it very slowly so that it has time to dissolve.

Lighten the fruit puree by folding in a little bit of the meringue. Then fold the remaining meringue very gently into the lightened puree—this makes for the highest rise.

Run the tip of your thumb around the inside edge of each ramekin to clean the edge so the batter will rise evenly up from the top of the ramekin.

The image of the cook rushing the soufflé from oven to table in a matter of seconds before it deflates is somewhat of a myth. Although these soufflés certainly may be served immediately, many of them may be cooled on a wire rack for a few minutes and then unmolded onto a platter. If you unmold a soufflé, you can garnish it beautifully, something you can't do if it is still in the dish. With certain recipes (those made with egg whites only, no yolks), you can even bake the soufflé ahead of time, refrigerate it, and then reheat it just before serving. It will magically rise again, just as it did the first time around.

WARM STRAWBERRY SOUFFLÉ

Serves 6

I use an Italian meringue in this recipe because it won't break, even when cooked with the very liquidy strawberries. It's not necessary to use a candy thermometer to determine whether your sugar syrup has reached the soft ball stage. Simply have a small bowl of ice water ready next to the cooktop, and after the sugar syrup has been boiling for 3 or 4 minutes, dribble a few drops into the ice water. If it dissolves immediately, continue to cook. Try again in another minute or two. When the sugar dropped into the ice water can be rolled into a soft ball, it is ready.

1 pint fresh strawberries, washed and
    stemmed
2 large egg whites
½ cup sugar, plus more for sprinkling

¼ cup water
½ cup Chunky Strawberry Sauce
    (page 518) or Vanilla Sauce
    (page 514)

1. Preheat the oven to 400 degrees. Butter six 6-ounce ramekins and sprinkle them generously with sugar.
2. Place the strawberries in the bowl of a food processor fitted with the metal blade, and process until smooth. Measure out 1 cup into a large bowl. Reserve any remaining puree for another use.
3. Place the egg whites in the bowl of an electric mixer fitted with the whisk attachment. Combine the ½ cup sugar and the water in a small saucepan and bring to a boil. When the sugar syrup reaches the soft ball stage (235 degrees on a candy thermometer), turn the mixer on high speed and dribble the syrup down the side of the bowl in a thin, steady stream. Decrease the speed to medium and continue to beat until the egg whites form stiff peaks.
4. Stir one third of the meringue into the strawberry puree to lighten it. Then fold the remaining meringue into the lightened puree, being careful not to deflate the egg whites. Fill each ramekin to the top, and smooth with a spatula. Run your thumb around the inside edge of each ramekin, and place them in the oven. Bake until just firm to the touch and well risen, no longer than 10 minutes. Don't overbake or the inside of the soufflé will become runny.
5. Remove the soufflés from the oven and serve immediately with Chunky Strawberry Sauce or Vanilla Sauce.

MANGO TROPICO SOUFFLÉ

Serves 6

I think of this as the perfect spa dessert: fat-free but completely satisfying and refreshing. Tropico, an unusual orange-flavored liqueur, complements and heightens the flavor of the mangoes.

FOR THE SAUCE:
1 large ripe mango, peeled and cut
   into 1-inch chunks
½ cup Tropico liqueur

FOR THE SOUFFLÉ:
1 large ripe mango, peeled and cut
   into chunks
⅓ cup Tropico liqueur

2 large egg whites, at room
   temperature
4½ tablespoons sugar, plus more for
   sprinkling
2 tablespoons confectioners' sugar
Fresh raspberries for garnish
   (optional)
Fresh mint leaves for garnish
   (optional)

1. For the sauce: Place the mango chunks in the bowl of a food processor fitted with the metal blade and process until smooth. Push the puree through a fine-mesh strainer into a bowl to remove any tough fibers. Stir the Tropico into the puree. Set the sauce aside while you make the soufflé.

2. For the soufflé: Preheat the oven to 400 degrees. Butter six 6-ounce ramekins and sprinkle them generously with sugar.

3. Place the mango in the food processor and process until smooth. Push the puree through a fine-mesh strainer into a large bowl to remove any tough fibers. Stir in the Tropico and set aside.

4. Place the egg whites in the bowl of an electric mixer fitted with the whisk attachment, and whip on high speed until they hold very soft peaks. With the mixer still on high, add the sugar in a very slow stream until they hold stiff peaks.

5. Stir one third of the egg whites into the mango mixture to lighten it. Then fold the remaining egg whites into the lightened puree, being careful not to deflate the egg whites. Fill each ramekin to the top, and smooth with a spatula. Sift 1 teaspoon of the confectioners' sugar over each ramekin. Run your thumb

around the inside edge of each ramekin, and place them in the oven. Bake until the soufflés are risen and set, about 10 minutes.

6. Serve immediately in the ramekins. Or for a dressier presentation, let the soufflés stand for 5 to 8 minutes, then run a sharp paring knife around each ramekin and unmold the soufflés onto dessert plates. Garnish the unmolded soufflés with fresh raspberries and mint leaves, and serve with the reserved sauce.

GRAND MARNIER SOUFFLÉ WITH CHUNKY STRAWBERRY SAUCE

Serves 8

Because this soufflé is made with pastry cream, it won't deflate as quickly as some, allowing you to spoon the strawberry sauce in before serving. Adding the strawberry sauce to the interior of the warm soufflés gives this dessert a very interesting mix of textures and flavors.

¾ cup granulated sugar, plus more for sprinkling

5 tablespoons cornstarch

4 large eggs

2 cups whole or 2 percent milk

8 store-bought ladyfingers, cut into 8 pieces each

3 tablespoons plus ½ cup Grand Marnier

3 large egg yolks

8 large egg whites, at room temperature

2 tablespoons plus 2 teaspoons confectioners' sugar

1 cup Chunky Strawberry Sauce (page 518)

1. Whisk 6 tablespoons of the granulated sugar and the cornstarch together in a medium bowl. Whisk in the whole eggs. Bring the milk to a boil in a medium saucepan. Slowly dribble ½ cup of the hot milk into the egg mixture, whisking constantly. Dribble another ½ cup of the milk into the egg mixture, again whisking constantly.

2. Whisk the egg mixture back into the remaining milk and return the pan to the heat. Bring to a full boil, whisking constantly. Then remove the pan from the heat and pour the mixture through a fine-mesh strainer into a large bowl. Let it cool completely.

3. Preheat the oven to 400 degrees. Place the ladyfinger pieces in a shallow baking pan and sprinkle with the 3 tablespoons Grand Marnier. Butter eight 8-ounce ramekins and sprinkle them generously with sugar. Whisk the egg yolks and the remaining ½ cup Grand Marnier into the cooled custard.

4. Place the egg whites in the bowl of an electric mixer fitted with the whisk attachment, and whip on high speed until just about to hold soft peaks. With the mixer still on high speed, slowly pour in the remaining 6 tablespoons granu-

lated sugar in a slow, steady stream. Whip until the meringue holds stiff peaks. Fold the whites into the custard mixture.

5. Fill each ramekin one-third full with soufflé mixture. Place 4 pieces of soaked ladyfinger on top of the mixture. Add more soufflé mixture, so that it reaches two thirds of the way to the top of each ramekin. Add 4 more pieces of soaked ladyfinger. Fill the ramekins all the way to the top with the remaining soufflé mixture, and smooth the tops with a small offset spatula so that the mixture is flush with the top of the ramekins. Sift 1 teaspoon confectioners' sugar over each ramekin. Run your thumb around the inside edge of each ramekin. Use a sharp knife to make a crosshatch pattern on the top of the soufflés.

6. Bake until the soufflés are risen and set, about 12 minutes. Cut an opening into the top of each soufflé and pour in 2 tablespoons of the Chunky Strawberry Sauce. Serve immediately.

BAKED APPLE SOUFFLÉ

Serves 12

Apples contain quite a lot of water, so I add cornstarch to this soufflé to help bind it together.

3 pounds Granny Smith apples, peeled, cored, and cut into 1-inch cubes

1 cup plus 2 tablespoons sugar

½ cup Cointreau or other orange-flavored liqueur

½ teaspoon pure vanilla extract

1 tablespoon cornstarch

5 large egg whites, at room temperature

1 cup Lemon Cream (page 510)

Prebaked Apple Slices (page 28, optional)

1. Preheat the oven to 375 degrees. Place the cubed apples on a rimmed baking sheet and bake, stirring two or three times to ensure even cooking, until tender, 25 to 30 minutes.

2. Meanwhile, butter two 4- to 5-cup soufflé dishes and sprinkle them generously with sugar.

3. Puree the baked apples in a blender. Measure out 3½ cups of the apple puree and place it in a large bowl. (Set aside any remaining puree for another use.) Stir in ¾ cup of the sugar. Combine the Cointreau, vanilla, and cornstarch and add to the puree.

4. Whip the egg whites with an electric mixer on high speed until they hold very soft peaks. Whipping constantly, add the remaining 6 tablespoons sugar in a very slow stream until they hold stiff peaks.

5. Stir about one third of the egg whites into the apple mixture to lighten it. Gently but thoroughly fold the remaining egg whites into the apple. Divide the mixture between the two soufflé dishes and smooth the tops with a spatula.

6. Pour 1 inch of hot tap water into a large roasting pan. Carefully place the soufflé dishes in the pan, and place the pan in the oven. Bake until the mixture is set and the soufflés have risen and are firm to the touch, 30 to 40 minutes. Remove them from the pan and let them cool on a wire rack for 10 to 15 minutes.

7. Place a serving dish upside down on top of one soufflé dish, invert the two together, and gently shake to release the soufflé. Repeat with the second soufflé dish. Spoon the Lemon Cream around the soufflés, decorate with apple slices if desired, and serve immediately.

DRIED PEAR SOUFFLÉ

Serves 8

When I need to make a low-fat but luscious dessert, I often turn to dried fruit. Dried pears have such concentrated flavor and richness that there is no need to add butter or egg yolks to this soufflé.

Dried apricots may be substituted with equally good results. Use Raspberry Sauce (page 516) instead of the Lemon Cream if you are really watching the calories. By contrast, for the most decadent version of this dessert, serve it right in the soufflé dish with Caramel Sauce (page 513) and Sweetened Whipped Cream (page 521).

A few preparation tips: Sprinkling the lemon juice directly onto the fresh pear slices will make them too tart; instead, moisten a paper towel or a tissue with lemon juice and rest the towel on top of the slices. This will prevent them from turning brown without affecting their flavor. Although this soufflé is best warm from the oven, it may be cooled to room temperature, refrigerated, and then reheated. When you are ready to serve it, reheat it in a 375-degree oven until it rises again, 10 to 15 minutes. You will have a do-ahead dessert that looks as if it was prepared à la minute!

1 pound dried pears	5 large egg whites, at room
½ cup granulated sugar, plus more	temperature
for sprinkling	1 tablespoon confectioners' sugar
2 teaspoons plus 1 tablespoon fresh	1 ripe pear
lemon juice	1 cup Lemon Cream (page 510)
1 teaspoon grated lemon zest	

1. Place the dried pears in a medium saucepan, cover with cold water, and bring just to a boil. Then lower the heat and cook, covered, at a bare simmer until tender, 30 to 40 minutes.

2. Preheat the oven to 375 degrees. Butter a 4- to 5-cup soufflé dish and sprinkle it generously with granulated sugar.

3. Drain the pears and puree them in a food processor fitted with the steel blade. You should have about 1 cup. Combine the pureed pears, ¼ cup of the granulated sugar, the 2 teaspoons lemon juice, and the lemon zest in a large bowl.

(continued)

4. Place the egg whites in the bowl of an electric mixer fitted with the whisk attachment and whip on high speed until they form soft peaks. Adding the remaining ¼ cup sugar in a slow stream, continue to beat until the egg whites hold very stiff peaks. Stir half of the egg whites into the pear mixture to lighten it. Then fold the remaining egg whites into the pear mixture, being careful not to deflate the whites. Pour the mixture into the soufflé dish, smooth the top with a spatula, and sift the confectioners' sugar over the top. Run the tip of your thumb around the inside edge of the soufflé dish to ensure the highest rise.

5. Bake until the soufflé is firm and well risen, 25 to 30 minutes.

6. Shortly before the soufflé is done, sprinkle a paper towel or tissue with the remaining 1 tablespoon lemon juice. Peel, core, and thinly slice the pear. Place the towel on top of the pear slices to keep them from turning brown.

7. Remove the soufflé from the oven, and if serving it right in the dish, serve it immediately, with the Lemon Cream and the pear slices on the side. If unmolding the soufflé, let it cool in the dish on a wire rack for 15 minutes. Then place a serving dish upside down on top of the soufflé dish, invert the two together, and gently shake to release the soufflé. Spoon the Lemon Cream around the unmolded soufflé, arrange the pear slices around the soufflé, and serve.

APRICOT SUNBURST

Serves 8

Like the Dried Pear Soufflé, this dessert relies on dried fruit rather than a lot of fat for richness. The glazed cherries add color; dried cherries may be substituted if you like. Any fresh fruit in season can be used to garnish the dessert. Add a Spun Sugar Sunburst for special occasions.

FOR THE SOUFFLÉ:
1 pound dried apricots
½ cup sugar, plus more for sprinkling
2 teaspoons fresh lime juice
½ teaspoon grated lime zest
Pinch salt
½ cup shelled unsalted pistachio nuts, chopped
½ cup Caramelized Pecans (page 503)
½ cup chopped red glazed cherries (available in supermarkets)

5 large egg whites, at room temperature

FOR THE SAUCE:
1 tablespoon cornstarch
2 tablespoons water
1 teaspoon finely chopped fresh mint leaves
About 3 cups cut-up fresh fruit (bite-size pieces)

Spun Sugar Sunburst (page 486, optional)

1. Place the apricots in a medium saucepan, cover with cold water, and bring just to a boil. Lower the heat, cover, and cook at a bare simmer until tender, 30 to 40 minutes. Drain the apricots, reserving the cooking liquid, and puree them in a food processor fitted with the metal blade. You should have about 1 cup of puree.

2. Preheat the oven to 375 degrees. Butter a 10-inch savarin mold and sprinkle it generously with sugar. Combine the pureed apricots, ¼ cup of the sugar, and the lime juice, lime zest, salt, pistachios, pecans, and cherries in a large bowl.

3. Place the egg whites in the bowl of an electric mixer fitted with the whisk attachment and whip on high speed until they form soft peaks. With the mixer on, add the remaining ¼ cup sugar in a slow stream. Continue to beat until the egg whites hold very stiff peaks. Carefully fold the whites into the apricot mix-

(continued)

ture. Scrape the mixture into the prepared savarin mold, and place it in the oven. Bake until firm, 10 to 15 minutes. Remove the dish from the oven and let it cool completely on a wire rack.

4. While the soufflé is cooling, make the sauce: Combine the cornstarch and water in a small bowl and whisk until smooth. Place ¾ cup of the reserved apricot cooking liquid in a small saucepan and bring to a boil. Whisk the cornstarch mixture into the liquid, lower the heat, and simmer, whisking constantly, until thickened, 2 to 3 minutes. Remove from the heat and stir in the mint.

5. Place a serving dish upside down on top of the mold, invert the two together, and gently shake to release the soufflé. Fill the center with the fresh fruit, and spoon the sauce around the base. Place the Spun Sugar Sunburst on top of the fruit if desired.

THREE

Versatile Mousses and Bavarians

MOUSSE IS A RATHER amorphous category. From the French word for "foam," it can mean any kind of whipped dessert. A mousse can be as simple as the combination of whipped cream and melted chocolate. More complicated versions, like the coconut recipe here, add gelatin and whipped egg whites for shape and volume.

Many mousses are casual desserts, simply spooned into dessert goblets and eaten like cold puddings. But others may be poured into molds and presented more elaborately on garnished dessert platters. They fit a variety of occasions. Lemon Mousse, folded together with fresh raspberries, is the perfect poolside dessert. Champagne Mousse is appropriate at a black-tie dinner.

Although it may be difficult to define exactly what a mousse is, one thing is certain: The mousse recipes in this chapter are among the most straightforward and useful for the everyday cook. Master the tasks of whipping cream and melting gelatin, and you can whip up a dessert in a matter of minutes. Some mousses, like the chocolate one, can be made on the spur of the moment. Others are made in advance and refrigerated or frozen, ready to serve whenever you need them.

Traditionally a Bavarian is a custard that has been folded together with whipped cream and gelatin. Although the basic technique is a bit trickier than that for most mousses, it is well worth mastering.

Bavarians don't get the attention they deserve, perhaps because they are usually thought of as cake filling. But a good Bavarian can be so much more than the glue between two layers of genoise! When made properly, a Bavarian is light, delicate, and flavorful. Poured into a pretty mold, it can be frozen and then unmolded when needed. Garnish it with fresh fruit or a sauce, and you have a simple, pretty, do-ahead dessert that will please any palate. Once you know how to make a basic Bavarian, you can vary its flavor to suit any season or occasion. When I began to work on this chapter, I listed the many ways I have enjoyed molded Bavarians as desserts in their own right. I was amazed at the range of flavors, from chocolate to chestnut, blackberry to passion fruit. I truly hope that you will not turn to the recipes in this section only when you need to fill a cake. Once you experience a properly made Bavarian, you just might give up baking in favor of these terrific stovetop creations!

THE RECIPES

*T*WO SIMPLE CHOCOLATE MOUSSES

Every cook should have a chocolate mousse recipe to rely on. I have two: one dark and one white. I don't fuss with beaten egg yolks or whipped egg whites in either recipe. Mousses made with whole uncooked eggs or yolks are too rich for my taste, but mousses made with just egg whites lack the luxury of added fat. I prefer the simple combination of chocolate and whipped cream. To me, this type of mousse is luxurious without being too rich.

The key to success with both versions is in the handling of the ingredients. The chocolate must still be warm to the touch when it is folded together with the cream. If it is too cool, it will seize up before it can be fully incorporated, making the mousse grainy. Likewise, bring the cream to room temperature before you whip it. You'll lose a little bit in volume, but if it is not icy cold there will be less of a chance that when it comes into contact with the chocolate, it will harden the chocolate. Whisk the chocolate all at once and quickly into the whipped cream for the smoothest result.

QUICK CHOCOLATE MOUSSE WITH CRYSTALLIZED GINGER

Serves 6

I am amazed at the number of unnecessarily complicated chocolate mousse recipes out there. Some people will make a sabayon to make mousse, or add butter. As far as I'm concerned, simpler is better. There is nothing more satisfying than the combination of cream and chocolate, with a little bit of crystallized ginger added for excitement. This mousse is very good on its own, served from a large bowl or spooned into individual goblets.

Although there are only three ingredients in this recipe, you must handle them carefully for the best results. The chocolate should be a little warm to the touch; otherwise it may set before you have a chance to fold it into the whipped cream, resulting in a grainy mousse. For the same reason, let the cream come to room temperature before you whip it. If it is too cold, it might cause the chocolate to harden too quickly.

> 4 ounces semisweet or bittersweet chocolate, finely chopped
> 1 cup heavy cream, at room temperature
>
> 2 teaspoons finely chopped crystallized ginger
> 6 Chocolate Cups (page 446, optional)

1. Pour 2 inches of water into a medium saucepan and bring to a bare simmer. Place the chocolate in a stainless steel bowl that is big enough to rest on top of the saucepan, and place it over the simmering water, making sure that the bowl doesn't touch the water. Heat, whisking occasionally, until the chocolate is completely melted. Remove from the heat and let cool until the chocolate is just warm to the touch, between 95 and 100 degrees on a candy thermometer.

2. Whip the heavy cream with an electric mixer until it holds soft peaks. Add the whipped cream and the ginger to the chocolate all at once, and quickly whisk together. Scrape the mousse into a large serving bowl or individual goblets, or pipe it into Chocolate Cups if desired. Serve immediately, or refrigerate, uncovered, for up to 1 day before serving.

WHITE CHOCOLATE MOUSSE WITH GRAND MARNIER

Serves 8

Most commercially available white chocolate barely tastes of chocolate and has an unpleasant aftertaste. When cooking at home, I rely on Lindt, a high-quality brand available in many supermarkets. Fold the melted chocolate in quickly and all at once so it doesn't have a chance to solidify and seize up before it is incorporated into the whipped cream.

6 ounces best-quality white chocolate

1 cup heavy cream, at room temperature

½ cup Grand Marnier or other orange-flavored liqueur

8 Chocolate Cups (page 446, optional)

1. Pour 2 inches of water into a medium saucepan and bring to a bare simmer. Place the chocolate in a stainless steel bowl that is big enough to rest on top of the saucepan, and place it over the simmering water, making sure that the bowl doesn't touch the water. Heat, whisking occasionally, until the chocolate is completely melted. Remove from the heat and let cool until the chocolate is just warm to the touch, between 95 and 100 degrees on a candy thermometer.

2. Whip the heavy cream with an electric mixer until it holds soft peaks. Gently but quickly fold the whipped cream and the Grand Marnier into the melted chocolate, adding it all at once. Scrape the mousse into a large serving bowl or individual goblets, or spoon it into Chocolate Cups if desired. Cover the bowl or goblets with plastic wrap, making sure that the plastic doesn't come in contact with the mousse. (If using Chocolate Cups, do not wrap in plastic.) Refrigerate for at least 3 hours or up to 1 day before serving.

MOLDED MOUSSES

Mousses made with gelatin keep their shape better than those made without gelatin, so they can be chilled and then unmolded. Try forming a layered mousse, with each layer a different flavor (making sure each layer sets before you add the next). You can also pour the mousse mixture over cake layers still in their pans, and then refrigerate until set.

LEMON MOUSSE

Serves 6

This is a very simple, refreshing mousse, especially with the berries folded in. I serve it poolside in the summer, with flutes of iced Champagne. The mousse needs gelatin to help keep its shape when unmolded. If you'd like to simply spoon it from a serving bowl into dessert goblets, omit the gelatin.

1 cup heavy cream, chilled
2 tablespoons cold water
½ envelope unflavored gelatin
    (or 2 sheets; see page 119)
1 cup Lemon Cream (page 510),
    at room temperature

1 cup fresh raspberries, blueberries,
    or blackberries, picked over,
    washed, and patted dry
    (optional)

1. Whip the heavy cream with an electric mixer until it holds soft peaks.
2. Pour 1 inch of water into a small saucepan and bring it to a bare simmer. Place the cold water in a small heatproof bowl and sprinkle the gelatin on top. Let stand to dissolve. Then place the bowl over the simmering water and heat, whisking constantly, just until the gelatin melts, 30 seconds to 1 minute.
3. Whisk the melted gelatin into the Lemon Cream, working quickly so that the gelatin doesn't have time to form rubbery strands. Fold in the whipped cream

(continued)

gently but thoroughly, so that no white streaks remain. Fold in the berries if desired.

4. Pour the mousse into a 4- or 5-cup mold, wrap it in plastic wrap, and refrigerate until completely set, at least 3 hours or up to 1 day. Or wrap it in plastic wrap and freeze for up to 3 weeks.

5. When you are ready to serve the mousse, dip the mold in hot water for 15 to 20 seconds (30 seconds for a frozen mousse). Place a serving platter upside down over the mold, invert the two together, and tap gently to unmold. Serve a refrigerated mousse immediately upon unmolding. Allow an unmolded frozen mousse to sit outside the refrigerator until defrosted, 3 to 4 hours, before serving.

Gelatin Basics

Gelatin gives certain mousses, and all Bavarians, stability and allows them to set. Mousses that contain gelatin will last longer in the refrigerator. Professionals use **sheet gelatin,** which resembles brittle strips of very thin clear plastic. Sheet gelatin is available by mail (see pages 523–24) and at baking supply shops. I like sheet gelatin because it is easier to dissolve and has less of an aftertaste than **powdered gelatin.** Powdered gelatin is a perfectly adequate substitute, however. All of the recipes in this book give quantities for both types of gelatin.

Gelatin is highly sensitive to temperature. Both powdered gelatin and sheet gelatin must be soaked in cold water until dissolved or softened, and then warmed until melted. If either step is skipped, your mousse or Bavarian will fail to gel. Place sheet gelatin in a bowl of cold water and let it stand for several minutes, until very soft. Squeeze the softened sheet gelatin to wring out most but not all of the excess water, and then melt it in a bowl set above a pan of barely simmering water. The melted gelatin is then ready to add to either a warm or a cold mixture.

Powdered gelatin must be dissolved in a small amount of cool water. Place a few tablespoons of water in a small bowl and sprinkle the gelatin on top. Let it stand for several minutes, until the white powder has turned into a clear, bumpy gel. Dissolved powdered gelatin is then melted over simmering water or heated by stirring into a warm liquid.

When stirring warmed gelatin, either the sheet or the powdered variety, into a room-temperature liquid (never stir it into cold liquid), make sure to whisk it in quickly and thoroughly. If the melted gelatin is not completely incorporated into the other ingredients before it begins to gel, it will form unappetizing strands.

LIME MOUSSE

Serves 6

Serve this mousse on its own or as part of Lime Mousse with Papaya (page 121).

2 tablespoons cold water
½ envelope unflavored gelatin
   (or 3 sheets; see page 119)
3 large egg yolks
6 tablespoons sugar

¾ cup whole milk
¼ cup fresh lime juice (from about
   3 limes)
1½ teaspoons grated lime zest
1 cup heavy cream, chilled

1. Place the water in a small bowl. Sprinkle the gelatin on top and let stand to dissolve. Prepare a large bowl of ice water.

2. Whisk the egg yolks and sugar together in a large bowl. Place the milk, lime juice, and lime zest in a small saucepan and bring to a boil. Pour the hot milk mixture into the yolk mixture in a slow stream, whisking constantly.

3. Return the mixture to the pan and bring just to a boil. As soon as the mixture begins to bubble, pour it through a fine-mesh strainer into a clean bowl. Whisk in the dissolved gelatin. Set the bowl into the bowl of ice water and let it cool, whisking occasionally, until it is just beginning to thicken but is still liquid.

4. While the lime mixture is cooling, whip the heavy cream with an electric mixer until it holds soft peaks. Gently but thoroughly fold the cooled lime mixture into the whipped cream. Pour the mousse into a 4- or 5-cup mold, wrap it in plastic wrap, and refrigerate it until completely set, at least 3 hours or up to 1 day. Or wrap the mousse in plastic wrap and freeze for up to 3 weeks.

5. When you are ready to serve the mousse, dip the mold in hot water for 15 to 20 seconds (30 seconds for a frozen mousse). Place a serving platter upside down over the mold, invert the two together, and tap gently to unmold. Serve a refrigerated mousse immediately upon unmolding. Allow an unmolded frozen mousse to sit outside the refrigerator until defrosted, 3 to 4 hours, before serving.

LIME MOUSSE WITH PAPAYA

Serves 8

This dessert has an exotic flair. Accompanied with a glass of Sauternes, it is a beautiful way to end a special meal.

1 medium-size ripe papaya
1 recipe Lime Mousse (page 120),
   prepared but not chilled

1 cup Lime Cream (page 511)
2 cups strawberries, washed and
   stemmed

1. Peel the papaya with a vegetable peeler or a sharp paring knife. Cut it in half lengthwise and scrape out the seeds.
2. Fill each papaya half with mousse, and refrigerate, uncovered, overnight. Pour the remaining mousse into a mold, cover it with plastic wrap, and freeze overnight.
3. When you are ready to serve the mousse, dip the mold in hot water for 30 seconds. Then invert it onto a large serving platter and tap gently to unmold. Allow the mousse to defrost to room temperature, 3 to 4 hours. Pour the Lime Cream around the the molded mousse. Cut the papaya halves lengthwise and then cut each piece diagonally. You should have 8 papaya wedges altogether. Arrange the wedges around the mousse, points facing out, and garnish with the strawberries. Serve immediately, or refrigerate uncovered for up to 1 day.

COCONUT MOUSSE

Serves 8

Homemade Coconut Puree gives this simple mousse a pure, strong coconut flavor. This is also one of my all-time favorite cake fillings. Half a recipe is enough for one cake: Layer the mousse between two ½-inch-thick rounds of Genoise (page 397) in a 9-inch cake pan. Cover with plastic wrap, freeze until firm, then unmold and glaze with Semi-sweet Chocolate Glaze (page 512). Bring the cake to room temperature before serving.

1½ cups heavy cream, chilled
4 large egg whites, at room
   temperature
¼ cup sugar
6 tablespoons cold water

1½ envelopes unflavored gelatin
   (or 8 sheets; see page 119)
2 cups Coconut Puree (page 42)
1½ tablespoons dark rum

1. Whip the heavy cream with an electric mixer until it holds soft peaks.
2. Place the egg whites in the clean bowl of an electric mixer fitted with the whisk attachment and whip on high speed until white, fluffy, and just about to hold soft peaks. With the mixer still on high, pour in the sugar in a slow, steady stream. Whip until the whites hold stiff peaks.
3. Pour 1 inch of water into a small saucepan and bring to a bare simmer. Place the cold water in a small heatproof bowl and sprinkle the gelatin on top. Let stand to dissolve. Place the bowl over the simmering water and heat, whisking constantly, just until the gelatin melts, 30 seconds to 1 minute.
4. Whisk the Coconut Puree and rum together in a large bowl. Whisk in the melted gelatin, working quickly so that no rubbery strands form. Add the egg whites and whipped cream to the coconut mixture, and fold them in together.
5. Pour the mousse into a 4- or 5-cup mold, wrap it in plastic wrap, and refrigerate until completely set, at least 3 hours or up to 1 day. Or wrap it in plastic wrap and freeze for up to 3 weeks.
6. When you are ready to serve the mousse, dip the mold in hot water for 15 to 20 seconds (30 seconds for a frozen mousse). Place a serving platter upside down over the mold, invert the two together, and tap gently to unmold. Serve a refrigerated mousse immediately upon unmolding. Allow an unmolded frozen mousse to sit outside the refrigerator until defrosted, 3 to 4 hours, before serving.

PASSION FRUIT MOUSSE

Serves 8

A lot of experimentation went into developing this very delicate mousse. Although I use it mainly to fill cakes, sometimes I will stir 1½ cups of clementine sections or diced mango into the mousse and pour it into a mold to make a refreshing and unusual dessert.

1 cup heavy cream, chilled	1 envelope unflavored gelatin
4 large egg whites	(or 5 sheets; see page 119)
1½ cups sugar	1 cup frozen passion fruit puree,
3 tablespoons cold water	thawed (see Note)

1. Whip the heavy cream with an electric mixer until it holds soft peaks.
2. Place the egg whites in a clean bowl of an electric mixer fitted with the whisk attachment and whip on high speed until white, fluffy, and just about to hold soft peaks. With the mixer still on high, slowly pour in ½ cup of the sugar in a slow, steady stream. Whip until the whites hold stiff peaks.
3. Pour 1 inch of water into a small saucepan and bring to a bare simmer. Place the cold water in a small heatproof bowl and sprinkle the gelatin on top. Let stand to dissolve. Then place the bowl over the simmering water and heat, whisking constantly, just until the gelatin melts, 30 seconds to 1 minute.
4. Whisk the passion fruit puree and the remaining 1 cup sugar together in a large bowl. Whisk in the melted gelatin, working quickly so that no rubbery strands form. Add the egg whites and whipped cream to the mixture, and fold them in together.
5. Pour the mousse into a 4-cup mold, wrap it in plastic wrap, and refrigerate until completely set, at least 3 hours or up to 1 day. Or wrap it in plastic wrap and freeze for up to 3 weeks.
6. When you are ready to serve the mousse, dip the mold in hot water for 15 to 20 seconds (30 seconds for a frozen mousse). Place a serving platter upside down over the mold, invert the two together, and tap gently to unmold. Serve a refrigerated mousse immediately upon unmolding. Allow an unmolded frozen mousse to sit outside the refrigerator until defrosted, 3 to 4 hours, before serving.

NOTE: Frozen passion fruit puree is available at most supermarkets.

MASCARPONE MOUSSE

Serves 8

This delicately flavored mousse, made with Italian-style double-cream cheese, pairs well with more lively fruit mousses, like passion fruit, when layered in a mold. It is also a delicious filling for a variety of cakes.

2 cups heavy cream, chilled
4 large egg whites
1 cup sugar
⅓ cup water
8 ounces best-quality white chocolate (see page 10)
3 tablespoons cold water

1½ envelopes unflavored gelatin (or 8 sheets; see page 119)
1 pound mascarpone, at room temperature
¼ cup Grand Marnier or other orange-flavored liqueur

1. Whip the heavy cream with an electric mixer until it holds soft peaks.
2. Place the egg whites in a clean bowl of an electric mixer fitted with the whisk attachment. Combine the sugar and the ⅓ cup water in a small saucepan and bring to a boil. When the sugar syrup reaches the soft ball stage (235 degrees on a candy thermometer), turn the mixer to high speed and dribble the syrup down the side of the bowl in a thin, steady stream while you whip the egg whites. Decrease the speed to medium and continue to beat until the whites hold stiff peaks and are completely cool.
3. Pour 1 inch of water into a medium saucepan and place over the lowest heat. Place the white chocolate in a heatproof bowl that is large enough to sit on top of the pan. Place the bowl over the hot water, making sure that the bottom of the bowl does not touch the water. Let the bowl stand over the water until the chocolate is melted, whisking often. Remove from the heat and let cool to warm room temperature, about 98 degrees on a candy thermometer.
4. Pour 1 inch of water into a small saucepan and bring to a bare simmer. Place the 3 tablespoons cold water in a small heatproof bowl and sprinkle the gelatin on top. Let stand to dissolve. Then place the bowl over the simmering water and heat, whisking constantly, just until the gelatin melts, 30 seconds to 1 minute.
5. Place the mascarpone in a large mixing bowl. Whisk in the melted gelatin,

working quickly so that no rubbery strands form. Whisk in the Grand Marnier and then the white chocolate. Add the egg whites and the whipped cream to the mixture, and gently but thoroughly fold them in together. Pour the mixture into a 4-cup mold. Cover it with plastic wrap and refrigerate until completely set, at least 6 hours or up to 2 days.

6. When you are ready to serve the mousse, dip the mold in hot water for 15 to 20 seconds. Place a serving platter upside down over the mold, invert the two together, and tap gently to unmold.

CHAMPAGNE MOUSSE

Serves 8

You should actually be able to taste and feel the Champagne bubbles in this mousse. To achieve this effect, make sure that both the cream and the Champagne are at room temperature. This will allow you to fold in all of the Champagne before the gelatin begins to thicken the mixture, making it lumpy rather than bubbly. A dessert made with Champagne may sound extravagant, but I have found that less expensive Champagnes (I usually use Cook's here) have large bubbles and actually make a better mousse.

2 cups heavy cream, at room
    temperature
¾ cup confectioners' sugar
2 cups dry Champagne or sparkling
    wine, at room temperature

2 tablespoons cold water
1 envelope unflavored gelatin
    (or 6 sheets; see page 119)

1. Whip the heavy cream with an electric mixer until it holds soft peaks. Beat in the confectioners' sugar, and set aside.
2. Prepare a large bowl of ice water, and set it aside. Place 1 cup of the Champagne in a large bowl, and set it aside.
3. Pour 1 inch of water into a small saucepan and bring to a bare simmer. Place the cold water in a small heatproof bowl and sprinkle the gelatin on top. Let stand to dissolve. Then place the bowl over the simmering water and heat, whisking constantly, just until the gelatin melts, 30 seconds to 1 minute. Slowly and gently fold the melted gelatin into the Champagne in the bowl, being careful not to beat the bubbles out of the mixture. Set the bowl in the bowl of ice water and stir slowly until the mixture begins to set, 10 to 15 minutes.
4. Add the whipped cream and the remaining 1 cup Champagne to the gelatin mixture, and fold them in together. Pour the mousse mixture into a 4- or 5-cup mold, cover it with plastic wrap, and refrigerate for at least 3 hours or up to 1 day.
5. When you are ready to serve the mousse, dip the mold in hot water for 15 to 20 seconds. Place a serving platter upside down over the mold, invert the two together, and tap gently to unmold.

THE BASIC BAVARIAN

Bavarians have not been done justice in the dessert world. Most chefs put too much gelatin into their Bavarians, which gives the mixture a dense texture and an unpleasant aftertaste. If the chef is rushing and folds the whipped cream into the custard when the custard is too warm, the cream will deflate and the Bavarian will be heavy. If the custard is too cool, it will become lumpy when folded with the cream.

Making the custard component of a Bavarian is a straightforward process, but as with all custards, there are moments when carelessness can lead to lumps:

When you are whisking the hot half-and-half into the uncooked eggs, do so slowly, drizzling the liquid in a slow stream. This will warm the eggs slowly and keep the mixture smooth. If you pour the hot liquid in all at once, it will cook the eggs into large curds.

Once the hot half-and-half has been incorporated into the eggs, return the mixture to the pan and bring it just to a boil. Then immediately remove the pan from the heat. Cook it too long and lumps will begin to form.

Don't forget to strain the custard once you remove it from the heat. This will remove any solids that may have formed in spite of your vigilance.

The key to finishing a Bavarian is folding the custard into the whipped cream at just the right moment. If the custard is too warm, it will deflate the cream, resulting in a heavy Bavarian. If it is too cold, lumps will form when it is folded into the cream. For a perfect Bavarian, fold the custard and cream together as soon as the custard has begun to thicken but is still liquid.

I use Bavarians as cake fillings, but these extremely light and delicate creations are also wonderful on their own: Pour a Bavarian into a mold and refrigerate or freeze it. Once unmolded, it can be decorated and served with the sauce and fresh fruit of your choice. In the summertime, I especially like frozen Bavarians that have been allowed to defrost for a little while on the counter and are served semi-frozen; they taste very much like ice cream but with a lighter-than-air texture.

BASIC BAVARIAN

Serves 8

There is my basic Bavarian formula, which I use when making any of the flavors on page 129.

¼ cup cold water	½ cup plus 2 tablespoons sugar
1 envelope unflavored gelatin	2 cups half-and-half
(or 5 sheets; see page 119)	2 cups heavy cream, chilled
5 large egg yolks	

1. Place the cold water in a small bowl. Sprinkle the gelatin on top and let stand to dissolve. Whisk the egg yolks and sugar together in a large bowl. Prepare a large bowl of ice water, and set it aside.

2. Bring the half-and-half to a boil in a medium saucepan. Pour the hot half-and-half into the yolk mixture in a slow stream, whisking constantly.

3. Return the mixture to the pan and bring it just to a boil. As soon as the mixture begins to bubble, pour it through a fine-mesh strainer into a clean bowl. Whisk in the dissolved gelatin. Set the bowl into the bowl of ice water and let the mixture cool, whisking occasionally, until it is just beginning to thicken but is still liquid.

4. While the Bavarian base is cooling, whip the heavy cream with an electric mixer until it holds soft peaks. Gently but thoroughly fold the cooled Bavarian base into the whipped cream. Pour the Bavarian into a 4- or 5-cup mold, wrap it in plastic wrap, and refrigerate until completely set, at least 3 hours or up to 1 day. Or wrap it in plastic wrap and freeze for up to 3 weeks.

5. When you are ready to serve the Bavarian, dip the mold in hot water for 15 to 20 seconds (30 seconds for a frozen Bavarian). Place a serving platter upside down over the mold, invert the two together, and tap gently to unmold. Serve a refrigerated Bavarian immediately upon unmolding. Allow an unmolded frozen Bavarian to sit outside the refrigerator until defrosted, 3 to 4 hours, before serving.

VARIATIONS:

VANILLA BAVARIAN. Split 2 vanilla beans lengthwise. Scrape the seeds into the half-and-half and add the pods to the pot also. Bring to a boil. Proceed with the recipe for Basic Bavarian, removing the vanilla pods after the Bavarian base has cooled.

ORANGE BAVARIAN. Add large strips of zest (not grated) from 2 oranges to the half-and-half. Bring to a boil. Proceed with the recipe for Basic Bavarian, stirring a drop of orange food coloring into the base as it cools over ice. Remove the orange zest after the Bavarian base has cooled.

CHOCOLATE BAVARIAN. Add ⅓ cup unsweetened cocoa powder to the half-and-half. Bring to a boil. Proceed with the recipe for Basic Bavarian.

COFFEE BAVARIAN. Add ¾ cup ground coffee beans to the half-and-half. Bring to a boil. Proceed with the recipe for Basic Bavarian.

HAZELNUT BAVARIAN. Whisk in 2 ounces unsweetened hazelnut paste (available at specialty food stores) to the Bavarian base before cooling it over ice (Step 3). Proceed with the recipe for Basic Bavarian.

PRALINE BAVARIAN. Decrease the sugar to 7 tablespoons. Whisk 3 ounces praline paste (available at specialty food stores) into the Bavarian base before cooling it over ice (Step 3). Proceed with the recipe for Basic Bavarian.

CHESTNUT BAVARIAN. Decrease the sugar to 7 tablespoons. Whisk 3 ounces sweet chestnut puree (available at specialty food stores) into the Bavarian base before cooling it over ice (Step 3). Proceed with the recipe for Basic Bavarian.

EGG WHITE BAVARIAN

Serves 8

In this variation on the Basic Bavarian recipe, I substitute whipped egg whites for the whipped cream. The result is a super-light dessert or cake filling with much less fat. Flavor and sweeten Egg White Bavarian using any of the versions on page 129.

¼ cup cold water
1 envelope unflavored gelatin
   (or 5 sheets; see page 119)
5 large egg yolks

½ cup plus 2 tablespoons sugar
2 cups half-and-half
12 large egg whites, at room
   temperature

1. Place the cold water in a small bowl. Sprinkle the gelatin on top and let stand to dissolve. Whisk the egg yolks and ½ cup sugar together in a large bowl. Prepare a large bowl of ice water, and set it aside.

2. Bring the half-and-half to a boil in a medium saucepan. Pour the hot half-and-half into the yolk mixture in a slow stream, whisking constantly.

3. Return the mixture to the pan and bring it just to a boil. As soon as the mixture begins to bubble, pour it through a fine-mesh strainer into a clean bowl. Whisk in the dissolved gelatin. Set the bowl into the bowl of ice water and let the mixture cool, whisking occasionally, until it is just beginning to thicken but is still liquid.

4. While the Bavarian base is cooling, place the egg whites in the bowl of an electric mixer fitted with the whisk attachment and whip on high speed just until they hold soft peaks. With the mixer still on high, slowly add the remaining 2 tablespoons sugar and whip until the whites hold stiff peaks. Gently but thoroughly fold the cooled Bavarian base into the whites. Pour the Bavarian into a 4- or 5-cup mold, wrap it in plastic wrap, and refrigerate until completely set, about 3 hours or up to 1 day. Or wrap it in plastic wrap and freeze for up to 3 weeks.

5. When you are ready to serve the Bavarian, dip the mold in hot water for 15 to 20 seconds (30 seconds for a frozen Bavarian). Place a serving platter upside down over the mold, invert the two together, and tap gently to unmold. Serve a refrigerated Bavarian immediately upon unmolding. Allow an unmolded frozen Bavarian to sit outside the refrigerator until defrosted, 3 to 4 hours, before serving.

$\mathcal{F}$RUIT BAVARIANS

Traditionally, fruit Bavarians are simply variations on the basic Bavarian, with fruit puree stirred into the mixture. This formula never pleased me, however, because the richness of the custard seemed to overshadow the fresh flavor of the fruit. After experimenting with reducing the proportion of custard to fruit, I decided to eliminate the custard altogether. What a difference! Without the eggs, the fruit took center stage. You might argue that the following recipes aren't Bavarians at all but fruit mousses, and you'd be right. But since they began as Bavarians, and I use them as I would a Bavarian, I categorize them as such even though they don't have the custard component.

These fruit Bavarians are simpler to make than any of the basic flavored versions. There is no worry about cooking the eggs. In most cases a simple fruit puree made in the food processor takes the place of the cooked custard.

But fruit Bavarians present their own challenges. A good fruit Bavarian has intense flavor, bright color, and just the right amount of added sugar. These qualities can be elusive.

First, choose your fruit carefully. Frozen fruit is a wonderful convenience, and it may seem that since you are going to puree and refrigerate or freeze it, you may as well not bother with fresh. In the case of raspberries and blackberries, this is certainly true. These frozen berries have a uniformly good flavor and are economical to boot. Frozen strawberries, on the other hand, are watery and tasteless. I have made recommendations in individual recipes as to which frozen fruit is acceptable and which should be avoided.

Individual recipes give recommendations for adding sugar, but I want to emphasize here that these are only recommendations. Fruits vary so much in sugar content, depending on how ripe they are. Taste your puree and add more sugar if needed. The puree should be rather sweet, because it will be folded into unsweetened whipped cream.

It is not necessary to cook softer fruits before pureeing them. In addition to berries, ripe mango and cantaloupe are soft enough to be pureed and folded directly into the cream. Peaches, apricots, pears, and apples, however, are too hard to be used uncooked. They must be poached before being pureed for use in Bavarians.

Many tropical fruits must be poached for a different reason. Pineapple and kiwi, for example, contain an enzyme that prevents gelatin from gelling. If added uncooked to a Bavarian mixture, they will prevent it from setting up. To break down this enzyme, these fruits must be cooked.

Poached fruit can lose some of its bright color, resulting in a drab-looking Bavarian. I use food coloring very sparingly in my kitchen, but I do find that a drop or two added to a peach, apricot, pineapple, or kiwi Bavarian makes it much more appetizing.

One last thing: I don't like to lace fruit Bavarians with liqueurs. Aside from the fact that too much alcohol inhibits the gelling of the mixture, I find that it mutes the clean, bright taste of fresh fruit.

Unmolding Bavarians

Bavarians cling to the sides of a mold with powerful suction. It is usually enough to dip the mold in hot water for 15 to 20 seconds (30 seconds for a frozen Bavarian) and then invert it onto a serving platter. If the Bavarian remains stuck in the mold, keep it inverted over the platter, lift one side of the mold a little bit, and insert your finger between the mold and the Bavarian to break the suction. The Bavarian should slip right out of the mold and onto the plate.

RASPBERRY BAVARIAN

Serves 8

I use frozen sweetened raspberries in this Bavarian. They make a more flavorful puree than either unsweetened frozen berries or fresh berries. Frozen sweetened raspberries are available in the freezer section of most supermarkets.

Two 12-ounce containers frozen
    sweetened raspberries
3 tablespoons cold water

1 envelope unflavored gelatin
    (or 5 sheets; see page 119)
1½ cups heavy cream, chilled

1. Place the raspberries in a blender or in the bowl of a food processor and puree until smooth. Push the puree through a fine-mesh strainer into a bowl to remove the seeds. Pour 2 cups into another bowl and reserve any remaining puree for another use.

2. Pour 1 inch of water into a small saucepan and bring to a bare simmer. Place the 3 tablespoons cold water in a small heatproof bowl and sprinkle the gelatin on top. Let stand to dissolve. Then place the bowl over the simmering water and heat, whisking constantly, just until the gelatin melts, 30 seconds to 1 minute. Whisk the melted gelatin into the puree, working quickly so that no rubbery strands form.

3. Whip the heavy cream with an electric mixer until it holds soft peaks. Fold the raspberry puree into the whipped cream. Pour the mixture into a 4- or 5-cup mold, cover it with plastic wrap, and refrigerate for at least 3 hours or up to 1 day. Or wrap it in plastic wrap and freeze for up to 3 weeks.

4. When you are ready to serve the Bavarian, dip the mold in hot water for 15 to 20 seconds (30 seconds for a frozen Bavarian). Place a serving platter upside down over the mold, invert the two together, and tap gently to unmold. Serve a refrigerated Bavarian immediately upon unmolding. Allow an unmolded frozen Bavarian to sit outside the refrigerator until defrosted, 3 to 4 hours, before serving.

STRAWBERRY BAVARIAN

Serves 8

For a strawberry Bavarian, I prefer fresh fruit to frozen. The amount of sugar will depend on how sweet the fruit is, so taste it and add more sugar, 1 teaspoon at a time, if necessary. Fresh lemon brightens and sharpens the flavors.

2 pints fresh strawberries, washed
   and stemmed
6 tablespoons sugar, or more to taste
2 tablespoons fresh lemon juice

3 tablespoons cold water
1 envelope unflavored gelatin
   (or 5 sheets; see page 119)
1½ cups heavy cream, chilled

1. Place the strawberries in the bowl of a food processor and puree until smooth. Measure 2 cups of puree into a bowl, and stir in the sugar and lemon juice. Reserve any remaining puree for another use.

2. Pour 1 inch of water into a small saucepan and bring to a bare simmer. Place the 3 tablespoons cold water in a small heatproof bowl and sprinkle the gelatin on top. Let stand to dissolve. Then place the bowl over the simmering water and heat, whisking constantly, just until the gelatin melts, 30 seconds to 1 minute. Whisk the melted gelatin into the puree, working quickly so that no rubbery strands form.

3. Whip the heavy cream with an electric mixer until it holds soft peaks. Fold the strawberry puree into the whipped cream. Pour the mixture into a 4- or 5-cup mold, cover it with plastic wrap, and refrigerate for at least 3 hours or up to 1 day. Or wrap it in plastic wrap and freeze for up to 3 weeks.

4. When you are ready to serve the Bavarian, dip the mold in hot water for 15 to 20 seconds (30 seconds for a frozen Bavarian). Place a serving platter upside down over the mold, invert the two together, and tap gently to unmold. Serve a refrigerated Bavarian immediately upon unmolding. Allow an unmolded frozen Bavarian to sit outside the refrigerator until defrosted, 3 to 4 hours, before serving.

MANGO BAVARIAN

Serves 8

Although you can buy frozen mango puree, I don't recommend it. The flavor is pallid compared with the vibrant flavor of fresh mango puree.

2 large ripe mangoes, peeled, pitted, and cut into chunks	3 tablespoons cold water
3 tablespoons sugar, or more to taste	1 envelope unflavored gelatin (or 5 sheets; see page 119)
1 tablespoon fresh lemon juice	1½ cups heavy cream, chilled

1. Place the mango chunks in the bowl of a food processor and puree until smooth. Push the puree through a fine-mesh strainer into a bowl to remove any strings. Measure 2 cups of puree into another bowl and stir in the sugar and lemon juice. Reserve any remaining puree for another use.

2. Pour 1 inch of water into a small saucepan and bring to a bare simmer. Place the 3 tablespoons cold water in a small heatproof bowl and sprinkle the gelatin on top. Let stand to dissolve. Place the bowl over the simmering water and heat, whisking constantly, just until the gelatin melts, 30 seconds to 1 minute. Whisk the melted gelatin into the puree, working quickly so that no rubbery strands form.

3. Whip the heavy cream with an electric mixer until it holds soft peaks. Fold the mango puree into the whipped cream. Pour the mixture into a 4- or 5-cup mold, cover it with plastic wrap, and refrigerate for at least 3 hours or up to 1 day. Or wrap it in plastic wrap and freeze for up to 3 weeks.

4. When you are ready to serve the Bavarian, dip the mold in hot water for 15 to 20 seconds (30 seconds for a frozen Bavarian). Place a serving platter upside down over the mold, invert the two together, and tap gently to unmold. Serve a refrigerated Bavarian immediately upon unmolding. Allow an unmolded frozen Bavarian to sit outside the refrigerator until defrosted, 3 to 4 hours, before serving.

BLACKBERRY BAVARIAN

Serves 8

Frozen berries work just as well as fresh in this pretty Bavarian.

3 pints fresh blackberries, washed
    and stemmed, or 2 pints frozen
    berries, defrosted
½ cup sugar, or more to taste
2 tablespoons fresh lemon juice

3 tablespoons cold water
1 envelope unflavored gelatin
    (or 5 sheets; see page 119)
1½ cups heavy cream, chilled

1. Place the blackberries in the bowl of a food processor and puree until smooth. Push the puree through a fine-mesh strainer into a bowl to remove the seeds. Measure 2 cups puree into another bowl and stir in the sugar and lemon juice. Reserve any remaining puree for another use.

2. Pour 1 inch of water into a small saucepan and bring to a bare simmer. Place the 3 tablespoons cold water in a small heatproof bowl and sprinkle the gelatin on top. Let stand to dissolve. Then place the bowl over the simmering water and heat, whisking constantly, just until the gelatin melts, 30 seconds to 1 minute. Whisk the melted gelatin into the puree, working quickly so that no rubbery strands form.

3. Whip the heavy cream with an electric mixer until it holds soft peaks. Fold the blackberry puree into the whipped cream. Pour the mixture into a 4- or 5-cup mold, cover it with plastic wrap, and refrigerate for at least 3 hours or up to 1 day. Or wrap it in plastic wrap and freeze for up to 3 weeks.

4. When you are ready to serve the Bavarian, dip the mold in hot water for 15 to 20 seconds (30 seconds for a frozen Bavarian). Place a serving platter upside down over the mold, invert the two together, and tap gently to unmold. Serve a refrigerated Bavarian immediately upon unmolding. Allow an unmolded frozen Bavarian to sit outside the refrigerator until defrosted, 3 to 4 hours, before serving.

CANTALOUPE BAVARIAN

Serves 8

I had trouble getting a Bavarian made with cantaloupe to set up properly until I tried warming some of the puree along with the gelatin before proceeding with the recipe. For some reason, heating some of the fruit at this stage helps it to gel when cooled. If you are at all worried that any of your fruit Bavarians won't set, it can't hurt to follow this procedure.

1 small cantaloupe (to make about 2 cups puree), cut into 1-inch chunks	3 tablespoons cold water
	1 envelope unflavored gelatin (or 5 sheets; see page 119)
6 tablespoons sugar, or more to taste	1½ cups heavy cream, chilled
2 tablespoons fresh lemon juice	

1. Place the cantaloupe in the bowl of a food processor and puree until smooth. Push the puree through a fine-mesh strainer into a bowl to remove any strings or fibers. Measure 2 cups of the puree into a medium bowl and stir in the sugar and lemon juice. Reserve any remaining puree for another use.

2. Pour 1 inch of water into a small saucepan and bring to a bare simmer. Place the 3 tablespoons cold water in a small heatproof bowl and sprinkle the gelatin on top. Let stand to dissolve. Then place the bowl over the simmering water and heat, whisking constantly, just until the gelatin melts, 30 seconds to 1 minute. Whisk about ½ cup of the cantaloupe puree into the melted gelatin and continue to stir until the mixture is just warm to the touch, about 1 minute. Remove from the heat and whisk into the remaining puree, working quickly so that no rubbery strands form.

3. Whip the heavy cream with an electric mixer until it holds soft peaks. Fold the cantaloupe puree into the whipped cream. Pour the mixture into a 4- or 5-cup mold, cover it with plastic wrap, and refrigerate for at least 3 hours or up to 1 day. Or wrap it in plastic wrap and freeze for up to 3 weeks.

4. When you are ready to serve the Bavarian, dip the mold in hot water for 15 to 20 seconds (30 seconds for a frozen Bavarian). Place a serving platter upside down over the mold, invert the two together, and tap gently to unmold. Serve a refrigerated Bavarian immediately upon unmolding. Allow an unmolded frozen Bavarian to sit outside the refrigerator until defrosted, 3 to 4 hours, before serving.

BANANA BAVARIAN

Serves 8

The lemon juice in this recipe prevents the bananas from browning.

6 to 8 bananas
2 tablespoons fresh lemon
   juice
¼ cup cold water

2 envelopes unflavored gelatin
   (or 9 sheets; see page 119)
2 cups heavy cream, chilled
¾ cup confectioners' sugar

1. Combine 6 bananas and the lemon juice in the bowl of a food processor and process until smooth. Scrape the puree into a large measuring cup. If it measures less than 3 cups, return it to the food processor, add the remaining 2 bananas, and process until smooth. Measure out 3 cups puree, and place it in a large bowl. Reserve the remaining puree, if there is any, for another use.

2. Pour 1 inch of water into a small saucepan and bring to a bare simmer. Place the ¼ cup cold water in a small heatproof bowl and sprinkle the gelatin on top. Let stand to dissolve. Then place the bowl over the simmering water and heat, whisking constantly, just until the gelatin melts, 30 seconds to 1 minute. Whisk the melted gelatin into the puree.

3. Whip the heavy cream with an electric mixer until it just begins to hold soft peaks. Add the confectioners' sugar and continue to whip until it holds stiff peaks. Gently fold the whipped cream into the banana mixture.

4. Pour the mixture into a 4- or 5-cup mold, cover it with plastic wrap, and refrigerate for at least 3 hours or up to 1 day. Or wrap it in plastic wrap and freeze for up to 3 weeks.

5. When you are ready to serve the Bavarian, dip the mold in hot water for 15 to 20 seconds (30 seconds for a frozen Bavarian). Place a serving platter upside down over the mold, invert the two together, and tap gently to unmold. Serve a refrigerated Bavarian immediately upon unmolding. Allow an unmolded frozen Bavarian to sit outside the refrigerator until defrosted, 3 to 4 hours, before serving.

POACHED FRUIT BAVARIAN

Serves 10

Bavarians made with poached fruit taste lovely, but their color can be a little drab. If you like, you can brighten the Bavarian by adding a touch of food coloring to the puree before folding in the whipped cream. Remember that the whipped cream will dilute the color, so make the puree a little bit brighter than you want your finished dessert to be.

2 cups pureed poached peaches, apricots, pears, apples, pineapples, or kiwis (see Chapter 1)

2 tablespoons sugar, or more to taste

2 tablespoons fresh lemon juice (optional)

3 tablespoons cold water

1 envelope unflavored gelatin (or 5 sheets; see page 119)

1½ cups heavy cream, chilled

1. Place the poached fruit in the bowl of a food processor and puree until smooth. Push the puree through a fine-mesh strainer into a medium bowl. You should have about 2 cups of puree. If you have more, set the extra puree aside for another use. Stir the sugar and lemon juice into the puree.

2. Pour 1 inch of water into a small saucepan and bring to a bare simmer. Place the 3 tablespoons cold water in a small heatproof bowl and sprinkle the gelatin on top. Let stand to dissolve. Then place the bowl over the simmering water and heat, whisking constantly, just until the gelatin melts, 30 seconds to 1 minute. Whisk in ½ cup of the puree. Continue to whisk until just warm to the touch, about 1 minute. Then remove from the heat and whisk into the remaining puree, working quickly so that no rubbery strands form.

3. Whip the heavy cream with an electric mixer until it holds soft peaks. Fold the puree into the whipped cream. Pour the Bavarian into a 4- or 5-cup mold, wrap it in plastic wrap, and refrigerate until completely set, at least 3 hours or up to 1 day. Or wrap it in plastic wrap and freeze for up to 3 weeks.

4. When you are ready to serve the Bavarian, dip the mold in hot water for 15 to 20 seconds (30 seconds for a frozen Bavarian). Place a serving platter upside down over the mold, invert the two together, and tap gently to unmold. Serve a refrigerated Bavarian immediately upon unmolding. Allow an unmolded frozen Bavarian to sit outside the refrigerator until defrosted, 3 to 4 hours, before serving.

$\mathcal{A}$ FEW FAVORITE
BAVARIAN-BASED DESSERTS

Once you have mastered the Bavarian technique, you can begin to use your imagination, garnishing favorite Bavarians in any way you choose to create your own stunning desserts. Here are three favorite recipes to give you an idea of the possibilities open to you once you know how to use gelatin to thicken cream. The first is a simple Bavarian flavored with maple syrup and garnished with chocolate sauce and almond nougat. The second is my version of an old-fashioned Jell-O mold—a delicious fresh banana Bavarian encased in a layer of sparkling lime gelatin. Finally, I include a recipe for Blancmange, a classic French gelatin and cream dessert that is well within your reach if you have studied the mousse and Bavarian basics outlined in this chapter.

MAPLE SYRUP BAVARIAN

Serves 8

This wonderful recipe reminds me of autumn in New England. I serve it to friends by the fireplace on a cool evening, while we sip some Port wine garnished with a twist of orange peel. Serve Poached Pears (page 61) or Whole Poached Apples (page 29) to accompany the Bavarian if you like.

6 large egg yolks
1½ cups pure maple syrup
3 large egg whites
¾ cup heavy cream, chilled
3 tablespoons cold water
¾ envelope unflavored gelatin
   (or 3½ sheets; see page 119)

2 cups chopped Nougat pieces
   (page 502)
1 cup Light Chocolate Sauce
   (page 512), at room temperature

1. Place the egg yolks in the bowl of an electric mixer fitted with the whisk attachment. Bring ½ cup of the maple syrup to a boil in a small saucepan. With the

mixer on high speed, dribble the hot syrup down the side of the bowl in a thin, steady stream. Lower the speed to medium and beat until the mixture is cool and fluffy. Transfer it to a large mixing bowl.

2. Place the egg whites in the cleaned and dried bowl of the electric mixer. Bring the remaining 1 cup maple syrup to a boil. When the syrup reaches the soft ball stage (235 degrees on a candy thermometer), turn the mixer on high speed and dribble the hot syrup down the side of the bowl in a thin, steady stream. Continue to beat until the egg whites hold stiff peaks. Lower the speed to medium and beat until completely cool.

3. Whip the heavy cream with an electric mixer until it holds soft peaks.

4. Pour 1 inch of water into a small saucepan and bring to a bare simmer. Place the cold water in a small heatproof bowl and sprinkle the gelatin on top. Let stand to dissolve. Then place the bowl over the simmering water and heat, whisking constantly, just until the gelatin melts, 30 seconds to 1 minute. Fold the melted gelatin into the yolk mixture, working quickly so that no rubbery strands form. Then add the egg whites and the whipped cream, and fold them in together. Pour the mixture into a 4- or 5-cup mold, cover with plastic wrap, and refrigerate overnight or for up to 2 days.

5. When you are ready to serve the Bavarian, dip the mold in hot water for 15 to 20 seconds. Place a serving platter upside down over the mold, invert the two together, and tap gently to unmold. Press the nougat pieces onto the sides of the Bavarian, spoon the chocolate sauce around the Bavarian, and serve.

BANANA CHARLOTTE

Serves 10

I call this a charlotte because it is constructed like that molded dessert. But instead of lining the dish with ladyfingers, here I line it with lime gelatin. The sparkling gelatin encases a rich banana-flavored Bavarian, making this dessert a real pleasure to look at. Although it's possible to make your own lime-flavored gelatin, it's easier and just as pretty to use commercial Jell-O.

One 3-ounce package lime Jell-O
2 cups cold water
3 to 4 bananas

1 recipe Banana Bavarian (page 138), prepared through Step 3
2 cups Raspberry Sauce (page 516)

1. Chill a 6-cup soufflé dish in the freezer for 2 hours.
2. Prepare a large bowl of ice water, and set it aside. Place the lime Jell-O in a medium bowl. Bring 1 cup of the water to a boil in a saucepan and stir it into the Jell-O, whisking until it is dissolved completely. Stir in 1 cup of the cold water.
3. Remove the soufflé dish from the freezer and pour the Jell-O into it. Move the dish in a circular motion to completely coat the bottom and sides. Pour the loose Jell-O back into the bowl, and place the soufflé dish in the bowl of ice water, leaving it until the Jell-O has completely solidified, about 5 minutes. Repeat this process with the remaining Jell-O until you have a ⅛-inch-thick layer of Jell-O on the bottom and sides of the soufflé dish.
4. After the soufflé dish has been coated, slice the bananas into ¼-inch-thick rounds. Arrange the bananas in one layer across the bottom and all the way up the sides of the dish.
5. Scrape the Banana Bavarian into the soufflé dish and smooth the top with a spatula. Wrap the dish in plastic wrap and refrigerate overnight or for up to 2 days.
6. When you are ready to serve the charlotte, dip the soufflé dish in a bowl of warm water for 1 minute (be careful not to overheat the dessert, or the Jell-O will dissolve). Place a serving dish upside down on top of the dish, invert the two together, and tap gently to unmold. Serve with the Raspberry Sauce.

BLANCMANGE WITH CRANBERRY JELLY AND POACHED PEARS

Serves 8 to 10

I'm including this gelatin-thickened dessert here, even though it isn't a Bavarian, because it is in the same category as the Maple Syrup Bavarian and the Banana Charlotte—a beautifully presented, very refreshing gelatin-based dessert.

This dessert looks more complicated than it really is. When you cut it, you will see lovely layers of blancmange, sponge cake, and cranberry jelly. The effect is simple to achieve but takes patience. The blancmange is poured into the cake pan little by little, with each layer allowed to set up in the freezer. Likewise, the cranberry jelly is chilled before the final layers of cake and blancmange are added. Serve the blancmange with a sweet dessert wine like a Sauternes.

3 tablespoons cold water	½ cup confectioners' sugar
1 envelope unflavored gelatin (or 6 sheets; see page 119)	2 rounds Genoise (page 397), ¼ inch thick and 8 inches in diameter
4 cups whole milk	1½ cups Cranberry Jelly Glaze (page 521)
4 ounces almond paste (see headnote, page 322)	8 Poached Pears (page 61)
¼ teaspoon almond extract	

1. Place an 8-inch round cake pan in the freezer. Prepare a large bowl of ice water, and set it aside. Place the 3 tablespoons cold water in a small bowl. Sprinkle the gelatin on top and let stand to dissolve.

2. Combine the milk and almond paste in a medium saucepan. Bring to a boil, whisking occasionally to dissolve the almond paste.

3. Remove the pan from the heat and whisk in the dissolved gelatin, almond extract, and confectioners' sugar. Pour the mixture through a fine-mesh strainer into a large bowl. Place the bowl in the bowl of ice water and let it stand, whisking occasionally, until the blancmange is completely cool and has just begun to thicken.

4. Remove the cake pan from the freezer and pour the blancmange into it. Move the pan in a circular motion to completely coat the sides. Pour the loose blanc-

(continued)

mange back into the bowl. Return the pan to the freezer and leave it until the blancmange layer has completely solidified, about 30 minutes. Repeat this process three to four times with the remaining blancmange, until you have a ½-inch-thick layer of blancmange on the bottom and sides of the pan. Reserve the leftover blancmange.

5. Place one of the cake layers in the blancmange-lined pan and pour the Cranberry Jelly Glaze over the cake. The pan will be about three-fourths full. Place the pan in the freezer again to allow the jelly to set, about 30 minutes. Then place the remaining sponge layer on top of the cranberry jelly and pour the remaining blancmange into the pan, smoothing the top with a spatula. Wrap the pan in plastic wrap and refrigerate until completely set, at least 3 hours or up to 1 day.

6. When you are ready to serve the dessert, dip the bottom of the cake pan in a bowl of warm water for 30 seconds. Run a sharp paring knife around the edge of the pan. Place a serving dish upside-down on top of the pan, invert the two together, and tap gently to unmold. Arrange the pears around the blancmange, and serve immediately.

FOUR

Frozen Desserts from Simple to Spectacular

LEGEND HAS IT that ice cream was introduced to Americans by Thomas Jefferson, who was probably our first gourmet president. Since then, frozen desserts have been a favorite at the White House and throughout the country. If the United States has a national dessert, it is ice cream. So I have taken particular interest in making it well, and in using it to create wonderful and unusual desserts.

As you shall see, the recipes for ice cream, as well as for sorbets and parfaits, are really quite simple. Layering them to create spectacular special-occasion desserts requires organization but no special skill. Compared with, say, a layer cake, a frozen dessert like Vodka and Lime Terrine with Iced Raspberry Vodka is relatively simple to make and just as impressive. If, like most of us, you have a passion for frozen desserts, you will be surprised and delighted at how beautifully these come together.

In this chapter I will take you through my favorite frozen desserts, from the simplest Banana Frozen Soufflé, which doesn't even require the use of an ice cream machine, to a spectacular Box of Chocolate Frozen Truffles served in a container made of puff pastry. I will explain the differences between a sorbet, a parfait, and ice cream, and I will show you how to layer them to make a dessert with deliciously contrasting flavors and textures.

EQUIPMENT

You will need a few basic pieces of equipment to make frozen desserts:

The parfait recipes, which are really just variations on frozen sabayon, require only an **electric mixer.**

For sorbet and ice cream, you will need an **ice cream machine.** The least expensive machines, costing less than $100, have a coolant-filled canister that must be frozen overnight before using. The frozen canister is then placed in a plastic housing, a lid with a handle that turns a paddle inside is placed on top of the housing, and the mixture is churned every few minutes over a 20-minute period until the proper consistency has been reached. The resulting ice cream or sorbet is usually too soft to serve at this point and must be placed in the freezer to firm up for a few hours. The canister must be refrozen before a new batch of ice cream can be made. These hand-cranked machines are a good choice if you make ice cream and other frozen desserts only occasionally, one batch at a time. Electric machines are more costly, ranging from about $300 to $1,000 depending on the brand and where you shop, but they can make batch after batch without any downtime. Electric machines also get colder than hand-cranked machines, so the ice cream can be served right from the machine. My suggestion is that you start with a hand-cranked machine and upgrade if you develop a strong interest in frozen desserts. During my time at the White House, I never invested in a professional ice cream machine. I used an electric machine designed for home use and made by Simac, an Italian company, that I purchased at Williams-Sonoma. So pleased was I with the results that I eventually bought two more identical Simacs, and with all three machines going at once I could produce 800 portions of ice cream over the course of a few days for a big dinner.

To make lump-free ice cream, two pieces of equipment are indispensable: a **fine-mesh strainer** and a **blender.** Custard that is destined to become ice cream should always be strained, no matter how smooth it looks, since tiny bits of cooked egg inevitably form no matter how careful you are as you cook. For badly curdled custards, the blender is a godsend. Whip the custard in the blender for a few seconds to break up the large curds, and then strain and freeze it for perfectly smooth ice cream.

To mold ice creams, sorbets, and parfaits into pretty shapes, you can purchase special **spherical ice cream molds** from pastry supply shops, but **two bowls of equal size** will do as well. I also use **decorative molds, soufflé dishes,** and **loaf pans** for layering and shaping frozen desserts. As long as the volume of your container is equal to the volume of the container suggested in the recipe, it makes no difference what shape it is. By all means use what you have if you'd rather not go out and purchase a new container.

Making Sorbets

The simplest frozen dessert is sorbet. Sorbets are usually made from sweetened fruit purees, sometimes diluted with water. Other liquids can be substituted—sweetened espresso or cocoa powder dissolved in sugar syrup, for example. Occasionally a sorbet may be enriched with a small quantity of heavy cream. But sorbets never contain eggs, as do most ice creams and all parfaits. Because of their simple, egg-free formulas, sorbets can be remelted and churned again if they become icy or too hard. Rechurned, sorbets will taste as creamy as they did the first time around.

The trickiest thing about making good sorbet is getting the sugar content right. Not only does sugar sweeten sorbet but it gives sorbet a smooth texture. A sorbet with too little sugar will be unpleasantly icy and hard, but a sorbet with too much sugar will not freeze properly and will have a slushy consistency, making it difficult to scoop. Luckily, the right amount of sugar for good consistency is also the right amount for sweetening. Chances are, if the sorbet tastes sweet but not too sweet, it will also freeze beautifully. In some cases, as with Chocolate Sorbet, the exact amount of sugar needed is quantifiable. But with fruit sorbets, where the sugar content of a particular fruit will vary from batch to batch depending on ripeness, you should taste the mixture before freezing it and add more sugar if necessary.

Making Parfaits

Parfait is less well known in the United States than sorbet or ice cream, but it is a common component of frozen desserts in France. Basically a parfait is a frozen sabayon custard.

Whipped cream is folded into the custard before it is frozen to stabilize it and prevent it from deflating. Even when frozen, parfait maintains its light, airy consistency. I vary the basic parfait recipe by sweetening it with either honey or maple syrup, or by flavoring the custard with liquor or a liqueur. These flavored parfaits are wonderful on their own as light frozen desserts, and they provide nice texture and flavor contrast when layered with complementary sorbets and ice creams.

The technique is simple: Egg yolks are placed in the bowl of an electric mixer fitted with the whisk attachment. Boiling sugar syrup is whisked quickly into the yolks to heat them to a safe temperature. (It is important to pour the syrup down the side of the bowl so that it doesn't fall on the moving whisk. If this happens, the syrup will be flung onto the sides of the bowl and will harden there before it has a chance to hit the egg yolks.) Once the syrup has been incorporated, the mixture is whipped on medium speed until cool and increased in volume. Then the whipped cream and liquor or liqueur are folded in and the parfait is frozen until thickened.

It is difficult to make a very small quantity of parfait, and in some cases you will have some left over. Look on this as a convenience: Leftover parfait can be stored in the freezer and later defrosted in the refrigerator to be used as a sauce for ice cream, cake, and many other desserts.

Making ice cream

Ice cream is simply frozen custard, made with egg yolks, sugar, milk, cream, and flavorings. Over the years I have experimented with the proportions of the ingredients to come up with a formula that I believe to be in perfect balance. Egg yolks add richness to ice cream, but too many make the ice cream taste eggy rather than creamy. As it turns out, I like ice cream made with whole or 2 percent milk and just a little bit of cream. Ice cream made with all cream or even half-and-half is too rich for my taste. All of my ice creams begin with this basic, balanced custard recipe. Making coffee, chocolate, or rum raisin ice cream is simply a matter of adding flavorings to the basic recipe.

The technique for making the custard is similar to the technique for making rice pudding, crème brûlée, or any other stovetop custard: Egg yolks and sugar are whisked until pale and increased in volume. Then milk that has been brought just to a boil is slowly dribbled over the eggs as they are being whisked, to warm them up so they won't curdle when heated. The warmed egg mixture is stirred back into the pan, and the custard is brought just to a boil over medium-low heat while being stirred constantly. Then it is poured through a strainer, cooled to lukewarm, and refrigerated until completely chilled. Stir in a little cold heavy cream, and it is ready for the ice cream machine.

The big trick with ice cream is that the custard has to be cooked sufficiently so that it will thicken properly when cooled and frozen, but not so much that the eggs will curdle— which can happen with just a little overcooking, making the custard lumpy and unusable. Most cooks err on the side of caution, undercooking the custard, with the result that their ice cream is not as creamy as it could be. I take the opposite approach, making sure that I bring the custard to a simmer before removing it from the heat. This way, I know the mixture has reached a high enough temperature to thicken properly when cooled in the ice cream machine. I don't concern myself with lumps in my custard. If there are just a few of them, they will be left behind when I strain the custard. If I have really gone too far and my custard is very lumpy, I don't throw it out. I put it in the blender, blend it until it is smooth, strain it, and proceed as if nothing has gone wrong. So far, people have not been able to tell the difference between the ice cream I have made from smooth custard and the ice cream that I have made from a curdled batch!

THE RECIPES

The recipes in this chapter are organized from the simplest frozen desserts to the most elaborate showpieces.

To begin, there are recipes that don't require an ice cream machine. Frozen Biscuit Tortoni, Banana Frozen Soufflé with Strawberries, and Nougat Glace are just mousses that are simply spooned into containers and placed in the freezer until firm.

Several simple sorbet and ice cream desserts follow. These consist of a single type of sorbet or ice cream garnished with fresh fruit or a quick sauce.

The largest section of the chapter consists of layered frozen desserts: ice creams, sorbets, and parfaits of complementary flavors, such as Corn Ice Cream with Tequila Parfait,

Pumpkin Ice Cream and Maple Syrup Parfait with Blackberry Sauce, and Chocolate Ice Cream and Honey Parfait. I love the way dense ice cream or icy sorbet contrasts with the softer parfait layer.

If you love drama, you will appreciate the three recipes I've grouped together under the heading "Warmed Ice Cream Desserts." Whether set aflame just before serving or slathered with meringue and baked until the topping is golden, these thrilling desserts have warm exteriors and cold interiors.

The last couple of desserts add a pastry component, which functions the same way that a crisp sugar cone enhances a scoop of ice cream—in a much more sophisticated fashion, of course. Rum Raisin Ice Cream encased in a golden phyllo shell and surrounded by Pears in Red Wine Sauce is a long way from the ice cream parlor but just as much fun in its own way. The same can be said for A Box of Chocolate Frozen Truffles with Orange Zest and Cranberry Sauce. The puff pastry box is a clever and pretty container that also adds buttery flavor and flaky texture to the dessert.

As a pastry chef, I usually consider my ice cream, sorbet, and parfait recipes to be building blocks for multi-layered and -textured desserts. Rather than group the building block recipes separately, I have placed them right after the dessert recipes in which they appear. Of course, any of the ice creams, sorbets, and parfaits may be served on their own. I hope you will page through these recipes even if you have no intention of making a layered, flamed, or pastry-encased frozen dessert. There are many suggestions for using just one component to create a simpler but still unusual and satisfying dish. Maple Syrup Parfait is easy to make and wonderful when served with Blackberry Sauce. If you don't have time to make a Cranberry and Grand Marnier Biscuit Glace, you might make just the Grand Marnier Parfait and serve it with orange segments or Orange Compote (page 56)—delicious!

Frozen Biscuit Tortoni

Banana Frozen Soufflé with Strawberries

Nougat Glace

Apple Sorbet with Caramel Sauce

Pineapple Champagne Sorbet

Espresso Sorbet with Walnut Sauce

Fresh Fig Ice Cream in Cantaloupe Bowls

Bailey's Irish Cream Ice Cream with
    Warm Chocolate Sauce

Red Wine Sorbet with Poached Peaches
    and Sabayon

Coffee Ice Cream with Tía Maria Sabayon and
    Almond Brittle

Corn Ice Cream with Tequila Parfait

Cranberry and Grand Marnier Biscuit Glace

Pumpkin Ice Cream and Maple Syrup Parfait
    with Blackberry Sauce

Snowball

Vodka and Lime Terrine with
    Iced Raspberry Vodka

Flaming Vanilla Brandied Prune Mold

Baked Alaska with Honey Vanilla Ice Cream
    and Raspberry Sorbet

Fruit Salad Surprise

Pears in Red Wine Sauce with
    Rum Raisin Ice Cream

A Box of Chocolate Frozen Truffles with
    Orange Zest and Cranberry Sauce

FROZEN DESSERTS MADE WITHOUT AN ICE CREAM MACHINE

You don't need an ice cream machine to make a great frozen dessert: You just need an electric mixer and a freezer. Mousses made with heavy cream, whipped egg whites, or both can often be frozen and served cold in place of ice cream. The texture is a little fluffier than ice cream, but these frozen mousses don't taste as rich. Some people even prefer frozen mousse to ice cream for its airy softness. Take the same care here as you would elsewhere not to overwhip the cream or the egg whites, and fold the ingredients together gently for the lightest dessert.

If you are looking for additional ways to make a frozen dessert without an ice cream machine, consider parfait. Any of the parfaits used in the layered frozen dessert recipes can also be served on their own with a sauce or garnish of your choice.

FROZEN BISCUIT TORTONI

Serves 12

This is a great do-ahead party dessert. The individual servings will keep for up to 2 weeks in the freezer, so you can serve some on one day and save the rest for another time. Serve it with one or all of the recommended sauces, which can also be made ahead.

1 cup heavy cream, chilled
¾ cup chopped Almond Macaroons (page 322) or store-bought macaroons
2 tablespoons brandy
2 large eggs, separated
½ cup sugar
2 teaspoons very hot water

Sweetened Whipped Cream (page 521) and Chocolate Shavings (page 436) for garnish
1½ cups Light Chocolate Sauce (page 512), Vanilla Sauce (page 514), Strawberry Sauce (page 517), or Raspberry Sauce (page 516)

1. Line a 12-cup muffin tin with paper liners. Whip the heavy cream with an electric mixer until it just holds soft peaks. Refrigerate until ready to use, up to 30 minutes.

2. Place the chopped macaroons in a medium bowl and sprinkle with the brandy. Set aside.

3. Combine the egg yolks, ¼ cup of the sugar, and the hot water in the bowl of an electric mixer and whip until pale yellow and increased in volume, about 5 minutes.

4. Place the egg whites in a clean bowl of an electric mixer fitted with the whisk attachment, and whip on high speed until just about to hold soft peaks. With the mixer still on high, gradually pour in the remaining ¼ cup sugar in a slow, steady stream. Whip until the whites hold stiff peaks.

5. Add the egg whites, whipped cream, and chopped macaroons to the yolk mixture, and fold them in together. Spoon the mixture into the muffin liners and freeze until firm, overnight. (Covered with plastic wrap, they can stay in the freezer for up to 2 weeks.)

6. To serve, peel the paper liners from the tortoni, and place each one on a dessert plate. Decorate with whipped cream rosettes and chocolate shavings. Spoon some sauce around each tortoni, and serve immediately.

BANANA FROZEN SOUFFLÉ WITH STRAWBERRIES

Serves 10

Here is another pretty, delicious frozen dessert that doesn't require an ice cream machine.

12 large egg yolks	¼ cup fresh lemon juice
1½ cups Heavy Syrup (page 506)	3 pints fresh strawberries
1½ cups heavy cream	⅓ cup sugar
8 ripe medium-size bananas	

1. Make a collar around a 6-cup (7-inch-diameter) soufflé dish: Wrap a piece of aluminum foil around the dish so that it extends 2 to 3 inches above the rim. Secure the collar with Scotch tape.
2. Place the yolks in the bowl of an electric mixer fitted with the whisk attachment.
3. Bring the Heavy Syrup to a boil in a small saucepan. With the mixer on high speed, quickly pour the syrup over the egg yolks in a steady stream, making sure that none of it falls on the whisk. Reduce the speed to medium and continue to beat until the mixture is cool, pale yellow, and increased in volume, 7 to 8 minutes.
4. In a clean bowl, whip the heavy cream with an electric mixer until it holds soft peaks. Set aside.
5. Combine the bananas and 3 tablespoons of the lemon juice in a blender, and puree. Measure out 3 cups of puree (set aside any extra for another use).
6. Gently fold the whipped cream and the banana puree into the egg mixture. Pour into the prepared soufflé dish and smooth the top with a spatula. The mixture should come up 1½ to 2 inches above the rim of the dish. Place the soufflé in the freezer overnight, or for up to 2 days.
7. Rinse the strawberries and remove the caps. Place 1 pint of the prepared strawberries in the blender with the sugar and the remaining 1 tablespoon lemon juice, and puree. Taste, and add more sugar if necessary.
8. Remove the soufflé from the freezer and peel away the foil collar. Warm a spoon under hot running water and dry it off. Use the warm spoon to scoop out about 1½ cups of the soufflé from the middle of the dish. Mound the remaining 2 pints strawberries in the cavity. Pour a little sauce on top of the berries. Serve immediately, with the remaining sauce on the side.

NOUGAT GLACE

Serves 10

Chopped nuts and candied fruit give this frozen mousse a chewy, candylike texture. I make an Italian meringue here because it is so stable and won't deflate under the weight of all the mixed-in ingredients. Making an Italian meringue also allows me to sweeten the dessert with cooked honey, which adds delicious flavor.

¼ cup golden raisins
6 red glazed cherries, chopped
2 tablespoons chopped unsalted pistachio nuts
2 tablespoons chopped candied orange peel
2 tablespoons chopped candied pineapple, apricots, or peaches
½ cup Grand Marnier

5 large egg whites, at room temperature
1 cup honey
1½ cups heavy cream, chilled
⅓ cup coarsely chopped Nougat (page 502)
Assorted fresh berries and fresh mint leaves for garnish
2 cups Raspberry Sauce (page 516)

1. Combine the raisins, cherries, pistachio nuts, orange peel, pineapple, and Grand Marnier in a small nonreactive bowl. Cover with plastic wrap and marinate at room temperature for 24 hours, stirring once or twice.
2. Place the egg whites in the bowl of an electric mixer fitted with the whisk attachment.
3. Place the honey in a small, deep saucepan and cook over medium-high heat, watching it carefully so that it doesn't boil over, until it reaches the soft ball stage (240 degrees on a candy thermometer).
4. Turn the mixer on high speed and pour the honey into the egg whites in a slow, steady stream, making sure that none of it falls on the whisk. Continue to whip on high speed until the whites hold stiff peaks and are completely cool.
5. Line a 4-inch deep, 6-cup soufflé dish with plastic wrap, making sure that the wrap is tucked into all the corners and that there is at least 1 inch overhanging on all sides.
6. Whip the heavy cream with an electric mixer until it just holds soft peaks.

(continued)

7. Combine the whipped cream, honey meringue, marinated fruit and nuts, and chopped nougat in a large bowl and fold together, being careful not to deflate the cream or the meringue.

8. Scrape the mixture into the prepared dish, smooth the top with a spatula, and cover it with plastic wrap. Freeze until completely solid, at least 1 day and up to 3 days.

9. To unmold, remove the outer plastic wrap and gently tug on the plastic wrap lining the dish to loosen the Nougat Glace. Place a serving plate upside down over the dish and invert the two together. Gently tap to release the Nougat Glace. Peel away the plastic wrap. Scatter the berries and mint around the dessert, and spoon the Raspberry Sauce over the berries. Spoon the Nougat Glace onto dessert plates and serve.

Simple Sorbet and Ice Cream Desserts

Here are a few ways to turn a single recipe of sorbet or ice cream into a real dessert. Pineapple Champagne Sorbet scooped into dessert goblets, splashed with some extra Champagne, and garnished with pineapple slices is a simple, elegant, light dessert. On the decadent end of the spectrum is Bailey's Irish Cream Ice Cream with Warm Chocolate Sauce. Use these recipes as a starting point to create your own simple desserts with other sorbets, ice creams, and parfaits.

APPLE SORBET WITH CARAMEL SAUCE

Serves 10

> *If you like the flavors of caramel-coated apples, here's a simple fall dessert you'll love. The icy sorbet is great with warm caramel sauce poured on top. If you already have Poached Apples on hand (see page 29), begin with Step 4; use 5 apples, halved.*

2 large lemons, halved
5 Granny Smith Apples
2 cups water
1½ cups sugar

1½ tablespoons fresh lemon juice
⅓ cup heavy cream
1 recipe Caramel Sauce (page 513),
   warmed

1. Fill a large bowl with ice water and squeeze the juice from the lemon halves into the water. Place the squeezed halves in the water. Peel, core, and halve the apples. Place each one in the ice water as soon as you have halved it.

2. Combine the water and sugar in a pot that is wide enough to hold all of the fruit in one layer. Cut a circle of parchment paper the same size as the poaching pot. Bring the water to a boil and place the apples in the pot. Cover with the parchment, pressing down on the paper to make sure that all of the apples are submerged. Lower the heat and cook, covered, at a slow boil until just a little soft to the touch, about 2 minutes.

3. Remove the pot from the heat and allow the fruit to cool completely in the syrup, making sure that the fruit is still submerged as it cools. Remove the parchment when the fruit has cooled. (The apples can be poached in advance; refrigerate them in the poaching liquid for up to 1 week.)

4. Remove the apples from the syrup and puree them in a blender. Measure 2½ cups puree into a bowl, setting aside any remaining puree for another use. Stir 1½ cups of the syrup into the puree. Stir in the lemon juice and the heavy cream. Freeze in an ice cream maker according to the manufacturer's instructions.

5. Scoop the sorbet into dessert goblets, top with the Caramel Sauce, and serve.

PINEAPPLE CHAMPAGNE SORBET

Serves 8

Serve this refreshing sorbet in a hollowed-out pineapple shell, surrounded by fresh fruit, for dessert. Or pipe it into cocktail glasses and serve it as an intermezzo between courses. Since they've come on the market, I've used golden pineapples from Costa Rica exclusively. Although they're a little more expensive than regular pineapples, you can always count on their sweetness. The Champagne doesn't have to be expensive—Korbel or Cook's gets great results.

1 golden pineapple, peeled, cored, and cut into chunks
6 tablespoons sugar
1 tablespoon fresh lemon juice

1 cup Champagne or sparkling wine, plus 2 cups for serving if desired
Fresh pineapple slices for garnish (optional)

1. Place the pineapple in the bowl of a food processor or in a blender and puree (in batches, if necessary) until smooth. Push the puree through a fine-mesh strainer into a large mixing bowl. Measure out 2 cups puree. (Set aside any remaining puree for another use.)
2. Stir the sugar and lemon juice into the puree. Mix in the Champagne very slowly so as not to break the bubbles. Freeze in an ice cream maker according to the manufacturer's instructions.
3. Spoon the sorbet into dessert goblets, and pour ¼ cup Champagne over each serving if desired. Garnish with pineapple slices if desired. Pineapple Champagne Sorbet will keep in an airtight container in the freezer for up to 3 days.

ESPRESSO SORBET WITH WALNUT SAUCE

Serves 8

This is an unusual sorbet, for people who seek out special flavors. Topped with the rich Walnut Sauce, it makes a simple but arresting ending to any meal. Spoon it into Chocolate Cups (page 446), if desired.

> 2 cups hot freshly brewed espresso or
>   very strong coffee
> ½ cup plus 2 tablespoons sugar
> Zest of 2 medium lemons, removed
>   in strips with a vegetable peeler
>
> 1 cup heavy cream
> Walnut Sauce (below)

1. Combine the espresso with the sugar and lemon zest in a nonreactive bowl, and let cool completely. Remove the zest and twist the strips over the espresso mixture to release their lemon fragrance. Refrigerate the espresso until cold.
2. Stir the heavy cream into the espresso mixture, and freeze in an ice cream maker according to the manufacturer's instructions.
3. Serve the sorbet in goblets, topped with Walnut Sauce. The sorbet will keep in an airtight container in the freezer for up to 1 week.

WALNUT SAUCE

Serves 8

This sauce turns Espresso Sorbet into a full-fledged dessert.

> 3 large egg yolks
> 3 tablespoons sugar
>
> 1 cup whole milk
> ½ cup chopped walnuts

1. Combine the egg yolks and sugar in the bowl of an electric mixer, and whip until pale yellow and increased in volume, about 5 minutes.

(continued)

2. Place the milk in a heavy saucepan and bring to a boil. Dribble the hot milk, a few tablespoons at a time, into the egg mixture, whisking constantly. Once you have whisked in all of the milk, return the mixture to the saucepan and cook over medium-low heat, stirring constantly with a wooden spoon, until the edges just begin to bubble and the mixture has the consistency of heavy cream.

3. Remove the pan from the heat and pour the mixture through a fine-mesh strainer into a bowl. Stir in the nuts and allow to cool to lukewarm.

4. Place the cooled mixture in a blender or food processor, and process until smooth. Pour the sauce through a strainer into a container, and refrigerate until ready to use. Serve the sauce cold or bring it to room temperature before serving. Walnut Sauce will keep in an airtight container in the refrigerator for 2 days.

FRESH FIG ICE CREAM IN CANTALOUPE BOWLS

Serves 8

Fresh figs and vermouth are an incredible combination. For a spectacular but simple dessert, scoop this ice cream over bowls of fresh fruit. At my farmers' market, I buy very small cantaloupe melons, about the size of a grapefruit. They are incredibly fragrant and sweet and make delicious edible serving bowls for the ice cream.

3 large egg yolks
5 tablespoons sugar
1 cup whole or 2 percent milk
2 pints black Mission figs, washed
   and dried

6 tablespoons fresh lemon juice
¾ cup red vermouth
4 small, ripe cantaloupes, halved
   and seeded
Mint sprigs (optional)

1. Combine the egg yolks and sugar in the bowl of an electric mixer and whip until pale yellow and increased in volume, about 2 minutes.
2. Place the milk in a heavy saucepan and bring to a boil. Dribble the hot milk, a few tablespoons at a time, into the egg mixture, whisking constantly. Once you have whisked in all of the milk, return the mixture to the saucepan and cook over medium-low heat, stirring constantly with a wooden spoon, until the edges just begin to bubble and the mixture has the consistency of heavy cream.
3. Remove the pan from the heat and pour the mixture through a fine-mesh strainer into a bowl. Allow it to cool to lukewarm, and then refrigerate the mixture until completely chilled, 2 to 3 hours.
4. Puree the figs in a food processor until smooth. Measure out 2 cups of puree, and set aside any remaining puree for another use. Stir the puree, lemon juice, and ¼ cup of the vermouth into the custard, and freeze in an ice cream maker according to the manufacturer's instructions.
5. Half an hour before serving, place the cantaloupe halves in the freezer to chill.
6. Scoop the ice cream into the cantaloupe halves, sprinkle each portion with 1 tablespoon vermouth, garnish with mint sprigs if desired, and serve immediately.

BAILEY'S IRISH CREAM ICE CREAM WITH WARM CHOCOLATE SAUCE

Serves 10

Adding Bailey's Irish Cream to coffee ice cream just before it is churned makes for a very grown-up treat. The ice cream is divine, especially when served with warm chocolate sauce. Because of its high alcohol content, this ice cream stays very soft, even after a couple of hours in the freezer.

2¼ cups whole or 2 percent milk
½ cup plus 1 tablespoon (1½ ounces) ground coffee beans
5 large egg yolks
½ cup sugar

½ cup heavy cream
1⅓ cups Bailey's Irish Cream liqueur
1 recipe Light Chocolate Sauce (page 512), warmed

1. Place the milk and ground coffee in a heavy saucepan, and bring to a boil slowly over medium heat, stirring occasionally. Remove the pan from the heat, and let stand 10 minutes. Then pour the mixture through a fine-mesh strainer into a clean saucepan.

2. Combine the egg yolks and sugar in the bowl of an electric mixer and whip until pale yellow and increased in volume, about 2 minutes.

3. Return the milk mixture to the heat and bring to a boil. Dribble the hot milk, a few tablespoons at a time, into the egg mixture, whisking constantly. Once you have whisked in all of the milk, return the mixture to the saucepan and cook over medium-low heat, stirring constantly with a wooden spoon, until the edges just begin to bubble and the mixture has the consistency of heavy cream.

4. Remove the pan from the heat and pour the mixture through a fine-mesh strainer into a bowl. Allow it to cool to lukewarm, and then refrigerate the mixture until completely chilled, 2 to 3 hours.

5. Stir the heavy cream and the Bailey's Irish Cream into the custard. Freeze in an ice cream maker according to the manufacturer's instructions.

6. Serve with the warmed Light Chocolate Sauce.

RED WINE SORBET WITH POACHED PEACHES AND SABAYON

Serves 10

I served this dessert to President Mitterand on one of his visits to the White House, knowing that its simple sophistication would please the leader of France—and everyone else who was dining with him that day.

1 recipe freshly churned Red Wine Sorbet (below)	1 recipe Poached Peaches (page 61)
½ cup cake or fresh bread crumbs	2 cups Vanilla Sauce (page 514)

1. Spoon the sorbet into a 10-inch savarin or ring mold. Cover it with plastic wrap and chill in the freezer until completely solid, overnight or for up to 2 days.

2. To serve, sprinkle the center of a serving platter with the cake crumbs. Dip the mold into a bowl of warm water for 20 seconds. Run a sharp paring knife around the edges of the mold to loosen it. Invert the mold on a work surface and tap one corner of it gently. The sorbet will slide right out. Use a spatula to position the sorbet on top of the cake crumbs. Mound some of the peaches in the center of the mold, and arrange the remaining peaches around the edges. Serve immediately, with the Vanilla Sauce on the side.

RED WINE SORBET

Makes 1 quart

Breaking up the cinnamon sticks allows them to release more flavor into this sorbet. If the sorbet is too soft, it is because the level of alcohol in the wine was too high. You can counter this by adding more water and refreezing.

(continued)

10 ounces frozen sweetened
  raspberries
2½ cups robust red wine
¾ cup sugar
½ cup water
Zest of 2 oranges, removed in strips
  with a vegetable peeler

Six 3-inch cinnamon sticks, broken
  into small pieces
6 whole cloves
½ cup fresh lemon juice (from
  2 medium lemons)

1. Combine the raspberries, wine, sugar, water, orange zest, cinnamon sticks, and cloves in a heavy saucepan and bring to a boil. Cook, stirring occasionally, until the sugar has dissolved.

2. Remove the pan from the heat, and pour the mixture through a fine-mesh strainer into a bowl. Stir in the lemon juice, and let it cool completely. Then refrigerate until completely chilled. Freeze in an ice cream maker according to the manufacturer's instructions. Red Wine Sorbet with keep in an airtight container in the freezer for several days.

COFFEE ICE CREAM WITH TÍA MARIA SABAYON AND ALMOND BRITTLE

Serves 10

This ice cream is best served shortly after it is churned. Just as brewed coffee loses its fresh flavor if it sits on a burner too long, coffee ice cream loses something when it sits too long in the freezer. No need to buy gourmet coffee beans for this recipe; supermarket coffee works very well.

The ice cream and the sabayon have two different textures that really complement each other. Their slightly different coffee flavors give nice depth to this simple dessert.

2¼ cups whole or 2 percent milk	½ cup heavy cream
½ cup plus 1 tablespoon (1½ ounces) ground coffee beans	1 recipe Tía Maria Sabayon (page 166)
5 large egg yolks	1 cup plus 2 tablespoons finely chopped Nougat (page 502)
½ cup sugar	

1. Place the milk and ground coffee in a heavy saucepan and bring to a boil slowly over medium heat, stirring occasionally. Remove the pan from the heat and let it stand for 10 minutes. Then pour the mixture through a fine-mesh strainer into a clean saucepan.
2. Combine the egg yolks and sugar in the bowl of an electric mixer and whip until pale yellow and increased in volume, about 2 minutes.
3. Return the milk mixture to the heat and bring to a boil. Dribble the hot milk, a few tablespoons at a time, into the egg mixture, whisking constantly. Once you have whisked in all of the milk, return the mixture to the saucepan and cook over medium-low heat, stirring constantly with a wooden spoon, until the edges just begin to bubble and the mixture has the consistency of heavy cream.
4. Remove the pan from the heat and pour the mixture through a fine-mesh strainer into a bowl. Allow it to cool to lukewarm, and then refrigerate the mixture until completely chilled, 2 to 3 hours.
5. Stir the heavy cream into the custard, and freeze in an ice cream maker according to the manufacturer's instructions.

(continued)

6. To serve, divide the ice cream among ten dessert goblets or sundae dishes. Spoon the Tía Maria Sabayon over the ice cream. Sprinkle each portion with chopped Nougat, and serve immediately.

Tía Maria Sabayon

Makes 3 cups

Sabayon is simply a parfait mixture that is refrigerated instead of frozen. Here I use sabayon flavored with Tía Maria (substitute Kahlúa if you like) to garnish goblets of coffee ice cream. You can use any other unfrozen parfait over ice cream in the same way.

4 large egg yolks
½ cup Heavy Syrup (page 506)

1½ cups heavy cream
½ cup Tía Maria liqueur

1. Place the egg yolks in the bowl of an electric mixer fitted with the whisk attachment.
2. Bring the Heavy Syrup to a boil in a small saucepan. With the mixer on high speed, pour the syrup over the egg yolks in a slow, steady stream, making sure that none of it falls on the whisk. Reduce the speed to medium and continue to beat until the mixture is cool, pale yellow, and increased in volume, 7 to 8 minutes.
3. In a clean bowl of the electric mixer, whip the heavy cream until it holds soft peaks. Gently fold the whipped cream and the Tía Maria into the egg mixture. Refrigerate until ready to serve, up to 2 hours.

$\mathcal{L}$AYERED FROZEN DESSERTS

Creating layered frozen desserts is sheer delight for me. I love to think about what kinds of ice creams, parfaits, and sorbets will taste good together, and what kinds of sauces and garnishes will further enhance the combinations. Flavor combinations can be as basic as chocolate and honey or as surprising as corn and tequila. I let my own preferences as well as the season and occasion inspire me.

In general I like contrasting textures, so I will pair creamy, dense ice cream with a fluffier parfait mixture. Icy sorbet also contrasts nicely with parfait. I often sprinkle crushed candied nuts into the parfait as I'm spooning it into the mold, to add a little crunch to the smooth dessert.

The ice cream, parfait, and sorbet recipes used in each dessert all make approximate amounts. Your actual yield will depend on how much air you beat into the mixture before you freeze it, and how much air your particular ice cream machine beats into the mixture during churning. In any case, you will have enough to use in any of the dessert recipes below. Leftover ice cream, parfait, and sorbet can be frozen and served separately. Leftover parfait may also be defrosted in the refrigerator and used as a dessert sauce.

Each of the recipes calls for a particular kind of container or mold, but feel free to use any container that you like, provided that it is approximately the same size as the one mentioned.

Make sure that your ice cream, sorbet, and parfait are softened before attempting to spoon them into a mold. Let each layer harden in the freezer for an hour or so before spooning in the next layer.

Before transferring your unmolded dessert to a serving platter, be sure to sprinkle bread crumbs or cake crumbs onto the platter. If you skip this step, your dessert will slide around on the platter instead of staying put. If the dessert has been in the freezer for more than a couple of hours and has become very hard, let it stand on the counter until it is soft enough to cut and serve.

CORN ICE CREAM WITH TEQUILA PARFAIT

Serves 10

This is a perfect example of how desserts were created at the White House. I developed this particular recipe for a state dinner given in honor of the President of Mexico. The ingredients—corn, tequila, and tropical fruit—all come from that country. Maybe because they are often served together or in proximity, the combination really works. Guests of honor were often very touched when they saw that we tried to create something new just for them, especially when it incorporated ingredients typical of their country.

1 recipe freshly made Corn Ice
  Cream (page 169)
1 recipe freshly made Tequila Parfait
  (page 170)
1 cup crushed Nougat (page 502)
½ cup cake or fresh bread crumbs

1 fresh pineapple, peeled, cored, and
  cut into half-rings
2 ripe mangoes, peeled, pitted, and
  cut into ¼-inch-thick slices
2 cups grated fresh coconut
  (see page 41)

1. Place a 5-cup decorative mold or bowl in the freezer until well chilled, about 30 minutes. Remove the mold from the freezer and place it into a bowl of ice. Using a soupspoon, line the mold with a 1-inch-thick layer of Corn Ice Cream. Then return the mold to the freezer and leave it until the ice cream is firm, about 1 hour.

2. Remove the mold from the freezer and slightly overfill it with the Tequila Parfait (it will settle over time), sprinkling the parfait with the Nougat as you spoon it into the mold. Return the mold to the freezer and leave it until firm, overnight, or for up to 4 days. Reserve any remaining parfait for another use.

3. Dip the mold in hot water for 5 seconds. Place a large plate upside down over the mold, invert the two together, and rotate the mold to release the ice cream.

4. Sprinkle the center of a serving platter with the cake crumbs, and use a spatula to place the ice cream on top of the crumbs. Place the dessert in the freezer, lightly draped with plastic wrap, until ready to serve, or for up to 2 days.

5. To serve, take the ice cream out of the freezer. If it is very hard, let it soften on the counter so that it can be cut or spooned. Arrange the pineapple, mango, and coconut around the ice cream just before serving.

CORN ICE CREAM

Makes 1 quart

Corn and mangoes go very well together, since both are very mild and sweet, and the lime juice perks them up. If I have some passion fruit puree on hand, I'll add a tablespoon of it along with the mango for an extra layer of tropical flavor, but it is by no means necessary.

8 ounces fresh or frozen corn kernels
2 cups whole or 2 percent milk
4 large egg yolks
¾ cup plus 2 tablespoons sugar
1½ cups strained fresh mango puree
   (from 1 very ripe mango)

1 tablespoon fresh lime juice
1 tablespoon frozen passion fruit
   puree, defrosted (optional)

1. Combine the corn and milk in a medium saucepan and bring to a simmer over medium heat. Cook until the corn is soft, about 20 minutes. Puree the corn mixture in a blender, and then push it through a fine-mesh strainer into a large measuring cup. You should have 2 cups (if you have more, set the extra aside for another use or discard it). Set aside to cool slightly.

2. Combine the egg yolks and ½ cup plus 2 tablespoons of the sugar in the bowl of an electric mixer and whip until pale yellow and increased in volume, about 2 minutes. Whisk the corn puree into the egg yolk mixture, and return it to the saucepan (there is no need to wash the pan). Cook over medium-low heat, stirring constantly with a wooden spoon, until the edges just begin to bubble and the mixture has the consistency of heavy cream.

3. Remove the pan from the heat and pour the mixture through a fine-mesh strainer into a bowl. Allow it to cool to lukewarm, and then refrigerate the mixture until completely chilled, 2 to 3 hours.

4. Stir the mango puree, the remaining ¼ cup sugar, the lime juice, and the passion fruit puree if desired into the custard, and freeze in an ice cream maker according to the manufacturer's instructions. Stored in an airtight container in the freezer, Corn Ice Cream will keep for a few days.

TEQUILA PARFAIT

Makes 1 quart

Consuming tequila this way is like sipping it; you can really taste it, so buy the best quality tequila possible.

4 large egg yolks
⅓ cup plus 1 tablespoon Heavy
    Syrup (page 506)

1¾ cups heavy cream
½ cup tequila

1. Place the egg yolks in the bowl of an electric mixer fitted with the whisk attachment.
2. Bring the Heavy Syrup to a boil in a small saucepan. With the mixer on high speed, pour the syrup over the egg yolks in a slow, steady stream, making sure that none of it falls on the whisk. Reduce the speed to medium and continue to beat until the mixture is cool, pale yellow, and increased in volume, 7 to 8 minutes.
3. In a clean bowl, whip the heavy cream with the electric mixer until it holds soft peaks. Gently fold the whipped cream and the tequila into the egg mixture. Place the bowl in the freezer and leave it until the Tequila Parfait is thickened, about 1 hour.
4. Spoon the parfait into dessert goblets and serve immediately, or freeze in an airtight container for up to 2 weeks.

CRANBERRY AND GRAND MARNIER BISCUIT GLACE

Serves 10

This is truly one of my favorite recipes. Because of its beautiful color, it makes a wonderful Christmas dessert. To make it truly stunning, add some green and gold to the presentation—holly leaves made of marzipan, gold marzipan Christmas balls, or gold sugar ribbons (see Chapter 12). I like to sip a glass of Grand Marnier as I enjoy it.

1 recipe Genoise (page 397), cut into three ⅜-inch-thick layers
⅔ cup Heavy Syrup (page 506)
⅓ cup Grand Marnier or other orange-flavored liqueur
1 recipe freshly made Cranberry Sorbet (page 172)
1 recipe freshly made Grand Marnier Parfait (page 172)
4 ripe pears, peeled, cored, and cut into ⅓-inch-thick slices
2 recipes Orange Sauce (page 517)

1. Line the bottom of a 9½ x 4-inch metal loaf pan with parchment paper, and chill it in the freezer for 30 minutes. Cut a 9 x 3-inch rectangle from the center of each Genoise layer. (Reserve the scraps to make cake crumbs or for another use.)
2. Stir the Heavy Syrup and Grand Marnier together in a small bowl. Place two of the Genoise rectangles on a baking sheet and brush them with the Grand Marnier syrup so that they are completely drenched.
3. Remove the loaf pan from the freezer and spread some of the Cranberry Sorbet in an even layer across the bottom so that the pan is one-third full. Using a cake board or a large spatula, carefully place one of the soaked Genoise layers on top of the sorbet. Return the pan to the freezer and leave it until the layers are firm, about 1 hour.
4. Remove the pan from the freezer. Spoon some of the Grand Marnier Parfait on top of the Genoise, smoothing it with a spatula, so that the pan is now two-thirds full. (Reserve any remaining parfait for another use.) Place the remaining soaked Genoise layer on top of the parfait, and return it to the freezer until firm, about 1 hour.
5. Remove the pan from the freezer again. Spread another layer of Cranberry Sorbet over the Genoise so that it fills the pan. Place the unsoaked layer of Genoise on top of the sorbet. (Reserve any remaining sorbet for another use.) Cover with plastic wrap and freeze until completely set, overnight, or for up to 2 days.
6. When you are ready to serve the dessert, dip the loaf pan into a bowl of warm water for 5 seconds. Run a sharp paring knife around the edges of the pan to loosen it. Invert the pan on a work surface and tap one corner of the pan gently. The loaf will slide right out. Use a spatula to position it on a serving platter. Garnish the platter with the pears. Cut the loaf into 1-inch-thick slices and serve with the Orange Sauce on the side.

CRANBERRY SORBET

Makes 1 quart

Here's one of the many uses I make of Cranberry Puree.

4 cups Cranberry Puree (page 43)

Freeze in an ice cream maker according to the manufacturer's instructions.

GRAND MARNIER PARFAIT

Makes 1 quart

To serve this on its own, spoon it into goblets and top it with fresh orange segments or Orange Compote (page 56).

4 large egg yolks
1½ teaspoons finely grated orange
    zest

½ cup Heavy Syrup (page 506)
1½ cups heavy cream
¼ cup Grand Marnier

1. Place the egg yolks and zest in the bowl of an electric mixer fitted with the whisk attachment.
2. Bring the Heavy Syrup to a boil in a small saucepan. With the mixer on high speed, quickly pour the syrup over the egg yolks in a steady stream, making sure that none of it falls on the whisk. Reduce the speed to medium and continue to beat until the mixture is cool, pale yellow, and increased in volume, 7 to 8 minutes.
3. In a clean bowl, whip the heavy cream with the electric mixer until it holds soft peaks. Gently fold the whipped cream and the Grand Marnier into the egg mixture. Place the bowl in the freezer and leave it until the parfait is thickened, about 1 hour.
4. Spoon the parfait into dessert goblets and serve immediately, or freeze in an airtight container for up to 2 weeks.

PUMPKIN ICE CREAM AND MAPLE SYRUP PARFAIT WITH BLACKBERRY SAUCE

Serves 12

This is a great autumn dessert. The color and taste will grace your table and delight your guests.

1 recipe freshly made and still soft Pumpkin Ice Cream (page 174)

1 recipe freshly made and still soft Maple Syrup Parfait (page 175)

1 cup chopped Caramelized Pecans (page 503)

½ cup cake crumbs or fresh bread crumbs

¼ cup marzipan, colored pale green (page 468)

1 recipe Blackberry Sauce (page 176), warmed

1. Place the two halves of a 6-cup metal sphere ice cream mold, or two 3-cup metal mixing bowls, in the freezer until well chilled, about 15 minutes. Remove the molds from the freezer and place them into a bowl of ice. Using a soupspoon, line each mold with a 1-inch-thick layer of the Pumpkin Ice Cream. Return the molds to the freezer and leave until the ice cream is firm, about 30 minutes. (Reserve any remaining ice cream for another use.)

2. Remove the molds from the freezer and slightly overfill each one with the Maple Syrup Parfait (it will settle over time), sprinkling each half of the parfait with ¼ cup of the pecans as you spoon it into the mold. Return the molds to the freezer and leave until firm, overnight or for up to 4 days. (Reserve any remaining parfait for another use.)

3. Dip one of the molds in hot water for 5 seconds. Place a large plate upside down over the mold, and invert the two together. Rotate the mold to release the ice cream. Repeat with the second mold.

4. Sprinkle a plate with the cake crumbs. Place one half of the ice cream sphere on top of the crumbs, flat side up. Place the other half on top of the first half to make a complete sphere. Place the ice cream in the freezer to firm up, about 1 hour.

5. When it has hardened, remove the sphere from the freezer. Using a conical zester or the dull side of a heavy chef's knife, make ⅛-inch-deep vertical mark-

(continued)

ings on the sphere, about 1 inch apart from each other all the way around, that look like the vertical indentations on a pumpkin. Place the "pumpkin" in the freezer until ready to serve, or for up 2 days.

6. Shape the marzipan into a 2-inch-long pumpkin stem and place it on top of the ice cream pumpkin. Scatter the remaining ½ cup pecans around the pumpkin base to cover the cake crumbs. Serve immediately, or if necessary, wait until the ice cream is soft enough to spoon, up to 20 minutes. Serve the Blackberry Sauce on the side.

PUMPKIN ICE CREAM

Makes 6 cups

If I'm going to make dozens of pumpkin pies or gallons of ice cream, I'll go to the trouble of making fresh pumpkin puree. But for a small quantity of puree, I go with canned.

5 large egg yolks
½ cup plus 2 tablespoons sugar
2 cups whole or 2 percent milk
1 cup canned pumpkin puree

½ teaspoon ground cinnamon
½ teaspoon ground ginger
½ teaspoon ground nutmeg

1. Combine the egg yolks and sugar in the bowl of an electric mixer and whip until pale yellow and increased in volume, about 2 minutes.
2. Place the milk in a heavy saucepan and bring to a boil. Dribble the hot milk, a few tablespoons at a time, into the egg mixture, whisking constantly. Once you have whisked in all of the milk, return the mixture to the saucepan and cook over medium-low heat, stirring constantly with a wooden spoon, until the edges just begin to bubble and the mixture has the consistency of heavy cream.
3. Remove the pan from the heat and pour the mixture through a fine-mesh strainer into a bowl. Allow it to cool to lukewarm, and then refrigerate the mixture until completely chilled, 2 to 3 hours.
4. Stir the pumpkin puree, cinnamon, ginger, and nutmeg into the custard. Freeze in an ice cream maker according to the manufacturer's instructions. Stored in an airtight container in the freezer, Pumpkin Ice Cream will keep for 2 or 3 days.

MAPLE SYRUP PARFAIT

Makes about 1 quart

You can serve this simple parfait on its own, with Blackberry Sauce on top.

4 large egg yolks
¾ cup pure maple syrup

1½ cups heavy cream

1. Place the egg yolks in the bowl of an electric mixer fitted with the whisk attachment. Bring the maple syrup to a boil in a small saucepan.
2. With the mixer on high speed, quickly pour the hot syrup over the egg yolks in a steady stream, making sure that none of it falls on the whisk. Reduce the speed to medium and continue to beat until the mixture is cool, pale yellow, and increased in volume, 7 to 10 minutes.
3. In a clean bowl, whip the heavy cream with the electric mixer until it holds soft peaks. Gently fold the whipped cream into the maple syrup mixture. Place the bowl in the freezer and leave it there until the parfait has thickened, at least 4 hours.
4. Spoon the parfait into dessert goblets and serve immediately, or freeze in an airtight container for up to 2 weeks.

BLACKBERRY SAUCE

Serves 10

I often double this recipe and use the sauce as cobbler filling and for fruit shortcakes.

1 pound frozen blackberries	1½ teaspoons water
2 tablespoons cornstarch	½ cup sugar, or more to taste

1. Set the blackberries in a strainer over a bowl to defrost. Reserve ½ cup of the juice. (Discard the remaining juice or save it for another use.)
2. Combine the cornstarch and water in a small bowl and stir to dissolve.
3. Combine the ½ cup reserved juice and the sugar in a medium saucepan, and bring to a boil. Stir in the dissolved cornstarch and continue to cook until the mixture is thickened, 3 to 4 minutes.
4. Gently stir in the defrosted blackberries, being careful not to break them up. Taste for sugar and add more if necessary. Scrape the sauce into a bowl or container, and cool to room temperature. Covered and refrigerated, the sauce will keep for 2 or 3 days.

SNOWBALL

Serves 8

The colors and the flavor combination make this dessert a real stunner.

1 recipe Chocolate Ice Cream (page 178), softened	1 cup heavy cream, chilled
1 recipe Honey Parfait (page 179), softened	2 tablespoons confectioners' sugar
1⅓ cups chopped Caramelized Pecans (page 503)	2 cups sweetened shredded coconut
¼ cup cake or fresh bread crumbs	1 pint fresh raspberries
	1½ cups Raspberry Sauce (page 516)
	1½ cups Light Chocolate Sauce (page 512), warmed

1. Place the two halves of a 6-cup metal sphere ice cream mold, or two 3-cup metal mixing bowls, in the freezer until well chilled, 30 minutes. Remove the molds from the freezer and place them into a bowl of ice. Using a soupspoon, line each mold with a 1-inch-thick layer of Chocolate Ice Cream. Return the molds to the freezer and leave until the ice cream is firm, about 1 hour.

2. Remove the molds from the freezer and slightly overfill each half with the Honey Parfait (it will settle over time), sprinkling each half of the parfait with ¼ cup of the pecans as you spoon it into the mold. Return the molds to the freezer and leave until firm, overnight, or for up to 4 days. (Reserve any remaining parfait for another use.)

3. Dip one of the molds in hot water for 5 seconds. Place a large plate upside down over the mold, and invert the two together. Rotate the mold to release the ice cream. Repeat with the second mold.

4. Sprinkle a serving platter with the cake crumbs. Place one half of the ice cream sphere on top of the crumbs, flat side up. Place the other half on top of the first half to make a complete sphere. Place the ice cream in the freezer.

5. Whip the heavy cream and the confectioners' sugar with an electric mixer until it just holds soft peaks. Spread the whipped cream over the ice cream sphere with an offset spatula, or pipe it with a pastry bag fitted with a #6 star tip. Sprinkle the coconut over the whipped cream. The Snowball can be frozen, loosely covered with plastic wrap, at this point for up to 1 week. Before serving, leave the Snowball on the kitchen counter until it is soft enough to cut, 30 to 40 minutes.

6. Arrange the raspberries around the Snowball, and serve it with Raspberry Sauce and warm Light Chocolate Sauce on the side.

CHOCOLATE ICE CREAM

Makes 6 cups

Melting the chocolate in the hot cream before incorporating it into the custard creates an extra-smooth chocolate ice cream.

½ cup semisweet or bittersweet
   chocolate, finely chopped, or
   ½ cup semisweet chocolate chips
1 ounce unsweetened chocolate,
   finely chopped

½ cup heavy cream
5 large egg yolks
½ cup plus 2 tablespoons sugar
2 cups whole or 2 percent milk

1. Place the chopped semisweet and unsweetened chocolate in a large heatproof bowl. Bring the cream to a near boil in a small saucepan. Pour the hot cream over the chocolate and whisk until smooth. Set aside to cool slightly.

2. Whisk the yolks and sugar together in a medium bowl. Place the milk in a heavy saucepan and bring to a boil over high heat. Dribble the hot milk, a few table-spoons at a time, into the egg mixture, whisking constantly. Once you have whisked in all of the milk, return the mixture to the saucepan and cook over medium heat, stirring constantly with a wooden spoon, until the edges just begin to bubble and the mixture has the consistency of heavy cream.

3. Quickly pour the custard over the chocolate mixture, whisking rapidly. Pour the mixture through a fine-mesh strainer into a bowl. Allow it to cool to lukewarm, and then refrigerate until completely chilled, 2 to 3 hours.

4. Freeze in an ice cream maker according to the manufacturer's instructions. Stored in an airtight container in the freezer, the ice cream will keep for 2 to 3 days.

HONEY PARFAIT

Makes 1 quart

You don't need an ice cream machine to make this simple but lovely frozen dessert.

4 large egg yolks
½ cup honey (preferably clover honey)

1½ cups heavy cream
1 tablespoon honey liqueur (optional)

1. Place the egg yolks in the bowl of an electric mixer fitted with the whisk attachment.
2. Bring the honey to a boil in a small saucepan. With the mixer on high speed, quickly pour the honey over the egg yolks in a steady stream, making sure that none of it falls on the whisk. Reduce the speed to medium and continue to beat until the mixture is cool, pale yellow, and increased in volume, 7 to 8 minutes.
3. In a clean bowl, whip the heavy cream with an electric mixer until it holds soft peaks. Gently fold the whipped cream, and the liqueur if desired, into the honey mixture. Place the bowl in the freezer and leave it until the parfait is thickened, about 1 hour.
4. Spoon the parfait into dessert goblets and serve immediately, or freeze it in an airtight container for up to 2 weeks.

VODKA AND LIME TERRINE WITH
ICED RASPBERRY VODKA

Serves 10

When First Lady Barbara Bush asked me to create a dessert to send on Air Force One all the way to Russia for a dinner she and the President were giving at the American Embassy, I sent this, with directions for the Navy chefs on how to finish it! I use frozen sweetened raspberries as a garnish, allowing them to defrost just slightly before arranging them around the terrine. This way they still have that icy flavor and texture that complements the dessert.

1 recipe freshly made Lime Sorbet (page 181)	¼ cup cake or fresh bread crumbs
1 recipe freshly made Vodka Parfait (page 181)	One 12-ounce bag frozen sweetened raspberries, partially defrosted
	2 tablespoons vodka for sprinkling

1. Line the bottom of a 9½ x 4-inch metal loaf pan with parchment paper, and place it in the freezer for 30 minutes.
2. Remove the pan from the freezer and spoon a layer of the Lime Sorbet into the pan, so that the pan is one-third full. Smooth the top with a spatula and return it to the freezer until firm, about 30 minutes.
3. Spoon some of the Vodka Parfait over the Lime Sorbet, so that the pan is now two-thirds full. Smooth with a spatula and return to the freezer until firm, about 1 hour. (Reserve any remaining parfait for another use.)
4. Spread another layer of the Lime Sorbet over the parfait so that it reaches the top of the pan. Cover with plastic wrap and freeze until completely set, overnight, or for up to 2 days.
5. When you are ready to serve the terrine, sprinkle the cake crumbs in the middle of a serving platter. Dip the loaf pan into a bowl of warm water for 5 seconds. Run a sharp paring knife around the edges of the pan to loosen the terrine. Invert the pan on a work surface and tap one corner of the pan gently. The terrine will slide right out. Use a spatula to position it on top of the crumbs. Cut the terrine into 1-inch-thick slices, keeping the slices standing upright together on the platter. Sprinkle the vodka over the half-frozen raspberries, and scatter the berries around the terrine. Serve immediately.

LIME SORBET

Makes about 1 quart

3 cups water
1¾ cups sugar
¾ cup fresh lime juice

¼ cup fresh lemon juice
1 tablespoon vodka (optional)
Green and yellow food coloring

1. Combine the water and sugar in a bowl and stir to dissolve the sugar. Stir in the lime juice, lemon juice, and vodka if desired. Stir in a few drops of green and yellow food coloring to create a lime color. Let stand for 15 minutes.
2. Stir the mixture, and then freeze it in an ice cream maker according to the manufacturer's instructions. Serve immediately in goblets, or freeze in an airtight container for up to 1 week.

VODKA PARFAIT

Makes 1 quart

Vodka isn't often used in desserts, but it works wonderfully here. Serve this with Raspberry Sauce (page 516) for a very refreshing summer dessert.

4 large egg yolks
7 tablespoons Heavy Syrup
   (page 506)

1¾ cups heavy cream, chilled
7 tablespoons vodka

1. Place the egg yolks in the bowl of an electric mixer fitted with the whisk attachment.
2. Bring the Heavy Syrup to a boil in a small saucepan. With the mixer on high speed, quickly pour the syrup over the egg yolks in a steady stream, making sure that none of it falls on the whisk. Reduce the speed to medium and continue to beat until the mixture is cool, pale yellow, and increased in volume, 7 to 8 minutes.

(continued)

3. In a clean bowl, whip the heavy cream with an electric mixer until it holds soft peaks. Gently fold the whipped cream and the vodka into the egg mixture. Place the bowl in the freezer and leave it until the parfait is thickened, about 1 hour.

4. Spoon the parfait into dessert goblets and serve immediately, or freeze in an air-tight container for up to 2 weeks.

WARMED ICE CREAM DESSERTS

This category of dessert is for daredevil chefs. It takes a little nerve, after all, to set an ice cream dessert aflame or to place it in a 450-degree oven just before serving! But the contrast between the warm exterior and the cold ice cream underneath is what makes this type of dessert exciting.

In reality, there is really very little danger that your ice cream will melt during the brief period that it is heated. The Flaming Vanilla Brandied Prune Mold is warmed just enough so that the outer layer of hardened chocolate melts into a sauce. The meringue layer covering the Baked Alaska and the Fruit Salad Surprise insulates the ice cream underneath from the heat of the oven. With both of these recipes, take care to turn the dessert in the oven every 20 seconds or so for even browning of the meringue.

FLAMING VANILLA BRANDIED PRUNE MOLD

Serves 8

This decadent dessert must have been created by the devil himself—and it's one of his best pieces of work! I have been known to wear a devil's cap on my head when I flame it, which gives people a good idea of what is to come. It's one ice cream dessert that's sure to warm you up in the dead of winter. Don't drain the brandied prunes too well—a little of the liquid makes the filling extra good. If too much of the glaze runs off when you pour it over the ice cream it means that the glaze was too warm. Simply return the mold to the freezer for 10 minutes and reglaze with the extra for a nice thick coating. The flame over the dessert melts the chocolate topping, turning it into a wonderful sauce. Do not be afraid to burn it well. Finally, make sure to warm the platter before lighting the brandy so you'll get a good flame.

1 recipe Vanilla Ice Cream
  (page 185), softened
18 to 20 Brandied Prunes (page 67),
  drained but still a little damp with
  brandy

1 recipe Semisweet Chocolate Glaze
  (page 512)
¼ cup cake or bread crumbs
½ cup Cognac, Armagnac, or brandy

1. Place a 4-cup metal mixing bowl, or one half of an 8-cup metal sphere ice cream mold, in the freezer and leave until well chilled, 30 minutes to 1 hour. Remove the mold from the freezer and place it into a bowl of ice. Using a soupspoon, line the mold with a 1-inch-thick layer of Vanilla Ice Cream. Return the mold to the freezer and leave it until the ice cream is firm, 1 to 2 hours.

2. Remove the mold from the freezer. Arrange a few prunes on top of the ice cream layer, and cover with more ice cream. Continue to layer the prunes and ice cream this way until there are no more prunes left and the ice cream is flush with the top of the mold. Cover with plastic wrap and freeze overnight or for up to 2 weeks.

3. Dip the mold in hot water for 5 seconds. Place a cardboard cake round or a plate over the mold, invert the two together, and rotate the mold to release the ice cream. Place the ice cream in the freezer for 30 minutes to firm up.

(continued)

4. Place the unmolded ice cream on a wire rack over a rimmed baking sheet. Pour the glaze over the ice cream, covering it completely. As soon as the chocolate has stopped dripping, return the covered ice cream to the freezer, on a cake board.

5. When you are ready to serve the ice cream, sprinkle the cake crumbs in the center of a silver or stainless steel serving platter (do not use china—it may crack when heated). Just before serving, slide the ice cream from the cake board to the platter. Place the platter on top of the stove and turn the burner heat to medium. Move the platter back and forth over the heat to warm it, about 30 seconds. Remove from the heat.

6. Heat the Cognac in a small saucepan, and then pour it into a large stainless steel ladle. Carefully heat the ladleful of brandy over the flame of a gas stove, or with a kitchen torch, until it ignites, and then pour the flaming brandy over the dessert. Allow it to burn out completely and melt the chocolate coating. Serve immediately.

Vanilla Ice Cream

Makes 1 quart

After whipped cream, this is the recipe I turn to most as a dessert garnish.

5 large egg yolks
½ cup plus 2 tablespoons sugar
2 cups whole or 2 percent milk

2 vanilla beans, split lengthwise
¼ cup heavy cream

1. Combine the egg yolks and sugar in the bowl of an electric mixer, and whip until pale yellow and increased in volume, about 2 minutes.
2. Place the milk in a heavy saucepan. Scrape the seeds from the vanilla beans into the pan, and then add the scraped beans to the pan. Slowly bring to a boil over medium heat. Dribble the hot milk, a few tablespoons at a time, into the egg mixture, whisking constantly. Once you have whisked in all of the milk, return the mixture to the saucepan and cook over medium-low heat, stirring constantly with a wooden spoon, until the edges just begin to bubble and the mixture has the consistency of heavy cream.
3. Remove the pan from the heat and pour the mixture through a fine-mesh strainer into a bowl. Allow it to cool to lukewarm, and then refrigerate the mixture until completely chilled, 2 to 3 hours.
4. Stir the heavy cream into the custard, and freeze in an ice cream maker according to the manufacturer's instructions. Stored in an airtight container in the freezer, the ice cream will keep for 2 or 3 days.

BAKED ALASKA WITH HONEY VANILLA ICE CREAM AND RASPBERRY SORBET

Serves 8

This is a glorious dessert. It may look like a lot of work, but the process can be broken up into stages: Make the cake one day, the ice cream the next day, and then put it all together a few hours before serving. I call for sponge cake (genoise) in this recipe, but any kind of cake will do—pound cake and chocolate cake both work well. You can make the cake well in advance, but wait to make the meringue until you are ready to use it.

1 recipe Genoise (page 397)
½ cup Heavy Syrup (page 506)
3 tablespoons Grand Marnier
2 cups Honey Vanilla Ice Cream
  (page 187), softened
2 cups Raspberry Sorbet (page 188),
  softened

1 recipe Meringue Topping for
  Frozen Desserts (page 211)
2 tablespoons confectioners' sugar
Fresh Fruit Salad (page 24) or
  Raspberry Sauce (page 516)
  for serving

1. Cut the Genoise into two ½-inch-thick layers. Trim one of the layers to form a 9 x 5-inch oval. Slice the remaining layer into two ¼-inch-thick layers. Slice the scraps from the first layer into ¼-inch-thick layers.

2. Place the oval Genoise on an ovenproof serving platter. Stir the Heavy Syrup and Grand Marnier together in a small bowl. Brush the oval cake with about half of the syrup.

3. Spread the Honey Vanilla Ice Cream evenly over the soaked sponge cake, making sure it reaches all the way to the edges. Repeat with the Raspberry Sorbet. Return to the freezer to firm up, about 30 minutes.

4. Remove the Alaska from the freezer and cover the top and sides with a ¼-inch-thick layer of Genoise, tearing the remaining layers and scraps in order to fit them so that no ice cream is visible on the top and sides. Brush the remaining syrup over the Genoise. Place the Alaska in the freezer until ready to proceed; it will keep for up to 3 days.

5. Remove the Alaska from the freezer. Spread freshly made Meringue Topping over it with a metal spatula, smoothing the top and sides.

6. Place the leftover meringue in a pastry bag fitted with a #6 star tip, and pipe a

border of rosettes around the base and top of the Alaska. (This has to be done fairly quickly, as you do not want the ice cream to melt.) Return the meringue-covered Alaska to the freezer until ready to bake, for up to 4 hours.

7. When you are ready to serve the dessert, preheat the oven to 425 degrees. Dust the Alaska lightly with the confectioners' sugar and bake until golden all over, 2 to 3 minutes, turning the platter every 20 seconds for even coloring. Watch it carefully, because once it is golden, it will burn very quickly.

8. Remove the Baked Alaska from the oven and spoon the fruit salad or fruit sauce around the base. Serve immediately.

HONEY VANILLA ICE CREAM

Makes 1 quart

This ice cream is sweetened with honey. Use this as you would plain vanilla ice cream, but be aware that it never gets as hard as plain vanilla.

5 large egg yolks	2 cups whole or 2 percent milk
¾ cup honey (preferably clover honey)	2 vanilla beans, split lengthwise
	¼ cup heavy cream

1. Combine the egg yolks and honey in the bowl of an electric mixer, and whip until pale yellow and increased in volume, about 2 minutes.

2. Place the milk in a heavy saucepan. Scrape the seeds from the vanilla beans into the pan, and then add the scraped beans to the pan. Slowly bring to a boil over medium heat. Dribble the hot milk, a few tablespoons at a time, into the egg mixture, whisking constantly. Once you have whisked in all of the milk, return the mixture to the saucepan and cook over medium-low heat, stirring constantly with a wooden spoon, until the edges just begin to bubble and the mixture has the consistency of heavy cream.

3. Remove the pan from the heat and pour the mixture through a fine-mesh strainer into a bowl. Allow it to cool to lukewarm, and then refrigerate the mixture until completely chilled, 2 to 3 hours.

4. Stir the heavy cream into the custard, and freeze in an ice cream maker according to the manufacturer's instructions. Stored in an airtight container in the freezer, Honey Vanilla Ice Cream will keep for 2 or 3 days.

Raspberry Sorbet

Makes 3 cups

3 cups fresh or frozen unsweetened
    raspberries

⅔ cup sugar
1 tablespoon fresh lemon juice

1. Puree the raspberries in a food processor or blender. Push the puree through a fine-mesh strainer into a bowl. Measure out 2 cups. (Reserve any remaining raspberry puree for another use.)
2. Stir the sugar and lemon juice into the strained raspberry puree. Freeze in an ice cream maker according to the manufacturer's instructions. Stored in an airtight container in the freezer, the sorbet will keep for 2 or 3 days.

Fruit Salad Surprise

Serves 10

If you love fruit salad, this is a terrific way to serve it. The meringue must be made at the last minute, and the dessert must be served as soon as it comes out of the oven, but the fruit salad can be made well in advance, and the ice cream can be shaped several hours ahead of time, making last-minute preparations minimal.

3 cups Vanilla Ice Cream (page 185),
    softened
1 cup apricot jam
⅓ cup Cointreau or other orange-
    flavored liqueur
1 recipe Fresh Fruit Salad (page 24),
    well drained
1 cup cake crumbs

1 recipe Meringue Topping for
    Frozen Desserts (page 211), made
    just before serving
Confectioners' sugar
Chunky Strawberry Sauce
    (page 518) or Raspberry Sauce
    (page 516, optional)

1. Line a 6-cup soufflé dish with plastic wrap so that at least 1 inch hangs over the edge. Pack the ice cream into the dish and smooth it with the back of a spoon to

make an even layer. Put the soufflé dish in the freezer for the ice cream to firm up, about 2 hours.

2. Remove the dish from the freezer, and remove the ice cream disk from the dish by pulling on the edges of the plastic. Transfer the molded ice cream to a baking dish and return it to the freezer until ready to use. Set the soufflé dish aside to use later.

3. Preheat the oven to 450 degrees. Position the oven rack at the bottom of the oven. Stir the jam and Cointreau together in a small bowl. Stir this mixture into the fruit salad until the fruit is well coated.

4. Place the fruit in the soufflé dish, and place the ice cream disk on top of the fruit. Sprinkle the cake crumbs over the ice cream in an even layer. Place the mixture back in the freezer while you make the meringue topping, but for no longer than 15 minutes.

5. Mound meringue topping on top of the ice cream, forming a dome shape. Place the remaining meringue in a pastry bag fitted with a #7 or #8 star tip and pipe arcs of meringue from the edge of the dish to the center point of the dome. Dust heavily with confectioners' sugar. Bake until golden, 1 to 1½ minutes, turning the dish every 20 seconds for even coloring. Remove the dish from the oven and serve immediately, with Chunky Strawberry Sauce or Raspberry Sauce if desired.

Ice cream and pastry showpieces

The following desserts are examples of ways to use ice cream, sorbet, and parfait to create visually stunning desserts for very special occasions, such as those at the White House. The pastry makes a beautiful container for the ice cream and also adds a textural element. These desserts have multiple components and are more time-consuming than others in this chapter, but there is nothing particularly difficult about each step. If you make the dessert in stages, the work is very manageable, and the results will be rewarding.

PEARS IN RED WINE SAUCE WITH RUM RAISIN ICE CREAM

Serves 8 to 10

This dessert is much more than the sum of its parts. The juicy fruit and rich ice cream play off each other perfectly. The phyllo covering provides the same satisfying crunch that you get from an ice cream cone but tastes much, much better. The phyllo shell, although very impressive to look at, is really rather simple to make: An aluminum foil mold is made, using the same bowl that will be used to mold the ice cream. The layers of phyllo dough, shaped around the foil mold and baked, then fit perfectly over the dome of ice cream. If you are using a metal bowl to mold the ice cream, you can shape and bake the phyllo on the outside of the bowl and skip the step of creating a mold with aluminum foil.

1 recipe freshly churned Rum Raisin
   Ice Cream (page 192)
6 tablespoons unsalted butter, melted
   and slightly cooled
10 sheets frozen phyllo dough,
   defrosted
5 tablespoons sugar

1 large egg, lightly beaten
1 recipe Pears in Red Wine
   (page 63)
Confectioners' sugar for dusting
1 pint fresh raspberries for garnish
   (optional)

1. To make the mold, line a 1-quart bowl with a piece of heavy-duty aluminum foil. Trim any overhanging edges. Tightly pack more aluminum foil into the foil-lined bowl, filling it firmly, to create a mold for the phyllo dough. Remove the foil mold from the bowl and set it aside.

2. Line the bowl with plastic wrap so that the wrap hangs over the sides by at least 1 inch. Pack the freshly churned ice cream into the bowl, cover in plastic wrap, and freeze for at least 2 hours or up to 1 day.

3. Preheat the oven to 350 degrees. Place the foil mold on a baking sheet. Brush the mold with some of the melted butter. Lay one of the phyllo sheets over the mold. Brush it with additional butter and sprinkle with ½ tablespoon sugar. Repeat with 4 more phyllo sheets. Trim any excess dough from the bottom of the mold.

4. Make the phyllo bow decoration: Place 1 sheet of phyllo on a work surface, brush it with butter, and sprinkle with ½ tablespoon sugar. Repeat, layering the remaining 4 phyllo sheets on top of the first. Cut 7 strips measuring 1½ inches wide and 6 inches long from the layered sheets. Lightly brush the top of the phyllo dome with beaten egg. Form 6 of the strips into loops and firmly press them into the top of the dome, forming a circle. Form 1 more loop and place it in the center of the circle. Tuck a small ball of foil inside each of the loops to prevent the phyllo from collapsing during baking.

5. Bake until golden, 15 to 17 minutes. Remove from the oven. Gently insert the tip of a paring knife between the phyllo shell and the mold to break the seal that will have formed during baking and to allow for easy removal of the shell when cooled. Cool the shell completely on the mold.

6. To assemble the dessert: Remove the pears from the poaching syrup and place them on paper towels. Heat the syrup until just warm. Remove the plastic covering from the bowl of ice cream. Place a large serving platter upside down over the bowl of ice cream, invert the two together, and gently tug on the overhanging plastic wrap to release the molded ice cream onto the platter. Peel off the plastic wrap. Remove the foil balls from the top of the phyllo dome and carefully lift the dome from the foil mold. Lower the phyllo dome over the molded ice cream. Dust it with confectioners' sugar. Arrange the pear halves in a circle around the ice cream, and spoon some of the warm syrup over the pears and on the platter around the ice cream. Garnish with fresh raspberries if desired. Serve immediately.

Form one more loop and place it in the center of the circle.

Rum Raisin Ice Cream

Makes 1 quart

The dark rum gives this ice cream great flavor and also prevents it from becoming too hard and icy in the freezer. Stir in the raisins at the end by hand so they don't get squashed in the machine.

5 large egg yolks	¼ cup heavy cream
½ cup sugar	½ cup dark rum
2 cups whole milk	1 cup golden raisins

1. Combine the egg yolks and sugar in the bowl of an electric mixer, and whip until pale yellow and increased in volume, about 2 minutes.
2. Bring the milk to a boil in a heavy saucepan. Dribble the milk, a few tablespoons at a time, into the egg mixture, whisking constantly. Once you have whisked in all of the milk, return the mixture to the saucepan and cook over medium-low heat, stirring constantly with a wooden spoon, until the edges just begin to bubble and the mixture has the consistency of heavy cream.
3. Remove the pan from the heat and pour the mixture through a fine-mesh strainer into a bowl. Allow it to cool to lukewarm, and then refrigerate the mixture until completely chilled, 2 to 3 hours.
4. Stir the heavy cream and ¼ cup of the rum into the custard, and freeze in an ice cream maker according to the manufacturer's instructions.
5. While the ice cream is churning, place the raisins in a small skillet and heat over high heat, shaking the pan so they don't burn, until they are very warm, about 2 minutes. Then carefully add the remaining ¼ cup rum to the pan. It will flame up, so be careful. Shake the pan as the rum burns, and continue to shake until the flame goes out. Transfer the raisins to a bowl, leaving any liquid behind, and set the bowl in the freezer to chill the raisins. Stir the raisins into the ice cream when it is fully churned. Stored in an airtight container in the freezer, Rum Raisin Ice Cream will keep for 2 or 3 days.

A BOX OF CHOCOLATE FROZEN TRUFFLES WITH ORANGE ZEST AND CRANBERRY SAUCE

Serves 8

I came up with this dessert for a black-tie White House affair. The presentation—Chocolate Sorbet and Grand Marnier Parfait molded into "truffles" and placed in individual puff pastry boxes—is delightful and elegant. If you want a show-stopping dessert for a very special occasion, this is one to consider. It takes some work, but much of it can be done in advance. The truffles can be put together a week ahead of time and kept in the freezer. Unbaked puff pastry can be rolled out and left in the freezer 3 days ahead; just bake the boxes on the morning of the day you're serving the dessert.

1½ tablespoons cornstarch
1 tablespoon water
2 cups Cranberry Puree (page 43)
1 recipe Grand Marnier Parfait
  (page 172), frozen overnight
1 recipe Chocolate Sorbet (page 194),
  freshly churned

1 cup unsweetened cocoa powder
8 Puff Pastry Boxes (page 282)
½ cup candied orange zest (page 505)
Mint sprigs for garnish (optional)

1. Combine the cornstarch and water in a small bowl and stir to dissolve. Bring the Cranberry Puree to a boil in a small saucepan, and stir in the dissolved cornstarch. Lower the heat to medium and cook, stirring constantly, until the mixture has thickened, about 2 minutes. Let cool completely. Refrigerate until ready to use, or for up to 3 days.

2. Make the frozen truffles: Line two baking sheets with parchment paper and place them in the freezer until well chilled, about 30 minutes. Working quickly, use a #100 ice cream scoop (which scoops out balls about the size of a marble) to scoop out 16 balls of Grand Marnier Parfait onto one of the chilled baking sheets. Return the parfait balls to the freezer for at least 15 minutes (or up to 3 days) to firm up. If the parfait gets too soft or the balls start to melt while you are working, return the baking sheet to the freezer until they are firm and then continue. Place the leftover parfait back in the freezer, to use later.

(continued)

3. Use a #50 ice cream scoop to scoop out one 1½-inch ball of Chocolate Sorbet. Make an indentation in the ball with your finger, and place a parfait ball in the indentation. Close the top so you don't see any parfait. Repeat with the remaining sorbet and parfait balls, working quickly and going in and out of the freezer so that nothing melts before the job is done. When you have made 16 truffles, let them harden in the freezer for at least 3 hours or for up to 3 days.

4. Once they have hardened, place the cocoa powder in a small bowl and roll each truffle in it to lightly coat, taking care that the truffles don't melt in the process. Return the truffles to the freezer. The coated truffles will keep in the freezer for up to 1 week.

5. Two to 3 hours before serving, take the leftover parfait out of the freezer and allow it to soften. Just before serving, place the puff pastry boxes on individual dessert plates. Spread 2 tablespoons of the softened parfait across the bottom inside each box, and place 2 truffles on top of the parfait. Arrange a few strands of candied orange zest around the truffles. Spoon 2 to 3 tablespoons of the cranberry sauce outside the base of each box. Place the cover at an angle on top of the box so that the truffles are still visible. Tuck a small sprig of mint into the box if desired, and serve immediately.

CHOCOLATE SORBET

Makes 1 quart

A triple dose of chocolate deeply flavors this sorbet.

2½ cups water	2 ounces unsweetened chocolate
¾ cup plus 2 tablespoons sugar	1½ ounces bittersweet chocolate
¼ cup unsweetened cocoa powder	

1. Combine the water, sugar, and cocoa powder in a heavy saucepan and bring to a boil. Cook, stirring occasionally, to dissolve the sugar and cocoa. Then remove the pan from the heat and whisk in all the chocolate until smooth. Let cool completely, and then refrigerate until chilled, 2 to 3 hours.

2. Freeze in an ice cream maker according to the manufacturer's instructions. Stored in an airtight container in the freezer, the sorbet will keep for 2 or 3 days.

FIVE

Magical Meringues

IN ITS BASIC FORM, a meringue is egg whites whipped together with sugar. There may be no skill more fundamental to the dessert chef's work than making a good meringue.

Although the recipe is simple, it is also magical. When whipped with care, egg whites can grow in volume by almost ten times. When baked or poached, a meringue becomes a featherweight dessert shell or an airy floating island. In either form, its ethereal texture contrasts beautifully with the heavier and richer ingredients in a variety of wonderfully balanced desserts. Adding a meringue to a mousse or buttercream, or to a muffin, cake, or soufflé batter, is like adding sweetened air. Mixtures that would have been unpleasantly heavy or dense are wonderfully lightened.

In this chapter, I will teach you how to make my versions of the three basic meringues. French meringue uses the most basic technique of simply whipping sugar into partially whipped egg whites. I add a little bit of flour to make sturdy cake layers from the mixture. For Swiss meringue, the sugar and egg whites are initially placed over a hot water bath and whisked before being whipped in the mixer. This slight cooking makes for a more stable meringue. Italian meringue, in which egg whites are whipped with a boiling sugar syrup rather than granulated sugar, is the strongest meringue. I use it when I need a very stable mixture that I'm not going to bake. It makes great buttercream frostings and other cake and pie toppings.

After demonstrating the techniques for making the basic types of meringues, I will show you how to use these techniques to create a number of containers, decorations, toppings, and cake layers. These items are dessert building blocks and are referred to in other recipes throughout the book, for everything from Warm Strawberry Soufflé, to Spiced Apple Meringue Cake, to Baked Alaska with Honey Vanilla Ice Cream and Raspberry Sorbet.

With a few embellishments, a simple meringue itself can become a terrific dessert. The last section of the chapter is devoted to demonstrating how to make a few easy meringue-based desserts like Chocolate Meringue Mousse and Raspberry Floating Island.

GETTING READY TO WHIP

Before getting to the recipes, let's review some basics of meringue-making:

- Save the just-laid eggs for omelets and custards, where the flavor really counts. Although fresher is generally better, slightly older egg whites always whip up smoother and higher than very fresh ones. If you make a practice of buying farm-fresh eggs, let them sit in the refrigerator for 3 to 5 days before using them in a meringue. This isn't an issue with supermarket eggs, which are always this old when you buy them.
- Separate your egg whites, one at a time, into a small bowl. Once you are sure that there is no speck of yolk or shell in the bowl, transfer the white to a larger mixing bowl. This way, if one of your eggs happens to be bad, or if a large quantity of yolk or shell winds up in the bowl along with the white, you won't have to throw everything out and start again.
- If you have used a quantity of yolks for, say, a custard or ice cream, don't throw out the whites! Egg whites will keep in the refrigerator for up to 2 days, and they freeze very well for up to 4 months (for use in a cooked meringue; for a meringue that is to be used unbaked, use freshly separated egg whites). Keep leftover egg whites in an airtight container and make sure to note how many you have stored in the container. Alternatively, you can measure out egg whites by the tablespoon or cup: Each large egg white is about 2 tablespoons of liquid. Convert the number of egg whites called for in a particular recipe to tablespoons, and measure out your refrigerated or defrosted egg whites accordingly.

- It is easier to separate eggs when they are cold from the refrigerator, but let the whites come to room temperature before whipping them for greatest volume.
- Be sure that your bowl and utensils are scrupulously clean. Even a speck of dirt or oil on your whip will prevent the whites from whipping to their highest peaks. Grease tends to cling to plastic mixing bowls and spatulas no matter how well they are washed, so avoid using plastic when whipping egg whites.
- Many cookbooks tell you to whip egg whites by hand with a balloon whisk. This is doable, but takes too much time and muscle for me. Definitely get out the electric mixer. A handheld mixer is fine, but if you have a standing mixer with a whisk attachment, the job will be even quicker.
- Many meringue recipes call for a little bit of cream of tartar to stabilize the meringue, but after years of whipping egg whites, I truly have not been able to tell the difference between whites whipped with cream of tartar and whites whipped without. So for the sake of simplicity I leave it out.
- I've also seen recipes that call for superfine sugar. I can't tell the difference between a meringue made with superfine sugar and one made with granulated sugar, so I stick with what I usually have on hand, which is granulated sugar.

How to whip egg whites and sugar

A properly made meringue is smooth, glossy, and of course wonderfully inflated. Achieving good volume and smooth texture depends on timing. Knowing when to begin adding the sugar, at what rate to pour it into the egg whites, and when to stop whipping will guarantee a successful meringue. Judge by the following cues when proceeding to the next step:

- Place the egg whites in the bowl of the electric mixer and whip them on high speed until they are just about to hold soft peaks. This means that when you pull the beaters or whisk attachment up from the whites, you will also pull up little points of whipped egg white that will quickly fall over.

- At this point, begin adding the sugar. Resist adding the sugar any sooner. If you whip egg whites too long with the sugar, the crystals will melt, weighting down the meringue. You want the sugar crystals to keep their shape for another reason: The crystals themselves help to aerate the whites, acting like tiny whips when whirling around.

- If you are making an Italian meringue with a hot sugar syrup, the timing is different. Turn the mixer on and immediately begin to pour the syrup into the bowl in a quick stream, making sure that none of it falls on the whisk. If the syrup falls on the whisk, it will be whipped onto the side of the bowl and will harden, throwing off the proportions of the recipe. Many chefs wait until the whites are partially whipped before adding the syrup, but there is a danger that the syrup will deflate the partially whipped egg whites as it is poured in. Starting the process with unbeaten egg whites means deflation is not a possibility. There is only one way to go: up.

- Once all of the sugar has been added, check often on the progress of your meringue. Stop whipping as soon as the mixture holds stiff peaks, which means that the little points pulled up by the beaters or whisk remain upright. Overbeaten egg whites, even those with added sugar, will deflate quickly.

- Some meringues call for additional ingredients to be folded into the beaten egg whites. When these ingredients are relatively lightweight, as with flour, cocoa powder, or ground nuts, they may be added directly to the bowl containing the meringue: Using a rubber spatula, scrape some of the meringue up from the bottom of the bowl and turn it over on top of the added ingredients. Give the bowl a slight turn and repeat. Continue to lift the meringue from the bottom of the bowl in this way, working all the way around the bowl, until the added ingredients and the egg whites are well combined. Be careful that you are gently lifting the mixture with the spatula and not stirring vigorously, which would deflate the whites. When a meringue calls for a thicker paste to be incorporated into the beaten eggs, stir a small amount of the meringue into the paste to lighten it, and then proceed as above, folding the lightened paste into the larger portion of beaten egg whites.

THE RECIPES

FRENCH MERINGUE

SWISS MERINGUE

ITALIAN MERINGUE

HONEY MERINGUE

MAPLE SYRUP MERINGUE

MERINGUE TOPPING FOR FROZEN DESSERTS

COCONUT MERINGUE

MERINGUE DACQUOISE

ALMOND MERINGUE

JAPONAISE MERINGUE

CHOCOLATE MERINGUE

CHOCOLATE MERINGUE MOUSSE

COFFEE MERINGUE COOKIES

LEMON PARISIAN MACAROONS

CHOCOLATE FLOATING ISLAND WITH
  PRALINE SAUCE

FLOATING HEARTS

RASPBERRY FLOATING ISLAND

THREE CLASSIC MERINGUES

Master the following recipes for French, Swiss, and Italian meringues and you will be able to make any number of meringue items and meringue-based desserts, from meringue mushrooms for a holiday Yule log to the layers for an Island Rum Cake.

French Meringue is the simplest recipe and the most common model upon which meringue cake layer recipes are based. Simply whip egg whites until they hold soft peaks, add some sugar in a slow, steady stream until the meringue holds stiff peaks, and then fold in flour and confectioners' sugar to give the baked meringue the structure and tenderness required of cake layers.

Swiss Meringue has that dry, powdery consistency and bright white color most people associate with meringue. Before the egg whites and sugar are whipped with an electric mixer, they are whisked together over a hot water bath until very warm. This cooking makes the finished meringue strong enough to become a reliable container for ice cream and juicy fruit salad.

With **Italian Meringue** this cooking process is taken one step further. Rather than simply warming the egg whites and sugar before beating them, you whip the whites with a boiling sugar syrup. The intense heat of the syrup cooks the egg whites as they whip, resulting in a very stable meringue that holds its shape even when unbaked. Buttercream frostings and meringue cake and pie toppings are commonly made using this method.

FRENCH MERINGUE

Makes four 10-inch round cake layers

My French Meringue has a bit of flour in it, and it bakes up very dry and crunchy. Because of its sturdy texture, I use it in ice cream cakes and other frozen desserts. It also makes perfect meringue mushrooms. It is not a pure, snowy white like Swiss meringue, but what it lacks in appearance it makes up for in flavor. Not simply sweet, it has a slightly caramelized taste that is delicious in a variety of desserts. For extra caramelization, set the oven at 300 degrees instead of 250 and bake for the same amount of time.

Don't forget to bake the meringue with the oven door slightly open. Moisture escapes from the oven this way, ensuring that the meringue is crisp.

2 cups granulated sugar
2 cups confectioners' sugar
3 tablespoons all-purpose flour

8 large egg whites, at room
temperature

1. Preheat the oven to 250 degrees. Position oven racks in the top and bottom thirds of the oven. Sift 1 cup of the granulated sugar with the confectioners' sugar and the flour in a bowl. Set aside.

2. Place the egg whites in the bowl of an electric mixer fitted with the whisk attachment, and whip on high speed until they are just about to hold soft peaks. With the mixer still on high, pour in the remaining 1 cup granulated sugar in a slow, steady stream. Whip until the meringue holds stiff peaks. Then fold the confectioners' sugar mixture in by hand.

3. Line four baking sheets with parchment paper. Scrape the meringue into a pastry bag fitted with a large plain tip (#7 or #8), and pipe the meringue into 10-inch rounds or any other shape you like (see pages 202 and 205). Pipe all of the cake layers at once; if you can't fit all the baking sheets into the oven at once, they can sit on the counter until the first batch comes out.

4. Place two baking sheets in the oven and leave the oven door cracked open about 1 inch. Bake for 30 minutes. Check the meringues: If they have begun to color, turn the heat down to 200 degrees. Continue to bake until the meringues are fully dry, another 1½ hours.

5. Remove the meringues from the oven and let them cool completely on the baking sheets. Repeat with the remaining meringue layers. Use immediately, or keep the meringues at room temperature, covered loosely with plastic wrap, for up to 3 weeks.

How to Pipe Meringue Cake Layers

There is no need to limit yourself to 10-inch rounds when piping French Meringue, Coconut Meringue, Chocolate Meringue, Japonaise Meringue, Almond Meringue, and Meringue Dacquoise to make cake layers. You may pipe squares, rectangles, hearts, or any other shape you desire.

For the cleanest shapes, draw your design with dark pencil on parchment paper. Flip the paper over so the pencil won't mix with the cake batter. Use a large plain tip (#7 or #8). Always start from the center, holding the pastry bag upright, and pipe in a spiral motion, moving outward toward the border you have drawn. Don't worry if the surface of the meringue is a little bumpy or if you occasionally go outside the lines. When you construct your cake, you will flip the top meringue upside down so its smooth surface is facing upward. Uneven outer edges can be trimmed with a sharp serrated knife when the meringue has fully dried and cooled.

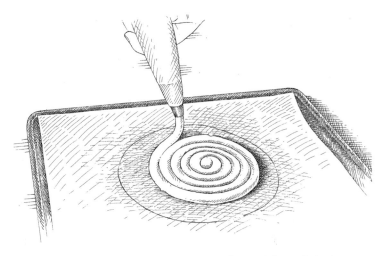

Always start from the center, holding the pastry bag upright, and pipe in a spiral motion, moving outward toward the border you have drawn.

Meringue Mushrooms

Most cookbooks give complicated directions for making dry, tasteless meringue mushrooms. I've come up with a way to make mushrooms that are still moist and flavorful inside, while simplifying the process. I use French Meringue, which has a much better flavor and texture than Swiss Meringue. Instead of gluing together the stems and caps with melted chocolate (a step I don't have the time or patience for), I simply stick the two parts together while they are still warm and soft. Here's how to do it:

1. Preheat the oven to 250 degrees. With a #6 plain tip, pipe mushroom stem shapes on parchment-lined baking sheets. Leaving the oven door cracked open 1 inch, bake until the outsides are firm, about 1 hour. Set them aside to cool.

2. Line a baking sheet with a wrung-out wet kitchen towel. Cover the towel with a sheet of parchment, dabbing a little meringue on the underside corners of the parchment to fix them to the towel. With the same #6 plain tip, pipe the mushroom caps onto the parchment. Then dust them with unsweetened cocoa powder and bake, leaving the oven door cracked open 1 inch, for 30 minutes. (The damp towel will keep the bottoms of the mushroom caps moist and sticky and the insides chewy rather than hard.) Let the caps cool slightly.

3. As soon as they are hard enough to handle, stick the caps on the cooled stems (work quickly, because the tops will still be sticky).

4. Lower the oven heat to 180 degrees, leave the oven door cracked open 1 inch, and bake the completed mushrooms until dry, 1 to 1½ hours. Meringue mushrooms will keep in an airtight container at room temperature for up to 1 month.

SWISS MERINGUE

Makes about twenty-four 4-inch dessert shells

Swiss Meringue, made of nothing more than egg whites and sugar, has the pure white color that comes to mind when you think of meringue. To keep it white, bake it at a very low temperature so that it doesn't so much cook (and caramelize) as just dry out. Baked Swiss Meringue has a dry, powdery texture that isn't right for cakes but is perfect for piped dessert shells and cake decorations. For pastel decorations, add a drop of food coloring after you've whipped it, just before you pipe.

8 large egg whites   **2 cups sugar**

1. Preheat the oven to 200 degrees. Position oven racks in the top and bottom thirds of the oven. Line two baking sheets with parchment paper.
2. Combine the egg whites and the sugar in the stainless steel bowl of an electric mixer. Pour enough water into the bottom of a large saucepan so that when the bowl is placed over it, the bottom of the bowl will come into contact with the water. Bring the water to a full boil. Place the mixing bowl over the boiling water. Heat, whisking constantly, until the egg whites are about 125 degrees on an instant-read thermometer, or feel like warm soup to the touch.
3. Remove the bowl from the heat and beat the whites with an electric mixer on high speed until the meringue is cool and stiff.
4. Pipe the meringue into the desired shapes on parchment-lined baking sheets.
5. Place the baking sheets in the oven and leave the oven door cracked open about 1 inch. Bake until completely dry, 2 to 3 hours.
6. Remove the meringues from the oven and let them cool completely on the baking sheets. Use immediately, or keep at room temperature, wrapped loosely in plastic wrap, for up to 3 weeks.

Shaping Swiss Meringue

To form Swiss Meringue into containers and cake decorations, follow these steps. All should be piped on parchment paper and then baked as directed on page 202:

Starting from the center and working outward, use a spiral motion to form a 4-inch round on a piece of parchment paper. Pipe a ring on top of the outer edge of the round. Pipe another ring on top of the first ring.

For individual dessert shells or nests: Use a plain tip, #5 or #6. Starting from the center and working outward, use a spiral motion to form a 4-inch round on a piece of parchment paper. Pipe a ring on top of the outer edge of the round, and then pipe another ring on top of the first ring.

To make birds: Use a plain #4 tip. Form the tail by piping three small teardrop shapes. For the body, form an oval shape attached to the tail. For the head, pipe a smaller round on top of the tip of the oval, pulling up at the end to

(continued)

For the wings, pipe three teardrop shapes in decreasing size, attached to one side of the body. Repeat on the other side.

create a beak. For the wings, pipe three tear shapes in decreasing size, attached to one side of the body. Repeat on the other side.

To make flowers: Use a plain #4 tip. Pipe a ½-inch ring for the center of the flower. For the petals, pipe six to eight open loops, 2 inches long, attached to the ring. After baking and cooling, fill the centers with melted chocolate and let harden.

A Large Swiss Meringue Container

A couple of steps beyond Swiss Meringue nests and birds is this impressive container. It is a real showpiece when set on a serving platter and surrounded by fresh fruit, with its lid askew to reveal an assortment of homemade ice creams and sorbets.

1. Use a plain #6 tip. For the container, starting from the center and, working outward, use a spiral motion to form an 8-inch round on parchment.
2. Pipe 6 separate 8-inch rings of meringue on parchment on three separate baking sheets.
3. The lid is a half-dome measuring 8 inches in diameter. Ball up aluminum foil until you have the shape you want. Cover the foil half-ball with a smooth piece of foil. Grease the foil dome with vegetable shortening, and dust it with flour. Pipe meringue over the dome, starting at the top and going around in a spiral until you reach the bottom. Pipe a small ball on top to use as a handle.
4. Bake the bottom, the rings, and the dome as directed on page 205.
5. When the meringues have cooled, pipe a thin line of meringue around the edge of the base. Place one of the rings on top; the uncooked meringue will fix it to the base. Pipe some more meringue on top of this ring, and place another ring on top. Continue to build the container this way until all the rings are stacked on the base. Make sure that the rings are nice and straight. Bake for another hour and then let cool completely.
6. Use a small offset spatula to smooth a thin layer of meringue over the container and the lid to create an even surface. Pipe decorations on the sides of the container and the lid with colored meringue, using a smaller tip, if desired. Return the container and lid to the oven and bake until dry, another 1½ hours.

ITALIAN MERINGUE

Makes enough to substitute for whipped cream in 1 Basic Bavarian recipe (see page 128).

This meringue makes very light Bavarians and mousses. If you like, you can substitute Italian Meringue for whipped cream in any Bavarian or mousse recipe. Just remember that the meringue contains a lot of sugar, whereas the whipped cream folded into Bavarians and mousses doesn't have any sugar at all. You'll need to adjust the sugar in your recipe accordingly.

Italian meringue also makes the lightest possible buttercream (see page 404). The cooked whites give this meringue more stability than Swiss or French meringue and will not deflate as quickly as those more delicate varieties.

6 large egg whites, at room temperature	½ cup water
1½ cups sugar	2 tablespoons light corn syrup

1. Place the egg whites in the bowl of an electric mixer fitted with the whisk attachment.
2. Combine the sugar, water, and corn syrup in a small saucepan and cook until the mixture reaches the soft ball stage (240 degrees on a candy thermometer).
3. Turn the mixer on high speed and pour the hot syrup into the bowl in a slow, steady stream, making sure that none of it falls on the whisk. Continue to whip on high speed until the meringue holds stiff peaks and is almost cool. Use immediately, or refrigerate in an airtight container for up to 2 days.

CAKE, PIE, AND ICE CREAM DESSERT TOPPINGS

I have never been a fan of marshmallow-like meringue toppings for pies, tarts, and ice cream desserts. They're pretty, but they don't add a lot of flavor to the finished product. I've experimented with meringue toppings to make them better-tasting.

The following three recipes are my favorite innovations. The first two are Italian meringues in which I've substituted honey or maple syrup for the sugar. The flavorful sweeteners give the meringues distinctive flavors and aromas.

The third is a French meringue that is folded together with a mixture of egg yolks, vanilla, and orange zest. If you have already read through my soufflé recipes, you'll recognize the combination; the topping is really a soufflé mixture. When briefly baked, it turns a wonderful golden color and has all the lightness and rich flavor of a soufflé.

HONEY MERINGUE

Makes enough to cover 1 cake or pie

Honey Meringue has great flavor and fragrance. Adding honey gives the meringue a slightly brown color, but this is not important since the meringue is designed to be browned in the oven or with a torch. Be careful when bringing the honey to a boil; it tends to bubble up and can be dangerous if not cooked in a pot that is deep enough to contain the bubbles.

4 large egg whites, at room temperature	**¾ cup plus 2 tablespoons (10 ounces) clover honey**

1. Place the egg whites in the bowl of an electric mixer fitted with the whisk attachment.

(continued)

2. Place the honey in a small, deep saucepan and cook over medium-high heat, watching it carefully so that it doesn't boil over, until it reaches the soft ball stage (240 degrees on a candy thermometer).
3. Turn the mixer on high speed and pour the hot honey into the bowl in a slow, steady stream, making sure that none of it falls on the whisk. Continue to whip on high speed until the meringue holds stiff peaks and is almost cool. Use immediately, or refrigerate in an airtight container for up to 2 days.

MAPLE SYRUP MERINGUE

Makes enough to cover 1 cake or pie

Maple syrup adds a rich flavor and fragrance to this meringue. It colors the meringue, too, but that won't matter when the meringue is browned. Like honey, maple syrup can boil over easily, so be sure to use a deep saucepan when heating it.

6 large egg whites, at room temperature   **1 cup pure maple syrup**

1. Place the egg whites in the bowl of an electric mixer fitted with the whisk attachment.
2. Place the maple syrup in a small, deep saucepan and cook over medium-high heat, watching it carefully so it doesn't boil over, until it reaches the soft ball stage (240 degrees on a candy thermometer).
3. Turn the mixer on high speed and pour the hot maple syrup into the bowl in a slow, steady stream, making sure that none of it falls on the whisk. Continue to whip on high speed until the meringue holds stiff peaks and is almost cool. Use immediately, or refrigerate in an airtight container for up to 2 days.

MERINGUE TOPPING FOR FROZEN DESSERTS

Makes enough to cover 1 Baked Alaska or other ice cream cake

This is the meringue I turn to when covering Baked Alaska with Honey Vanilla Ice Cream and Raspberry Sorbet (page 186) and other ice cream cakes. The egg yolks give it a wonderful texture and a rich flavor.

2 large egg yolks
1 teaspoon grated orange zest
2 teaspoons cornstarch
1 vanilla bean, split lengthwise

8 large egg whites, at room
   temperature
1¼ cups sugar

1. Combine the egg yolks, orange zest, and cornstarch in a small bowl. Using a sharp paring knife, scrape the seeds from the vanilla bean into the bowl. Lightly beat together. (Reserve the vanilla pods for another use.)
2. Place the egg whites in the bowl of an electric mixer fitted with the whisk attachment, and whip on high speed until just about to hold soft peaks. With the mixer still on high, pour in the sugar in a slow, steady stream. Whip until the meringue holds stiff peaks.
3. With the mixer on low speed, slowly pour the egg yolk mixture into the bowl, mixing until just combined. Use immediately as directed in Baked Alaska or as a topping for any other ice cream cake or frozen dessert.

Meringue Cake Layers

For basic cake layers, I use French Meringue (page 200) and the technique described on page 202. But there are many ways to vary that recipe. Introducing ingredients like coconut, almond flour, or chocolate enhances the basic recipe. Adjusting the ratios of sugar, flour, and egg whites changes the texture. Sometimes I'll want very dry, crisp layers to contrast with very creamy fillings and frostings, as in Marjolaine (page 426). In that case my meringue of choice is Almond Meringue, for its shatteringly delicate texture. Sometimes a soft, moist meringue is called for, and then I'll turn to Meringue Dacquoise, which has the same almond flavor but couldn't be more different in texture.

Although each recipe for meringue cake layers gives a yield, this yield may vary, depending on how much volume you whip into your egg whites. If your meringue is under- or over-whipped, you may not be able to pipe as many cake layers as you would like. For best results, read the tips for maximizing volume (page 197) carefully before beginning to whip your whites.

When coming up with cake layer, filling, and frosting combinations of your own, keep texture in mind as well as flavor. A good cake will have enough contrasting but complementary flavors and textures to make it interesting. But don't make your cakes so complicated that the different elements seem to compete for your attention! In the end, the elements should harmonize.

In the recipes that follow I give some suggestions on constructing simple cakes from meringue layers. See Chapter 10 for specific cake recipes using these and other cake layers.

COCONUT MERINGUE

Makes four 10-inch cake layers

These meringue layers have a lot of flavor, courtesy of an abundant use of unsweetened grated coconut. For a different take on coconut cake, sandwich the layers with Pastry Cream (page 509) and cover the cake with French Meringue or Swiss Meringue and toasted coconut. Other favorite combinations are coconut meringue filled and covered with chocolate ganache, or coconut meringue filled with vanilla-flavored Italian Meringue Buttercream (page 404) and fresh raspberries and then covered with more buttercream.

1 cup sugar	8 large egg whites, at room
2 cups grated unsweetened	temperature
coconut	Confectioners' sugar for dusting
¼ cup all-purpose flour	

1. Preheat the oven to 325 degrees. Position oven racks in the top and bottom thirds of the oven. Line four sheet pans with parchment paper.
2. In a medium bowl, combine ½ cup of the sugar with the coconut and flour. Mix well.
3. Place the egg whites in the bowl of an electric mixer fitted with the whisk attachment, and whip on high speed until just about to hold soft peaks. With the mixer still on high, pour in the remaining ½ cup sugar in a slow, steady stream. Whip until the meringue holds stiff peaks.
4. Fold half of the meringue into the coconut mixture. Then gently fold in the remaining meringue, being careful not to deflate it.
5. Using a #6 tip (or a tip measuring about ½ inch in diameter), pipe the meringue into 10-inch rounds, or any other shape you like, on the prepared baking sheets. Pipe all of the cake layers at once. If you can't fit all of the baking sheets into the oven at once, just let them sit on the counter until the first batch comes out. Dust the rounds with confectioners' sugar right before baking.
6. Place two baking sheets in the oven and leave the oven door cracked open about 1 inch. Bake until firm but not dry, about 1 hour.
7. Remove the baking sheets from the oven and invert onto a wire rack. Carefully peel the parchment from the meringues, and allow to cool completely. Repeat with the remaining meringue rounds. Use immediately, or keep at room temperature, covered loosely with plastic wrap, for up to 1 week.

MERINGUE DACQUOISE

Makes four 10-inch cake layers

The dacquoise is a soft, moist meringue used in many cakes, including one of my fa-vorites, Chocolate-Vanilla Dacquoise (page 423).

1 cup almond flour (see page 523)
1½ cups granulated sugar
2 tablespoons all-purpose flour
5 tablespoons whole milk

8 large egg whites, at room
   temperature
Confectioners' sugar for dusting

1. Preheat the oven to 350 degrees. Line four baking sheets with parchment paper. Position oven racks in the top and bottom thirds of the oven.

2. In a large bowl, combine the almond flour, ½ cup of the sugar, and the all-purpose flour. Stir in the milk. The mixture should have the consistency of mashed potatoes.

3. Place the egg whites in the bowl of an electric mixer fitted with the whisk attachment, and whip on high speed until just about to hold soft peaks. With the mixer still on high, pour in the remaining 1 cup sugar in a slow, steady stream. Whip until the meringue holds stiff peaks.

4. Fold half of the meringue into the almond flour paste to lighten it. Then gently fold in the remaining meringue, being careful not to deflate it.

5. Using a #8 tip (or a tip measuring ¾ inch in diameter), pipe the meringue into the desired shape on the prepared baking sheets (see page 202). Dust with confectioners' sugar just before baking.

6. Place the baking sheets in the oven and leave the oven door cracked open about 1 inch. Bake for 20 minutes. Then turn the temperature down to 300 degrees and bake until firm and golden, about 40 minutes more.

7. Remove the meringues from the oven and slide them off the baking sheets onto wire racks, parchment-lined side down. Allow to cool completely. Then use immediately, or leave the meringues on the parchment paper, drape them loosely with plastic wrap, and store at room temperature for up to 1 week.

ALMOND MERINGUE

Makes one 12 x 16-inch layer

This delicious meringue is used as the base for Marjolaine (page 426). The finished meringue is quite fragile, so handle it carefully when removing it from the sheet pan and peeling away the parchment paper. Toasted almond flour is available at pastry supply shops and by mail from the Baker's Catalogue (see page 523).

1½ cups toasted almond flour
1½ tablespoons all-purpose flour
1½ cup plus 3 tablespoons sugar

4 large egg whites, at room
  temperature

1. Preheat the oven to 300 degrees. Grease a 12 x 16-inch rimmed sheet pan with vegetable shortening. Place a sheet of parchment paper in the pan and grease the parchment as well. Dust the parchment and the sides of the pan with all-purpose flour.
2. In a medium bowl, sift together the toasted almond flour, all-purpose flour, and ¾ cup plus 1 tablespoon of the sugar.
3. Place the egg whites in the bowl of an electric mixer fitted with the whisk attachment, and whip on high speed until just about to hold soft peaks. With the mixer still on high, pour in the remaining 6 tablespoons sugar in a slow, steady stream. Whip until the meringue holds stiff peaks.
4. Gently fold in the almond flour mixture.
5. Scrape the meringue into the parchment-lined pan and smooth with an offset spatula.
6. Place the baking sheet in the oven and leave the oven door cracked open about 1 inch. Bake for 1 hour. Remove the pan from the oven, and use a sharp paring knife to cut the meringue into four 3 x 16-inch rectangles. Return it to the oven and bake until very dry, about 30 minutes longer.
7. Remove the meringue from the oven and let it cool completely on the baking sheet. Use it immediately, or wrap the cooled meringue, still on the baking sheet, in plastic wrap and store it in a dry place for up to 3 weeks. To unmold it, place another sheet pan on top of the meringue and carefully invert the two together. Then carefully peel the parchment away from the meringue.

JAPONAISE MERINGUE

Makes four 10-inch round cake layers

Japonaise Meringue falls somwhere between Meringue Dacquoise and Almond Meringue in texture. I use it in a variety of cakes and pastries, as well as frozen desserts, whenever I'm looking for extra crunch. Sometimes I'll substitute hazelnut (filbert), pecan, or peanut flour for the almond flour, depending on how I'm going to use the meringue. Japonaise Meringue is piped thinner than dacquoise. I call for a #6 tip here, but be aware that actual tip sizes vary from manufacturer to manufacturer. Make sure that yours measures just under ½ inch in diameter for the best results.

1 cup toasted almond flour
  (see page 523)
3 tablespoons all-purpose flour
1½ cups granulated sugar

8 large egg whites, at room
  temperature
Confectioners' sugar for dusting

1. Preheat the oven to 300 degrees. Arrange 2 oven racks in the top third and bottom third of the oven. Line 2 12 x 16-inch sheet pans with a piece of parchment paper.
2. In a medium bowl, sift together the toasted almond flour, all-purpose flour, and ¾ cup of the sugar.
3. Place the egg whites in the bowl of an electric mixer fitted with the whisk attachment, and whip on high speed until just about to hold soft peaks. With the mixer still on high, pour in the remaining ¾ cup sugar in a slow, steady stream. Whip until the meringue holds stiff peaks.
4. Fold the almond flour mixture in by hand.
5. Using a #6 tip (or a tip measuring a little less than ½ inch in diameter), pipe the meringue into the desired shape on the prepared sheet pan. Dust with confectioners' sugar.
6. Place the baking pans in the oven and leave the oven door cracked open about 1 inch. Bake until very dry, about 1½ hours, switching the position of the pans every ½ hour.
7. Remove the meringue from the oven and let it cool completely on the baking sheet. Use it immediately, or wrap the cooled meringue in plastic wrap and store it in a cool, dry place for up to 3 weeks.

CHOCOLATE MERINGUE

Makes three 10-inch cake layers or about 80 small meringue shells

I use the Italian meringue technique here because it produces a chewier meringue. This simple chocolate meringue can be baked into luscious chocolate cookies, and it also makes wonderful cakes. For something simple but luxurious, I'll layer Chocolate Meringue with chocolate Ganache (page 482). When I have more time, I like to place a layer of chocolate meringue between two layers of vanilla genoise that have been soaked with a light syrup and a liqueur and then spread with chocolate or vanilla buttercream. The sponge is soft and moist, the buttercream is rich and creamy, and the meringue adds crunch to the mix.

8 ounces bittersweet chocolate	2 cups sugar
2 ounces unsweetened chocolate	½ cup water
5 large egg whites	

1. Preheat the oven to 250 degrees. Line three or four baking sheets with parchment paper. Pour 2 inches of water into a medium saucepan and bring to a bare simmer. Place the bittersweet and unsweetened chocolate in a stainless steel bowl that is big enough to rest on top of the saucepan, and place the bowl over the simmering water, making sure that it doesn't touch the water. Heat, whisking occasionally, until the chocolate is completely melted. Remove the bowl from the heat and let cool slightly.
2. Place the egg whites in the bowl of an electric mixer fitted with the whisk attachment.
3. Combine the sugar and water in a small saucepan, and cook until the mixture reaches the soft ball stage (240 degrees on a candy thermometer).
4. Turn the mixer on high speed and pour the hot syrup into the bowl in a slow, steady stream, making sure that none of it falls on the whisk. Continue to whip on high until the meringue holds stiff peaks and is almost cool. Then fold in the melted chocolate.
5. Using a #6 tip (or a tip measuring about ½ inch in diameter), pipe the meringue into 10-inch rounds, or any other shape you like, on the prepared baking sheets. Pipe all of the cake layers at once. For cookies, pipe into teardrops, S-shapes, or

(continued)

rosettes with a #5 star tip. If you can't fit all the baking sheets into the oven at once, just let them sit on the counter until the first batch comes out.

6. Place the baking sheets in the oven and leave the oven door cracked open about 1 inch. Bake until firm around the edges but still a little soft in the center, about 1½ hours for both cake layers and cookies.

7. Remove the meringues from the oven and let them cool completely on the baking sheets. Use cake layers immediately, or keep at room temperature, covered loosely with plastic wrap, for up to 3 weeks. Keep cookies in an airtight container.

Meringue Mousses

When I need a lower-fat mousse, I turn to meringue. Like whipped cream, meringue can provide an airy base for a variety of flavorings, including coffee, orange, hazelnut, and chestnut (see Egg White Bavarian, page 130, for gelatin-enhanced low-fat mousses). I also

What to Do with Leftover Meringue

Leftover meringue, chopped up and toasted, is a wonderful addition to buttercream and many other cake fillings. It adds flavor and texture, and it lightens the buttercream. Or sprinkle it over ice cream instead of using nuts.

Preheat the oven to 375 degrees. Break up leftover meringue into finger-size pieces. (Don't make the pieces any smaller or they may crumble to dust.) Place the meringue pieces on a parchment-lined baking sheet and bake until just golden, 5 to 7 minutes. Don't let the pieces brown too much or they will become bitter. Remove from the oven and let cool completely. Store in an airtight container at room temperature for up to 2 weeks.

use meringue in combination with whipped cream for extra-delicate fruit mousses such as Passion Fruit Mousse (page 123). The following chocolate mousse recipe relies even more heavily on meringue than any of these examples. There is no cream or half-and-half; whipped egg whites alone aerate the chocolate. With just three ingredients—egg whites, sugar, and chocolate—it is an easy way to make a meringue-based mousse if you've never tried one.

CHOCOLATE MERINGUE MOUSSE

Serves 8 to 10

This meringue-based chocolate mousse is wonderfully light and a good choice if you are avoiding dairy products and butterfat. Although the egg whites make it low in calories compared with heavy cream-based mousses, it is surprisingly rich-tasting, with a pure, strong chocolate flavor. It is also shockingly quick to put together—just the thing for unexpected guests or an impromptu treat. It can be served right away or chilled for up to 8 hours before serving.

As with Quick Chocolate Mousse with Crystallized Ginger (page 115), the temperature of the ingredients and the way you fold them together will determine the success of the recipe. The chocolate should be warm to the touch. If it is too cool, it will seize before you have a chance to smoothly incorporate it into the meringue. Likewise, the egg whites should be at room temperature. Not only will this give you better volume, but warmer egg whites won't cool down the melted chocolate too quickly, another cause of grainy mousse. Fold the egg whites into the chocolate, not vice versa, since the chocolate bowl is probably warmer than the egg white bowl, and a cold bowl could chill and harden the chocolate.

For an almost fat-free chocolate cake, sandwich this mousse between layers of Chocolate Meringue (page 217) and then cover the sides and top with the remaining mousse. You can even pipe extra mousse along the base and top of the cake to decorate it. If you are going to use the mousse this way, be sure to do so as soon as you prepare it, when it will spread and pipe beautifully. If you keep it in the refrigerator for any amount of time, it will taste great when spooned but will quickly deflate when handled with a spatula or squeezed through a pastry bag.

(continued)

| 7 ounces semisweet or bittersweet chocolate or semisweet chocolate chips | 8 large egg whites, at room temperature |
| | ¾ cup sugar |

1. Pour 2 inches of water into a medium saucepan and bring to a bare simmer. Place the chocolate in a stainless steel bowl that is big enough to rest on top of the saucepan and place it over the simmering water, making sure that the bowl doesn't touch the water. Heat, whisking occasionally, until the chocolate is completely melted. Remove the bowl from the heat and let it cool slightly until the chocolate is just warm to the touch, between 95 and 100 degrees on a candy thermometer.
2. Place the egg whites in the bowl of an electric mixer fitted with the whisk attachment, and whip on high speed until just about to hold soft peaks. With the mixer still on high, pour in the sugar in slow, steady stream. Whip until the meringue holds stiff peaks.
3. Add the egg whites to the chocolate all at once, and quickly but gently fold them in. Scrape the mousse into a large serving bowl or into individual goblets. Serve immediately, or cover the container or goblets with plastic wrap, making sure that the plastic doesn't come in contact with the mousse, and refrigerate for up to 8 hours.

Meringue cookies

Meringues have the potential to be very dry. This is good in some cases—crisp cake layers, for example—but not so great for cookies. The best meringue cookies are crisp on the outside but moist on the inside. There are couple of things you can do to achieve this consistency.

Baking meringue cookies on a piece of parchment that sits on a wet kitchen towel is a venerable technique that allows moisture to seep into the undersides of the cookies even as the tops turn crunchy. Alternatively, you can pour water between the parchment paper and the baking sheet as soon as the cookies come out of the oven.

In the following recipes, I use some confectioners' sugar, rather than all granulated sugar, to give the cookies some added softness.

COFFEE MERINGUE COOKIES

Makes 36 cookies

If you'd like to dress these cookies up, let them cool completely, top sides down, on wire racks. Then hollow out the insides with a small spoon, fill with buttercream, Ganache (page 513), or even ice cream, and sandwich them together. The filling will act like glue. Coffee Meringues filled with buttercream should be refrigerated and then allowed to come to room temperature before serving. Ice cream–filled meringues may be frozen for up to 1 week before serving straight from the freezer.

½ tablespoon instant espresso
   powder
½ tablespoon hot tap water
½ cup granulated sugar

3 large egg whites, at room
   temperature
1 cup confectioners' sugar, sifted

1. Preheat the oven to 250 degrees. In a large bowl, combine the espresso powder and hot water and stir to dissolve. Add ¼ cup of the granulated sugar, stirring until the mixture resembles a thick paste.
2. Place the egg whites in the bowl of an electric mixer fitted with the whisk attachment, and whip on high speed until just about to hold soft peaks. With the mixer still on high, pour in the remaining ¼ cup granulated sugar in a slow, steady stream. Whip until the meringue holds stiff peaks.
3. Fold one third of the meringue into the coffee mixture to lighten it. Then gently fold in the remaining meringue, being careful not to deflate it. Gently fold in the confectioners' sugar until it is fully incorporated.
4. Wet a clean, thick kitchen towel and wring out so that it is thoroughly moistened but no longer dripping. Place the towel on a baking sheet. Dab a little bit of the meringue on each corner of the towel, and place a sheet of parchment paper on top of the towel, pressing on each corner to fix the paper to the towel (the meringue will act like glue).

(continued)

5. Using a #7 star tip, pipe 72 walnut-size rounds onto the parchment.
6. Place the baking sheet in the oven and leave the oven door cracked open about 1 inch. Bake until firm enough to be handled, 30 to 40 minutes. The cookies should be dry on the outside but still soft on the inside.
7. Remove the cookies from the oven. As soon as they are cool enough to handle, sandwich them together (the bottoms will still be sticky). Let cool completely. Coffee Meringues will keep in an airtight container for 2 to 3 days.

LEMON PARISIAN MACAROONS

Makes about 45 cookies

These cookies are a challenge to make but well worth the effort. Baking conditions have to be just right or they will spread and crack on top. Baking the cookies on doubled baking sheets, one stacked on top of the other, ensures that the cookies will be crisp on the outside but soft on the inside. Make sure that you use rimmed baking sheets so that when you pour the water under the parchment paper, it doesn't spill out onto the counter and the floor! If you'd like, omit the Lemon Cream and sandwich the macaroons together while their bottoms are still wet. Or omit the Lemon Cream and food coloring and sandwich the cookies together with Ganache (page 513) or the jam of your choice.

1 cup plus 2 tablespoons almond flour (see page 523)
1½ cups confectioners' sugar
3 large egg whites, at room temperature

6 tablespoons granulated sugar
1 teaspoon grated lemon zest
1 drop yellow food coloring
¼ cup Lemon Cream (page 510)

1. Preheat the oven to 375 degrees. Line two rimmed baking sheets with parchment paper. Place each baking sheet on top of another unlined baking sheet. Sift the almond flour and confectioners' sugar together in a medium bowl, and set aside.

2. Place the egg whites in the bowl of an electric mixer fitted with the whisk attachment, and whip on high speed until just about to hold soft peaks. With the mixer still on high, pour in the granulated sugar in a slow, steady stream. Whip until the meringue holds stiff peaks. Stir in the lemon zest and food coloring.

3. Fold the almond flour mixture into the egg whites, making sure everything is well combined but being careful not to deflate the mixture.

4. Spoon the batter into a pastry bag fitted with a plain #6 tip, and pipe quarter-size portions on the prepared baking sheets, leaving ½ inch between cookies. You should have about 90 cookies. Bake until the cookies are risen and lightly colored, 10 to 12 minutes.

5. As the baking sheets come out of the oven, place them on wire racks, lift one end of the parchment, and carefully pour about ½ cup water between the parchment paper and the baking sheet to moisten the paper. Let stand for 2 minutes, and then transfer the cookies to a dry baking sheet, flat side up, and cool completely.

6. Sandwich the cookies together, using ¼ teaspoon Lemon Cream as the "glue" between two flat sides. Lemon Parisian Macaroons will keep in an airtight container at room temperature for 2 days, or in the freezer for up to 1 week.

$\mathcal{F}$LOATING ISLANDS

Floating Island is an old-fashioned dessert that has recently been taken up by younger chefs. There is much to attract a new generation to this dessert, in which scoops of meringue are quickly poached in water and then "floated" in a dessert sauce and garnished with fresh fruit, chocolate, or chopped nuts. The sweet but neutral-tasting meringue puffs are a perfect foil for a variety of sauces.

Floating Island can be a terrific low-fat dessert. The Floating Hearts version was created during the Reagan administration, when the demand for healthy cooking really took off. But Floating Island can also be a decadent treat. Chocolate Floating Island with Praline Sauce consists of chocolate-covered meringues floated on a rich almond caramel sauce and garnished with nougat. It is like an ice cream sundae without the ice cream, for grown-up kids.

Use a shallow saucepan for this project. It is easier to slide the meringues in and out of a wide, shallow pot than a narrow, deep one. An ice cream scoop is the perfect implement for making uniformly sized floating islands. Dip it in cold water between scoops to rinse it and cool it off.

Poaching meringues takes some practice; you want them to be firm to the touch on the outside, but if you overcook them they will deflate as they cool. If you've never done it before, you might try practicing with one or two scoops to see exactly how long the meringues will take to cook properly on your cooktop before cooking them in larger batches.

One of the wonderful things about this dessert is that the meringues can be poached well in advance of serving. Remove the cooked meringues from the pot with a slotted spoon and transfer them to a sheet pan lined with a clean kitchen towel, to allow excess water to drain off. Then refrigerate them, uncovered, for up to 24 hours.

CHOCOLATE FLOATING ISLAND WITH PRALINE SAUCE

Serves 10

I love the combination of colors, flavors, and textures in this dessert. The soft white meringues are encased in a thin layer of dark chocolate. The dessert is completed by a rich-looking and even richer-tasting Praline Sauce and sprinkled with crunchy, sparkling nougat candy. Simple, but perfect.

6 large egg whites, at room
   temperature
¾ cup sugar
9 ounces semisweet or bittersweet
   chocolate, finely chopped

1 cup heavy cream or crème fraîche
3 cups Praline Sauce (page 515),
   at room temperature
1 cup Nougat, crushed (page 502)

1. Place the egg whites in the bowl of an electric mixer fitted with the whisk attachment, and whip on high speed until they hold soft peaks, 2 to 3 minutes. With the mixer still on high, pour in the sugar in a slow, steady stream. Whip until the meringue holds stiff peaks but is not dry or lumpy.

2. Pour 3 to 4 inches of water into a large shallow pot, and bring to a bare simmer. Dip a large oval ice cream scoop in cold water, and scoop up some meringue. Gently drop the meringue into the simmering water. Repeat with 3 or 4 more scoops. Cook the meringues for 30 seconds, and then turn them over in the water and cook for another 30 seconds. The exteriors of the meringues should be firm to the touch.

3. Remove the meringues with a slotted spoon and place them on a sheet pan lined with a clean kitchen towel. Allow the cooked meringues to cool in the refrigerator. Repeat, cooking the meringues in batches of 4 or 5, until you have used all the meringue mixture. (Poached meringues can be stored in the refrigerator, uncovered, for up to 1 day before using.)

4. Place the chopped chocolate in a heatproof bowl. In a medium saucepan, heat the cream or crème fraîche just until it comes to a bare simmer (do not allow the cream to come to a boil or you will cook off its fresh flavor). Pour the hot cream over the chopped chocolate, cover the bowl with plastic wrap, and let stand for

(continued)

5 minutes. Then whisk until smooth. Let this ganache stand until cool to the touch but still fluid.

5. Place the meringue "islands" on a wire rack set over a rimmed baking sheet. Spoon some of the ganache over each meringue to coat it completely. Let the covered meringues stand until the ganache is hardened, 10 to 15 minutes.

6. To serve: Pour the Praline Sauce onto a large serving dish, and place the glazed meringue "islands" on top of the sauce so that they touch each other. Sprinkle the crushed Nougat over the meringues, and serve.

FLOATING HEARTS

Serves 8 to 10

I have developed many versions of Floating Island, usually as a response to a request for a light, low-fat dessert. This is one of the simplest and prettiest, perfect for Valentine's Day or any other occasion. The meringue is piped into heart shapes, poached in simmering water, and floated on a simple raspberry sauce. Sliced strawberries, which themselves look like hearts, garnish the dessert and add fresh fruit flavor.

For the lightest meringue, whip the egg whites until they are quite white and fluffy before adding any sugar. I have found that sugar added too early will dissolve during whipping and weight down the meringue, making it heavier and less voluminous.

Unlike the other Floating Islands, these are poached covered. The tops steam until they are cooked, so you don't have to flip them and risk ruining their heart shapes.

8 large egg whites, at room temperature
1 cup plus 1½ tablespoons sugar
2 cups Raspberry Sauce (page 516)

1 pint fresh strawberries, washed, stemmed, and cut lengthwise into ¼-inch-thick slices
Fresh mint leaves for garnish

1. Place the egg whites in the bowl of an electric mixer fitted with the whisk attachment, and whip on high speed until white, fluffy, and just about to hold soft peaks. With the mixer still on high, pour in the sugar in a slow, steady stream. Whip until the meringue holds stiff peaks.

2. Cut out a round piece of parchment just a little bit smaller in diameter than the large, wide sauté pan that you will use to cook the meringues. Grease the parchment with vegetable shortening. Pour 3 to 4 inches of water into the pan and bring it to a bare simmer.

3. Fit a pastry bag with a #8 or #9 plain tip, and fill the bag about halfway with meringue. Form hearts by piping two teardrops, each about 3 inches long, side by side on the greased parchment.

4. Carefully slide the parchment onto the surface of the simmering water, and pull it out from under the hearts. The hearts should just slide off as soon as the paper comes in contact with the hot water. Simmer, covered, for 45 seconds. Lift the hearts from the water with a slotted spoon, and drain them on paper towels. Repeat until you have 16 to 20 hearts. (Meringue hearts can be refrigerated uncovered for up to 1 day.)

5. To assemble the dessert: Pour the Raspberry Sauce onto a shallow platter that is large enough to hold all of the meringue hearts. Using a slotted spatula, carefully float the meringues on top of the sauce. Arrange the strawberry slices around the rim of the platter and decorate with the mint leaves. Serve immediately.

Form hearts by piping two teardrops, each about 3 inches long, side by side on the greased parchment.

RASPBERRY FLOATING ISLAND

Serves 6 to 8

Most Floating Islands depend on sauces and other accompaniments to add flavor, but in this recipe Raspberry Sauce gives a jolt of flavor to the meringue itself.

4 large egg whites, at room
   temperature
½ cup sugar
¾ cup Raspberry Sauce (page 516)
3 cups Vanilla Sauce (page 514),
   or 2 cups Vanilla Sauce mixed
   with 1 cup Lemon Cream
   (page 510)

45 fresh raspberries
Fresh mint leaves for garnish

1. Place the egg whites in the bowl of an electric mixer fitted with the whisk attachment, and whip on high speed until they hold soft peaks, 2 to 3 minutes. With the mixer still on high, pour in the sugar in a slow, steady stream. Whip until the meringue holds stiff peaks but is not dry or lumpy. Gently fold the Raspberry Sauce into the meringue.
2. Pour 2 to 3 inches of water into a large shallow pan, and bring to a bare simmer. Dip a large oval ice cream scoop in cold water, and scoop up some meringue. Gently drop the meringue into the simmering water. Repeat with 3 or 4 more scoops. Cook the meringues for 30 seconds and then turn them over in the water and cook for another 30 seconds. The exteriors of the meringues should be firm to the touch.
3. Remove the meringues with a slotted spoon and place them on a sheet pan lined with a clean kitchen towel. Allow the cooked meringues to cool in the refrigerator. Repeat the process, cooking meringues in batches of 4 or 5 until you have used all the meringue mixture. (Poached meringues can be stored in the refrigerator, uncovered, for up to 1 day before serving.)
4. Pour the Vanilla Sauce onto a large serving dish, and place the meringue "islands" on top of the sauce so they touch each other. Place 3 raspberries on top of each meringue, and garnish each meringue with a mint leaf. Serve immediately, or refrigerate the platter, uncovered, for up to 3 hours before serving.

SIX

Delicate Crêpes and Delectable Fillings

THERE WAS A TIME when a cook was judged by the transparency of his or her crêpes. Proper crêpes, it was said throughout the pastry world, had to be so thin that one could read a newspaper through them. And I'm not talking about the large print edition!

Young pastry apprentices are no longer held to this standard. In fact, crêpes don't appear very often at all on dessert menus or at the home table anymore. You are more likely to find them at the county fair or served by a street vendor. This is too bad, because crêpes make absolutely fantastic, quite sophisticated desserts when cooked correctly and filled thoughtfully. I served them frequently at the White House, where they were always received with surprise and pleasure, partly because they were considered so out-of-the-ordinary.

It is still true that the best crêpes are delicate and light in the extreme. Over the years, I have refined two crêpe recipes. My Basic Crêpe batter cooks up thin enough to pass the newspaper test but is so easy to work with that a beginner can be confident of success the first time out. Use Basic Crêpes any time, with any kind of filling, sweet or savory. Beer Batter Crêpes are very thin, with a slightly tangy flavor. These tear easily, so they are best used in recipes where the crêpes aren't handled or otherwise treated roughly.

Whichever recipe you choose, there are a few things you can do to guarantee success:

MIXING: Make sure that your eggs, milk, and beer are at room temperature. If they are too cool, they will cause the melted butter to solidify, making the batter lumpy. Strain the batter before using it (in the case of Beer Batter Crêpes, before folding in the egg whites) to eliminate any lumps of unmixed flour.

RESTING: Although you may cook Basic Crêpes right away, it is best to let the batter rest for at least 1 hour at room temperature or for several days in the refrigerator. This downtime allows the protein in the flour to relax, making a softer crêpe. For Beer Batter Crêpes, let the batter rest for about an hour, but make sure to use it on the day you make it, or the batter will begin to ferment and become overly yeasty.

COOKING: A special crêpe pan is nice but not necessary for making crêpes. A 6-inch skillet, preferably nonstick, will work just as well. Brush the pan with melted butter before you begin cooking the first crêpe. Butter the pan again only if the crêpes start to stick. Pour about 2 tablespoons batter into the pan and very quickly tilt the pan to the right and then in a circular motion to coat it completely with the batter. Temperature is the key to making good crêpes: If your pan is too cool, your crêpes will be rubbery. If your pan is too hot, the crêpes will be too thick because the batter will cook before you can swirl it across the entire cooking surface. Cool your pan down between crêpes by dipping the bottom of the pan in a bowl of cool water standing right next to your cooktop. The first crêpe is usually not the best of the bunch. I call it the test crêpe. If it's not perfectly shaped, just take this as a sign to sample it right from the pan. The rest will look progressively better.

FLIPPING: My crêpes are quite fragile, not the type you can turn over in the pan with a flick of your wrist. Grasp the edge of the crêpe with your thumb and index finger and carefully lift and flip it.

FILLING AND BAKING: In keeping with their light texture, crêpes should be filled with modest amounts of delicate fillings. They should never be filled to bursting or contain large chunks of fruit that might tear them or make them appear lumpy. They are not burritos or giant wrap sandwiches, after all. I like to fill and fold my crêpes, arrange them on a heatproof serving dish, and warm them through in a very hot oven for just a few minutes. If you overfill your crêpes, you will not be able to heat them adequately without drying them out.

FREEZING: Crêpes freeze amazingly well. Somehow they taste just as good or even better after some time in the freezer. Freeze the crêpes right on the sugared sheet pan that you've flipped them onto after cooking. Place a clean, damp kitchen towel over them, wrap the whole pan, including the towel, in plastic wrap, and freeze. When you need the crêpes, remove the plastic wrap and place the sheet pan in a 375-degree oven with the towel still in place; then cook for 5 to 7 minutes, so the towel just becomes hot to the touch. The towel will release some steam onto the crêpes, making them very pliable and easy to work with as they thaw. Carefully lift the defrosted crêpes from the sheet pan and fill as desired.

If you aren't sure you will be using all of your frozen crêpes at once, freeze them in smaller quantities on separate baking sheets.

The Recipes

Unlike, say, cake recipes, crêpe recipes can very successfully be cut down by half or even a fourth if you'd like to make just a couple of servings. This makes them ideal for small dinner parties and intimate celebrations.

Basic Crêpes

Beer Batter Crêpes

Chocolate Crêpes

Apple Butter Crêpes with Marsala-Laced
   Vanilla Sauce

Crêpes Parisiennes

Crêpes Japonaises

Christmas Tree Crêpes

Lemon Soufflé Crêpes with Strawberry Sauce

Yogurt Apricot Purses

Pear Crêpes

Gâteau of Crêpes

BASIC CRÊPES

Makes about 20 crêpes

If you've never made crêpes before, start with this recipe, which is easier to work with than the beer batter recipe. This recipe is also a better match for savory fillings, if you want to fill some of them for a lunch or light dinner. This amount of batter will produce a few more crêpes than you will need for any of the crêpe recipes in this chapter, just in case of tearing, overcooking, or any other mishap that might occur.

1 large egg, at room temperature
1 large egg yolk, at room temperature
¼ cup sugar
¾ cup all-purpose flour
1¼ cups whole or 2 percent milk, at room temperature

½ teaspoon pure vanilla extract
4 tablespoons unsalted butter, melted and cooled, plus a little more for greasing the pan
Pinch salt

1. Combine the egg, egg yolk, 2 tablespoons of the sugar, the flour, and ½ cup of the milk in a medium bowl. Stir until it forms a smooth paste. Add the remaining ¾ cup milk and the vanilla, melted butter, and salt. Stir until smooth. Pour the mixture through a fine-mesh strainer into a measuring cup or bowl. Let the batter rest for 1 hour, or refrigerate for up to 4 days. Warm the batter slightly over a pot of barely simmering water before using.
2. Sprinkle a rimmed sheet pan with the remaining 2 tablespoons sugar. Fill a shallow bowl or cake pan with cool water.
3. Heat a nonstick crêpe pan or 6-inch skillet over medium-high heat until a few drops of water drizzled onto the surface sizzle and evaporate. Brush the bottom of the pan lightly with some of the extra melted butter.
4. Use a small ladle to pour 2 tablespoons of the batter into the pan. Quickly tilt the pan to the right and then in a circular motion to coat it completely with the batter. Cook until the edges begin to color, about 30 seconds. Carefully lift the edge of the crêpe with a sharp paring knife and grasp the edge between your thumb and index finger. Carefully flip, and cook for another 30 seconds. Invert the pan over the sugared sheet pan so the crêpe will fall out flat. Dip the bottom

(continued)

of the pan into the cool water. Repeat with the remaining batter (it's not necessary to butter the pan after every crêpe).

5. Rather than stacking the crêpes one on top of the other, overlap them slightly so that they are easier to separate. Let the crêpes cool to room temperature. To keep them nice and moist, place a clean, very damp kitchen towel over the crêpes until ready to use, up to 8 hours; or refrigerate for up to 2 days.

    If you want to keep them longer, wrap the whole sheet pan, including the towel, in plastic wrap and freeze for up to 2 months. When you need the crêpes, remove the plastic wrap and place the pan in a 375-degree oven with the towel still in place; bake for 5 to 7 minutes, so the towel just becomes hot to the touch. The towel will release some steam onto the crêpes, making them very pliable and easy to work with as they thaw. Carefully lift the defrosted crêpes from the sheet pan and fill as desired.

BEER BATTER CRÊPES

Makes about 30 crêpes

The beer and the whipped egg whites make these crêpes delightfully airy and very tender. Use a light-colored lager-style beer. Dark beer is too strong for this delicate batter.

2 large egg yolks, at room
    temperature
¼ cup sugar
¾ cup flour
1¼ cups whole or 2 percent milk,
    at room temperature
4 tablespoons unsalted butter, melted
    and cooled, plus a little more for
    greasing the pan

¼ cup lager-style beer, at room
    temperature
½ teaspoon pure vanilla extract
Pinch salt
3 large egg whites, at room
    temperature

1. Combine the egg yolks with 1 tablespoon of the sugar, the flour, and ½ cup of the milk in a medium bowl. Stir until it forms a smooth paste. Add the remaining ¾ cup milk and the melted butter, beer, vanilla extract, and salt. Stir until smooth. Pour the mixture through a fine-mesh strainer into a bowl.

2. Whip the egg whites with an electric mixer on high speed until they just hold soft peaks. With the mixer still on high, add 1 tablespoon sugar in a slow, steady stream. Beat until the whites just hold stiff peaks. Fold the egg whites into the batter and let rest at room temperature for 1 hour.

3. Sprinkle a rimmed sheet pan with the remaining 2 tablespoons sugar. Fill a shallow bowl or cake pan with cool water.

4. Heat a nonstick crêpe pan or 6-inch skillet over medium-high heat until a few drops of water drizzled onto the surface sizzle and evaporate. Brush the bottom of the pan lightly with some of the extra melted butter.

5. Use a small ladle to pour 2 tablespoons of the batter into the pan. Quickly tilt the pan to the right and then in a circular motion to coat it completely with the batter. Cook until the edges begin to color, about 30 seconds. Carefully lift the edge of the crêpe with a sharp paring knife and grasp the edge between your thumb and index finger. Carefully flip, and cook for another 30 seconds. Invert the pan over the sugared sheet pan so the crêpe will fall out flat. Dip the bottom of the pan into the cool water. Repeat with the remaining batter (it's not necessary to butter the pan after every crêpe).

6. Rather than stacking the crêpes one on top of the other, overlap them slightly so that they are easier to separate. Let the crêpes cool to room temperature. To keep them nice and moist, place a clean, very damp kitchen towel over the crêpes until ready to use, up to 8 hours; or refrigerate for up to 2 days.

    If you want to keep them longer, wrap the whole sheet pan, including the towel, in plastic wrap, and freeze it for up to 2 months. When you need the crêpes, remove the plastic wrap and place the pan in a 375-degree oven with the towel still in place; bake for 5 to 7 minutes, so the towel just becomes hot to the touch. The towel will release some steam onto the crêpes, making them very pliable and easy to work with as they thaw. Carefully lift the defrosted crêpes from the sheet pan and fill as desired.

CHOCOLATE CRÊPES

Serves 8

This classic recipe is a favorite with children. Use store-bought ice cream to save time if you'd like.

2 tablespoons sugar
1½ cups Ganache (page 513)
16 Basic Crêpes (page 233)

1 pint Vanilla Ice Cream (page 185),
    slightly softened

1. Preheat the oven to 375 degrees. Butter a heatproof serving platter and sprinkle it with the sugar.
2. Spread 1½ tablespoons of the Ganache over a crêpe, leaving a ½-inch border all the way around. Fold the crêpe in half and place it on the prepared platter. Repeat with the remaining crêpes, slightly overlapping them on the platter. (At this point you can cover the platter lightly with plastic wrap and let it stand at room temperature for up to 8 hours before baking.)
3. Bake for 3 to 4 minutes or until the chocolate starts to melt. Serve immediately, with the ice cream on the side.

APPLE BUTTER CRÊPES WITH
MARSALA-LACED VANILLA SAUCE

Serves 8

Sparkling cider is a must to accompany this dessert. Vanilla Sauce mixed with Marsala is a wonderful garnish.

2 tablespoons sugar
2 cups apple butter
16 Beer Batter Crêpes (page 234)
1 recipe Prebaked Apple Slices
   (page 28)

1 cup strained apricot jam
2 tablespoons Marsala wine
2 cups Vanilla Sauce (page 514),
   at room temperature

1. Preheat the oven to 375 degrees. Butter a heatproof serving platter and sprinkle it with the sugar.
2. Place 2 tablespoons of the apple butter in the center of a crêpe. Fold the edges inward to create a rectangle measuring 2 x 2½ inches. Place the filled crêpe, folded side up, on the prepared platter and place an apple slice on top of the crêpe to keep it closed. Repeat with the remaining crêpes, apple butter, and apple slices. (At this point you can drape the platter lightly with plastic wrap and let it stand at room temperature for up to 8 hours before baking.)
3. Bake the crêpes until very hot, about 4 minutes. While they are baking, bring the apricot jam to a boil. Brush the hot crêpes with the hot jam as soon as they come out of the oven.
4. Mix the Marsala into the Vanilla Sauce. Pour the sauce around the crêpes, and serve immediately.

CRÊPES PARISIENNES

Serves 8

This dessert does it every time. It serves eight, but I guarantee that if you have only six people over, they'll be competing for the seconds. Beer Batter Crêpes contribute to the delicacy of the dessert.

6 tablespoons granulated sugar
40 large strawberries, washed and
    stemmed
2 cups Pastry Cream (page 509)
2 tablespoons plus 1 teaspoon
    Grand Marnier

1 cup Melba Sauce (page 518)
16 Beer Batter Crêpes (page 234)
2 tablespoons plus 1 teaspoon butter,
    cut into small pieces
Confectioners' sugar for dusting

1. Preheat the oven to 375 degrees. Butter a heatproof serving platter and sprinkle it with 2 tablespoons of the granulated sugar.

2. Reserve 8 strawberries, and slice the remaining strawberries into 8 thin slices each. Stir the Pastry Cream and Grand Marnier together in a medium bowl. Stir the sliced strawberries and the Melba Sauce together in a large bowl.

3. Spread about 2 tablespoons of the pastry cream mixture over a crêpe. Arrange some of the Melba Sauce–covered strawberries in a row across the center of the crêpe. Roll the crêpe up tightly, as if it were a roulade. Place it, seam side down, on the prepared platter. Repeat with the remaining crêpes and filling. (At this point, the platter may be loosely covered with plastic wrap and refrigerated for up to 8 hours.)

4. Dot the crêpes with the butter, and sprinkle with the remaining ¼ cup granulated sugar. Bake the crêpes until very hot, about 4 minutes (a minute or two longer if the crêpes have been refrigerated). Dust with confectioners' sugar, garnish the platter with the reserved whole strawberries, and serve immediately.

CRÊPES JAPONAISES

Serves 8

Serve this heart- and soul-warming dish in the middle of winter, with or without glasses of orange liqueur. Be sure to remove as much of the tough and bitter membrane from the orange segments as possible.

2 tablespoons sugar	2 cups strained apricot jam
8 small navel oranges	2 tablespoons Grand Marnier
1 tablespoon grated orange zest	16 Beer Batter Crêpes (page 234)

1. Preheat the oven to 375 degrees. Butter a heatproof serving platter and sprinkle it with the sugar.
2. Peel the oranges, and use a sharp paring knife to cut each segment free from the surrounding membrane. Place the zest, orange segments, apricot jam, and Grand Marnier in a large bowl and toss to combine.
3. Place the coated orange segments from about half an orange in a row down the middle of a crêpe. Roll the crêpe up tightly and place it on the prepared platter, seam side down. Repeat with the remaining crêpes, using about half an orange per crêpe. (At this point you can drape the platter lightly with plastic wrap and let it stand at room temperature for up to 4 hours until ready to bake.)
4. Bake the crêpes until very hot, about 4 minutes (a minute or two longer if they have been refrigerated). Serve immediately.

CHRISTMAS TREE CRÊPES

Serves 6

Feather-light crêpes spread with Lemon Cream make a wonderful holiday dessert when arranged on a platter in the shape of a Christmas tree. Of course you can serve them any time of the year, arranged in any way you like. In spring and summer, substitute straw-berries, blueberries, or raspberries for the cranberries.

16 Beer Batter Crêpes (page 234)
2 cups Lemon Cream (page 510)
2 tablespoons grated lemon zest

1 cup fresh or frozen cranberries
  for garnish
1 Golden Marzipan Star (page 469)

1. Working on one crêpe at a time, spread about 1 tablespoon of the Lemon Cream over each crêpe. Fold the crêpe in half and then in half again, to form a triangle shape. Repeat, using 15 of the crêpes. Spread about 1 tablespoon of the Lemon Cream over the remaining crêpe. Fold the top toward the bottom, as if folding a letter. Fold the bottom toward the top in the same way. Fold the folded crêpe in half lengthwise to form a square.
2. Spread the remaining Lemon Cream across the surface of a large oval serving dish.
3. Arrange the triangles in the shape of a Christmas tree. Place the serving dish on the counter so that the shorter side is closest to you. About one-fourth of the way up from the bottom of the dish, arrange 4 of the folded crêpes in a row, overlapping one another slightly. Then arrange 3 crêpes in a row directly above the first row so that they overlap just about ½ inch of the top of the first row. Arrange 3 crêpes above the second row, 2 crêpes above the third row, 2 crêpes above the fourth row, and one final crêpe above the fifth row. You should have a pyramid of crêpes. Place the 16th crêpe, folded into a square shape, at the bottom of the tree to form the trunk.
4. Sprinkle the zest across the bottom edge of each row of crêpes. Arrange the cranberries around the edge of the platter to form a frame for the tree. Place a Golden Marzipan Star at the top of the tree. Serve immediately.

LIME CREAM CHRISTMAS TREE CRÊPES. Substitute Lime Cream (page 511) for the Lemon Cream. Decorate the tree with Golden Marzipan Stars (page 469), fresh red currants, and Candied Lime Zest (page 505).

LEMON SOUFFLÉ CRÊPES WITH STRAWBERRY SAUCE

Serves 8

This is just a magical recipe. Soufflé batter is baked inside the crêpes, puffing them up in the oven. The pale lemon of the soufflé and the red of the strawberry sauce are beautiful together.

3 egg yolks	½ tablespoon cornstarch
1 teaspoon grated lemon zest	8 Beer Batter Crêpes (page 234)
¼ cup fresh lemon juice	Confectioners' sugar for dusting
3 large egg whites	1 cup Chunky Strawberry Sauce
6 tablespoons granulated sugar	(page 518)
2 tablespoons water	

1. Preheat the oven to 425 degrees. Butter eight individual heatproof plates, and sprinkle them lightly with granulated sugar.
2. Combine the egg yolks, lemon zest, and lemon juice in a small bowl. Place the egg whites in the bowl of an electric mixer fitted with the whisk attachment.
3. Combine the sugar and water in a small saucepan and cook until the mixture reaches the soft ball stage (240 degrees on a candy thermometer). Watch it carefully, since such a small amount of syrup will heat up quickly.
4. Turn the mixer on high speed and pour the hot syrup into the bowl in a slow, steady stream, making sure that none of it falls on the whisk. Continue to whip on high speed until the meringue holds stiff peaks and is almost cool.

(continued)

5. With the mixer on low, add the cornstarch. Turn it to high speed and whip for 10 seconds. Then fold in the egg yolk mixture with a rubber spatula.

6. Place one eighth of the soufflé mixture on the center of each crêpe. Lightly fold one half of the crêpe over the other, taking care not to press on or deflate the soufflé batter. Place each crêpe on a prepared plate. Dust with confectioners' sugar, and bake until the crêpes are puffed, 5 minutes. Pull the plates out of the oven, place 2 tablespoons Chunky Strawberry Sauce in front of each crêpe, and return to the oven for 1½ minutes. Serve immediately.

YOGURT APRICOT PURSES

Serves 8

Use the recipe for Basic Crêpes here. They cook up a little bit sturdier than Beer Batter Crêpes and won't tear when you tie them with the strips of orange zest.

1 medium orange	One 8-ounce container plain yogurt
One 15-ounce can apricots in syrup, drained	4 tablespoons plus 2 teaspoons sugar
	2 tablespoons cream cheese, softened
8 Basic Crêpes (page 233)	½ pint fresh raspberries

1. Preheat the oven to 375 degrees. Use a vegetable peeler to remove the zest of the orange in one long strip. Reserve the orange for another use. Cut the strip into 6-inch lengths. Cut each 6-inch length into ⅛-inch-wide strips. Set them aside.

2. Cut 2 apricot halves into ¼-inch cubes. Place them in the middle of a crêpe, and spoon 2 teaspoons of the yogurt over the apricots. Sprinkle with 1 teaspoon of the sugar. Gather the edges of the crêpe together around the apricot mixture to form a little bundle. Tie the bundle with a strip of orange zest.

3. Repeat with the remaining 7 crêpes.

4. Combine any leftover apricots, the cream cheese, the remaining yogurt, and the remaining 2 tablespoons sugar in a blender and blend until smooth. Pour the puree into a heatproof shallow 7 x 12-inch oval baking dish. Arrange the purses on top of the puree. Bake until very warm, about 4 minutes. Garnish with the raspberries, and serve immediately.

PEAR CRÊPES

Serves 10

In this recipe, pears are cooked together with the crêpe batter in the pan. It is a rustic dessert, very simple but tasty. I usually serve them warm, but Pear Crêpes are also excellent at room temperature for a picnic or any other casual meal. Be sure you are using a crêpe pan or skillet with a metal handle, since you will be placing the whole pan under the broiler—a plastic or rubber handle would melt.

1½ cups Vanilla Sauce (page 514)
1 tablespoon Poire Williams
   (pear brandy; optional)
5 ripe pears

2 tablespoons sugar
1 tablespoon unsalted butter, melted
1 recipe Basic Crêpe batter
   (page 233), uncooked

1. Combine the Vanilla Sauce and the pear brandy, if desired, in a small bowl.
2. Preheat the broiler to high. Position the oven rack close the broiler. Butter a heatproof serving platter and sprinkle it lightly with sugar.
3. Peel, core, and halve the pears. Cut them lengthwise into ½-inch-thick slices.
4. Sprinkle a rimmed sheet pan with the 2 tablespoons sugar. Fill a shallow bowl or cake pan with cool water. Heat a nonstick crêpe pan or 6-inch skillet over medium-high heat until a few drops of water drizzled onto the surface sizzle and evaporate. Brush the bottom of the pan lightly with some of the melted butter.
5. Use a small ladle to pour 2 tablespoons of the batter into the pan. Quickly tilt the pan to the right and then in a circular motion to coat it completely with the batter. When the batter has begun to set, remove the pan from the heat and place some pear slices, about half a pear's worth, on top of the crêpe, flat sides down. Return the pan to the heat and cook until the edges begin to color, about 30 seconds. Ladle another 2 tablespoons batter over the pears. Place the pan under the broiler and broil until golden. Then invert the pan over the prepared sheet pan so the crêpe will fall out flat. Dip the bottom of the pan into the cool water. Repeat with the remaining batter and pears (it's not necessary to butter the pan after every crepe).
6. Serve immediately with the Vanilla Sauce, or let cool and keep at room temperature, lightly covered with plastic wrap, for up to 8 hours. Reheat in a 375-degree oven until very warm, about 5 minutes.

GÂTEAU OF CRÊPES

Serves 8

Here is a variation on Summer Pudding, using crêpes instead of white bread. The result is a little more elegant but just as refreshing.

1 tablespoon unsalted butter
¾ cup plus 2 tablespoons sugar
2 ripe pears, peeled, cored, and thinly sliced
1 cup cake or fresh bread crumbs
1 tablespoon cornstarch
1 tablespoon water

1 pound fresh strawberries, washed and stemmed
2 cups fresh blueberries, picked over and washed
10 Beer Batter Crêpes (page 234)
2 cups Vanilla Sauce (page 514)

1. Combine the butter and 1 tablespoon of the sugar in a medium saucepan and cook over medium-high until the sugar is dissolved and golden, 1 to 2 minutes. Add the pear slices and sauté for 2 minutes, stirring once or twice. Remove from the heat and let cool in the pan. When cool, transfer the pears to a bowl and toss with ½ cup of the cake crumbs.
2. Combine the cornstarch and water in a small bowl. Stir to dissolve.
3. Combine the strawberries and ½ cup of the sugar in a small saucepan. Cover and slowly bring to a boil over low heat, shaking the pan every minute so the bottom does not burn. After about 10 minutes the strawberries should release a lot of water. Simmer without stirring (stirring will break up the fruit), shaking the pan occasionally, until the strawberries are soft but not falling apart, 5 to 6 minutes.
4. Pour the strawberry mixture into a strainer set over a bowl. Return the juice to the pan and whisk in the dissolved cornstarch. Cook over medium-high heat until slightly thickened, 1 to 2 minutes. Add the strawberries and allow them to cool in the pan.
5. In another saucepan, combine the blueberries and the remaining 5 tablespoons sugar. Cover and slowly bring to a boil over low heat, shaking the pan every minute so the bottom does not burn. Cook until the blueberries are soft but still whole, about 3 minutes. Transfer the blueberries to a bowl and let cool. Stir in the remaining ½ cup cake crumbs.

6. Line a 1-quart mixing bowl with plastic wrap so that at least 2 inches overhang the rim. Line the bowl with 4 crêpes so that they are overlapping each other and overhanging the rim by about 1 inch. Place the pears in the bowl, pack them tightly, and smooth the surface with the back of a spoon. Place 1 crêpe on top of the pears. Spoon the strawberry mixture on top of the crêpe and smooth it with the back of a spoon. Cover the strawberries with 2 crêpes, and spoon the blueberry mixture on top. Cover with the remaining 3 crêpes. Pull the edges of the plastic wrap toward the center of the bowl, so that the overhanging crêpe edges fold inward toward the center also. Press lightly on the plastic wrap to compact the layers. Refrigerate for 2 hours or up to 2 days.

7. Preheat the oven to 200 degrees. Carefully peel the plastic away from the surface of the gâteau. Place a heatproof serving platter upside down on top of the bowl, and invert the two together. Tug on the edges of the plastic wrap to release the gâteau. Peel the plastic from the surface of the cake. Bake in the oven until warm, about 30 minutes. Pour the Vanilla Sauce around the gâteau, and serve.

SEVEN

Memorable Breakfast Pastries and Perfect Pastry Doughs

I WILL NEVER FORGET the first time I stepped off a train at the station in the small town of Tours in the Loire Valley. My first impression was not of sight or sound but of the incredible, instantly recognizable smell of baking brioche. I followed my nose to the source, a bake shop across from the station that specialized in the dough. Obviously I was not the only one lured to the spot by the fabulous bouquet—there was a line of people running halfway down the block, all waiting to buy still-warm brioche. As we waited, we could peek into the kitchen to watch the busy bakers weighing, shaping, and baking the brioche, which only increased our anticipation. When I finally got my hands on a loaf and tore off a piece to taste it, I was not disappointed. It was the best brioche I had ever had. I can still conjure up its flavor, texture, and aroma.

It is rare to find brioche, not to mention muffins, biscuits, Danish pastries, or croissants, as memorable as that. You may wonder why. After all, the batters and doughs contain just a few ingredients, in some cases only flour, butter, and water. But it's the way you work with those ingredients, the techniques and tricks you apply to get the most out of them, that transform them into something really special.

For the best carrot or pumpkin muffins, I whip oil and eggs together to create an emulsion. These muffins have a light texture and a very fine crumb, unlike the muffins you buy at the local coffee shop, which are usually so heavy they could be used as doorstops. Instead of using chilled butter for sweet pie dough, I cream the butter and sugar together before adding the eggs and flour, as with cookie dough. This gives the finished crust a tender texture that more conventional methods won't. I use bread flour in my croissants because I like the extra crunch that a higher protein content gives them.

Just as important as technique are experience and intuition. The bakers in Tours could see and feel that on a humid day their dough would take more flour. If it was a little on the cool side in the kitchen, they would wait patiently until the brioche dough had risen enough, rather than going by the clock. Working with any of the recipes in this chapter, try to get a feel for the batter or dough. It might not come naturally to you, and it might take a few tries before you recognize when choux paste is well mixed but not overly mixed. You might bake a few batches of puff pastry before you trust yourself to bake it long enough so that it is fully dry. Every time you make dough, you have a fresh opportunity to observe how it works and to learn something from the process. I know that I am still learning, but I love the challenge, even after all these years.

Batters and doughs are the workhorses of pastry. Master perfect biscuit dough, puff pastry, and brioche, and you can create an infinite number of pastries, cakes, and pies. But there is great satisfaction in making many of these batters and doughs for their own sake. Just watching madeleines rise and brown in the oven and enjoying their delicious scent makes me smile. Baking and serving wonderful Danish and croissants to the thousands of people who passed through the White House for all the years I was there was more than a job. It was a celebration of life. Now that I am baking primarily for friends and family, it is just as much of a joy.

$\mathscr{T}$HE RIGHT INGREDIENTS

It goes without saying that the freshest ingredients, properly handled, will make the best batters and doughs.

Buy organic eggs and keep them in the coldest part of the refrigerator. I never store my eggs on the shelf inside the door because they go bad more quickly there.

Butter should always be unsalted and as fresh as possible. If you are not going to use your butter within a day or two of purchasing it, store it in the freezer.

Buy flour at a store where you know the turnover is high. Flour that has been sitting around on the market shelf too long is more likely to be rancid or contaminated by insects than is flour that has just been delivered from the producer. Once you get it home, keep it in a cool, dry place in an airtight container.

Flour is the common denominator in these recipes. It gives fats and liquids something to hang on to, and thus gives structure to baked goods. How much structure depends on how much protein, or gluten, a particular flour contains. In the following recipes, I use all-purpose flour, cake flour, or bread flour, depending on the result I'm after.

Soft **cake flour,** with a gluten content of about 8 percent, produces delicately textured baked goods. I wouldn't use it to make a chewy loaf of French bread, but it is what I put into All-American Pie Dough. When developing that recipe, I wanted a dough with very little elasticity, that when baked would have a soft, flaky, almost crumbly texture. Cake flour provides just enough structure so that the dough holds together and holds the pie ingredients. Even when very well browned, though, the dough never gets tough or hard.

For most recipes, **all-purpose flour** works very well. As a pastry chef working in the United States, I have always counted on the consistent results I get with any brand of all-purpose flour made in this country. Its uniform quality takes a lot of the guesswork and anxiety out of baking. With a reliable gluten content of 9 to 11 percent, it makes muffins that are tender but won't fall apart when you hold them. It makes wonderfully light but not cottony Danish pastries and brioche with crisp but yielding crusts. If you are trying for pastry that is soft but with some character, all-purpose flour will suit most of your needs.

Although I bake primarily pastries and not bread, I occasionally use **bread flour.** This harder flour, with a gluten content of 12 to 14 percent, is great for recipes where you want a little bit of toughness. I use some in my croissant dough because I like the very crackly, well-defined layers that this harder flour produces.

Nut flours are not really flours at all, but very finely ground and processed nuts that are used in addition to flour to give flavor to linzer and other doughs.

On occasion I've been asked to make pastries without wheat flour for people who are allergic to gluten. I've successfully substituted **spelt flour** in a variety of recipes, including the recipe for Carrot Muffins and the recipe for All-American Pie Dough.

Many of the batter and dough recipes here contain a little bit of **sugar.** Sugar gives baked goods a golden crust, adds flavor, and feeds the yeast.

Fat in the dough gives it a soft texture and adds the richness that you want for most pastries and desserts. In the case of doughs that are rolled and folded many times over— Danish dough, croissant dough, and puff pastry—the fat is partly or wholly responsible for the amazing rise of the dough into flaky layers. As the butter sandwiched between the layers of dough melts and the water contained in the butter turns to steam, the pressure from the steam pushes the layers higher and higher. **Vegetable shortening** or **vegetable oil** will do these jobs, but in most cases I prefer **butter** for its outstanding flavor. The exception is pie dough. I find that most pie fillings have enough added butter to give them good flavor, so I use vegetable shortening for superior texture.

Eggs give muffins, brioche, Danish, and pâte sucrée structure with a little bit of softness. The yolks add richness and flavor where you want it. Doughs that don't have eggs, like croissant dough or puff pastry, are crunchier and more brittle. They are also more neutral in flavor.

Some doughs require a liquid, either **water** or **milk**; the choice depends on the dough. Puff pastry should showcase the rich flavor of butter. Milk would interfere, so water is used. With pâte à choux, milk gives the dough its good flavor; water would make the choux puffs bland. In the case of blueberry muffins, **buttermilk** provides a tangy flavor that balances the sugar in the batter.

Salt plays a very important role in all of the recipes in this chapter. At the very least, it enhances the flavors of the other ingredients. Just as in the preparation of savory dishes, the proper use of salt brings the flavors of any batter or dough into focus without making the dough taste salty. In recipes containing yeast, salt also plays the crucial role of controlling its growth. If yeast ferments too quickly, the resulting dough will have a spongy texture rather than a silky, smooth crumb when baked. Salt inhibits the growth of yeast, so that big air bubbles cannot form in the dough and create large, unattractive holes in your brioche or Danish pastry. I use iodized table salt for baking. It is cheap and convenient. Some cooks prefer kosher salt because it has no additives. However, I have not found that the small quantities of iodized salt that I use in baking impart any unwanted flavor.

Leaveners cause a batter or dough to rise. In the case of muffins, madeleines, shortcakes, and scones, **baking powder, baking soda,** or a combination of the two is used. Baking powder is a commercial mixture of baking soda and acids that cause it to form bubbles when it comes in contact with liquid ingredients. As these bubbles expand in the heat of the oven, they cause the batter to rise. Baking soda is used when a recipe already contains acidic ingredients to activate the soda. The distinction is important, because the two cannot be used interchangeably.

Yeast is a living organism that produces air bubbles when fed with simple sugars found in dough. The air bubbles expand at room temperature and continue to do so in the oven until the yeast is killed when the temperature of the dough rises above 130 degrees, at which point they have done their job and caused the dough to rise to its finished height. You may use either compressed yeast, which comes in cakes and must be refrigerated, or active dry yeast, which is compressed yeast that has been dehydrated so that it can be stored at room temperature and has a longer shelf life. Personally, I prefer compressed yeast for its superior aroma. **Dry yeast** should also be kept in a cool, dry place. **Compressed yeast,** which I prefer, will keep in the refrigerator for 2 to 3 weeks. If you see surface mold on compressed yeast, scrape it away with a sharp paring knife before using the yeast. Pay attention to the expiration date on the packaging of either type, or you may be disappointed when your dough fails to rise. Both types of yeast should be dissolved in warm water before being added to the dough. Take care that the water is not too hot. Let the yeast stand in the water for 5 minutes. It should become foamy and develop a yeasty aroma. If it doesn't, it is no longer viable and you should purchase new yeast and start again. The yeast in these recipes will work best if your kitchen is between 70 and 90 degrees. The amount of time it will take for your dough to rise will depend on the relative warmth of your kitchen. Judge a yeast dough's rise by sight, rather than by the clock, for best results.

TEMPERATURE AND THE RECIPES

It is imperative when making batters and doughs that you take care with the temperature of your ingredients at every stage. This is true not only for yeast but also for butter, eggs, and liquids. If a recipe calls for eggs and butter at room temperature, it is because room-temperature eggs and butter blend best with the flour, sugar, and other ingredients, resulting in a properly aerated mixture that won't bake up heavy and greasy. On the other hand, if a recipe calls for chilled butter, take heed. Shortcake dough made with softened rather than chilled butter will not rise properly. Butter that is too warm will not be able to withstand the pounding required to create the butter-and-flour packet to be folded inside puff pastry, croissant, or Danish dough.

Once the dough is mixed, follow the recipe instructions about chilling it before shaping and baking. Dough that is not properly chilled will be difficult to roll. Sometimes dough must rest in the refrigerator after rolling to relax it before shaping it further. Sometimes rolled dough must be chilled before baking to ensure that it will keep its shape in the oven.

The Recipes

This chapter is divided into sections based on different types of batters and doughs. The first section, on **muffins** and their French relation, the **madeleine,** describes how to make baking powder breakfast pastries that are light and flavorful.

The second section describes how to make a wonderfully versatile **cobbler dough** that can also be cut into scones and shortcakes or filled with fruit for turnovers.

Three varieties of **pie and tart dough** are discussed next. Pâte sucrée, a crisp and cookielike sweet dough, is perfect for most fruit tarts. Pâte brisée, unsweetened and buttery, holds up well when filled with very wet sweet and savory combinations. All-American Pie Dough is just what you will need to make perfect pumpkin pie and other traditional American favorites.

A section on **choux paste** will teach you how to make this underused batter and how to bake it into perfect cream puffs and éclairs.

If you love **puff pastry, croissants,** and **Danish** but have always thought they were out of your reach, you can gain some courage by reading the step-by-step instructions for these.

Finally, yeast-risen **brioche** is discussed in depth and accompanied by some simple but truly delectable recipes that will transport you from your kitchen to that bakery in Tours.

LIGHT AND AIRY MUFFINS

Muffins were a staple at the White House for all the years I was there, both at family breakfasts and at morning and afternoon receptions for large crowds. But just because they were everyday items doesn't mean that I didn't take the time to perfect my recipes. I would have been horrified to serve anything like the heavy, sticky shrink-wrapped pastries sold beside the cash register at convenience stores and coffee shops. As a matter of pride, I refined basic recipes until I felt my muffins were fit for presidents, prime ministers, and kings.

Every step I take when making muffin batter is focused on creating the lightest muffins possible. The carrot and pumpkin muffin recipes are lightened by emulsifying eggs, oil, and sugar before stirring the mixture into the dry ingredients. Whipping the ingredients this way gives the muffins a very fine crumb, like a delicate chiffon cake.

For Blueberry Muffins, I separate the eggs and whip the whites. This gives the batter an extra lift in the oven. It takes a few extra minutes but the difference is worth the time.

I've included a recipe for Madeleines along with the muffins. I serve these buttery little cakes alongside or instead of muffins, and I often bake them in mini muffin tins if I don't have enough special madeleine pans. The trick to making light Madeleines, I've found, is to beat the butter and sugar until just smooth. Avoid overzealously whipping the mixture. Too much air beaten in at this stage will cause the Madeleines to rise and then fall before they are finished baking. I've also found that letting the batter sit overnight in the refrigerator contributes to the beautiful bump on top that indicates a light pastry. Another characteristic of good Madeleines is a crispy, brown, caramelized edge. Lemon glaze, my own innovation, adds extra crunch as well as bright flavor to the finished morsels.

CARROT MUFFINS

Makes 12 muffins or 36 mini muffins

When I make muffins with oil rather than butter, I take care to whip the eggs, oil, and sugar together until they are emulsified, resembling a runny mayonnaise. This mixing results in a fine crumb and a delicate texture that you won't get by simply stirring all of the ingredients together. If you have time, let the finished batter stand at room temperature for 1 hour before baking; this will yield the finest crumb.

This batter may also be baked in a bundt or loaf pan and frosted with the Cream Cheese Frosting below.

1 cup all-purpose flour	1 cup sugar
1 teaspoon baking soda	1½ cups shredded carrots (about
½ teaspoon ground cinnamon	4 medium carrots, or 8 ounces)
2 large eggs, at room temperature	½ cup coarsely chopped pecans
¾ cup canola or sunflower oil	Cream Cheese Frosting (page 256,
1 teaspoon pure vanilla extract	optional)

1. Preheat the oven to 350 degrees. Line a 12-cup muffin tin, or a 36-cup mini muffin tin, with paper liners.
2. Combine the flour, baking soda, and cinnamon in a medium bowl.
3. Place the eggs, oil, vanilla, and sugar together in the bowl of an electric mixer fitted with the whisk attachment, and whisk on high speed until the mixture resembles a runny mayonnaise, about 5 minutes. Stir in the flour mixture until just combined. Stir in the carrots and pecans.
4. Divide the batter among the muffin cups, and bake until a toothpick inserted into the center of a muffin comes out clean, 18 to 20 minutes, or 8 to 10 minutes for mini muffins. Cool in the pan for about 5 minutes. Then invert the muffins onto a rack, re-invert them onto another rack so they are right side up, and allow to cool completely. (Carrot Muffins may be individually wrapped in plastic wrap and then in foil, and frozen for up to 3 weeks.) Frost with Cream Cheese Frosting if desired.

CREAM CHEESE FROSTING

Makes enough to frost 12 large or 36 mini muffins

8 ounces cream cheese, softened
½ cup confectioners' sugar

1 teaspoon pure vanilla extract

Combine the cream cheese, confectioners' sugar, and vanilla in the bowl of an electric mixer fitted with the paddle attachment, and mix until smooth.

PUMPKIN MUFFINS WITH COCONUT TOPPING

Makes 12 muffins or 36 mini muffins

As a naturalized American citizen, I love all things pumpkin, especially these wholesome-tasting muffins. As a French pastry chef, I like to top them with a sweet, rich coconut custard. Serve Pumpkin Muffins with Coconut Topping for breakfast or brunch, or call them cupcakes and serve them as a casual dessert.

FOR THE PUMPKIN MUFFINS:
1½ cups all-purpose flour
1 teaspoon baking soda
¼ teaspoon salt
1 teaspoon ground cinnamon
½ teaspoon ground cloves
½ teaspoon ground nutmeg
2 large eggs, at room temperature
½ cup corn oil
1 cup sugar
1 cup canned pumpkin puree

FOR THE COCONUT TOPPING:
½ cup evaporated milk
½ cup sugar
2 large egg yolks
4 tablespoons unsalted butter
¾ cup unsweetened grated
coconut
½ teaspoon pure vanilla extract

1. Preheat the oven to 350 degrees. Butter and flour a 12-cup muffin tin or a 36-cup mini muffin tin, or line it with paper liners.
2. Combine the flour, baking soda, salt, cinnamon, cloves, and nutmeg in a medium bowl.
3. Whisk the eggs, oil, and sugar together in a large bowl. Stir in the pumpkin. Stir in the flour mixture until just combined.
4. Divide the batter among the muffin cups and bake until a toothpick inserted into the center of a muffin comes out clean, about 25 minutes, or 8 to 10 minutes for mini muffins. Cool in the pan for about 5 minutes. Then invert the muffins onto a rack, re-invert them onto another rack so they are right side up, and allow to cool completely. (Unfrosted Pumpkin Muffins may be individually wrapped in plastic and then in foil, and frozen for up to 3 weeks.)
5. For the Coconut Topping: Combine the evaporated milk, sugar, egg yolks, and butter in a medium saucepan and cook over medium heat, whisking constantly, until the mixture boils, 3 to 4 minutes. Remove the pan from the heat and stir in the coconut and vanilla. Let cool to room temperature before spreading on the muffins.

BLUEBERRY MUFFINS

Makes 12 extra-large muffins or 36 mini muffins

My blueberry muffins were a morning favorite at the White House for years. What makes them rise above the garden variety? It's all in the details.

There's nothing worse than a heavy muffin, especially a large heavy muffin. Here egg whites are whipped and then folded into the batter to make the muffins extra-light, and buttermilk gives them a little tang. Abundant blueberries make them nice and juicy, and the cinnamon sugar sprinkled on top midway through baking gives the crust extra crunch. You'll notice that I bake these muffins at 400 degrees; the high heat caramelizes the tops while baking the muffins quickly so they aren't dry inside.

If you have everything on hand except the buttermilk, make your own by mixing 2 teaspoons lemon juice with ½ cup plus 2 tablespoons milk and letting it stand at room temperature for 30 minutes.

1 cup all-purpose flour
1 teaspoon baking powder
Pinch salt
½ cup plus 2 tablespoons buttermilk
1 large egg yolk, at room temperature
½ tablespoon pure vanilla extract
4 tablespoons unsalted butter, softened
½ cup sugar

2 large egg whites, at room temperature
1½ cups fresh blueberries
½ teaspoon grated lemon zest
¼ cup pecan pieces, coarsely chopped
3 tablespoons Cinnamon Sugar (page 502)

1. Preheat the oven to 400 degrees. Line a 12-cup extra-large muffin tin, or a 36-cup mini muffin tin, with paper liners. Place the flour, baking powder, and salt in a medium bowl and whisk to combine. Place the buttermilk, egg yolk, and vanilla in another medium bowl or in a large glass measuring cup, and whisk to combine.

2. Place the butter and 6 tablespoons of the sugar in the bowl of an electric mixer fitted with the paddle attachment, and cream on medium-high speed until fluffy, about 3 minutes. With the mixer on low speed, slowly pour in one fourth of the buttermilk mixture and mix until combined, scraping down the sides of the bowl once or twice as necessary. Stir in one fourth of the flour mixture until

just combined. Repeat three more times with the remaining buttermilk and flour mixtures.

3. Place the egg whites in a clean bowl of the electric mixer fitted with the whisk attachment, and whip on high speed until just about to hold soft peaks. With the mixer still on high, slowly pour in the remaining 2 tablespoons sugar in a slow, steady stream. Whip until the whites hold stiff peaks.

4. Fold the blueberries, lemon zest, and nuts into the batter. Gently fold the egg whites into the batter, being careful not to deflate them. Divide the batter among the prepared muffin tins and bake for 5 minutes. Sprinkle the tops with the Cinnamon Sugar and bake until a toothpick inserted into the center comes out dry, about another 10 minutes for extra-large muffins, another 5 minutes for mini muffins. Allow the muffins to cool in the pan for 5 minutes. Then invert them onto a wire rack, turn them right side up, and allow to cool completely. The muffins may be individually wrapped in plastic wrap and then in foil, and frozen for up to 3 weeks. Reheat in a 325-degree oven for 10 minutes before serving.

MADELEINES

Makes 32 madeleines

This is a very traditional French breakfast or tea cake. Most Americans who have tried my version have happily accepted the buttery little cakes in lieu of the usual muffins.

Perfect madeleines should have a nice hump at the top, indicating a good rise and a resulting lightness in texture. The thinner edges should be golden brown, caramelized, and crunchy. Don't overwhip the butter, or the air bubbles you whip in will deflate during baking and you'll lose the rise. I've found that letting the batter rest overnight in the refrigerator also contributes to a full rise.

I've added a lemon glaze, brushed on as soon as the madeleines come out of the oven, which gives them even more of a crunch and a delightful lemon flavor. If you want to vary the glaze, substitute grapefruit juice and zest. This, too, is delicious.

A special madeleine pan, which will shape the dough into the traditional madeleine shape, is nice but not necessary. The dough can be baked in miniature nonstick muffin tins. If you are using muffin tins, you might like to top the dough with some fruit instead of the glaze. Miniature muffins made with madeleine dough and topped with fresh blueberries, cherries, apricots, pineapple, plums, or apples make a dazzling addition to breakfast baskets.

The dough can be made ahead of time and refrigerated or frozen in small portions so that you may enjoy a few freshly baked madeleines any morning you choose.

FOR THE MADELEINE DOUGH:
1½ cups plus 2 tablespoons all-purpose flour
2¼ teaspoons baking powder
1 cup (2 sticks) unsalted butter, softened
1 cup granulated sugar
1 teaspoon grated lemon zest
Pinch salt

4 large eggs
1 large egg yolk

FOR THE LEMON GLAZE (OPTIONAL):
¾ cup confectioners' sugar
2 tablespoons strained fresh lemon juice
1 teaspoon grated lemon zest

1. Place the flour and baking powder in a medium bowl and whisk to combine.
2. Combine the butter, sugar, lemon zest, and salt in the bowl of an electric mixer fitted with the paddle attachment, and mix until smooth. Be careful not to over-

beat. With the mixer on low speed, add the eggs and then egg yolk, one at a time, scraping down the sides of the bowl as necessary, and mix until well combined. Stir in the flour mixture and mix until the dough is smooth, 1 minute. Cover the bowl with plastic wrap and refrigerate for at least 1 hour or up to 3 days. The dough will keep in an airtight container, or portioned out in zipper-lock bags, in the freezer for up to 1 month.

3. Preheat the oven to 425 degrees. Make the lemon glaze: Combine the confectioners' sugar, lemon juice, and lemon zest in a medium bowl and whisk to dissolve the sugar.

4. Butter the madeleine or muffin pans and flour them. (If you are using nonstick pans, there is no need to butter and flour them.) Spoon the batter into the pans until each cup is about three-fourths full. Bake until risen and golden, about 8 minutes. Remove the pans from the oven, immediately turn the madeleines out of the pans, and brush them with lemon glaze if desired. Madeleines are best eaten on the day they are baked.

TENDER SCONES, SHORTCAKES, AND COBBLER TOPPING

Tender baking powder biscuit dough is wonderfully useful in making a variety of breakfast pastries and desserts. Quick to mix and bake, it can be sweetened and rolled into scones, cut to fit the top of a cobbler, or baked in rounds and used for fruit shortcakes.

Traditionally this dough is eggless, which contributes to its meltingly soft texture. I always liked the texture, but as a Frenchman used to rich-tasting baked goods I found this typical American dough a little flavorless. To get a richer-tasting biscuit dough that would still bake up soft and crumbly like a biscuit, I turned to a typically French method for adding flavor without changing texture.

A couple of hard-boiled egg yolks stirred into the dough gave it a lot of flavor without changing its texture. Raw eggs undergo a chemical reaction while baking in dough, giving the dough a strong structure and resulting crispness. Since the eggs in this dough have already been cooked, they don't react in this way, and thus lend their rich flavor without influencing the structure of the dough.

You might wonder why I use a combination of baking soda and cream of tartar here instead of simply using baking powder. Baking powder would give the dough a good rise, but cream of tartar, which is an acid that activates the baking soda in the absence of an acidic ingredient like buttermilk or sour cream, gives the mixture a slightly tangy flavor as well as the required lift.

COBBLER, SCONE, SHORTCAKE, OR TURNOVER DOUGH

Makes enough dough for 1 cobbler, 16 scones, 12 shortcakes, or 24 turnovers

I use this wonderfully versatile and delicious dough to make fruit shortcakes and to top fruit cobblers (see Peach and Blackberry Cobbler, page 370).

2 large eggs, hard-boiled and cooled
2 cups all-purpose flour
3½ tablespoons sugar
1 teaspoon baking soda
½ tablespoon cream of tartar

Pinch salt
8 tablespoons (1 stick) unsalted
   butter, chilled and cut into 8 pieces
¾ cup plus 2 tablespoons heavy
   cream

1. Separate the egg yolks from the whites and set the whites aside for another use. Push the yolks through a fine-mesh strainer into a small bowl, and set aside.
2. Combine the flour, sugar, baking soda, cream of tartar, and salt in the bowl of an electric mixer fitted with the paddle attachment. Add the butter and mix on low speed until the mixture resembles coarse meal.
3. Add the egg yolks and the heavy cream, and mix until the dough just comes together. Cover the bowl with a kitchen towel until ready to use, up to 1 day.

Making Turnovers

This dough makes terrific turnovers: Just roll out the dough to ¼-inch thickness and cut it into 3 x 3-inch squares. Place 1 tablespoon Prebaked Apple Chunks (page 27) or canned mincemeat in the center of each square. Brush the edges with egg wash, fold over, and pinch to seal. Brush with melted butter and sprinkle with Cinnamon Sugar (page 502) before baking, following the instructions for Dried Fruit Scones (page 265).

BLUEBERRY SHORTCAKES

Makes 12 shortcakes

I like warm, lightly cooked fruit rather than uncooked fruit in my shortcakes. To vary this recipe, use warm Oven-Poached Apricots (page 34) or Rhubarb Compote (page 69) instead of the Blueberry Sauce.

½ recipe Cobbler Dough
   (page 263)
1 tablespoon unsalted butter, melted
1½ tablespoons Cinnamon Sugar
   (page 502)

Confectioners' sugar
1 recipe Blueberry Sauce (page 38),
   warmed
2 cups Sweetened Whipped Cream
   (page 521)

1. Preheat the oven to 375 degrees. Scrape the dough onto a lightly floured surface and roll it out to ½-inch thickness. Use a 3- to 3½-inch round biscuit cutter to cut the dough into rounds. Place the dough rounds at least 2 inches apart on an ungreased, unlined baking sheet. Brush with the melted butter and sprinkle with the Cinnamon Sugar. Bake until golden, about 20 minutes.

2. Remove the baking sheet from the oven. Turn the broiler on high. Dust the shortcakes heavily with confectioners' sugar, and place them under the broiler for a few seconds, just until the sugar melts and turns golden. Watch the shortcakes carefully, because the sugar will begin to burn quickly.

3. Remove the shortcakes from the oven and let cool for 5 minutes on a wire rack. Split the warm shortcakes in half, and place them on individual dessert plates. Spoon some Blueberry Sauce over each bottom half, top with the whipped cream, and then set the shortcake tops on top. Serve immediately.

DRIED FRUIT SCONES

Makes 8 scones

To make scones, I simply stir some raisins, dried blueberries, or dried cherries into cobbler dough and shape it in the traditional triangles. I like to sandwich the fruit between two layers of dough. If you simply mix the dried fruit into the dough, the bits on top will burn and become bitter when baked. Confectioners' sugar sprinkled on and broiled at the end of baking gives the scones a nice crunchy crust. Make sure your baking sheet is not lined with parchment paper or it may catch fire under the broiler!

½ recipe Cobbler Dough
   (page 263)
2 tablespoons butter, melted, for
   brushing
1 cup raisins, dried blueberries, or
   dried cherries

3 tablespoons Cinnamon Sugar
   (page 502)
Confectioners' sugar

1. Preheat the oven to 375 degrees. Turn the dough onto a lightly floured work surface and divide it into 4 pieces. Shape each piece into a 6-inch disk about ¼ inch thick. Brush 2 of the disks with 1 tablespoon of the melted butter, and sprinkle with the dried fruit. Place the remaining disks on top of the fruit and press lightly. With a sharp chef's knife, cut each disk into 4 wedges. Place the wedges ½ inch apart on an ungreased and unlined baking sheet. Brush with the remaining 1 tablespoon melted butter and sprinkle with the Cinnamon Sugar. Bake the scones until they are light golden, about 15 to 20 minutes.

2. Remove the baking sheet from the oven and turn the broiler on high. Sift confectioners' sugar heavily over the scones and place them under the broiler. Broil for just a few seconds, until the sugar is melted and golden. Watch the scones carefully, because the sugar will begin to burn quickly.

3. Cool the scones on a wire rack. Dried Fruit Scones will keep for up to 3 days in an airtight container at room temperature. Wrapped in plastic wrap and then foil, they can be frozen for up to 3 weeks. Defrost them on the counter and then reheat in a 325-degree oven for 7 to 8 minutes before serving.

PIE AND TART DOUGHS FOR EVERY FILLING

I am somewhat of an iconoclast when it comes to pie and tart dough. I've read all of the treatises on making flaky pie dough, and I must say that my own recipes don't follow most of the rules.

My favorite recipe is a pâte sucrée, or sweet dough. Conventionally, sweet pie dough is made by cutting cold butter into flour and a little bit of sugar and then stirring in a lightly beaten egg to hold the mixture together. I never liked this method because I found the baked dough to be a little too hard and brittle. Instead, I found myself returning to an old-fashioned German recipe that I was taught early in my career, in which softened butter and sugar are creamed together before the egg and then flour are stirred in, similar to cookie dough. The resulting crust is like a tender butter cookie—the perfect foil for pastry cream, fruit, and nut fillings of all kinds.

I also have a pâte brisée recipe that deviates from convention. Pâte brisée is usually an unsweetened short crust made with chilled butter, flour, and a little bit of ice water. When baked it has a tender, almost melting texture. I love the buttery, unsweetened flavor of this dough with savory fillings made with lots of juicy or wet ingredients (see Summer Tomato Pie, page 357) and with very sweet fruit and custard combinations (see Rhubarb Custard Tart, page 355). But the standard pâte brisée quickly becomes soggy when baked with these moist fillings. My solution was to add some egg yolks to the mixture, which keeps the crust crisp for up to 3 days after it is filled and baked.

In France I would probably be sent to jail for the pie dough that I became famous for at the White House. All-American Pie Dough is made with vegetable shortening rather than butter, the fat preferred by most of my countrymen. But I have been won over by Crisco, which is easy to work with and makes the kind of flaky dough that people expect in a Thanksgiving Day pumpkin pie. The flavor of vegetable shortening is neutral. I will often brush the top crust of a pie with melted butter before baking it. Combined with a rich filling, this brushing gives enough of a butter flavor to compensate for the lack of butter in the crust.

As a bonus, I've included a recipe for Linzer dough. Made with nut flour rather than wheat flour, it goes beyond even the richness of pâte sucrée or pâte brisée.

PÂTE SUCRÉE, OR SWEET DOUGH

Makes enough dough for one 10-inch tart crust

I have worked with this dough for the last thirty years and I have never found anything better for tarts, cookies, and deep-dish-pie topping. Softened butter is creamed together with sugar, as in cookie dough, a technique that I learned early in my career at a German pastry shop. The resulting crust is wonderfully buttery and tender but with a good crunch—just like a good rolled butter cookie. Pâte sucrée freezes well and is just as easy to make in large quantities as in small, so I've included a large-yield recipe for professional bakers with large mixers at their disposal.

½ cup sugar	1 teaspoon grated lemon zest
1 cup (2 sticks) unsalted butter, softened	Pinch salt
	1 large egg
½ tablespoon pure vanilla extract	2¼ cups all-purpose flour

1. Combine the sugar and butter in the bowl of an electric mixer fitted with the paddle attachment. Cream together until smooth. Stir in the vanilla, lemon zest, and salt. Then stir in the egg, scraping down the sides of the bowl once or twice as necessary. Stir in the flour until just combined.
2. Turn the dough out onto a lightly floured work surface, and wrap it in plastic wrap. Refrigerate the dough for at least 1 hour or up to 2 days. Pâte sucrée may be frozen, wrapped in plastic and then in aluminum foil, for up to 2 months. Defrost it in the refrigerator overnight.

VARIATION

FOR FIVE 10-INCH TART CRUSTS:	1 tablespoon grated lemon zest (from
2½ cups sugar	3 medium lemons)
5 cups (10 sticks) unsalted butter, softened	1 teaspoon salt
	4 large eggs
3 tablespoons pure vanilla extract	11¼ cups all-purpose flour

Follow the directions for the single crust.

PÂTE BRISÉE

Makes enough dough for two 10-inch tart crusts

This dough stands up well to any filling that will release a lot of liquid. Not quite as tender as pâte sucrée, it is nonetheless delicious. I use it for savory pies and tarts such as Summer Tomato Pie (page 357).

Usually pâte brisée doesn't include eggs, but I find that adding them makes the baked dough less crumbly, which is a good thing when you want to fill your pie or tart with a juicy filling.

1 teaspoon salt
½ cup water
3¼ cups all-purpose flour
1 cup (2 sticks) unsalted butter,
   chilled and cut into small pieces

1 large egg
3 large egg yolks

1. Combine the salt and 1 tablespoon of the water in the bowl of an electric mixer fitted with the paddle attachment. Stir to dissolve the salt. Add the flour and butter, and mix on low speed until the mixture feels like sand. With the mixer still on low, add the egg and then the egg yolks, one at a time. Then add the remaining 7 tablespoons water. Mix until the dough just comes together, about 2 minutes. Do not overmix.

2. Turn the dough out onto a lightly floured work surface and divide it into 2 pieces. Press each ball out to form a 6-inch disk and wrap them in plastic wrap. Refrigerate the dough for at least 1 hour or for up to 3 days. Pâte brisée may be frozen, wrapped in plastic and then in aluminum foil, for up to 2 months; defrost it in the refrigerator overnight.

ALL-AMERICAN PIE DOUGH

Makes enough dough for 1 double-crust 9-inch pie

I have used this recipe for years. The dough is easy to make, easy to work with, and has a nice flaky texture. It will keep in the freezer, wrapped well in plastic wrap, for 2 to 3 months. Crisco shortening makes the flakiest dough I've ever had and doesn't leave any aftertaste. I do love the taste of butter, but since my pie fillings often include a lot of butter and I brush my top crusts with melted butter, I don't miss it in the dough. The butter flavor is prominent in the finished pie even though there's none in the dough.

3½ cups cake flour
⅓ cup sugar
Pinch salt

½ cup water
1½ cups solid vegetable shortening

1. Combine the flour, sugar, salt, water, and shortening in the bowl of an electric mixer fitted with the paddle attachment. Mix on low speed until the ingredients are well combined and the dough is smooth.
2. Divide the dough into 2 pieces. Press each piece out to form a 6-inch disk and wrap them in plastic wrap. Refrigerate the dough for at least 1 hour or for up to 1 week. All-American Pie Dough may be frozen, wrapped in plastic and then in aluminum foil, for up to 3 months. Defrost it in the refrigerator overnight before rolling it out.

Rolling Pin Basics

I find that rolling pins with thin handles keep me at a distance from the dough, so I use a straight, untapered wooden rolling pin without handles. This dowel-style pin allows for the best feel for the dough and the most control of the pressure the pin will exert on the dough. It is like an extension of the body. I don't recommend marble rolling pins, which are very heavy and may toughen delicate doughs by exerting too much pressure on them.

I prefer to roll dough out on a wooden surface, not a marble surface. As long as the dough is well chilled, you don't need the added coolness of a marble surface to keep it workable. Marble itself is fine for rolling, but it is tough on knives and cutters, which will become dull over time when used on marble. Wood surfaces like butcher block, in contrast, will save your knives.

Any pressure exerted on the dough will develop the gluten in the flour, making the crust tough, so you actually want to achieve the desired size and shape with as little rolling as possible. To do so, follow these steps:

1. Press the pie dough into flat disks as soon as it comes out of the mixer and before it goes into the refrigerator to chill. If you begin with a flat piece of dough rather than a rounded ball, you will have to do less rolling.

2. Many novice bakers are afraid that excess flour on the work surface will be absorbed by the dough, increasing its flour-to-fat ratio and making it tougher. But the danger in underflouring the work surface is that the dough will stick, and as a result the dough will require additional flour and more handling in the long run. Don't be afraid to dust your surface liberally with flour. Excess flour can always be brushed off with a pastry brush before the dough is pressed into the tart or pie pan.

3. Pâte sucrée and Linzer dough require a brief kneading before they are rolled. Kneading will not toughen these doughs. If you attempt to roll them without softening them up first, they will crumble into large pieces rather than rolling out into a smooth sheet.

4. Instead of beginning to roll right away, press the pin down into the dough to flatten it without rolling.

5. As you roll, periodically fold the dough over the rolling pin, sprinkle the surface with more flour, and give the dough a quarter turn on the freshly floured table. Turning the dough as you roll it will help you to roll out a circle instead of a long strip. If you turn the dough frequently and roll it in all directions, rather than just up and down and side to side, it will shrink evenly in the oven, giving you a uniform crust rather than a crust with sides that are alternately too thick and too thin.

6. Don't make the mistake of stopping too soon. For a 9-inch pie pan or a 10-inch tart pan, roll the crust to a good 14 inches, to make sure you have enough to make decent sides.

LINZER DOUGH

Makes enough dough for one 10-inch Linzer Tart

This delicate and fragrant dough is used in Linzer Tart (page 272). It also makes wonderful mini tart shells, which I fill with buttercream and fruit. At Christmastime, I cut this dough into star and tree shapes for tender cookies. Its spicy aroma always evokes happy feelings about winter. Linzer dough crumbles easily but is well worth the trouble. Just patch any tears with a bit of extra dough.

1 cup (2 sticks) unsalted butter, softened
½ cup sugar
2⅓ cups toasted almond flour or hazelnut flour (see Note, page 249)
2 large egg yolks

¼ teaspoon salt
2 teaspoons grated lemon zest (from 2 medium lemons)
1½ teaspoons ground cinnamon
1½ cups plus 1 tablespoon all-purpose flour

(continued)

1. Combine the butter, sugar, and nut flour in the bowl of an electric mixer fitted with the paddle attachment. Mix together on medium speed until smooth. Do not overmix.
2. Add the egg yolks, salt, lemon zest, and cinnamon and continue to stir on low speed until combined. Add the all-purpose flour and stir until just combined.
3. Turn the dough out onto a lightly floured work surface, press it out to form a 6-inch disk, and wrap it in plastic wrap. Refrigerate for at least 4 hours or up to 1 day before using. Linzer dough may frozen, wrapped in plastic wrap and then in aluminum foil, for up to 2 months. Defrost it in the refrigerator overnight.

NOTE: Toasted nut flours are available by mail from The Baker's Catalogue and other bakers' supply catalogues (see page 523).

LINZER TART

Serves 10 to 12

I like to serve this very sweet tart with unsweetened whipped cream dusted with a little ground cinnamon.

| 1 recipe Linzer Dough (page 271), chilled | 2 cups seedless raspberry jam |
| | 2 tablespoons fresh lemon juice |

1. Preheat the oven to 400 degrees. Butter the bottom and sides of a 10-inch tart pan with removable bottom.
2. Cut out two 12-inch rounds of parchment paper. Take two thirds of the dough and place it between the parchment rounds, rolling the dough until it is an even 12-inch round. Set aside the top circle of parchment and carefully flip the dough onto the tart pan. Set aside the second circle of parchment. Press the dough firmly against the bottom and sides of the pan, and trim away any excess. Patch any tears with the excess dough. Prick the bottom of the tart shell with a

fork. Place the tart shell in the refrigerator for at least 30 minutes to chill completely.

3. Mix together the raspberry jam and lemon juice. Using a small offset spatula, spread the mixture evenly across the bottom of the tart shell.

4. Place the remaining dough between the parchment rounds and roll it out to form an even 10-inch round. Cut the dough into ½-inch-wide strips. Place the strips on top of the jam-filled tart shell in a lattice pattern. Press the ends of the strips lightly into the sides of the tart shell, and trim any excess dough.

5. Bake until dark golden, about 40 minutes. Cool completely on a wire rack before removing the sides of the pan. Linzer Tart will keep, covered, at room temperature for up to 3 days.

CHOUX PASTE

Pâte à choux is as versatile as puff pastry but requires less time and elbow grease to make. Small baked choux puffs filled with savory fillings make elegant hors d'oeuvres. Filled with pastry cream or ice cream, they become cream puffs, éclairs, and profiteroles.

Choux paste consists of a liquid, flour, and butter mixture that is cooked on the stove, then mixed with eggs to make a batter that is just thick enough to pipe. While many recipes call for water, I like to use milk. Choux puffs made with water just don't taste as rich and buttery and don't brown as well as those made with milk. It is crucial that you stir the flour in all at once and very quickly to dissolve it. If you don't, your choux paste will have lumps that you won't be able to get rid of.

Choux puffs and éclair shells rise quickly in the oven, becoming hollow containers for fillings. But they must remain in the oven well after they puff, in order to completely dry out. If you don't bake your choux puffs or éclairs long enough, they will collapse as they cool. To avoid this, prop open the oven door slightly with the handle of a wooden spoon to release any moisture after the pâte à choux has puffed, and bake until they are golden brown and feel dry to the touch. If the surface still gives, put them back in the oven until completely dry on the outside.

PÂTE À CHOUX

Makes enough choux paste for about 24 éclairs, 24 cream puffs,
or 110 small petit-four-size puffs

1 cup whole or 2 percent milk
8 tablespoons (1 stick) unsalted
butter
½ teaspoon salt

1 cup plus ½ tablespoon all-purpose
flour
4 large eggs
1 large egg yolk

1. Preheat the oven to 425 degrees. Combine the milk, butter, and salt in a large saucepan and bring to a boil over medium-high heat.
2. Remove the pan from the heat and quickly stir in the flour all at once, using a wooden spatula. When the flour is dissolved and the mixture is smooth, return the pan to the heat and cook, stirring constantly, for 1 minute. The mixture will be quite thick, the consistency of dry mashed potatoes.
3. Transfer the mixture to the bowl of an electric mixer fitted with the paddle attachment. With the mixer on low speed, add the eggs and then the yolk, one at a time, mixing until each is just incorporated and scraping down the sides of the bowl once or twice as necessary. Do not overmix the dough or it will become oily and will not puff in the oven the way it should. (Alternatively, you may mix the eggs in by hand with the wooden spatula.) The dough will be a thick liquid. To test for the proper consistency, spoon some up with your wooden spatula and tip the spatula to see how fast it runs down the flat surface. It should run very slowly. If it is too thick and not running at all, stir in a little water, a tablespoon at a time, until it is a little bit looser.
4. Use the pâte à choux right away, or cover the bowl with a wet kitchen towel and let it stand at room temperature until ready to use, up to 6 hours.

CHOCOLATE ÉCLAIRS AND COFFEE CREAM PUFFS

Makes 12 éclairs and 12 cream puffs

One recipe of choux paste will make about two dozen pastries, so it is easy to make two different shapes and fillings at the same time and offer your guests a choice. Of course you can pipe just éclairs or just cream puffs and make a double portion of the chocolate or coffee filling if you prefer. If you like, glaze the éclairs with tempered dark chocolate and the cream puffs with tempered milk or white chocolate instead of the fondant icing.

1 recipe Pâte à Choux (page 275)
1 recipe Pastry Cream (page 509)
1 cup heavy cream, chilled
3½ ounces bittersweet or semisweet chocolate, melted cooled (½ cup)
1½ tablespoons instant espresso powder
1 tablespoon hot tap water

FOR THE FONDANT ICING:
3 cups icing fondant (see Note)
1 tablespoon Heavy Syrup (page 506), or more if necessary
1½ tablespoons unsweetened cocoa powder
Red food coloring
½ tablespoon instant espresso powder
1 teaspoon hot tap water

1. Preheat the oven to 375 degrees. Arrange oven racks in the top and bottom thirds of the oven. Line two baking sheets with parchment paper.

2. Use a #7 plain tip to pipe twelve 4-inch-long éclair shapes onto one of the prepared baking sheets. Use a #7 plain tip to pipe 12 cream puff shapes, each about the size of half a lemon, onto the other baking sheet. Bake until golden brown and dry, 25 to 30 minutes, reversing the positions of the baking sheets after 15 minutes to ensure even baking. Cool completely on the baking sheets.

3. Divide the Pastry Cream in half and place each portion in a medium bowl. Whip the heavy cream in an electric mixer until it holds stiff peaks.

4. To make the chocolate filling, stir the cooled melted chocolate into one portion of the Pastry Cream. Fold in half of the whipped cream.

5. To make the coffee filling, dissolve the espresso powder in the hot water, and then stir this mixture into the remaining portion of Pastry Cream. Fold in the remaining whipped cream.

6. To fill the éclairs with chocolate, use the tip of a paring knife, making a twisting motion, to make a small hole about the diameter of a pencil at each end of the

éclairs. Use a #2 or #3 plain tip to pipe the chocolate filling into one end of an éclair. Continue to fill until you can see that the filling is about to come out the other end. Repeat, filling all the éclairs.

7. To fill the cream puffs with coffee filling, use the tip of a paring knife, making a twisting motion, to make a small hole about the diameter of pencil in the bottom of each puff. Use a #2 or #3 plain tip to pipe the coffee filling into the puffs.

8. Prepare the glaze: Place the icing fondant and the Heavy Syrup in a glass bowl and microwave on high power for 5 seconds. Mix well. The icing should be thick but still fluid and slightly warm to the touch. If necessary, return it to the microwave for a few more seconds until it is the right consistency and temperature. If it is still too thick, stir in another tablespoon of Heavy Syrup.

9. Divide the fondant in half and place each portion in a small bowl. Whisk the cocoa powder and 2 drops of red food coloring into one portion. Dissolve the espresso powder in the hot water and then whisk the mixture into the other portion of fondant.

10. Dip the tops of the éclairs into the bowl of cocoa-flavored fondant, allowing the excess to drip back into the bowl. Smooth the icing with your index finger. The glaze should harden quickly, staying on the pastry and not running off. (On a humid day, heat the fondant so that it is a little warmer, or it won't harden sufficiently.) Repeat with the cream puffs, dipping them in the espresso-flavored fondant. Let stand at room temperature until ready to serve, up to 6 hours.

NOTE: Icing fondant is available at pastry supply shops and by mail (see page 524).

$\mathcal{D}$OUGHS CONTAINING BUTTER PACKETS

Puff pastry, croissant dough, and Danish dough are three different mixtures with one thing in common: each consists of a dough that encloses a large packet of butter. The dough, with the butter packet inside of it, is rolled and "turned" a number of times to create very thin layers of dough and butter. When baked, the steam that rises between the layers of dough separates them while the melting butter crisps them up and gives them incredible flavor.

The character of each dough is quite distinct, due to the different ingredients that are used. Puff pastry consists of just flour, butter, and water. It gets all of its flavor from the butter and all of its height from the steam created when the butter and water heat up in the oven. It is crisp and almost crackerlike, with no crumb at all.

Croissant dough is a bread dough made with flour, yeast, and milk that is rolled and folded around a butter packet. Croissants taste like very rich, flaky dinner rolls. They are the buttery cousins of humbler milk-based bread.

Danish dough is more like brioche than bread dough. It contains eggs, which give it more flavor and structure than croissants when baked.

PUFF PASTRY

Makes 2½ pounds dough

Homemade puff pastry is challenging but also exciting. Whenever I make a batch, I can't wait to see how high I can get it to rise, trying to top myself every time. Puff pastry can be put to so many uses—tarts, turnover, napoleons, savory hors d'oeuvres, wrapping fish or beef, or just as a fleuron, a small puff pastry shape used as a garnish with a main course.

Make sure your puff pastry is always completely baked; otherwise the center will look and taste like cardboard. I like to prop the oven door open slightly with the handle of a wooden spoon, to release any moisture from the oven and really dry the pastry out.

FOR THE DOUGH:
1½ teaspoons salt
1½ cups water
3¼ cups all-purpose flour
3 tablespoons unsalted butter

FOR THE BUTTER LAYER:
2 cups (4 sticks) unsalted butter, chilled
¾ cup all-purpose flour, plus more for sprinkling

FOR THE EGG WASH:
1 egg, lightly beaten

1. For the dough: Place the salt and ¼ cup of the water in the bowl of an electric mixer fitted with the paddle attachment, and stir to dissolve the salt. Add the flour and butter, and mix on low speed until the butter is completely mixed in and no pieces are visible. Add 1 cup of the water and continue to mix until the dough comes together; it should be very firm but not hard. If it won't come together or is too hard, add some of the remaining ¼ cup water, 1 tablespoon at a time, until the dough has the consistency of pie dough.

2. Turn the dough out onto a lightly floured work surface and roll it into a ball. With a sharp paring knife, make a cut about ¼ inch deep across the top of the dough ball to release its elasticity. Place the dough on a baking sheet, cover it with plastic wrap, and let it rest in the refrigerator for 2 hours.

3. For the butter layer: Sprinkle 2 or 3 tablespoons of flour on a work surface. Place the chilled sticks of butter on the surface and sprinkle with the ¾ cup flour. Pound the butter with a rolling pin until it comes together in one mass, turning it over often and sprinkling it with more flour as necessary so it does not stick to the work surface or to the rolling pin. Continue to pound and turn until the butter is a soft and pliable doughy square measuring about 6 x 6 inches, with no cracks or crumbling around the edge. If the butter begins to get sticky or begins to melt, cover it loosely with plastic wrap and place it in the refrigerator until chilled, about 1 hour; then begin to work it again. Place the floured butter on a plate and refrigerate it.

4. Scrape the work surface with a dough scraper to remove any remaining butter. Lightly flour the surface, and roll the puff pastry dough out to form a 10 x 10-inch square. Place the pounded butter in the center of the square at a 45-degree angle, so that each corner of the butter square is pointing to the middle of a side of the dough. Fold the corners of the dough in until they meet in the center of the butter square, enclosing the butter.

5. Sprinkle the folded dough with a little flour, and roll it out to form a rectangle measuring about 22 x 10 inches. With one narrow edge facing you, fold the bottom third of the dough over the middle third, and then fold the top third of the dough over these two layers, as if you were folding a letter to be placed in an envelope. This is called a single turn—it should give you three layers of dough. Put the dough back on the sheet pan, cover it with plastic wrap, and refrigerate for 30 minutes for it to rest and firm up.

6. Flour the work surface again. Remove the dough from the refrigerator and place it on the work surface with the narrow edge facing you. Roll it out again into a 22 x 10-inch rectangle. Fold the top edge down so that it comes to the middle of the dough. Fold the bottom edge up so that it meets the top edge in the middle of the dough. Fold the dough in half again, from top to bottom. This is called a double turn—it should give you four layers of dough. Return the dough to the baking sheet, cover it, and refrigerate for another 30 minutes.

Fold the bottom third of the dough over the middle third, and then fold the top third of the dough over these two layers, as if you were folding a letter to be placed in an envelope. This is called a single turn—it should give you three layers of dough.

7. Roll the dough out again and give it another single turn. Let it rest in the refrigerator again, for 30 minutes to 1 hour. Then roll it out again and give it a double turn. You will have given the dough 1 single turn, 1 double turn, 1 single turn, and 1 double turn in total.

8. Wrap the dough in plastic wrap and let it rest in the refrigerator for 2 to 3 hours, or up to 1 week, before using. Puff pastry dough, wrapped in plastic wrap and then in aluminum foil, may be frozen for up to 2 months. Defrost it in the refrigerator overnight before using.

9. To bake: Roll the puff pastry dough out to form the desired shape or shapes (see pages 282–83). If you are planning on making decorative cuts, brush the shapes with egg wash now, and place the shapes in the refrigerator for 45 minutes before making the cuts.

10. Preheat the oven to 450 degrees. Make decorative cuts, or brush any uncut dough with egg wash, taking care not to brush the edges, which would seal them and inhibit the rising. Bake until the dough just starts to get some color. Lower the heat to 375 degrees, prop the oven door open with the long handle of a wooden spoon to release the oven's moisture, and continue to bake until the top is dark golden brown and the pastry is completely cooked through.

11. To add a sweet glaze, sift some confectioners' sugar over the baked puff pastry and place it under the broiler for a few seconds until it melts and caramelizes.

12. Allow the puff pastry to cool completely on a wire rack before using.

Fold the bottom edge up so that it meets the top edge in the middle of the dough. Fold the dough in half again, from top to bottom. This is called a double turn—it should give you four layers of dough.

Puff Pastry Boxes

Makes 8 boxes

1½ pounds Puff Pastry (page 278), prepared through Step 8, chilled	1 egg, lightly beaten
	1 tablespoon whole or 2 percent milk

1. Preheat the oven to 425 degrees. Lightly butter a baking sheet, and set it aside. Turn the chilled puff pastry out onto a lightly floured work surface and sprinkle it with a little flour. With a lightly floured rolling pin, roll the pastry out to form a rectangle measuring about 20 x 3 inches and ¼ inch thick, rotating the dough as you roll it and sliding a flat metal spatula underneath occasionally to make sure that the dough does not stick to the work surface.
2. With a ruler and a sharp paring knife, cut the pastry into 8 rectangles measuring 2½ x 3 inches. Transfer the rectangles to the prepared baking sheet. Combine the egg and milk. Lightly brush the rectangles with the egg wash. Place the baking sheet in the freezer for 15 minutes.
3. Using a sharp paring knife, make a cut all the way around each rectangle, about ¼ inch in from the edge and about 1/16 inch deep. Do not cut all the way through the dough. (This cut will later allow you to remove the top from the pastry to form the box.)
4. Bake for 10 minutes. Then lower the heat to 375 degrees and bake until the rectangles are golden brown, about 20 minutes longer.
5. Remove the pastry from the oven and let the rectangles cool on a wire rack for 5 minutes. Then carefully remove the cut-out tops of the boxes, releasing them from the sides with a sharp paring knife and lifting them away from the bottom with a small offset spatula. Scrape out the wet, unbaked puff pastry from the center of the boxes. Let the boxes and lids cool completely. Puff Pastry Boxes will keep at room temperature, lightly draped with plastic wrap, for up to 3 days.

Making Decorative Cuts on Puff Pastry Dough

To make beautiful designs on puff pastry, first roll the dough out and cut out the desired shapes. Then brush the pieces lightly with beaten egg. Refrigerate uncovered for 45 minutes. Then, with a small sharp paring knife, draw your design by cutting into the dough slightly and at an angle. When baked, the cuts in the dough will open up to reveal your design.

Decorative cuts on a rectangular piece of puff pastry.

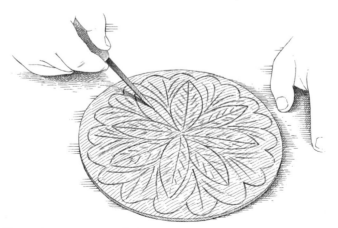

Decorative cuts on a round of puff pastry.

Single and Double Turns

When you are working with dough that contains a butter packet, you roll it and fold it a number of times to end up with a many-layered piece of dough that will bake up high and flaky. Depending on the dough you are working with and the desired result, you use either single turns, double turns, or a combination of the two.

For a **single turn,** the bottom third of the dough is folded over the middle third, then the top third of the dough is folded over these two layers, as when you fold a letter. A single turn results in three layers of dough.

For a **double turn,** the top edge is folded down so that it comes to the middle of the dough. The bottom edge is folded up to meet the top edge in the middle of the dough. Then the dough is folded in half again. A double turn creates four layers of dough.(See illustrations on pages 280–81.)

There is a logic to deciding what kind and how many turns to give your dough: The more layers you fold, the higher the dough will rise. The fewer layers the dough has, the crisper and more distinct the leaves of pastry will be when they bake.

But you also want to take into consideration how much work it will take to roll out the dough, because you don't want to overwork puff pastry, Danish dough, and croissant dough or the end product will be tough. A single turn will not give dough as many layers, but because it is thinner, it will require less work to roll out. A double turn adds layers, but if you give the dough too many double turns you may toughen it up.

Puff pastry takes 2 double turns and 2 single turns, which create over 1,000 very fine layers of dough. These layers are necessary to give the pastry its characteristic height.

In contrast, Danish pastry takes just 2 double turns. It will never rise as high as puff pastry, but it isn't supposed to. It should be enjoyed for its large, crisp flakes.

Croissant dough bakes up somewhere between puff pastry and Danish in height. I give my croissant dough just 3 single turns. Because it is made with bread flour, which contains more gluten than the all-purpose flour used in the other doughs, it is more elastic and more difficult to roll. Single turns work the dough less, so it is still very tender when baked.

CROISSANT DOUGH

Makes 24 croissants

Bread flour makes this croissant dough a little more elastic than conventional croissant dough. A more elastic dough results in a crisper, flakier texture.

1½ cups plus 2 tablespoons milk, warmed

1 ounce fresh yeast, or 1⅓ packages active dry yeast

1½ cups bread flour

1¾ cups all-purpose flour, plus more for sprinkling

⅓ cup sugar

1 teaspoon salt

1 cup (2 sticks) unsalted butter, chilled

1. Place 2 tablespoons of the warm milk in a small bowl and mix in the yeast. Let stand for several minutes, allowing the yeast to dissolve and become foamy.
2. Combine the bread flour, 1¾ cups all-purpose flour, sugar, and salt in the bowl of an electric mixer fitted with the dough hook. Add the remaining 1½ cups warm milk, and mix on medium-low speed until the dry ingredients are moistened. Add the yeast mixture and mix on low speed until incorporated. Increase the speed to medium-low and beat until smooth and firm. The dough will not be too soft—just about the consistency of pasta dough. If the dough is too sticky, add more flour, 1 tablespoon at a time, until it just comes together.
3. Cover the bowl with plastic wrap and let it stand at room temperature until dough has about doubled in size, 45 minutes to 1 hour. Punch down the dough, cover the bowl with plastic wrap again, and let it rest in the refrigerator for 2 hours.

(continued)

4. Sprinkle 2 or 3 tablespoons flour on a work surface. Place the chilled sticks of butter on the surface and sprinkle with more flour. Pound the butter with a rolling pin until it comes together in one mass, turning it over often and sprinkling it with more flour as necessary so that it does not stick to the work surface or to the rolling pin. Continue to pound and turn until the butter is a soft and pliable doughy square measuring about 6 x 6 inches, with no cracks or crumbling around the edge. If the butter begins to get sticky or to melt, lightly cover with plastic wrap, place it in the refrigerator until chilled, and then begin to work it again. Place the floured butter on a plate and refrigerate.

5. Scrape the work surface with a dough scraper to remove any remaining butter. Lightly flour the surface, and roll the croissant dough out to form a 10 x 10-inch square. Place the pounded butter in the center of the square at a 90-degree angle, so that each corner of the butter square is pointing to the middle of a side of the dough. Fold the corners of the dough in until they meet in the center of the butter square, enclosing the butter.

6. Sprinkle the folded dough with a little flour, and roll the dough out to form a rectangle measuring about 10 x 16 inches. With a narrow edge facing you, fold the bottom third of the dough over the middle third, and then fold the top third of the dough over these two layers, as if you were folding a letter to be placed in an envelope. This is called a single turn—it should give you three layers of dough. (See the illustration at top of page 280.) Transfer the dough to a floured baking sheet, lightly cover with plastic wrap, and refrigerate it for 30 minutes.

7. Remove the chilled dough from the refrigerator and roll it out to form a 10 x 16-inch rectangle. Give it a single turn as before. Cover the dough with a floured dish towel and refrigerate it for another 30 minutes.

8. Remove the chilled dough from the refrigerator, roll it out to form a 10 x 16-inch rectangle, and give it one more single turn. Cover it with a floured dish towel and chill for at least 2 to 3 hours or overnight.

CROISSANTS

Makes 20 croissants

Once you've rolled these croissants, lightly drape them with plastic wrap and let them rise. (A kitchen towel is too heavy and might hold them down.) Wait until the croissants have doubled in size before baking them. If you don't give them a chance to rise completely, they will be heavy and hard.

> 1 recipe Croissant Dough (page 285), chilled   1 egg, lightly beaten

1. Line two baking sheets with parchment paper and set them aside. Roll the croissant dough out on a lightly floured surface to form a 24 x 12-inch rectangle. Cut the rectangle into 2 long strips, each strip measuring 6 x 24 inches. Cut each strip into 10 triangles, each triangle having a base of 4 inches and sides of about 6 inches. Transfer the triangles to the prepared baking sheets, placing them at least 1 inch apart.

2. Place one of the triangles on a lightly floured work surface, with the long point facing you. Gently pull the two corners of the short side to stretch that side so that it measures about 6 inches. With one hand, roll the stretched edge toward you while gently pulling on the point facing you with the other hand. Place the rolled croissant back on the parchment-lined baking sheet, curving the ends inward to make a crescent shape and making sure that the point is tucked underneath. Repeat with the remaining dough triangles, placing them in rows on the baking sheets and making sure to leave 2 inches between croissants. (If the triangles become too soft to work with, place them in the freezer for 5 minutes to firm up.) Lightly drape the croissants with plastic wrap, and let stand in a warm (about 75 degrees), draft-free place until they have doubled in size, about 1 hour.

3. Preheat the oven to 425 degrees. Lightly brush the croissants with the beaten egg, and bake until deep golden and well risen, 15 to 20 minutes. Cool on a wire rack. Croissants are best eaten on the day they are baked. I don't recommend freezing either unbaked or baked croissants.

PAINS AU CHOCOLAT

Makes 16 pains au chocolat

Beaten egg brushed on the inside of the croissant dough before it is rolled into individual pains ensures that your pastries won't unroll during baking.

½ recipe Croissant Dough
(page 285), chilled
1 egg, lightly beaten

6 ounces (1 cup) semisweet
chocolate chips

1. Line a baking sheet with parchment paper and set it aside. Roll the croissant dough out to form a 24 x 6-inch rectangle. Cut the rectangle into 2 long strips, each strip measuring 24 x 3 inches. Brush each strip with beaten egg; reserve the leftover egg. Arrange 1 tablespoon of chocolate chips in a row 1 inch in from the short edge, and fold the edge over the chocolate. Then fold once more, so that you have three layers of dough and one layer of chocolate. Trim the dough right at the edge with a sharp paring knife. Place the *pain* on the prepared baking sheet, and flatten it slightly with the palm of your hand. Repeat with the remaining dough, making 8 *pains* out of each strip. Place the *pains au chocolat* 2 inches apart on the baking sheet. Drape plastic wrap loosely over them and let stand in a warm (about 75 degrees), draft-free place until they have doubled in size, about 1 hour.

2. Preheat the oven to 425 degrees. Lightly brush the *pains au chocolat* with the remaining egg wash, and bake until deep golden and well risen, 15 to 20 minutes. Cool on a wire rack. *Pains au chocolat* are best eaten on the day they are baked. I don't recommend freezing them either unbaked or baked.

DANISH PASTRY DOUGH

Makes about 2 pounds dough, enough for 26 large or 50 small Danish

While doughnut and coffee shops across the country claim to sell Danish, it is in fact very rare to find the real thing. Most of what passes for Danish pastry is just sweetened bread dough with little texture or character. To make matters worse, this characterless dough is often rolled into huge, appetite-killing portions and loaded with overly sweet frosting and fillings. Like puff pastry and croissant dough, Danish dough consists of two components: an egg and flour mixture that encloses a packet of butter. The dough is then rolled and folded in on itself a couple of times so that there are thin layers of butter between thin layers of dough. To my mind Danish dough should be not only sweet and buttery but also very flaky, with a little bit of crunch. The more folds you give to a dough like this, the finer the flakes will be. I give my dough just two full double turns so that it bakes up not with fine flakes but with large crisp leaves that you can see and almost lift one by one. After tasting my Danish pastry, I think you'll agree that it is an indulgence well worth the fat and calories. I like small Danish pastries better than large ones for a couple of reasons. If you want to indulge just a little, one small pastry will not destroy your diet. If you want to try a variety (many people find a tray of small different pastries irresistible), you will always have room for a few small ones.

¼ cup lukewarm water
1 ounce fresh yeast or 1½ envelopes
    active dry yeast
3¼ cups all-purpose flour, plus more
    if necessary
¼ cup sugar
½ teaspoon salt

2 large eggs, at room temperature
¼ cup whole milk, at room
    temperature
1 tablespoon unsalted butter, melted
1 cup (2 sticks) unsalted butter,
    chilled

1. Place the lukewarm water in a small bowl and mix in the yeast. Let stand for several minutes, allowing the yeast to dissolve and become foamy.
2. Combine the 3¼ cups flour, the sugar, and the salt in the bowl of an electric mixer fitted with the dough hook. Add the eggs and milk, and mix on medium-low speed until the dry ingredients are moistened. Then add the yeast mixture and the melted butter, and mix on low speed until incorporated. Raise the speed

(continued)

to medium-low and beat until smooth and firm. The dough will not be too soft—just about the consistency of pasta dough. If it is too sticky, add more flour, 1 tablespoon at a time, until it just comes together.

3. Cover the bowl with plastic wrap and let it stand at room temperature until the dough has about doubled in size, 45 minutes to an hour. Punch down the dough, cover the bowl with plastic wrap again, and let it rest in the refrigerator for 2 hours.

4. Sprinkle 2 or 3 tablespoons of flour on a work surface and place the chilled sticks of butter on the surface. Sprinkle the butter with more flour. Pound the butter with a rolling pin until it comes together in one mass, turning it over often and sprinkling it with more flour as necessary so that it does not stick to the work surface or to the rolling pin. Continue to pound and turn until the butter is a soft and pliable doughy square measuring about 6 x 6 inches, with no cracks or crumbling around the edge. If the butter begins to get sticky or to melt, place it in the refrigerator until chilled and then begin to work it again. Place the floured butter on a plate and refrigerate.

5. Scrape the work surface with a dough scraper to remove any remaining butter. Lightly flour the surface and roll the dough out to form a 10 x 10-inch square. Place the pounded butter in the center of the square at a 90-degree angle, so that each corner of the butter square is pointing to the middle of a side of the dough. Fold the corners of the dough in until they meet in the center of the butter square, enclosing the butter.

6. Sprinkle the folded dough with a little flour, and roll the dough out to form a rectangle measuring about 10 x 16 inches, with a narrow edge facing you. Fold the top edge down so that it comes to the middle of the dough. Fold the bottom edge to meet the top edge in the middle of the dough. Fold the dough in half again, from top to bottom. (See the bottom illustration on page 281.) This is called a double turn—it should give you four layers of dough. Transfer the dough to a floured baking sheet, lightly cover it with plastic wrap, and refrigerate for 30 minutes.

7. Remove the chilled dough from the refrigerator and roll it out to form a 10 x 16-inch rectangle. Give it a double turn as before. Cover the dough with a floured dish towel and leave it in the refrigerator for 2 to 3 hours or overnight. This dough will keep in the refrigerator up to 1 day. Or wrap it in plastic wrap and freeze it for up to 2 weeks; defrost it in the refrigerator overnight.

Shaping and Baking Small Danish Pastries

Over the years I've abandoned complicated ways of folding and twisting Danish dough. It is much more modern and less fussy to simply roll the dough out to a ⅛-inch thickness, cut it with a biscuit or cookie cutter, and top it with a filling. These simple shapes are less labor-intensive and more fun to eat, and you and your guests don't have to guess which filling you are choosing. Top the dough with some Cream Cheese Frosting (page 256), Frangipane (page 508), Almond Paste Filling (page 507), Hazelnut Filling (page 509), or Pastry Cream (page 509). Then top the filling with canned apricot halves, sour cherries, or pineapple chunks. Small turnovers filled with Prebaked Apple Chunks (page 27) and sealed with an egg wash are another simple alternative.

1. After cutting and topping the Danish, or filling and folding the turnovers (see page 263), place them on a baking sheet, leaving 2 inches between pastries. Drape them lightly with plastic wrap and let them stand in a warm (about 75 degrees), draft-free place until they have doubled in size, about 1 hour.
2. Preheat the oven to 425 degrees. Bake the Danish until golden and well risen, 15 to 20 minutes. Remove them from the oven. Brush cut-out shapes with heated, strained apricot jam and then Vanilla Glaze (page 519). Brush hot turnovers with melted butter and then sprinkle them generously with Cinnamon Sugar (page 502). Serve warm or at room temperature. Danish pastries are best eaten on the day they are baked.

Making Memorable Brioche Pastries

Great brioche is not difficult to make. Basically it is bread dough that has been enriched with a little bit of sugar and a lot of eggs and butter. Many recipes call for making a sponge—a mixture made with all of the yeast and just some of the liquid and flour from the recipe—to quickly grow the yeast and hurry along the process. But this is not necessary. Just mixing together the ingredients and letting the dough rise slowly is fine. The dough won't rise as quickly as with a sponge—it will take a whole night versus just a couple of hours. But if you take the time to do it the long way, you'll get a better result. Slow fermentation gives a nice, yeasty flavor to the dough, flavor that doesn't have time to develop if you try to hurry the process. Active dry yeast works fine, but try using fresh cake yeast to experience the ultimate brioche—with a yeasty aroma and character.

Brioche dough is very useful to the pastry chef and home baker. It makes incomparable French toast, which can be served for breakfast, brunch, or, as in France, for dessert. Bread pudding (see page 89) made with brioche has a wonderful body and flavor that the same dish made with plain white bread can't match. Brioche dough can also form the base for any number of coffee cakes, dessert pastries, and tarts, like Italian Plum Tart (page 363) or Brioche and Crème (page 296).

BRIOCHE DOUGH

Makes 2 pounds, 6 ounces dough

Brioche dough is used in many recipes, sweet and savory, throughout this book. If you are using the dough for a savory dish, use half the amount of sugar.

1½ teaspoons salt
5 tablespoons sugar (or
   2½ tablespoons for a
   savory recipe)
6 tablespoons warm water
3 cups all-purpose flour

1 ounce fresh yeast, or 1⅓ envelopes
   active dry yeast
5 large eggs
1 cup (2 sticks) unsalted butter,
   softened

1. Combine the salt, sugar, and 2 tablespoons of the warm water in the bowl of an electric mixer fitted with the dough hook. Stir on low speed to dissolve the salt and sugar. Add the flour and stir to combine.
2. Combine the remaining 4 tablespoons warm water and the yeast in a small bowl and let stand to dissolve and become foamy.
3. With the mixer on medium speed add 4 of the eggs, one at a time. Continue to stir for 5 to 7 minutes, until the dough is smooth and very firm.
4. With the mixer on medium, slowly add the remaining egg and then the yeast mixture to the dough. Mix on low speed until the dough is silky and elastic and detaches from the sides of the bowl, about 15 minutes.
5. With the mixer still on low, add the butter, 4 tablespoons at a time, making sure that it is incorporated before adding more. The addition of all of the butter should take about 3 to 4 minutes. When it is all incorporated, the dough should be glossy and elastic.
6. Cover the bowl with a clean kitchen towel and let it stand in a warm (about 75 degrees), draft-free place until it has doubled in size, about 1½ hours.
7. Deflate the dough by flipping it over in the bowl five or six times. Cover it again with the towel, place it in the refrigerator, and leave overnight or no longer than 24 hours.

BRIOCHE LOAF

Serves 8

12 ounces Brioche Dough (page 293)   1 egg, lightly beaten

1. Butter an 8 x 4-inch, 2½-inch-deep nonstick brioche pan.
2. Divide the dough into six 2-ounce pieces. Roll each piece into an egg shape.
3. Place the dough eggs inside the loaf pan, one against the other. Lightly drape the pan with plastic wrap, and let it stand in a warm (about 75 degrees), draft-free place until the loaf has doubled in size, about 1½ hours.
4. Preheat the oven to 450 degrees. Brush the loaf lightly with the beaten egg. Snip the middle of the loaf with sharp scissors, making a ½-inch-deep cut to allow the brioche to expand while baking. Bake for 10 minutes. Then reduce the heat to 375 degrees and bake until the brioche is golden and fully risen, 50 to 60 minutes. Unmold it immediately and let it cool on a wire rack. Brioche Loaf will keep, wrapped in plastic wrap at room temperature, for up to 2 days.

ALMOND BRIOCHE

Serves 8 to 10

Serve this simple cake, made from brioche dough, for brunch or tea.

¾ cup sliced almonds
½ cup apricot jam
½ cup confectioners' sugar
½ tablespoon pure vanilla extract

½ tablespoon water
12 ounces Brioche Dough (page 293)
1 cup Frangipane (page 508)
1 large egg, lightly beaten

1. Preheat the oven to 375 degrees. Spread the almonds on a baking sheet and bake, stirring every few minutes, until lightly browned, about 5 minutes. Set the almonds aside.
2. Place the jam in a small saucepan and bring it to a boil. Push the hot jam through a strainer into a bowl.
3. Whisk together the confectioners' sugar, vanilla, and water in a small bowl. Set this glaze aside.
4. Butter a 9-inch tube pan. Roll the dough out to form a rectangle measuring 18 x 9 inches. Spread the Frangipane over the dough, leaving a ¾-inch border all around. Brush the border with the beaten egg. With the long edge facing you, roll the dough up away from you. Tightly pinch the long edge to seal the cylinder.
5. Pinch together one end of the cylinder. Spread open the other end. Place the cylinder in the prepared pan, seam side up. Fit the two ends together, inserting the pinched end into the open end to form a solid ring. Lightly drape the pan with plastic wrap and let it stand in a warm (about 75 degrees), draft-free place until the loaf has doubled in size, about 1½ hours.
6. Preheat the oven to 450 degrees. Bake for 10 minutes. Then reduce the heat to 375 degrees and bake until the loaf is golden and fully risen, 50 to 60 minutes. Unmold it immediately onto a cake circle or serving plate.
7. While the cake is baking, rewarm the strained jam. As soon as the cake is unmolded, brush it with the warm jam, and then brush the reserved vanilla glaze over the jam. Sprinkle the almonds all over the cake. Serve warm or at room temperature. Almond Brioche will stay fresh under a cake saver at room temperature for 2 days. It can also be wrapped in plastic wrap and frozen for up to 3 weeks; defrost it on the counter for several hours and then rewarm it in a 325-degree oven for 10 minutes before serving.

BRIOCHE AND CRÈME

Serves 10

My mother baked this free-form custard tart every Sunday—what a treat! It is simple but delicious, perfect after a casual meal or even for breakfast or tea. Even though I've made a career of preparing elaborate desserts, it was traditional recipes like this one that inspired me to become a pastry chef. There is nothing fancy here—just a basic construction of brioche dough and vanilla custard—but sometimes the most rustic desserts offer the greatest pleasure.

1 pound Brioche Dough (page 293)

FOR THE CUSTARD FILLING:
1 cup heavy cream
¼ cup plus 2 teaspoons sugar
1 large egg, lightly beaten

3 large egg yolks, lightly beaten
Pinch salt
2 teaspoons pure vanilla extract

3 tablespoons Vanilla Sugar
  (page 502)

1. Line a rimmed baking sheet with parchment paper. On a lightly floured surface, roll the dough out to form a round about 12 inches in diameter and about ⅓ inch thick. Roll about ½ inch of the edge inward to create a lip to hold the filling. The rolled dough should resemble a pizza, with a flat surface and a thicker rounded edge. Carefully transfer the dough to the prepared baking sheet, and lightly drape plastic wrap over it. Let the dough stand in a warm (about 75 degrees), draft-free place until doubled in size, 45 minutes to 1 hour.

2. Preheat the oven to 425 degrees. Whisk together the cream, sugar, whole egg, yolks, salt, and vanilla in a medium bowl. Pour the custard mixture into the center of the dough. Bake until the custard is shiny and just set, about 15 minutes. Then sprinkle the Vanilla Sugar over the custard and bake until the sugar has begun to form a crust, the edges of the brioche are golden brown, and the custard is set, another 15 minutes. Let it stand for 20 minutes. Serve warm.

BRIOCHE, FRUIT, AND CRÈME. After shaping the dough into a rimmed round, arrange 2 cups of pitted sour cherries or Prebaked Apple Slices made with 4 apples (page 28) on top of the dough. Let the dough double in size as described. Then pour the custard mixture on top of the fruit and bake for 15 to 20 minutes before sprinkling with the Vanilla Sugar and baking for another 15 minutes.

SAVARIN

Serves 10

The old-fashioned Savarin is among my favorite desserts. Judging by the response when I served this at the White House, the marriage of yeast-risen dough, rum, fresh fruit, and whipped cream is as popular today as it was 100 years ago.

This dough is related to brioche. It is a combination of butter, eggs, flour, and yeast, but there is much less flour in the Savarin. The mixture is very loose, almost liquid, and more like a batter than brioche dough. When baked, it is lighter and spongier than brioche, perfect for soaking up a flavorful syrup.

One of the nice things about this dessert is that the difficult part—baking the cake and soaking it—can be done up to 2 days in advance. In fact, the cake just gets better as it sits in the refrigerator. Depending on the type of fruit salad or compote you've chosen, the fruit may also be prepared ahead of time. When you are ready to serve the dessert, simply put the two parts together, garnish with whipped cream, and serve.

Other liquors or liqueurs may be substituted for the rum. If you prefer a nonalcoholic dessert, substitute orange juice for the water in the soaking liquid, omit the rum, and heat but don't boil it to dissolve the sugar, since boiling will make the juice bitter.

(continued)

FOR THE DOUGH:

½ cup warm water

½ ounce fresh yeast, or ¾ envelope
   active dry yeast

½ teaspoon salt

2 tablespoons sugar

1½ cups plus 2 tablespoons all-
   purpose flour

2 large eggs, at room temperature

1 large egg yolk, at room temperature

8 tablespoons (1 stick) unsalted
   butter, melted and cooled

½ cup dried currants

FOR THE SOAKING LIQUID:

1 quart water

2 cups sugar

2 oranges, halved

1 lemon, halved

Six 3-inch cinnamon sticks

⅓ cup dark rum

½ cup apricot jam

1 quart fruit salad or fruit compote
   of your choice (see Chapter 1)

2 cups Sweetened Whipped Cream
   (page 521)

1. Place 2 tablespoons of the warm water in a small bowl. Sprinkle with the yeast
    and let stand 5 minutes to dissolve and become foamy.

2. Combine the salt, sugar, and 2 tablespoons of the warm water in the bowl of an
    electric mixer fitted with the dough hook. Stir on low speed to dissolve the salt
    and sugar. Add the flour and stir to combine.

3. With the mixer on medium speed, add the whole eggs and the yolk, one at a
    time. Continue to stir until the dough is smooth and very firm, about 5 min-
    utes. Stir in the yeast mixture.

4. With the mixer on low speed, slowly add the remaining 6 tablespoons water,
    1 tablespoon at a time. Mix on low speed until the dough is silky and elastic and
    detaches from the sides of the bowl, about 15 minutes.

5. With the mixer still on low, add the cooled melted butter in a slow, steady
    stream. The addition of all the butter should take about 3 minutes. When it is all
    incorporated, the dough should be very silky and runny, with a lot of elasticity.
    Stir in the currants.

6. Cover the bowl with a clean kitchen towel and let it stand in a warm (about
    75 degrees), draft-free place until it has doubled in size, about 1 hour.

7. Deflate the dough by punching it down five or six times. It is now ready to be
    molded.

8. Butter two 8-inch Savarin molds. Divide the dough in half and fill the molds
    halfway with the dough. Place them in a warm, draft-free place and allow to rise
    by about one third, about 45 minutes. (Do not let them double in size.)

9. Preheat the oven to 400 degrees. Bake the Savarins until dark golden and risen up to the top of the molds, about 45 minutes.

10. Remove the molds from the oven, and turn the heat down to 375 degrees. Immediately invert the cakes onto a baking sheet and return them to the oven for 15 minutes to dry out. Let them cool completely on a wire rack.

11. Make the soaking liquid: Combine the water, sugar, orange halves, lemon halves, and cinnamon sticks in a medium saucepan and bring to a boil. Remove the pan from the heat. Using the back of a wooden spoon, press the orange and lemon halves into the syrup to extract their juices, and discard the rinds. Pour the syrup through a fine-mesh strainer into a large glass measuring cup. Add the rum.

12. Return the cooled Savarins to the baking pans. Set the pans on rimmed baking sheets. Slowly drizzle some of the soaking liquid over the Savarins, and let stand for 5 minutes to let the cake absorb the liquid. Drizzle more syrup over the Savarins and again let stand 5 minutes to absorb. Continue to soak the cake this way until it will not absorb any more liquid. Allow the Savarins to rest for 30 minutes.

13. Turn the Savarins onto serving plates. Bring the apricot jam to a boil in a small saucepan. Strain the hot jam and brush it over the Savarins. Allow them to cool. At this point, the Savarins may be refrigerated, uncovered, for up to 2 days. When ready to serve, place the fruit salad or compote of your choice in the centers of the Savarins, and decorate with whipped cream.

EIGHT

Cookies You Can Count On

WHENEVER I HAD SOME DOWNTIME at the White House, I'd spend it making cookie dough. It was like putting money in the bank. If a dessert was needed on the spur of the moment, I could pull out some of the dough, bake it, and serve my freshly baked cookies with leftover sorbet, Quick Chocolate Mousse, or a fruit salad improvised from what I had on hand. If I had a particularly good selection of doughs, I'd just serve a platter of cookies. With three or four varieties, plus a bar or two thrown in for good measure, it would look as if I had been baking all week.

Although I count on cookies to come through for me in a crunch, I truly enjoy baking them and eating them for their own sake. Cookies spread joy—they are a pleasure to bake, make your whole house smell great, and put smiles on the faces of people who are eating them.

The best cookies are loaded with flavor but are light and delicate. I gather my ingredients and design my techniques to achieve this goal. Although I see giant cookies in coffee shops and bakery windows, I much prefer bite-size versions. I don't want to feel full after eating just one Chocolate Chip Cookie, because then I might not feel like trying an Oatmeal Cookie, Shortbread Cookie, or Walnut Square! The idea is to bake the cookies so that they are small and delicious, and then everyone will be tempted to try one of each.

Equipment

Cookies require the minimum amount of equipment:

- An **electric mixer** mixes dough quickly and efficiently. I use a standing mixer, but a handheld mixer is fine.
- Heavy, good-quality **baking sheets** are important so that the cookies don't burn on the bottom before they cook on the top. Some people swear by insulated baking sheets, which are available at cookware shops. The idea is that the air trapped between the layers of the sheet temper the heat of the oven so that the cookie bottoms won't become scorched. You can improvise an insulated baking sheet by stacking one baking sheet on top of another.
- For portioning out dough, I use either an **ice cream scoop** or a **pastry bag.** A tablespoon may be substituted for the scoop. Ice cream scoops in different sizes are available at pastry supply shops. They have numbers (#70, #100) that indicate how many scoops you get to the quart. A good quality plastic-coated canvas pastry bag and a set of basic tips are a good investment, as you will use them for many tasks besides cookie-making.
- Unless otherwise directed, bake cookies on **parchment paper** or a **Silpat pad** (see page 17). You'll never have a problem with sticking, and you'll save time on cleanup.
- A **flexible metal spatula** is good for removing delicate cookies from baking sheets. Place warm cookies on **wire racks,** which allow air to circulate all around them, to cool.

Mixing

Very often cookie recipes will direct you to cream together the butter and sugar until fluffy. If you follow these instructions to the letter, you will beat a lot of air into the mixture. As the cookies bake, the air bubbles will expand, causing your cookies to rise, but as soon as they come out of the oven, they will fall flat. I recommend turning off the mixer as soon as the sugar and butter are thoroughly combined. Your cookies will be much shapelier if you use a little restraint during the creaming phase.

When incorporating dry ingredients, mix only until everything is combined. Over-mixing at this stage will encourage the development of the gluten in the flour and may result in tough cookies.

I often like to give the dough a rest and chill it in the refrigerator before baking. I have found that chilled dough keeps its shape better and bakes up higher than dough that's baked as soon as it is mixed. The exception is piped cookie dough. This type of dough will become too hard to pipe if refrigerated and must be piped right away. However, you can refrigerate or even freeze piped cookies, provided they don't contain whipped egg whites, and bake them later at your convenience.

$\mathcal{B}$AKING AND STORAGE

Although there are exceptions, I like to bake my cookies at a relatively high heat—375 or 400 degrees. Cookies are small and will cook through quickly regardless of the temperature. But the best cookies are crisp on the outside and moist on the inside, and only a high oven temperature will adequately brown the crusts before the insides dry out. Watch the cookies carefully as the timer winds down. As soon as the outsides are golden, pull them from the oven. Their small size puts cookies at risk. If left in the oven just a minute or two too long, they will burn and dry out.

Ideally, I like to serve my cookies very soon after they have come out of the oven so that my guests can enjoy the baking aroma as well as the taste of the cookies. Most cookies will keep for a few days in an airtight container at room temperature, but they will lose a little fresh flavor every day. You can freeze baked cookies, but they just won't taste as good as a freshly baked batch.

It's not always practical to make cookie dough just before you want to eat your cookies. Luckily, most cookie dough freezes very well. If you make the dough, portion it out, and then freeze it, you have the option of removing as many cookies as you need and baking them just before serving. This way, you can conjure up an impressive selection of cookies in very little time.

When it comes to freezing, bar cookies are the exception. For most of my bar cookie recipes, I prebake a pâte sucrée crust before filling it with the bar dough, so freezing them before baking wouldn't work. In the case of brownies, which are made with a simple batter and no crust, I find that freezing after baking has no effect on flavor or texture. Frozen cookies may get soggy when defrosted, but brownies are supposed to be soft and fudgy, so a little condensation doesn't affect them. Cookies lose their crisp crust when they are frozen, but brownies are frosted, so the crispness of the top doesn't matter in the end. Depending on the recipe, I either cut baked bars and wrap them individually in plastic wrap before freezing them, or I just wrap the whole sheet pan's worth, freeze it, and cut the bars after defrosting.

The Cookie Plate

When I'm putting together a selection of cookies, I try to vary the flavors and textures so that there's something for everyone. Depending on how much time I have or what I have in the freezer, I'll bake something thin and dry (Lacy Orange Tuiles, for example), something chocolatey and chewy (Chocolate Chip Cookies or Brownies), something with caramel and nuts (Florentine Squares), and a rich and tender butter cookie (Palais Raisin).

THE RECIPES

CHOCOLATE CHIP COOKIES

OATMEAL COOKIES

SHORTBREAD COOKIES

ICEBOX SABLÉS

WALNUT SQUARES

PECAN GALETTE

ALMOND CRESCENTS

HAZELNUT CRESCENTS

LACY ORANGE TUILES

ORANGE BUTTER COOKIES

ALMOND MACAROONS

HAZELNUT SOUFFLÉ COOKIES

PALAIS RAISIN

BROWNIES

PECAN DIAMONDS

COCONUT CHOCOLATE BARS

FLORENTINE SQUARES

Simple, Classic Cookies

These cookies are the ones I baked on an almost daily basis at the White House.

CHOCOLATE CHIP COOKIES

Makes about 70 cookies

Molasses keeps my chocolate chip cookies chewy for more than a day. It also gives them a more intense brown sugar flavor than Toll House–type cookies. I bake these cookies at 400 degrees for a good reason: High heat browns the outside while keeping the inside moist and almost gooey. Don't overbake these, or they will overbrown on the outside and dry out on the inside.

3 cups plus 3 tablespoons all-purpose flour
1 teaspoon baking soda
¼ teaspoon salt
1 cup (2 sticks) unsalted butter, softened
1 cup granulated sugar
⅔ cup packed light brown sugar
2 large eggs
¼ cup molasses
1 tablespoon pure vanilla extract
2 cups (one 12-ounce bag) chocolate chips
1 cup chopped walnuts

1. Combine the flour, baking soda, and salt in a medium mixing bowl.
2. In the bowl of an electric mixer fitted with the paddle attachment, cream together the butter, granulated sugar, and brown sugar until thoroughly combined. Beat in the eggs, molasses, and vanilla, scraping down the sides of the bowl once or twice as necessary. Stir in the flour mixture until just incorporated. Then stir in the chocolate chips and walnuts. Place the bowl in the refrigerator and allow the dough to chill for 1 hour.
3. Preheat the oven to 400 degrees. Line several baking sheets with parchment paper or Silpat pads.

4. Drop heaping tablespoons or #40 ice cream scoops of the dough 2 inches apart on the prepared baking sheets, flattening them slightly by hand. (Balls of dough may be placed next to each other on parchment-lined baking sheets, frozen, transferred to zipper-lock plastic freezer bags, and stored in the freezer for up to 1 month. Place frozen cookies on prepared sheets as above, and defrost on the counter for 30 minutes before baking.)
5. Bake until just light golden, 8 to 10 minutes. Cool the cookies for 5 minutes on the baking sheets before using a metal spatula to transfer them to a wire rack to cool completely. Chocolate Chip Cookies will keep in an airtight container for 2 to 3 days.

OATMEAL COOKIES

Makes about 65 cookies

Here's my version of an American classic. I chill the dough to make it easier to work with; your hands won't stick to it when you flatten the dough balls.

1½ cups all-purpose flour
1 teaspoon baking soda
3 cups quick-cooking (not instant) rolled oats
1 cup (2 sticks) unsalted butter, softened
1 cup granulated sugar

1 cup packed light brown sugar
2 large eggs
1 tablespoon pure vanilla extract
½ cup raisins, dried cherries, or semisweet chocolate chips (optional)

1. Sift the flour and baking soda together in a medium mixing bowl. Stir in the oats.

2. In the bowl of an electric mixer fitted with the paddle attachment, cream together the butter, granulated sugar, and brown sugar until smooth. Beat in the eggs one at a time, scraping down the sides of the bowl after each addition. Stir in the vanilla. Stir in the flour and oat mixture until just incorporated. Stir in the raisins, cherries, or chocolate chips if desired. Place the bowl in the refrigerator and allow the dough to chill for 1 hour.

3. Preheat the oven to 375 degrees. Line several baking sheets with parchment paper or Silpat pads.

4. Drop heaping tablespoons or #70 scoops of the dough 2 inches apart on the prepared baking sheets. With a moistened palm, flatten the dough balls slightly. (Balls of dough may be placed next to each other on parchment-lined baking sheets, frozen, transferred to zipper-lock plastic freezer bags, and stored in the freezer for up to 1 month. Defrost frozen cookie dough on the counter for 30 minutes before baking.)

5. Bake until golden, 12 to 15 minutes. Cool the cookies for 5 minutes on the baking sheets before using a metal spatula to transfer them to a wire rack to cool completely. Oatmeal Cookies will keep in an airtight container for 2 to 3 days.

Sunflower Tart (PAGE 344)

Champagne Crème Brûlée with Green Grapes (PAGE 95)

Chocolate Chip Cookies (PAGE 306), *Shortbread Cookies* (PAGE 309),

Coconut Chocolate Bars (PAGE 330), *and Hazelnut Crescents* (PAGE 317)

 Christmas Tree Crêpes (PAGE 240)

Orange Bavarian Cake (PAGE 410)

 Marjolaine (PAGE 426)

SHORTBREAD COOKIES

Makes 32 cookies

I go against the grain when it comes to shortbread. I just don't like very pale cookies that looked underbaked. My shortbread cookies have the same basic ingredients as Scottish shortbread—butter, flour, and sugar—but I bake them at a higher heat than is traditional because I like the caramelization that such heat gives the cookies. Sometimes, instead of sprinkling them with plain or cinnamon sugar, I'll dust shortbread cookies with confectioners' sugar and briefly broil them until the sugar becomes a beautiful, crunchy glaze. I also like to dip them in chocolate or cut them with a smaller round cutter and sandwich them with jam, ganache, lemon filling, or buttercream.

1 cup (2 sticks) plus 4 tablespoons
   unsalted butter, softened
1 cup confectioners' sugar
½ teaspoon salt
1 vanilla bean

1½ cups all-purpose flour
6 tablespoons granulated sugar,
   Vanilla Sugar (page 502), or
   Cinnamon Sugar (page 502)

1. Combine 1 cup of the butter, the confectioners' sugar, and the salt in the bowl of an electric mixer fitted with the paddle attachment. Use a sharp paring knife to split the vanilla bean in half lengthwise. Scrape the seeds from each half into the bowl. (Reserve the pods for another use.) Cream together on medium speed until smooth but not fluffy. Do not overbeat.

2. Add the flour to the bowl and stir on low speed until just combined. Do not overmix or your cookies will be tough.

3. Shape the dough into 2 disks, wrap them in plastic wrap, and refrigerate until firm, at least 2 hours and up to 1 day. (Shortbread dough may be wrapped in plastic wrap and frozen for up to 1 month. Defrost the dough in the refrigerator overnight before proceeding with the recipe.)

4. Preheat the oven to 375 degrees. Line several baking sheets with parchment paper or Silpat pads.

5. Remove the dough from the refrigerator. On a lightly floured work surface, using a lightly floured rolling pin, roll the dough out to a ¼-inch thickness. Use a fluted 4-inch round cutter to cut the dough into rounds. Place the rounds on

(continued)

the prepared baking sheets and refrigerate for 30 minutes. Refrigerate the scraps, and when they are well chilled, repeat the rolling and cutting.

6. Melt the remaining 4 tablespoons butter in a small pan and let it cool to room temperature. Remove the rounds from the refrigerator. Lightly brush them with the melted butter, and sprinkle with sugar, Vanilla Sugar, or Cinnamon Sugar. With a sharp paring knife, cut each round into 4 wedges. Bake them until very light golden, 7 to 9 minutes. Remove the shortbread from the oven and let it cool completely on the baking sheets. Shortbread will keep for 3 to 4 days, stored at room temperature in an airtight container.

$\mathcal{I}$CEBOX COOKIES

Slice-and-bake cookies saved me many times when I got a message that the First Lady had invited last-minute guests for tea and would like some freshly baked cookies on the table in less than an hour. I was always prepared—I just had to pull my dough logs out of the freezer to get ready for company. Convenience aside, there's a lot to love about these recipes. Both cookies are full of flavor but tender and delicate. Because they are sliced instead of dropped, the cookies have a pleasingly uniform shape and appearance, ideal for times when you want something a little more tailored than a chocolate chip cookie.

ICEBOX SABLÉS

Makes 40 cookies

Hard-boiled egg yolks add richness to the dough but don't make the baked cookies hard, as raw yolks as would. To color-coordinate your cookies with a particular holiday, roll the dough logs in the colored sugar of your choice instead of plain sanding sugar.

3 large hard-boiled eggs
12 tablespoons unsalted butter, softened
1 cup plus 2 tablespoons confectioners' sugar
Pinch salt
½ teaspoon almond extract

2 teaspoons finely grated lemon zest
¼ cup almond flour (see page 523)
1½ cups plus 2 tablespoons all-purpose flour
Coarse sanding sugar (see Resources, page 523) for rolling
1 large egg, lightly beaten

1. Separate the egg yolks from the whites and set the whites aside for another use. Push the yolks through a fine-mesh strainer into a small bowl, and set aside.

(continued)

2. In the bowl of an electric mixer fitted with the paddle attachment, cream the butter and confectioners' sugar together until well combined. Do not overmix. Stir in the salt, almond extract, and lemon zest. Stir in the almond flour. Add the reserved egg yolks and mix until well combined, scraping down the sides of the bowl several times as necessary. Stir in the all-purpose flour and mix until well combined.

3. Turn the dough out onto a lightly floured work surface and divide it into 2 portions. Shape each portion into a 1½-inch-thick log. Make sure that each log is tightly rolled so that it won't have any holes in the center when cut. Roll each log in a piece of parchment paper, and then roll it up in plastic wrap and freeze it until needed. Dough logs may be frozen like this for up to 3 months.

4. When ready to bake, remove the dough logs from the freezer and let stand at room temperature for 30 minutes. Preheat the oven to 375 degrees. Line several baking sheets with parchment paper or Silpat pads. Place the sanding sugar in a rimmed baking sheet.

5. Brush the logs lightly with the beaten egg and then quickly roll them in the sugar to coat. Slice the logs into ⅓-inch-thick rounds and place them on the prepared baking sheets, leaving ½ inch between cookies. Bake until light golden. Remove the cookies from the oven and let them cool completely on the baking sheets. Ice Box Sablés will keep for 3 to 4 days, stored at room temperature in an airtight container.

WALNUT SQUARES

Makes about 80 cookies

These icebox cookies are simple to make and surprisingly delicate and elegant. They make a good teatime snack; combined with fruit or ice cream, they make a quick dessert. Take care to coat the walnuts with a little bit of egg white before stirring them into the dough. If left uncoated, the nuts tend to fall out of the cookies when baked.

1½ cups walnut pieces
2 large egg whites, in separate bowls
14 tablespoons unsalted butter,
    softened

1½ cups confectioners' sugar
1 teaspoon ground cinnamon
Pinch salt
2 cups all-purpose flour

1. Place the walnut pieces in a medium bowl and stir in 1 tablespoon of one of the egg whites, just moistening the nuts. Discard what is left of the egg white.
2. Combine the butter and confectioners' sugar in the bowl of an electric mixer fitted with the paddle attachment, and cream together until light and fluffy. Stir in the remaining egg white until well combined. Stir in the cinnamon and salt. Stir in the flour until the dough just comes together. Stir in the walnuts.
3. On a lightly floured surface, shape the dough into a rectangle measuring 12 x 3 inches, about 1 inch thick. Wrap it in plastic wrap and let it rest for 2 hours in the refrigerator. (The dough can be frozen for up to 3 months and thawed briefly on the countertop before using.)
4. Preheat the oven to 375 degrees. Line several baking sheets with parchment paper or Silpat pads. Cut the dough rectangle into 2 pieces, each one measuring 12 x 1½ inches. Slice each piece into individual cookies about ¼ inch thick. Bake until the cookies just begin to color around the edge, about 10 minutes. Slide the parchment onto a wire rack and let the cookies cool completely. Walnut Squares will keep at room temperature in an airtight container for up to 5 days.

EUROPEAN-STYLE DROP AND SHAPED COOKIES

The cookies in this category are a little bit more refined than chocolate chip or oatmeal cookies. Flavored with nuts, spices, or citrus zest, they are tasty enough to serve on their own but light enough to serve as garnishes for fruit salad or ice cream.

PECAN GALETTE

Makes about 50 cookies

These simple cookies are wonderful on their own or as a garnish for more elaborate desserts such as Coconut Custard (page 84). The cookie dough can be frozen for up to 1 month, making it very handy to have around for times when you need an instant dessert. The food processor is handy for finely grinding nuts, but be careful not to grind them too much or they will release their oil and become like nut butter. You want them to be nice and dry to the touch.

1¾ cups pecan halves	½ cup sugar
8 tablespoons (1 stick) unsalted butter, softened	1 large egg white
	¼ cup all-purpose flour

1. Preheat the oven to 375 degrees. Line two baking sheets with parchment paper or Silpat pads, and set them aside. Place the pecans on a baking sheet and toast until fragrant, 7 to 10 minutes. Remove them from the oven and allow to cool completely.
2. Place the cooled pecans in the bowl of a food processor and process until finely ground but not powdery or oily.
3. Combine the butter and sugar in the bowl of an electric mixer fitted with the paddle attachment, and cream until well combined. Don't beat too much air into the mixture. Stir in the egg white. Stir in the ground pecans and the flour until just combined.

4. Using a #70 ice cream scoop or a tablespoon, place balls of dough at least 3 inches apart on the prepared baking sheets. (Balls of dough may be placed next to each other on a parchment-lined baking sheet, frozen, transferred to zipper-lock plastic freezer bags, and stored in the freezer for up to 1 month. Defrost on the counter for 30 minutes before baking.)

5. Bake for 6 minutes. Remove the baking sheet from the oven, and tap it on a work surface to make the cookies deflate. Return the baking sheet to the oven and bake until golden brown, another 4 minutes. Allow the cookies to cool completely on the baking sheets. Pecan Galette will keep in an airtight container at room temperature for up to 3 days.

ALMOND CRESCENTS

Makes about 36 cookies

These cookies are rich and tasty even though they contain no egg yolks or butterfat. I use a #100 ice cream scoop to get uniform-size cookies, but if you don't have a scoop, just use a scant tablespoon and roll the dough between your palms to form a ball.

8 ounces almond paste
   (see headnote, page 322)
½ cup plus 2 tablespoons sugar
3 large egg whites, 2 in one small
   bowl and 1 in another small bowl

3 tablespoons chopped store-bought
   candied orange peel
2½ cups sliced almonds
¼ cup Heavy Syrup (page 506)

1. Preheat the oven to 400 degrees. Line several baking sheets with parchment paper or Silpat pads.

2. Place the almond paste and ½ cup of the sugar in the bowl of an electric mixer fitted with the paddle attachment, and mix on low speed until well combined. With the mixer still on low, add the 2 egg whites, a little at a time so that no lumps form, and mix well, scraping down the sides of the bowl as necessary. Stir in the candied orange peel.

(continued)

3. Sprinkle a work surface with the remaining 2 tablespoons sugar. Place the remaining egg white in a cake pan or pie plate and lightly beat it with a fork. Place the almonds in another cake pan or pie plate.

4. Roll scant tablespoonfuls of the batter into balls, or scoop them out with a #100 ice cream scoop. Roll the balls first in the egg white and then in the almonds. Shape the coated cookies between your palms into 2-inch-long logs and place them on the prepared baking sheets, leaving at least ¾ inch between cookies and bending the ends toward each other slightly to form crescents. (Shaped cookies can be placed next to each other on parchment-lined baking sheets, frozen, transferred to zipper-lock plastic freezer bags, and stored in the freezer for up to 1 month. Defrost frozen cookie dough on the counter for 30 minutes before baking.)

5. Bake until golden brown, 12 to 15 minutes. Remove the cookies from the oven and lightly brush them with the Heavy Syrup. Let them cool completely on the baking sheets. Almond Crescents will keep in an airtight container at room temperature for 5 to 6 days.

VARIATION:

PINE NUT–ORANGE COOKIES. Substitute 2½ cups (10 ounces) pine nuts for the sliced almonds. After coating the cookies with the nuts, leave them rounded instead of shaping as crescents. Bake as directed.

HAZELNUT CRESCENTS

Makes about 80 cookies

Here is my version of the melt-in-your-mouth Mexican Wedding Cakes. I use hazelnut flour in my version, along with a good dose of cinnamon. These were always the first to go on the holiday cookie platters I put together at the White House.

1 cup (2 sticks) unsalted butter, softened
7 tablespoons sugar
1 large egg
1 large egg yolk
1 tablespoon pure vanilla extract
1 tablespoon ground cinnamon
Pinch salt

2 cups all-purpose flour
1½ cups plus 2 tablespoons toasted hazelnut flour (see Note)

1 cup (2 sticks) unsalted butter, melted and slightly cooled
1 pound confectioners' sugar for dusting

1. In the bowl of an electric mixer fitted with the paddle attachment, cream the softened butter and the sugar together until smooth. Beat in the egg, egg yolk, vanilla, cinnamon, and salt, scraping down the sides of the bowl once or twice as necessary. Stir in the all-purpose flour and the hazelnut flour until just incorporated. Cover the bowl with plastic wrap and refrigerate until the dough is firm, at least 2 hours and up to 3 days.

2. Preheat the oven to 375 degrees. Line several baking sheets with parchment paper or Silpat pads. Roll heaping tablespoonfuls of batter into balls (or use a #100 ice cream scoop if you have one). Shape the cookies between your palms into 2-inch-long logs and place them on the prepared baking sheets, leaving ¾ inch between cookies and bending the ends toward each other slightly to form crescents. (Shaped cookies can be placed next to each other on parchment-lined baking sheets, frozen, transferred to zipper-lock plastic freezer bags, and stored in the freezer for up to 1 month. Defrost frozen cookie dough on the counter for 30 minutes before baking.)

3. Bake until light golden, about 15 minutes. Brush the hot cookies with the melted butter, dust heavily with the confectioners' sugar, and let cool com-

(continued)

pletely on the baking sheets. Hazelnut Crescents will keep in an airtight container at room temperature for up to 3 days.

NOTE: Nut flours are available at bakery supply shops and also by mail order (see page 523).

LACY ORANGE TUILES

Makes about 30 cookies

Make sure to bake these cookies until they are browned all over—undercooked tuiles will not crisp up the way that they should. Tuiles are highly sensitive to moisture, so to prevent them from getting soggy, store them in an airtight container away from any humidity. I recommend serving these cookies with a sorbet or ice cream.

6 tablespoons fresh orange juice
1½ teaspoons grated orange zest
1½ cups sugar
½ cup all-purpose flour

8 tablespoons (1 stick) unsalted
   butter, melted and slightly cooled
1½ cups sliced almonds

1. Preheat the oven to 400 degrees. Line several baking sheets with parchment paper or Silpat pads.
2. Combine the orange juice, zest, and sugar in a large bowl and mix well. Stir in the flour, melted butter, and almonds. Cover with plastic wrap and refrigerate until well chilled, at least 1 hour and up to 1 week. (The batter can be frozen in an airtight container for up to 1 month. Defrost in the refrigerator overnight before using.)
3. Place teaspoon-size portions on the prepared baking sheets, leaving them at least 3 inches apart because the cookies will spread quite a bit. Flatten each cookie with the tines of a fork that has been dipped into cold water. Bake the cookies until they are light brown, 7 to 8 minutes.
4. Remove the baking sheet from the oven. Use a large round biscuit cutter to gather the cookies, which will have spread, into nice rounds. Return the shaped

tuiles to the oven and cook an additional minute or two, until they are brown all over.

5. Remove the cookies from the oven and let them stand until they begin to firm up but are still pliable, about 1 minute. Then carefully lift each cookie from the baking sheet with a metal spatula and drape it over a rolling pin or an empty wine bottle. After 30 seconds or so it should hold the shape of the rolling pin. (If some cookies harden before you are able to shape them, return them to the oven for 20 to 30 seconds to soften.) Let the tuiles cool completely, and then store them in an airtight container at room temperature for up to 3 days.

$\mathcal{P}$IPED COOKIES

Getting out the pastry bag for cookies might seem like a hassle, but piping the dough onto baking sheets is actually a very quick way to make a large quantity of pretty cookies. The biggest issue with piped cookies is keeping the dough soft enough to pipe. I use a couple of different tricks, depending on the result I'm after. For the Orange Butter Cookies, cake flour makes a very soft dough with no elasticity, important when you're pushing it through the tip of the pastry bag. Almond Macaroons have no flour at all. Palais Raisin cookies contain quite a few eggs, which make the dough soft. Whatever kind of cookie dough you are making, be sure that your ingredients are at room temperature. Cold eggs and butter will make a stiff dough that will be difficult to handle.

ORANGE BUTTER COOKIES

Makes about 50 cookies

It's important that all the ingredients be at room temperature in this recipe, so that the dough will be soft enough to pipe. Cake flour makes the dough soft for piping as well as making the finished cookies extra tender.

To vary the recipe, make an indentation in the center of each portion of cookie dough and fill it with jam before baking. Or fill the indentations with Ganache (page 513) after the cookies have baked and cooled. You could also place a hazelnut, walnut half, or pecan half on top of each unbaked rosette for a simple garnish.

3 ounces almond paste, at room temperature (see headnote, page 322)
¾ cup confectioners' sugar
4 large egg yolks
14 tablespoons unsalted butter, softened

1½ teaspoons finely grated orange zest
Pinch salt
2¼ cups cake flour

1. Preheat the oven to 375 degrees. Line several baking sheets with parchment paper or Silpat pads.
2. Combine the almond paste, confectioners' sugar, and 1 of the egg yolks in the bowl of an electric mixer fitted with the paddle attachment, and mix on low speed until the mixture is a soft, smooth paste.
3. With the mixer running, add another egg yolk and mix until smooth.
4. Add the butter to the bowl and mix on medium speed until well combined. Do not overbeat. Mix in the remaining 2 egg yolks. Stir in the orange zest and salt. Stir in the cake flour until just combined. Do not overmix.
5. Spoon the batter into a pastry bag fitted with a large (#7 or #8) star tip or rosette tip, and pipe half-dollar-size portions onto the prepared baking sheets, leaving ¾ inch between cookies. Bake until light golden, 12 to 14 minutes. Let the cookies cool for 5 minutes on the baking sheets, then use a metal spatula to transfer them to a wire rack to cool completely. Orange Butter Cookies will keep in an airtight container at room temperature for 2 to 3 days.

Filling and Using a Pastry Bag

If you have never used a pastry bag, now is a good time to try. Piping cookie dough is simple, and there's less at stake than when you are piping cake decorations. Disposable plastic pastry bags are convenient, but I prefer the feel of a plastic-coated canvas bag that can be reused.

1. If using a disposable bag, snip off just enough of the end so that the bottom half of the tip will fit snugly in the hole and not slide through.
2. Place the desired tip in the bag and fill the bag no more than halfway to the top with dough. (If you fill it any higher than this, you will have trouble twisting it closed and the dough will come out the top as you work.)
3. Push the dough toward the bottom of the bag by holding the top of the bag closed with one hand and sliding the fingers of your other hand down the sides of the bag toward the bottom. Once all of the dough is in the bottom of the bag, twist the top tightly to seal it.
4. Hold the bag in your right hand (or in your left, if you are left-handed), grasping it with your thumb and forefinger at the point where it has been twisted. Hold the bag at a 90-degree angle and an inch or so above the prepared cookie sheet. Use your other three fingers to squeeze the dough from the bag. Use your other hand to steady the bottom of the bag as you move it over the cookie sheet.
5. Practice a few times on a work surface. You can scrape the batter back into the bowl and reuse it once you've gotten the hang of it.

ALMOND MACAROONS

Makes about 40 cookies

Almond Macaroons are delicious on a cookie plate and also very good when coarsely chopped and stirred into a variety of parfaits. Make sure that you buy almond paste, which is just a mixture of 50 percent sugar and 50 percent almonds. Marzipan, which is processed with other ingredients and made for decoration, should not be substituted.

8 ounces almond paste
1 cup confectioners'
    sugar

2½ large egg whites, at room
    temperature
1 teaspoon grated lemon zest

1. Preheat the oven to 375 degrees. Line several baking sheets with parchment paper or Silpat pads. Place the almond paste and confectioners' sugar in the bowl of an electric mixer fitted with the paddle attachment, and mix on low speed until well combined. With the mixer still on low, add 2 of the egg whites, a little bit at a time, scraping down the sides of the bowl after each addition. Mix well, but do not whip, until very smooth and no lumps remain. Add the remaining ½ egg white and mix well. Stir in the lemon zest.

2. Spoon the batter into a pastry bag fitted with a #6 plain tip and pipe quarter-size portions onto the prepared baking sheets, leaving ¾ inch between cookies. Place the baking sheets in the oven and leave the door open about ½ inch (prop it open with the handle of a wooden spoon). Bake until light golden, 20 to 25 minutes. Let the macaroons cool completely on the baking sheets. Almond Macaroons will keep in an airtight container in the refrigerator for up to 1 week, or in the freezer for up to 2 months.

HAZELNUT SOUFFLÉ COOKIES

Makes about 40 cookies

This very flavorful cookie is relatively low in calories—a good choice for when I'm watching my weight. Usually when I make a batch, I can't resist dipping the bottoms of the cookies in tempered chocolate, making them less dietetic but that much more tasty! If you like, you can substitute almond, pecan, or any other nut flour for the hazelnut flour called for here (see Mail-Order Resources, page 523).

To toast and skin hazelnuts, place the nuts on a baking sheet and bake them in a pre-heated 350-degree oven until fragrant, about 10 minutes. Wrap the hot nuts in a clean kitchen towel and let steam for 10 to 15 minutes. Then rub the nuts with the towel to remove the skins.

1 cup toasted hazelnut flour	2 large egg whites
½ cup sugar	40 whole hazelnuts, skinned
1 large egg white, lightly beaten, plus more if necessary	Confectioners' sugar for dusting

1. Preheat the oven to 375 degrees. Combine the hazelnut flour and 6 tablespoons of the sugar in a large mixing bowl. Add the 1 beaten egg white, a little at a time, and mix by hand until the mixture becomes a paste with the consistency of thick mashed potatoes. (You may or may not have to use the whole egg white to achieve this consistency. If the mixture is too dry after the entire egg white has been added, add a little more egg white, a teaspoon at a time, until the desired consistency has been reached.)

2. Place the remaining 2 egg whites in the bowl of an electric mixer fitted with the whisk attachment and whip on high speed until just about to hold soft peaks. With the mixer still on high, pour in the remaining 2 tablespoons sugar in a slow, steady stream. Whip until the whites hold stiff peaks.

3. Stir half of the egg whites into the flour paste to lighten it. Fold the remaining egg whites into the mixture, making sure everything is well combined but being careful not to deflate the mixture.

(continued)

4. Spoon the batter into a pastry bag fitted with a #5 plain tip, and pipe the batter into small paper baking cups, filling the cups to the top. Place a hazelnut on top of each cup; dust with confectioners' sugar. Bake until golden, 7 to 10 minutes.

5. Let the cookies cool completely in the baking cups, and then peel away the paper. Hazelnut Soufflé Cookies will keep in an airtight container for 2 to 3 days.

PALAIS RAISIN

Makes about 60 cookies

This piped butter cookie dough is incredibly versatile. Because it has so many eggs, the dough is very soft, even though it is not made with cake flour. Sometimes I substitute candied orange peel for the currants and Grand Marnier for the rum. You could also leave out the currants and the glaze, bake the cookies plain and then sandwich them together with Ganache (page 513).

1 cup (2 sticks) unsalted butter, softened	Pinch salt
1 cup sugar	2 cups all-purpose flour
4 large eggs	1¼ cups dried currants
1 tablespoon pure vanilla extract	2 cups apricot jam
	1 recipe Rum Glaze (page 520)

1. Preheat the oven to 375 degrees. Line several baking sheets with parchment paper or Silpat pads.

2. In the bowl of an electric mixer fitted with the paddle attachment, cream the butter and sugar together until smooth. Beat in the eggs one at a time, scraping down the sides of the bowl after each addition. Stir in the vanilla and salt. Add the flour and mix until well combined. Stir in the currants.

3. Spoon the batter into a pastry bag fitted with a #6 or #7 plain tip, and pipe quarter-size mounds onto the prepared baking sheets, leaving ¾ inch between cookies.

4. Bake until the edges of the cookies are golden brown but the centers are still pale, 8 to 10 minutes.

5. Meanwhile, bring the jam to a boil in a small saucepan. Strain the jam. As soon as the cookies come out of the oven, brush each one with a light coating of hot jam and then brush the Rum Glaze over the jam. Serve warm, or allow to cool on the baking sheets and serve at room temperature. Palais Raisin will keep in an airtight container at room temperature for 3 days.

ℬAR COOKIES

Bar cookies are an efficient way to feed a large number of people without scooping or piping out cookie dough. I make mine in large quantities even if I'm not planning on having a lot of people over; they freeze well, and I can defrost them as I need them.

I am rather proud of my brownies, which I have served to literally thousands of people over the years. I have an easy trick for making them extra fudgy, and I never skip the chocolate glaze, which adds another texture and more chocolate flavor.

The other bar cookie recipes all call for a crust made from pâte sucrée. This cookielike dough makes a great base for gooey fillings like pecan and caramel or chocolate and coconut. It's a little extra work, but the pastry elevates these bars so that they taste like tartlets.

BROWNIES

Makes 32 brownies

For the absolute fudgiest brownies, I remove the pan from the oven midway through baking and tap it on the counter to deflate the rising batter. If you prefer a cakier brownie, skip the tapping step and just let the brownies continue to rise as they bake. Well wrapped in plastic wrap, unglazed and uncut brownies will keep in the freezer for up to 2 months. Defrost them overnight in the refrigerator, and then cut and glaze them the day you want to serve them.

10 tablespoons unsalted butter, softened

1¼ cups sugar

3 large eggs

1 large egg yolk

1 tablespoon pure vanilla extract

Pinch salt

5 tablespoons unsweetened cocoa powder

1 cup all-purpose flour

1½ cups pecan pieces

1 recipe Semisweet Chocolate Glaze (page 512), warmed

1. Preheat the oven to 400 degrees. Grease a 9 x 13-inch baking pan and line the bottom with parchment paper.

2. In a large mixing bowl with an electric mixer on medium speed, cream the butter and sugar together until fluffy, 2 to 3 minutes. Add the eggs and the egg yolk one at a time and beat until smooth, scraping down the sides of the bowl after each addition. Add the vanilla, salt, and cocoa powder and mix well. Beat in the flour until well combined. Stir in the nuts. Remove the bowl from the mixer, scrape down the sides, and give the batter a few more stirs by hand to make sure that all the ingredients are well incorporated.

3. Scrape the batter into the prepared pan and smooth the top with a spatula. Bake for 10 minutes. Then, for fudgy brownies, remove the pan from the oven and tap it on the counter to make the rising brownies collapse. Return the pan to the oven and bake until firm to the touch, 8 to 10 minutes more. (For cakey brownies, bake for 18 to 20 minutes without interruption.) Do not overbake or your brownies will be dry. Remove the pan from the oven, place it on a wire rack, and let the brownies cool completely in the pan.

4. Invert the cooled brownies onto a baking sheet and peel off the parchment paper. (Uncut brownies may be wrapped in plastic wrap and frozen for up to 2 months. Defrost them in the refrigerator overnight before continuing with the recipe.)

5. Place uncut brownies back in the pan. Rewarm the glaze if necessary, and pour the glaze over the brownies, smoothing it evenly with a spatula. Refrigerate until the glaze has hardened, about 30 minutes. Slice into 32 brownies. Brownies will keep in the refrigerator, loosely draped with plastic wrap, for up to 1 week.

PECAN DIAMONDS

Makes 120 diamonds

This recipe makes a half-sheet-pan's worth of bars, which is a lot. They freeze well, so if this is more than you can use at one time, cut the baked dough in quarters and freeze some in large pieces. Defrost in the refrigerator and cut into diamonds before serving.

2 recipes Pâte Sucrée (page 267), chilled
1 cup (2 sticks) unsalted butter
1¼ cups packed light brown sugar
¼ cup granulated sugar
½ cup honey
½ cup heavy cream
1½ tablespoons pure vanilla extract
Pinch salt
4 cups pecan pieces

1. Butter a 16 x 12-inch rimmed sheet pan.
2. Turn the chilled dough out onto a lightly floured work surface and sprinkle it with a little flour. With a lightly floured rolling pin, roll the dough out to form a ⅛-inch-thick rectangle measuring roughly 18 x 14 inches, rotating the dough as you roll it and occasionally sliding a flat metal spatula underneath to make sure that it does not stick to the work surface. Lift the dough by folding it in half over the rolling pin, and gently place it in the prepared pan. Trim the dough with a sharp paring knife so that it covers the bottom and comes flush up the sides of the pan. Prick the dough all over with a fork. Place it in the refrigerator for at least 30 minutes to chill completely. (Wrapped in plastic wrap, the dough can stay in the refrigerator for up to 2 days.)
3. Preheat the oven to 400 degrees. Cut an 18 x 14-inch piece of aluminum foil and place it on top of the chilled dough. Pour pie weights or 6 cups dried beans on top of the foil. Bake until the edges of the dough just start to brown, about 15 minutes. Carefully remove the foil and beans, return the dough to the oven, and bake until light brown all over, about 15 minutes more. Keep an eye on the dough as it bakes, and if a bubble appears, pierce it with a sharp paring knife to deflate it. Remove the pan from the oven and turn the heat down to 375 degrees.
4. While the crust is baking, prepare the filling: Combine the butter, brown sugar, granulated sugar, honey, heavy cream, vanilla, and salt in a heavy saucepan and bring to a boil over medium-high heat, stirring occasionally, until the mixture reaches the thread stage (the mixture will pull into a thread when stretched be-

tween two fingers but will not yet form a ball, 225 degrees on a candy thermometer), 6 to 8 minutes.

5. Stir the pecans into the mixture and pour it over the baked pâte sucrée, smoothing it evenly with a metal spatula or the back of a spoon. Bake until the surface bubbles all over, about 20 minutes. Remove the pan from the oven and place it on a wire rack. Let the pastry cool completely.

6. Using a sharp chef's knife, cut the pastry into diamond shapes approximately 1½ inches long and 1 inch across. Pecan Diamonds will keep in an airtight container at room temperature for 2 to 3 days. Uncut, they will keep in the freezer for 3 months.

COCONUT CHOCOLATE BARS

Makes about 60 bars

These irresistible bar cookies taste just like candy bars. The recipe makes a large quantity, but individual bars can be wrapped in plastic wrap and frozen for up to 1 month. If you like, cut the recipe in half and bake the bars in a 9 x 13-inch baking pan.

2 recipes Pâte Sucrée (page 267), chilled
4 cups sugar
12 large egg whites
5½ cups grated unsweetened coconut
½ teaspoon salt

1 tablespoon pure vanilla extract
¾ cup all-purpose flour
½ cup bitter orange marmalade
4 cups (two 12-ounce bags) semisweet chocolate chips
2½ cups heavy cream

1. Butter a 16 x 12-inch rimmed sheet pan.
2. Turn the chilled dough out onto a lightly floured work surface and sprinkle it with a little flour. With a lightly floured rolling pin, roll the dough out to form a ⅛-inch-thick rectangle measuring roughly 18 x 14 inches, rotating the dough as you roll it and occasionally sliding a flat metal spatula underneath to make sure that it does not stick to the work surface. Lift the dough by folding it in half over the rolling pin, and gently place it in the prepared pan. Trim the dough with a sharp paring knife so that it covers the bottom and comes flush up the sides of the pan. Prick the dough all over with a fork, and place it in the refrigerator for at least 30 minutes to chill completely. (Wrapped in plastic wrap, the dough can stay in the refrigerator for up to 2 days.)
3. Preheat the oven to 400 degrees. Cut an 18 x 14-inch piece of aluminum foil and place it on top of the chilled dough. Pour pie weights or 6 cups dried beans on top of the foil. Bake until the edges of the dough just start to brown, about 15 minutes. Carefully remove the foil and beans, return the dough to the oven, and bake until light brown all over, about 15 minutes. Keep an eye on the dough as it bakes, and if a bubble appears, pierce it with a sharp paring knife to deflate it. Remove the pan from the oven and turn the heat down to 300 degrees.
4. While the crust is baking, prepare the filling: Combine the sugar, egg whites, coconut, salt, and vanilla in a large stainless steel bowl set over a saucepan containing an inch or two of simmering water. Heat, stirring constantly, until the

mixture is very hot to the touch but not yet simmering. Remove from the heat and stir in the flour.

5. Spread the marmalade evenly over the crust. Spread the coconut mixture on top of the marmalade. Bake until golden, 45 minutes to 1 hour. Remove from the oven and let cool completely on a wire rack.

6. Place the chocolate chips in a large heatproof bowl. Bring the heavy cream just to a simmer, pour it over the chocolate, and stir until smooth. Pour this ganache over the cooled coconut filling, smooth it evenly with a spatula, and refrigerate the pan overnight.

7. Heat a sharp chef's knife in hot water, dry it well with a clean kitchen towel, and slice the pastry into 60 bars, reheating and drying the knife as necessary. Coconut Chocolate Bars will keep in an airtight container at room temperature for 2 to 3 days. Individually wrapped in plastic wrap, the bars can be frozen for up to 1 month.

FLORENTINE SQUARES

Makes about 60 squares

To make these squares more elegant and to give them an added flavor dimension, you can dip them in Tempered Chocolate (pages 433, 435): Insert a toothpick in the middle of each square and dip the square into the chocolate up to the top edges. Scrape off the excess chocolate on the edge of the pot, and place the dipped squares on a parchment-lined baking sheet. Remove the toothpicks and let stand until the chocolate has completely hardened.

2 recipes Pâte Sucrée (page 267), chilled
1 cup (2 sticks) unsalted butter
1 cup sugar
½ cup honey
½ cup heavy cream
1 tablespoon pure vanilla extract

Pinch salt
1 pound sliced almonds
⅓ cup chopped unsalted pistachio nuts
⅓ cup dried currants or raisins
⅓ cup chopped red glazed cherries
⅓ cup chopped candied orange peel

1. Butter a 16 x 12-inch rimmed sheet pan.
2. Turn the chilled dough out onto a lightly floured work surface and sprinkle it with a little flour. With a lightly floured rolling pin, roll the dough out to form a ⅛-inch-thick rectangle measuring roughly 18 x 14 inches, rotating the dough as you roll it and occasionally sliding a flat metal spatula underneath to make sure that it does not stick to the work surface. Lift the dough by folding it in half over the rolling pin, and gently place it in the prepared pan. Trim the dough with a sharp paring knife so that it covers the bottom and comes flush up the sides of the pan. Prick the dough all over with a fork. Place the pan in the refrigerator for at least 30 minutes to chill completely. (Wrapped in plastic wrap, the dough can stay in the refrigerator for up to 2 days.)
3. Preheat the oven to 400 degrees. Cut an 18 x 14-inch piece of aluminum foil and place it on top of the chilled dough. Pour pie weights or 6 cups dried beans on top of the foil. Bake until the edges of the dough just start to brown, about 15 minutes. Carefully remove the foil and beans, return the dough to the oven, and bake until light brown all over, about 15 minutes more. Keep an eye on the

dough as it bakes, and if a bubble appears, pierce it with a sharp paring knife to deflate it. Remove the pan from the oven and turn the heat down to 375 degrees.

4. While the crust is baking, prepare the filling: Combine the butter, sugar, honey, and heavy cream in a heavy saucepan, and bring to a boil over medium-high heat, stirring occasionally, until the mixture reaches the thread stage (the mixture will pull into a thread when stretched between two fingers but will not yet form a ball, 225 degrees on a candy thermometer), 6 to 8 minutes.

5. Stir the vanilla, salt, sliced almonds, pistachios, currants, glazed cherries, and candied orange peel into the mixture. Mix all together and pour the filling over the baked pâte sucrée, smoothing it evenly with a metal spatula or the back of a spoon. Bake until the surface bubbles all over, about 20 minutes. Then bake an additional 2 to 3 minutes until the surface is golden. Remove the pan from the oven and place it on a wire rack. Let the pastry cool completely. The filling will be the consistency of soft caramel when cooled.

6. Cut into squares with a sharp chef's knife. Florentine Squares will keep in an airtight container at room temperature for 2 to 3 days. Freeze uncut squares, wrapped in plastic wrap, for up to 3 months.

NINE

Favorite Tarts and Pies

WHEN I WAS GROWING UP, we were on a limited budget, and because fruit was plentiful and cheap in the summertime, my mother became quite an expert at making fruit tarts, always with a delectable crust and with whatever fruit was coming to market on the days that she shopped. I used to wait at her side for the leftover dough so I could make myself a tartlet. Nothing gave me more pleasure than eating my own little fruit and pastry creation, warm from the oven. I should have known then that I'd wind up a pastry chef! To this day, nothing conjures up feelings of home more than a just-baked fruit tart.

Perhaps because they do remind us of home, we love tarts and pies in all of their incarnations. They can be as simple as some cut-up fruit topped with a layer of pâte sucrée, as in Strawberry Deep Dish Pie, or they can be as beautifully decorated as Swan Tart with Winter Fruit Salad. Plain or fancy, for many people a combination of crust and filling is the ultimate dessert.

When made right, these desserts do indeed have it all. But the elements must be in balance for full enjoyment. I have spent many days in the kitchen experimenting with crust and filling combinations, discovering what kinds of fillings go best with pâte sucrée and which ones taste better with All-American Pie Dough, puff pastry, or brioche. I have tried different techniques for finishing tarts and pies. Sometimes a shell needs to be partially or completely baked before filling; sometimes it is better to fill before baking. After filling tart shells with frangipane and fruit with unsatisfactory results, I have even decided that some tarts are better off *without* crusts. My recipe for Crustless Almond Peach and Almond Pear Tartlets is an example.

THE RIGHT DOUGH FOR THE RIGHT FILLING

I have grouped the recipes in this chapter according to the type of dough I use, since each type is handled and baked a little differently. For information on making and working with the various doughs, see Chapter 7.

Recipes with **pâte sucrée** come first. I have found that this is the most versatile dough when it comes to tarts. It is also the easiest to roll. Pleasantly sweet and crisp, it can be blind-baked and filled with pastry cream and fruit, partially baked and filled with lemon custard before being baked some more, or filled with apples or sweetened nut filling before going into the oven at all.

Pâte brisée is the dough I turn to for savory tarts and pies, as well as fruit tarts and pies with very moist fillings. Not quite as tender as pâte sucrée, it will stay crisp for much longer, even when filled with tomatoes and cheese or rhubarb and custard.

While preparing Thanksgiving dessert for five different First Families over the years, I had plenty of time to consider the type of flaky pie crust that people across the country hope for on this day. If I weren't already a naturalized citizen, I would argue that my recipes for pumpkin and apple pie, made with **All-American Pie Dough,** would qualify me for that honor!

Puff pastry, when baked up tall and crisp, makes a spectacular container for cream and mousse fillings.

Brioche dough rises around fruit for comforting and homey tarts that are wonderful for breakfast or at teatime.

Included in this chapter are some of my favorite recipes for not-quite tarts or pies. **Cobblers, crumbles,** and **charlottes** are each composed of crisp topping and juicy filling. None of them requires rolling pastry dough and fitting it into a pan, but each delivers pleasure similar to the pleasure you get from a real tart or pie.

GETTING READY TO BAKE

For general tips on working with a rolling pin and rolling out dough, see page 270. Here are a few rules to follow once you've begun to roll out your tart or pie dough:

- For my tarts, I use a 10-inch tart pan with removable bottom. These pans come either polished or with a black finish. For these recipes, it makes no difference which you use. For pies, any 9-inch pie pan will do, although a clear glass Pyrex pan has the advantage of giving you a view of the bottom crust, so you can be sure that it is well browned before you pull your pie from the oven.

- When it comes to pies and tarts, I prefer thicker dough to dough that's been rolled paper-thin. When I bite into a slice of pie, I want to taste the crust as well as the filling. An eighth of an inch is about as thin as I want to go with Pâte Sucrée, Pâte Brisée, or All-American Pie Dough.

- Many beginning bakers make the mistake of rolling out a round of dough that they think will be just big enough to cover the bottom and sides of the pan with a little left over for a doubled edge. Invariably, part of the circle will fall a little short of expectations, and a section of the edge will be shrunken and thin as a result. I recommend that you roll out dough for a 10-inch tart shell or a 9-inch pie pan so that it measures at least 13 and up to 14 inches in diameter (the dough recipes in Chapter 7 will provide you with more than enough to do so).

- Once you have rolled out your dough to the desired shape and thickness, fold it in half over the rolling pin and place it over your greased tart or pie pan. (I always grease the pan because I find that it helps keep the dough in place while I'm working with it.) Be sure to press the dough firmly against the bottom and sides of the pan, but be careful not to pull or stretch it, since if you do so it will just shrink back to its original position when it is baking.

- I like to make a double layer of dough on the sides of pie and tart pans, whether I'm using Pâte Sucrée, Pâte Brisée, or All-American Pie Dough. For the same reasons that I like a thicker bottom crust, I like thicker sides. They hold fillings better than thin ones, and they taste good besides. Trim off all but ½ inch of the dough along the edge of the tart or pie pan. Fold the extra dough into the pan and press it firmly against the sides.

- Pie and tart crusts made with butter should be chilled for at least 30 minutes before baking. If the dough is too warm when it goes into the oven, it will lose its shape before it begins to crisp up.

- When prebaking a tart or pie crust, do not neglect to line the pan with greased parchment and fill it with dried beans or pie weights. If you don't grease the side of the parchment that touches the dough, the paper might stick to it. The beans perform the job of a baked filling, weighting down the crust as it bakes and helping it to keep its shape.

THE RECIPES

RICE PUDDING TART WITH
   FRESH PEACHES AND PLUMS
APRICOT TART
SUNFLOWER TART
LEMON TART
RUM WALNUT TART
SWAN TART WITH WINTER FRUIT SALAD
FRENCH APPLE TART
STRAWBERRY DEEP DISH PIE
RHUBARB CUSTARD TART
SUMMER TOMATO PIE
PUMPKIN PIE WITH GINGER
ALL-AMERICAN APPLE PIE
ITALIAN PLUM TART (ZWETSCHEGENTORTE
   MIT SAHNE)
BANANA STRAWBERRY TART
PEAR AND CRANBERRY CRUMBLE
PEACH AND BLACKBERRY COBBLER
APPLE-MANGO CHARLOTTE
INDIVIDUAL YOGURT TARTS
CRUSTLESS ALMOND PEAR OR
   ALMOND PEACH TARTLETS

Tarts made with sweet dough

The majority of tarts coming out of my kitchen are made with pâte sucrée. This easy-to-roll dough has the flavor and texture of a good butter cookie. It marries well with most sweet fillings, the exceptions being particularly juicy fruits, which need a stronger and thicker dough like pâte brisée or brioche to soak up the excess liquid.

It is particularly important that you not roll your pâte sucrée too thin. While not fragile, it will not support heavier fillings if it isn't at least ⅛ inch thick. Not only that, but of all the pie and tart doughs I work with, I enjoy the flavor of pâte sucrée the most. It adds great flavor to tarts as long as you don't skimp.

Whether you partially or completely bake the shell before filling it depends on what that filling is. The recipes in this section run the gamut.

For Rice Pudding Tart with Fresh Peaches and Plums, the shell is fully baked. The pudding is completely cooked on top of the stove and would dry out and thicken too much if it spent any time in the oven.

When making Lemon Tart, I partially bake the tart shell to crisp it up and then pour in the lemon custard to bake in the oven. For the Apricot and Sunflower tarts I spread pastry cream across the bottom of unbaked tart shells. In these cases, baking the custard inside the tart shell makes the two elements come together as if they were a single layer. When they are just spread on a prebaked shell, pastry cream and custard fillings taste unfinished to me.

Tart shells that are to be filled with relatively dry fillings needn't be prebaked at all. Rum Walnut Tart has a candylike filling that won't leak any moisture into the crust. The apples in French Apple Tart have been prebaked to remove excess moisture, so there is no need to prebake the shell.

With a partially or wholly prebaked crust, you always know that you've browned the dough sufficiently. With a tart that you fill before baking, it's a little harder to tell if the bottom and sides are fully cooked and crisp. I like to push the bottom of the tart pan up a little bit and away from the sides to take a peek at the outer edges of the shell before I take the tart out of the oven. If the edges are still pale, I know to return it to the oven until golden.

Last but not least, don't neglect to glaze the top of your tart if it is called for in the recipe. A glaze makes a tart visually appealing, but more important, these glazes enhance the flavors of the filling: raspberry jelly for the Rice Pudding Tart with Fresh Peaches and Plums, apricot jam for the Apricot Tart, and honey-walnut topping for the Rum Walnut Tart.

RICE PUDDING TART WITH FRESH PEACHES AND PLUMS

Serves 10

Anyone familiar with French pastry shops knows that the fruit tart reigns supreme where I come from. Usually these tarts are filled with pastry cream. One day, after many years of observing American tastes, it struck me that a beloved American custard, rice pudding, might be substituted for traditional pastry cream with interesting results. Everyone who has tried this tart is delighted by it, and I am especially proud of it since it is the combined product of my European training and my experience in the United States.

1 recipe Pâte Sucrée (page 267), chilled

1 recipe Rice Pudding (page 92), still hot

3 ripe plums, halved, pitted, and cut into 8 wedges each

6 ripe peaches, peeled, pitted, and cut into 8 wedges each

1½ cups Raspberry Jelly Glaze (page 520)

1. Butter the bottom and sides of a 10-inch tart pan with removable bottom. Turn the chilled dough out onto a lightly floured work surface and sprinkle it with a little flour. With a lightly floured rolling pin, roll the dough out to form a 13-inch round about ⅛ inch thick, rotating the dough as you roll it and occasionally sliding a flat metal spatula underneath to make sure that it does not stick to the work surface. Lift the dough by folding it in half over the rolling pin, and gently place it on top of the prepared tart pan. Press the dough firmly against the bottom and sides of the pan; be careful not to stretch the dough, or the tart shell will shrink as it bakes. Trim off all but ½ inch of the dough along the edge of the tart pan. Fold the extra dough into the pan and press it firmly against the sides. Prick the bottom of the tart shell about 12 times with a fork. Place in the refrigerator for at least 30 minutes, or for up to 3 days, to chill completely.
2. Preheat the oven to 400 degrees.

(continued)

3. Cut out a 12 x 12-inch square of parchment paper. Remove the tart shell from the refrigerator and line it with the parchment. Fill the parchment-lined tart shell with pie weights or 3 cups dried beans. Bake for 15 minutes. Then remove the pan from the oven, lift the parchment and beans from the shell, and return the tart pan to the oven. Cook the shell until it is golden brown, another 15 minutes. Let it cool completely on a wire rack.

4. Pour the hot rice pudding into the shell and allow it to cool to room temperature.

5. Arrange the fruit in concentric circles on top of the rice pudding, making one small circle of peach slices in the center, a larger circle around this one with plum slices, and an even larger circle around this one with peach slices.

6. Spoon the glaze over the fruit, refrigerate, and allow it to set, 2 to 3 hours.

7. Remove the tart from the ring, transfer it to a platter, and serve chilled or at room temperature. The tart will keep, refrigerated, for up to 2 days.

APRICOT TART

Serves 10

This summertime tart has a beautiful color and a wonderful balance of sweet and tart flavors. A layer of cake crumbs or genoise, whichever you prefer, absorbs excess moisture and guarantees that the crust stays crisp.

1 recipe Pâte Sucrée (page 267), chilled

2 cups Pastry Cream (page 509), chilled

1 cup cake crumbs, or one ⅟₁₆-inch-thick slice Genoise (page 397)

3 pounds fresh apricots, halved and pitted, or 3 pounds canned apricot halves, drained and patted dry

1 cup apricot jam

1. Butter the bottom and sides of a 10-inch tart pan with removable bottom. Turn the chilled dough out onto a lightly floured work surface and sprinkle it with a little flour. With a lightly floured rolling pin, roll the dough out to form a

13-inch round about ⅛ inch thick, rotating the dough as you roll it and occasionally sliding a flat metal spatula underneath to make sure that it does not stick to the work surface. Lift the dough by folding it in half over the rolling pin, and gently place it on top of the prepared tart pan. Press the dough firmly against the bottom and sides of the pan; be careful not to stretch the dough, or the tart shell will shrink as it bakes. Trim off all but ½ inch of the dough along the edge of the tart pan. Fold the extra dough into the pan and press it firmly against the sides. Prick the bottom of the tart shell about 12 times with a fork. Place the tart shell in the refrigerator for at least 30 minutes, or for up to 2 days, to chill completely.

2. Preheat the oven to 425 degrees. Position the oven rack in the middle of the oven.

3. Spread the Pastry Cream evenly over the bottom of the chilled tart shell. Sprinkle the cake crumbs evenly over the Pastry Cream, or place the Genoise on top of the Pastry Cream. Arrange the apricots upright and very close together, in concentric circles on top of the cake crumbs or Genoise, leaving no gaps between them. Bake until the edges of the pastry are golden brown, about 50 minutes. Cool completely on a wire rack.

4. Heat the apricot jam until boiling. Strain the jam, and then lightly and evenly brush it over the top of the tart. Remove the tart from the ring, transfer it to a platter, and serve. Lightly covered with plastic wrap, Apricot Tart will keep at room temperature for up to 2 days.

SUNFLOWER TART

Serves 10

This dessert, which looks like a giant sunflower, appeals to my inner Van Gogh. Beautiful as it is, it is also simple and fun to make. It's a good family project if your children like to bake.

1 recipe Pâte Sucrée (page 267), chilled

2 cups Pastry Cream (page 509), chilled

2 large ripe mangoes, peeled, flesh removed and cut into long, thin slices

½ cup apricot jam

⅓ cup chocolate sprinkles

1. Butter the bottom and sides of a 10-inch tart pan with removable bottom. Turn the chilled dough out onto a lightly floured work surface and sprinkle it with a little flour. With a lightly floured rolling pin, roll the dough out to form a 13-inch round about ⅛ inch thick, rotating the dough as you roll it and occasionally sliding a flat metal spatula underneath to make sure that it does not stick to the work surface. Lift the dough by folding it in half over the rolling pin, and gently place it on top of the prepared tart pan. Press the dough firmly against the bottom and sides of the pan; be careful not to stretch the dough, or the tart shell will shrink as it bakes. Trim off all but ½ inch of the dough along the edge of the tart pan. Fold the extra dough into the pan and press it firmly against the sides. Prick the bottom of the tart shell about 12 times with a fork. Place it in the refrigerator for at least 30 minutes, or for up to 2 days, to chill completely.

2. Preheat the oven to 425 degrees.

3. Spread the Pastry Cream evenly over the bottom of the chilled tart shell. Bake until the edges of the dough are golden brown, about 30 minutes. Remove the tart from the oven and let it cool slightly on a wire rack. While the tart is still slightly warm, peel away and discard the skin that has formed on top of the Pastry Cream. Allow it to cool completely.

4. Place a 3-inch round biscuit cutter in the center of the Pastry Cream. Arrange the mango slices on top of the Pastry Cream, placing one tip of the slice at the

edge of the cutter so that the other tip extends to the edge of the tart. Make several layers around the cutter so that the mango slices look like sunflower petals.

5. Bring the apricot jam to a boil in a small saucepan. Strain the jam, and then brush it lightly and evenly over the mango slices.

6. Scatter the chocolate sprinkles in an even layer inside the biscuit cutter, and carefully remove the cutter. Remove the tart from the ring, transfer it to a platter, and serve. Sunflower Tart will keep for 8 hours under a cake dome at room temperature.

LEMON TART

Serves 10

This is a wonderful dessert that can be served at any time and for any occasion. I like to top the tart with fresh raspberries and a dusting of confectioners' sugar just before serving. The filling for this tart is quite liquidy, so if the prebaked shell develops cracks, patch them with leftover dough before pouring in the lemon mixture. Otherwise, the mixture will leak through and make your crust soggy.

1 recipe Pâte Sucrée (page 267), chilled

¾ cup plus 2 tablespoons sugar

4 large eggs

2 large egg yolks

8 tablespoons (1 stick) unsalted butter, melted and cooled

3 seedless lemons, peeled and cut into 1-inch chunks

1 navel orange, peeled and cut into 1-inch chunks

½ cup heavy cream

Pinch salt

Fresh raspberries for garnish (optional)

Confectioners' sugar for garnish (optional)

1. Butter the bottom and sides of a 10-inch tart pan with removable bottom. Turn the chilled dough out onto a lightly floured work surface and sprinkle it with a little flour. With a lightly floured rolling pin, roll the dough out to form a 13-inch round about ⅛ inch thick, rotating the dough as you roll it and occasionally sliding a flat metal spatula underneath to make sure that it does not stick to the work surface. Lift the dough by folding it in half over the rolling pin, and gently place it on top of the prepared tart pan. Press the dough firmly against the bottom and sides of the pan; be careful not to stretch the dough, or your tart shell will shrink as it bakes. Trim off all but ½ inch of the dough along the edge of the pan (save the trimmings in case you need them for patching). Fold the extra dough into the pan and press it firmly against the sides. Prick the bottom of the tart shell about 12 times with a fork. Place the tart shell in the refrigerator for at least 30 minutes, or for up to 3 days, to chill completely.

2. Preheat the oven to 400 degrees.

3. Cut out a 12-inch square of parchment paper. Remove the tart shell from the refrigerator and line it with the parchment. Fill the parchment-lined tart shell

with pie weights or 3 cups dried beans. Bake for 15 minutes. Then remove the pan from the oven, lift the parchment and beans from the shell, and return the tart pan to the oven. Cook the shell until it is just beginning to turn golden, another 10 minutes. Remove the pan from the oven and patch any cracks on the bottom of the shell with leftover Pâte Sucrée.

4. While the tart shell is baking, make the filling: Combine the sugar, eggs, egg yolks, butter, lemons, orange, heavy cream, and salt in a large blender and blend until smooth. Press the mixture through a fine-mesh strainer into a bowl or measuring cup.

5. Turn the oven heat down to 350 degrees. Pour the lemon mixture into the warm tart shell and return it to the oven. Bake until just set, about 1 hour. Cool completely on a wire rack.

6. Remove the tart from the ring, transfer it to a platter, and serve at room temperature, topped with raspberries and confectioners' sugar if desired. The tart may be refrigerated, uncovered, for up to 1 day before serving; or wrap it in plastic wrap and freeze it for up to 1 month before unmolding it from the pan.

RUM WALNUT TART

Serves 10

I serve this love-warming dessert in winter, with either ice cream or a glass of Port wine.

1 recipe Pâte Sucrée (page 267), chilled

Pinch salt

½ cup seedless raspberry jam

FOR THE RUM WALNUT FILLING:

1¾ cups walnut halves

¾ cup sugar

12 tablespoons (1½ sticks) unsalted butter, softened

3 large eggs

3 tablespoons all-purpose flour

1 tablespoon pure vanilla extract

1 teaspoon grated lemon zest

⅓ cup dark rum

FOR THE HONEY-WALNUT TOPPING:

3 cups walnut halves

12 tablespoons (1½ sticks) unsalted butter

¼ cup honey

⅓ cup heavy cream

1 tablespoon pure vanilla extract

Pinch salt

1. Butter the bottom and sides of a 10-inch tart pan with removable bottom. Turn the chilled dough out onto a lightly floured work surface and sprinkle it with a little flour. With a lightly floured rolling pin, roll the dough out to form a 13-inch round about ⅛ inch thick, rotating the dough as you roll it and occasionally sliding a flat metal spatula underneath to make sure that it does not stick to the work surface. Lift the dough by folding it in half over the rolling pin, and gently place it on top of the prepared tart pan. Press the dough firmly against the bottom and sides of the pan; be careful not to stretch the dough, or your tart shell will shrink as it bakes. Trim off all but ½ inch of the dough along the edge of the tart pan. Fold the extra dough into the pan and press it firmly against the sides. Prick the bottom of the tart shell about 12 times with a fork. Place the tart shell in the refrigerator for at least 30 minutes, or cover with plastic wrap and refrigerate for up to 2 days, to chill completely.

2. For the filling: Combine the walnuts and sugar in the bowl of a food processor and process until finely ground. Place the butter in the bowl of an electric mixer fitted with the paddle attachment, and cream until fluffy. Add the walnut mix-

ture and mix until well blended. Add the eggs, one at a time, and beat until smooth. Add the flour, vanilla, lemon zest, rum, and salt, and mix well.

3. Preheat the oven to 375 degrees.

4. Spread the raspberry jam evenly over the bottom of the chilled tart shell. Spread the walnut filling evenly on top of the jam. Bake the tart until golden brown, about 45 minutes. Remove the tart from the oven and allow it to cool completely on a wire rack.

5. For the topping: Arrange the walnut halves in concentric circles on top of the cooled tart. Combine the butter, honey, heavy cream, vanilla, and salt in a small saucepan and cook over medium heat until the mixture reaches the soft ball stage (240 degrees on a candy thermometer), about 8 minutes. Drizzle the caramel over the walnuts and let cool.

6. Remove the tart from the ring, transfer it to a platter, and serve. Rum Walnut Tart will keep at room temperature, under a cake dome, for 2 to 3 days.

SWAN TART WITH WINTER FRUIT SALAD

Serves 8

In the winter, I rely on dried fruit to add flavor to fresh fruit salad. Here is a wonderful way to present such a fruit salad—arranged in a beautiful tart shell made from Pâte Sucrée and embellished with swans whose necks are piped from choux paste. If you want to save time, skip the swans and simply decorate the top of each wedge with the date halves.

1 recipe Pâte Sucrée (page 267), chilled
1 recipe Pâte à Choux (page 275)
2 cups Fresh Fruit Salad made with apples, pears, oranges, and kiwis (page 24)
¼ cup chopped walnuts
¼ cup chopped dried figs
¼ cup chopped dried dates, plus 8 beautiful whole dried dates
¼ cup chopped dried prunes
¼ cup dried cherries
¼ cup dried blueberries
2 cups Pastry Cream (page 509)
1 cup apricot jam
Confectioners' sugar

1. Lightly butter a baking sheet. Turn the chilled dough out onto a lightly floured work surface and sprinkle it with a little flour. With a lightly floured rolling pin, roll the dough out to form an 11-inch round about ¼ inch thick, rotating the dough as you roll it and occasionally sliding a flat metal spatula underneath to make sure that it does not stick to the work surface. Using a cake pan or cardboard cake circle as your guide, trim the dough to a 10-inch round. Lift the dough by folding it in half over the rolling pin, and place it on the prepared baking sheet. Use a pizza wheel or the dull edge of the paring knife to mark the dough, without cutting completely through it, into 8 equal wedges. Prick the dough about 12 times with a fork. Cover it lightly with plastic wrap and place the baking sheet in the refrigerator for at least 30 minutes, or for up to 2 days, to chill the dough completely.

2. Preheat the oven to 400 degrees. Place the choux paste in a pastry bag fitted with a #5 plain tip. Pipe the choux paste along the lines traced on the Pâte Sucrée round, beginning at the center and going down one side of a wedge and around the edge. Repeat until the wedges are all outlined with choux paste. Bake until the pastry is golden and the choux paste is puffed and dry to the touch, about

25 to 30 minutes. Remove the pan from the oven and set it aside. Lower the heat to 375 degrees.

3. While the tart shell is baking, make the swan heads: Line a baking sheet with parchment paper. Using a #1 plain tip, pipe ten swan necks on the sheet (it's a good idea to make a couple extra) by making 5-inch-long S-shapes. To make the heads of the swans, pipe a small teardrop shape at the top of each S, pulling toward you with the pastry bag as you finish to make a point for the beak.

4. Bake the swan heads until golden brown and dry, about 8 minutes.

5. At least 1 hour and up to 4 hours before serving, place the fruit salad in a large bowl. Stir in the walnuts, figs, chopped dates, prunes, cherries, and blueberries one ingredient at a time, mixing well after each addition. Once the salad is well mixed, place it in a colander over the sink and stir several times to drain off the excess liquid. Spoon ¼ cup of the Pastry Cream into each wedge of the tart, and smooth it with a spatula. Top each portion of pastry cream with fruit salad. Refrigerate for up to 4 hours before serving.

6. Just before serving, place a swan neck in the middle of each wedge, beak facing out. Place the jam in a small saucepan and bring it to a boil.

(continued)

With a #5 plain tip, pipe the choux paste along the lines traced with the pizza wheel, beginning at the center and going down one side of a wedge and around the edge.

For the necks of the swans, use a #1 plain tip to pipe 5-inch-long S-shapes. To make the heads of the swans, pipe a small teardrop shape at the top of each S, pulling toward you with the pastry bag as you finish to make a point for the beak.

Strain the hot jam, and then lightly brush it over the fruit salad. Place 2 date halves on either side of each swan neck, cut side down. Dust with confectioners' sugar, and serve immediately.

NOTE: The tart shell can be baked ahead of time (through Step 2), cooled thoroughly, and then wrapped in plastic wrap and frozen for up to 2 weeks.

FRENCH APPLE TART

Serves 10

A simple filling of prebaked apples delivers pure apple flavor. Baking the apples ahead of time ensures that your filling will not be watery and your pastry will be crisp. Serve this with Vanilla Ice Cream (page 185).

1 recipe Pâte Sucrée (page 267), chilled

Prebaked Apple Chunks (page 27) made with 8 apples, cooled

Prebaked Apple Slices (page 28) made with 4 apples, cooled

1 cup apricot jam

1. Butter the bottom and sides of a 10-inch tart pan with removable bottom. Turn the chilled dough out onto a lightly floured work surface and sprinkle it with a little flour. With a lightly floured rolling pin, roll the dough out to form a 13-inch round about ⅛ inch thick, rotating the dough as you roll it and occasionally sliding a flat metal spatula underneath to make sure that it does not stick to the work surface. Lift the dough by folding it in half over the rolling pin, and gently place it on top of the prepared tart pan. Press the dough firmly against the bottom and sides of the pan; be careful not to stretch the dough, or the tart shell will shrink as it bakes. Trim off all but ½ inch of the dough along the edge of the tart pan. Fold the extra dough into the pan and press it firmly against the sides. Prick the bottom of the tart shell about 12 times with a fork. Lightly cover the tart shell with plastic wrap and place it in the refrigerator for at least 30 minutes, or for up to 2 days, to chill completely.

2. Preheat the oven to 400 degrees. Remove the tart shell from the refrigerator and spread the cooled apple chunks evenly across the bottom of the shell. Arrange the apple slices decoratively on top of the apple chunks. Bake for 35 minutes. Remove the tart from the oven and carefully push the bottom of the pan up a little bit to check on the bottom crust; it should be golden. If the bottom crust is pale, continue to bake until it is sufficiently colored, another 10 to 15 minutes. Remove the tart from the oven and allow it to cool for 30 minutes on a wire rack.

3. Place the apricot jam in a small saucepan and bring to a boil; strain. Lightly and evenly brush the top of the tart with the hot jam. Remove the tart from the ring, transfer it to a serving platter, and serve. French Apple Tart will keep, under a cake saver, at room temperature for up to 2 days.

EEP DISH PIES

When you reverse the positions of pie filling and crust, you get a deep dish pie: Fruit is spread across the bottom of a baking dish and then topped with a sheet of pâte sucrée. It is a homey rather than an elegant presentation, great for casual occasions when you don't want to spend a lot of time constructing a pie shell.

Pâte sucrée, with its delicate texture and buttery flavor, is my choice for the top crust. Because it sits on top of the fruit in a deep dish pie, it becomes beautifully caramelized and crisp. I almost enjoy it more as a pie covering than as a pie shell.

The fruit in deep dish pies isn't protected from the heat of the oven by a pastry crust bottom, so I bake my deep dish pies in a water bath. This ensures that the fruit won't overcook while the pastry topping crisps up.

STRAWBERRY DEEP DISH PIE

Serves 8

This is the deep dish pie I make every year when local strawberries arrive at the farmers' market. Serve it warm with Sweetened Whipped Cream or crème fraîche. If you like, substitute 2 tablespoons Vanilla Sugar (page 502) for the 3 tablespoons regular sugar in Step 3.

3 pints fresh strawberries, washed, dried, stemmed, and halved
4 tablespoons unsalted butter, cut into small pieces
¾ cup plus 1 tablespoon sugar
1 recipe Pâte Sucrée (page 267)

1 large egg
1 tablespoon whole or 2 percent milk
Sweetened Whipped Cream (page 521) or crème fraîche for serving

1. Preheat the oven to 400 degrees. Place the strawberries in an oval ceramic baking dish measuring 10 x 6 inches. Dot with the butter, and sprinkle with ½ cup plus 2 tablespoons of the sugar.

2. Turn the chilled dough out onto a lightly floured work surface and sprinkle it with a little flour. With a lightly floured rolling pin, roll the dough out to form an oval measuring about 13 x 9 inches and about ⅓ inch thick, rotating the dough as you roll it and occasionally sliding a flat metal spatula underneath to make sure that it does not stick to the work surface.

3. Lightly beat the egg and milk together in a small bowl. Brush the edge of the baking dish with this egg wash. Lift the dough by folding it in half over the rolling pin, and gently place it on top of the baking dish (it will be resting on the strawberries), letting the excess dough hang over the edge. Trim the dough so that it overhangs the dish by ½ inch all the way around. Brush the dough with the egg wash and sprinkle with the remaining 3 tablespoons sugar.

4. Line a rimmed baking sheet with brown paper. Place the baking dish on the paper. Place the pan on the oven rack and carefully pour ½ inch of hot tap water into the pan. Bake until the dough is crisp and golden, about 45 minutes. Cool slightly and serve warm; or let stand at room temperature for up to 1 day and reheat for 15 minutes in a 325-degree oven. Serve with whipped cream or crème fraîche.

TARTS MADE WITH PÂTE BRISÉE

Once it is filled and baked, Pâte Brisée will stay crisp much longer than Pâte Sucrée. It is the only choice when making a tart or pie that may give off a lot of water during and after baking. Because it is unsweetened, pâte brisée is also the dough to use for savory pies and tarts such as quiche Lorraine and the Summer Tomato Pie on page 357.

I like the way the filling ingredients and the shell bake up together as one. The bottom crust stays crisp, but the dough itself bakes right into the filling so that it's difficult to say where the crust ends and the filling begins.

RHUBARB CUSTARD TART

Serves 10

I particularly like the tart flavor of rhubarb. It marries well with sweet, creamy custard. Rhubarb can give off a lot of juice and the custard needs a sturdy container, so I use pâte brisée for the shell.

½ recipe Pâte Brisée (page 268), chilled
1¼ cups sugar
2½ tablespoons all-purpose flour
4 large eggs
2 large egg yolks
1 teaspoon pure vanilla extract

¼ teaspoon freshly grated nutmeg
Pinch salt
4 cups cut-up peeled rhubarb (1-inch cubes)
¼ cup Vanilla Sugar (page 502) or Cinnamon Sugar (page 502)

1. Butter the bottom and sides of a 10-inch tart pan with removable bottom. Turn the chilled dough out onto a lightly floured work surface and sprinkle it with a little flour. With a lightly floured rolling pin, roll the dough out to form a 13-inch round about ⅛ inch thick, rotating the dough as you roll it and occasionally sliding a flat metal spatula underneath to make sure that it does not

(continued)

stick to the work surface. Lift the dough by folding it in half over the rolling pin, and gently place it in the prepared tart pan. Press the dough firmly against the bottom and sides of the pan; be careful not to stretch the dough, or the tart shell will shrink as it bakes. Trim off all but ½ inch of the dough along the edge of the tart pan. Fold the extra dough into the pan and press it firmly against the sides. Prick the bottom of the tart shell about 12 times with a fork. Place the pan in the refrigerator for at least 30 minutes, or for up to 2 days, to chill completely.

2. Preheat the oven to 375 degrees.

3. Combine the sugar, flour, eggs, egg yolks, vanilla, nutmeg, and salt in a medium bowl and whisk until smooth. Remove the tart shell from the refrigerator and arrange the rhubarb cubes evenly over the bottom of the chilled tart shell. Pour the egg mixture over the rhubarb. Bake until the custard is set around the edges but still jiggly in the center, 50 to 60 minutes. Remove the tart from the oven and place it on a wire rack to cool a bit. Sprinkle with the Vanilla Sugar or Cinnamon Sugar while still warm. Serve warm, or refrigerate for up to 1 day and serve chilled.

SUMMER TOMATO PIE

Serves 8

This is obviously not a dessert recipe, but it is one of my favorite ways to use Pâte Brisée. I make it at home using tomatoes from my garden. The combination of very juicy tomatoes, custard, and cheese could result in a terribly soggy pie crust. But I guarantee that my Pâte Brisée will hold this filling very well, staying crisp for 2 days in the refrigerator. In fact, the pie tastes even better after this amount of time, because the flavors of the filling have been allowed to develop. Bruise the basil leaves by twisting them between your fingers to release their fragrance.

½ recipe Pâte Brisée (page 268),
   chilled
1½ cups plain fresh bread crumbs
1 tablespoon finely chopped garlic
3 tablespoons finely chopped parsley
4 ripe medium-size beefsteak
   tomatoes, peeled, cored, and cut
   into ¾-inch-thick slices

6 large egg yolks
1 large egg
2 cups heavy cream
Pinch ground nutmeg
Salt
Pepper
6 large basil leaves, bruised
2 cups shredded Gruyère cheese

1. Butter the bottom and sides of a 9-inch pie pan. Turn the chilled dough out onto a lightly floured work surface and sprinkle it with a little flour. With a lightly floured rolling pin, roll the dough out to form a 13-inch round about ⅛ inch thick, rotating the dough as you roll it and occasionally sliding a flat metal spatula underneath to make sure that it does not stick to the work surface. Lift the dough by folding it in half over the rolling pin, and gently place it on top of the prepared pie pan. Press the dough firmly against the bottom and sides of the pan; be careful not to stretch the dough, or the pie shell will shrink as it bakes. Trim off all but 1 inch of the dough along the edge of the pie pan. Fold the extra dough into the pan and press it firmly against the sides so that it extends a half inch or so upward from the edge of the pan. Prick the bottom of the pie shell about 12 times with a fork. Place the pie shell in the refrigerator for at least 30 minutes, or for up to 2 days, to chill completely.

2. Preheat the oven to 375 degrees.

(continued)

3. Cut out a 12 x 12-inch square of parchment paper. Remove the pie shell from the refrigerator and line it with the parchment. Fill the parchment-lined pie shell with pie weights or 3 cups dried beans. Bake for 15 minutes. Remove the pie pan from the oven, lift the parchment and beans from the shell, and return the pan to the oven. Bake the shell until it just begins to turn golden, another 15 minutes. Remove the pie shell from the oven and turn the heat up to 400.

4. Stir the bread crumbs, garlic, and parsley together in a medium bowl. Spread the mixture evenly across the bottom of the still-hot pie shell. Arrange the tomato slices so that they are overlapping in concentric rings. Bake for 20 minutes.

5. While the tart is baking, make the custard: In a mixing bowl, whisk together the egg yolks, egg, heavy cream, nutmeg, and salt and pepper to taste.

6. Remove the pie from the oven and place the bruised basil leaves on top of the tomatoes. Sprinkle the cheese over the tomatoes, and pour the custard mixture on top of the cheese. Return the pan to the oven and bake until the custard is just set, 20 to 25 minutes. Let cool slightly and serve warm; or let cool completely, refrigerate for up to 2 days, and reheat in a 325-degree oven for 15 minutes before serving.

ALL-AMERICAN PIES

European pastry chefs are somewhat shocked to hear that I regularly make pie dough with vegetable shortening instead of butter. They just don't have the experience that I do with American tastes and expectations. Above all, when people in this country think of pie, they think of flaky crust. And butter does not make a flaky crust. Only vegetable shortening will do that.

It is true that you sacrifice flavor when you pass on the butter. So when I come up with fillings for All-American pies, I make sure that they are sufficiently rich-tasting. Pumpkin Pie with Ginger has a good dose of heavy cream. The apples for the filling of All-American Apple Pie are prebaked with a generous amount of butter. No one leaves the table feeling deprived.

So if you want to have it both ways, flaky crust *and* rich flavor, just make sure to match an All-American Pie Dough crust with a filling that doesn't skimp on butterfat.

PUMPKIN PIE WITH GINGER

Serves 8

The Thanksgiving menu at the White House varies from administration to administration, but the dessert is always the same. This pumpkin pie has been a presidential favorite for twenty-five years, so don't be surprised if it becomes a family tradition in your own home. This crust can get sticky while prebaking, so grease the parchment to avoid tearing the shell when removing the beans.

1 disk (½ recipe) All-American Pie
    Dough (page 269), chilled
2 large eggs
3 large egg yolks
1 teaspoon vanilla
½ cup sugar
¼ teaspoon salt
¾ teaspoon ground cinnamon

⅓ teaspoon ground ginger
Pinch ground cloves
2 cups heavy cream
1½ cups plain canned pumpkin
    puree
1½ tablespoons confectioners' sugar
2 tablespoons finely chopped
    crystallized ginger

1. Preheat the oven to 375 degrees. Butter the bottom and sides of a 9-inch pie pan. Turn the chilled dough out on a lightly floured surface and sprinkle it with a little flour. With a lightly floured rolling pin, roll the dough out to form a 13-inch round about ⅛ inch thick, rotating the dough as you roll it and occasionally sliding a flat metal spatula underneath to make sure that it does not stick to the work surface. Lift the dough by folding it in half over the rolling pin, and gently place it on top of the prepared pie pan. Press the dough firmly against the bottom and sides of the pan; be careful not to stretch the dough, or the tart shell will shrink as it bakes. Trim the crust at the edge of the pan (it will later be covered with whipped cream).

2. Prick the bottom and sides of the crust with a fork. Cut out a 12 x 12-inch square of parchment paper. Crumple the parchment; then open it up and grease one side of the paper with vegetable shortening. Place the greased side down on the crust, and add pie weights or dried beans to fill the bottom and a little up the sides.

3. Bake for 15 minutes. Remove the pie pan from the oven and carefully lift out the paper and beans. If the crust tears, patch it by pressing it together with your

fingers. Bake the crust for another 10 minutes, until it is brown, and then remove it from the oven. It is not necessary to wait for the crust to cool before filling it.

4. In a large mixing bowl, beat the eggs, egg yolks, and vanilla together lightly. Stir in the sugar, salt, cinnamon, ginger, cloves, and 1 cup of the heavy cream until thoroughly blended. Stir in the pumpkin. Pour into the prebaked pie shell.

5. Bake until a toothpick inserted in the center comes out clean, about 1 hour. Do not jiggle the pie while it is baking. Allow the pie to cool on a wire rack, then refrigerate it, uncovered, for up to 3 days.

6. When you are ready to serve the pie, whip the remaining 1 cup heavy cream with the confectioners' sugar in an electric mixer until it holds stiff peaks. Pipe the whipped cream around the edge of the pie, and decorate it with the candied ginger.

ALL-AMERICAN APPLE PIE

Serves 8

The melted butter brushed on the top crust of this pie gives it a buttery flavor even though the crust itself is made with vegetable shortening. Since this pie crust is not pre-baked, I like to use a clear Pyrex pan so that I can see if the bottom is well browned before taking it out of the oven.

1 recipe All-American Pie Dough
(page 269), chilled
1 recipe Prebaked Apple Chunks
(page 27), made with 8 apples

½ cup golden raisins
3 tablespoons unsalted butter, melted
and cooled
¼ cup Cinnamon Sugar (page 502)

1. Preheat the oven to 375 degrees. Butter the bottom and sides of a 9-inch pie pan. Turn 1 dough disk out on a lightly floured surface and sprinkle it lightly with flour. With a lightly floured rolling pin, roll the dough out to form a 14-inch round about ⅛ inch thick, rotating the dough as you roll it and occasionally sliding a flat metal spatula underneath to make sure that it does not stick to the work surface. Lift the dough by folding it in half over the rolling pin, and gently place it on top of the prepared pie pan. Press the dough firmly against the bottom and sides of the pan; be careful not to stretch the dough, or the pie shell will shrink as it bakes. Let the extra dough hang over the edges of the pan.

2. Arrange the apple chunks in an even layer across the bottom of the dough. Sprinkle the raisins over the apple chunks.

3. Roll the other half of the dough out to form a 12-inch round. Place it on top of the apples.

4. Trim the bottom and top crusts so they extend ½ inch beyond the edge of the pan. Fold the ½ inch of dough over on itself all around, so that it forms a thick edge flush with the edge of the pan. Crimp the thick edge with your fingers, or press it together with the tines of a fork to seal it. Cut a 1½-inch-long X in the top crust.

5. Brush the top crust and the edges with the melted butter, and sprinkle with the Cinnamon Sugar. Bake until well browned, 50 minutes to 1 hour.

Tarts Made with Brioche Dough

Tarts made with brioche dough are quite different from tarts made with pâte sucrée or pâte brisée. The dough is a much more prominent part of the dessert, rising up and surrounding the fruit rather than staying put at the bottom of the pan. In fact, these desserts are more like coffee cakes than tarts. I often serve brioche-based tarts for breakfast, brunch, or tea. For other examples of this very different but delicious tart, see Brioche and Crème (page 296).

Italian Plum Tart (Zwetschegentorte mit Sahne)

Serves 10

Italian plums, the small, purple oval-shaped variety available in late August and September, are better for baking than for eating out of hand. Here I remove the pits and quarter the fruit, leaving the quarters attached at one end so that each plum looks like a lovely purple flower. Then I arrange the plums on top of brioche dough, bake it, and brush the baked tart with butter and Cinnamon Sugar. This simple combination makes an extraordinary tart, wonderful for dessert but also perfect at brunch or teatime. The tart freezes well wrapped in plastic wrap, for up to 1 month. Slice it into wedges while it is still partially frozen and reheat the slices in a 350-degree oven until warmed through before serving.

14 ounces Brioche Dough (page 293), chilled
3 to 4 pounds Italian plums
4 tablespoons unsalted butter, melted
¾ cup Cinnamon Sugar (page 502)
Sweetened Whipped Cream (page 521, optional)

1. Butter the bottom and sides of a 10-inch tart pan with removable bottom. Turn the chilled dough out onto a lightly floured work surface and sprinkle it with a little flour. With a lightly floured rolling pin, roll the dough to form a 12-inch

(continued)

round about ¼ inch thick, rotating the dough as you roll it and occasionally sliding a flat metal spatula underneath to make sure that it does not stick to the work surface. Lift the dough by folding it in half over the rolling pin, and gently place it on top of the prepared tart pan. Press the dough firmly against the bottom and sides of the pan. Let the excess dough hang over the sides of the ring.

2. Use a sharp paring knife to cut each plum open almost all the way around from top to bottom on both sides, leaving one end intact so that the two halves are still attached. Remove the pit. Cut each half almost in half again, leaving the four quarters of the plum attached to each other. Arrange as many plums as will fit, very tightly, standing up with the quarters opened a bit, on the brioche dough in concentric circles. Drape the tart loosely with plastic wrap and let it stand at room temperature until the dough has doubled in size, about 2 hours.

3. Preheat the oven to 375 degrees. Bake the tart until the dough is golden brown and the plums are soft, about 1 hour. Remove the tart from the oven and place it on a wire rack. Brush it with the melted butter and sprinkle with the Cinnamon Sugar. Let it cool completely.

4. Before removing the tart from the ring, trim the excess dough from the edge of the ring with a sharp paring knife. Serve at room temperature, with Sweetened Whipped Cream if desired. Italian Plum Tart is best served the day it is baked. Wrapped in plastic wrap, it can be frozen for up to 2 weeks; defrost the tart on the counter and then reheat it for 10 minutes in a 325-degree oven.

$\mathcal{T}$ARTS MADE WITH PUFF PASTRY

Because it is so light and delicate, puff pastry cannot support very heavy fillings. But it makes a wonderful container for extra-light fillings such as mousse or Bavarian cream.

The following recipe is an example of my favorite way to use puff pastry as a tart base. I roll the dough to ¼-inch thickness and then cut it into the shape of a strawberry, or any other shape that strikes my imagination. About ½ inch from the edge of the dough, I use a sharp paring knife to make a shallow cut all the way around. When the dough is baked, I am able to lift off the top of the dough and scrape away the insides of the puffed shape. I now have a container and lid for any filling I choose.

BANANA STRAWBERRY TART

Serves 8

Puff pastry, cut to resemble a large strawberry, becomes a container for a luscious banana mousse topped with strawberries in this beautiful tart. It takes a little work to cut the puff pastry, but you will feel well compensated with the stunning result. Not only is this dessert beautiful but it is also delicious, the crisp and flaky pastry contrasting with the creamy banana mousse and the juicy strawberries.

1 pound Puff Pastry (page 278), chilled
1 large egg
1 tablespoon whole or 2 percent milk
2 tablespoons confectioners' sugar

½ recipe Banana Bavarian (page 138)
1 cup red currant jelly
2 pints fresh strawberries, washed, stemmed, and halved

1. Lightly butter a baking sheet. Turn the chilled puff pastry out onto a lightly floured work surface and sprinkle it with a little flour. With a lightly floured rolling pin, roll the pastry out to form an 11 x 9-inch rectangle about ¼ inch thick, rotating the dough as you roll it and occasionally sliding a flat metal spatula underneath to make sure it does not stick to the work surface. Transfer the dough to the prepared baking sheet and place it in the freezer for 15 minutes.

2. Draw a strawberry about 10 inches long and 8 inches wide, with a 3 x 1-inch stem and two 2 x 3-inch leaves, on a piece of cardboard. Place the cutout on top of the chilled puff pastry and use it as a template to cut the dough into the shape of the strawberry, using a sharp paring knife. Set aside the excess pastry for another use. Place the strawberry-shaped puff pastry back in the freezer for another 15 minutes.

3. Using a sharp paring knife, make a ¹⁄₁₆-inch-deep cut about ½ inch in from the edge all the way around the strawberry. Do not cut all the way through the dough. (This cut will allow you to remove the top from the baked pastry to form the container for the Bavarian.)

4. Combine the egg and milk in a small bowl, and brush this egg wash very lightly over the dough, avoiding the cut and the outside ½ inch around the edge.

(continued)

(Brushing egg on the cut would prevent the dough from rising and separating properly in the oven.) Brush the egg wash over the leaves and stem as well.

5. Using sharp scissors, make small cuts at ½-inch intervals all over the inner portion of the strawberry. (These small cuts will open up during baking to resemble strawberry seeds.) With a paring knife, make a cut down the center of each leaf and make smaller V-shaped cuts extending from these center cuts. (These cuts will look like the veins of leaves.) Place the pastry in the refrigerator for 30 minutes.

After you have egg-washed the center of the strawberry and the leaves and stem, use sharp scissors to make small cuts at ½-inch intervals all over the inner portion of the strawberry.

6. Preheat the oven to 400 degrees. Bake the pastry for 25 minutes. Turn the heat down to 375 degrees and bake for another 10 minutes. Then raise the heat to 450 degrees, dust the pastry with the confectioners' sugar, and bake until the sugar melts, 2 to 3 minutes. Watch the pastry carefully, because the sugar will begin to burn as soon as it is melted.

7. Remove the pastry from the oven and let it cool on a wire rack for 5 minutes. Then carefully remove the cut-out top of the strawberry, releasing it from the sides with a sharp paring knife and lifting it away from the bottom with a small offset spatula. Scrape out the wet, unbaked puff pastry from the center of the container. Let the container cool completely.

8. Place the bottom of the puff pastry strawberry on a serving platter. Fill the container with the Banana Bavarian and smooth it with a spatula. The layer of Bavarian should be about 1 inch thick. Place it in the refrigerator for 15 minutes to set.

9. Push the red currant jelly through a fine-mesh sieve. Brush the top of the puff pastry container with 3 tablespoons of the jelly. Combine the remaining 13 tablespoons jelly and the strawberries in a bowl and toss gently to coat. Arrange the strawberries on top of the Bavarian. Place the top of the container on top of the strawberries, at a slight angle so that the filling is visible. Serve immediately, or refrigerate for up to 4 hours before serving.

CRUMBLES, COBBLERS, AND CHARLOTTES

Crumbles, cobblers, and charlottes have the fruity fillings of our favorite pies and tarts, but instead of time-consuming pastry doughs, they are topped with bread crumbs, biscuit batter, or toasted white bread. The recipes are simple but the results are very satisfying.

While most pastry recipes require strict adherence to the ingredients lists, there is room for improvisation and substitution with these very casual desserts. Once you have made a Pear and Cranberry Crumble, there is no reason why you couldn't make a Peach and Blackberry Crumble. You can fill your cobbler with any fresh fruit that's in season and appealing.

PEAR AND CRANBERRY CRUMBLE

Serves 8

In this simple, traditional American dessert with autumn flavors, the pears are not pre-cooked, so it is imperative to use ripe, flavorful fruit. Cake or bread crumbs spread across the bottom of the dish absorb the extra fruit juices and prevent the crumble from becoming watery. If you like nuts in your topping, use only 1 cup flour and add ½ cup chopped nuts.

FOR THE TOPPING:
1½ cups all-purpose flour
½ cup plus 2 tablespoons sugar
1 teaspoon ground cinnamon
1 teaspoon grated lemon zest
Pinch salt
1½ teaspoons baking powder
10 tablespoons unsalted butter, melted

FOR THE FRUIT:
2 tablespoons cornstarch
½ cup plus 1 tablespoon water
1 pound fresh or frozen cranberries, picked over and washed
1½ cups sugar
1 teaspoon grated lemon zest
4 ripe pears
¼ cup fresh lemon juice
1 cup cake crumbs or plain fresh bread crumbs

Vanilla Ice Cream (page 185) or Sweetened Whipped Cream (page 521, optional)

1. Make the topping: Combine the flour, sugar, cinnamon, lemon zest, salt, baking powder, and melted butter in a large bowl and mix well. Cover the bowl with plastic wrap and refrigerate for 30 minutes.

2. Prepare the fruit: Place the cornstarch in a small bowl and stir in the 1 table-spoon water to dissolve. Place the cranberries and the remaining ½ cup water in a medium saucepan and cook over medium-high heat, stirring occasionally, until they begin to pop, about 6 minutes. Stir in the cornstarch mixture and

bring to a boil. Cook for 1 minute. Remove the pan from the heat and stir in the sugar and lemon zest. Set aside.

3. Preheat the oven to 375 degrees. Peel and core the pears, and cut them into ¼-inch-thick slices. Place them in a bowl and sprinkle them with the lemon juice.

4. Sprinkle the cake crumbs on the bottom of a 1½-quart soufflé dish. Spoon half of the cranberry mixture into the dish, and then half of the pear slices. Repeat with the remaining cranberry mixture and pear slices.

5. Crumble the chilled topping over the pears and bake until the topping is golden brown and the fruit is bubbling around the edges, about 30 minutes. Let cool slightly and serve warm, with ice cream or whipped cream if desired.

PEACH AND BLACKBERRY COBBLER

Serves 10

Cobbler is a simple dessert—just fruit filling with a pastry crust topping. But it can still be remarkable if made with care. I like to thicken the berries on top of the stove and spread them over uncooked peaches. I use frozen berries because as they thaw they release a lot of juice, which you need to moisten the filling. I take the extra step of baking the crust separately before placing it on top of the fruit, and then I just warm the assembled cobbler in the oven. This way the peaches are softened up but don't become mushy, and the crust stays nice and crisp because it's already been baked.

The filling can be made and the topping baked up to 8 hours before serving time. Keep them separate until you are ready for dessert. Then simply place the topping on top of the filling, bake, and serve warm.

Leftover dough can be rolled and cut into biscuits or scones.

FOR THE FILLING:
5 ripe peaches
1 tablespoon fresh lemon juice
1 cup cake or fresh bread crumbs
2 recipes Blackberry Sauce (page 176)

FOR THE CRUST:
1 recipe Cobbler Dough (page 263)
3 tablespoons unsalted butter, melted
¼ cup Cinnamon Sugar (page 502)

Sweetened Whipped Cream
(page 521), crème fraîche, or
Vanilla Ice Cream (page 185)
for serving

1. Preheat the oven to 375 degrees.
2. Peel, pit, and slice the peaches. Place them in a shallow bowl and toss with the lemon juice.
3. Sprinkle the cake crumbs over the bottom of an 11 x 7-inch baking dish. Arrange the peach slices on top of the crumbs. Cover the peaches with the Blackberry Sauce.
4. Turn the dough out onto a lightly floured work surface and sprinkle it with a little flour. With a lightly floured rolling pin, roll the dough out to form a rectangle a little bit bigger than the baking dish, rotating the dough as you roll it and

occasionally sliding a flat metal spatula underneath to make sure that the dough does not stick to the work surface.

5. Trim the dough so that it is the same size as the baking dish. Slide the dough onto a baking sheet. Brush with the melted butter, and sprinkle with the Cinnamon Sugar. With a sharp paring knife, score the dough with lengthwise and crosswise cuts about ⅟₁₆ inch deep to make a pattern of little squares.

6. Place the dough in the oven and bake until golden brown and firm, about 25 minutes. Remove the crust from the oven, and let it cool on the baking sheet on a wire rack for 10 minutes. Turn the oven heat down to 250 degrees.

7. Place the slightly cooled crust on top of the fruit in the baking dish. Place the dish in the oven and bake until the fruit is warmed through, about 30 minutes. Serve warm, with Sweetened Whipped Cream, crème fraîche, or Vanilla Ice Cream.

APPLE-MANGO CHARLOTTE

Serves 10

Apple-Mango Charlotte is an impressive-looking dessert but simple to make. It is won-derful in winter, when both fruits are available. I love the surprising combination of comforting, warm apples and exotic mango. Lemon Sauce, Vanilla Sauce, or Vanilla Ice Cream finishes off the dish. Crucial to the success of the charlotte is that the bread be nice and brown. Check on it as directed and return it to the oven if it is the least bit pale. The filling just needs to be heated through; the apples are precooked, and you don't want the mango to get too soft.

8 tablespoons (1 stick) unsalted butter, softened	2 ripe mangoes, peeled and cut into ¾-inch-thick slices
16 slices white bread, crusts removed	Light Lemon Sauce (page 515),
Prebaked Apple Chunks (page 27) made with 7 apples, cooled	Vanilla Sauce (page 514), or Vanilla Ice Cream (page 185)
1 cup fresh bread or cake crumbs	for serving

1. Preheat the oven to 375 degrees. Spread ½ tablespoon of the butter on one side of each of the bread slices. Cut each slice in half lengthwise. Cut 10 of the halves into 2 triangles each; you should have 20 triangles and 22 rectangles.

2. Butter the bottom of a 7½-inch round baking dish with 3-inch sides. Cut out a round of parchment the same diameter as the dish, and place it on the bottom of the dish.

3. Arrange the bread triangles in a circle on the bottom of the dish, buttered side down, so that they overlap slightly and their points meet at the center. Place 1 rectangle in the middle, butter side down, where all the points meet. Arrange the remaining rectangles along the sides of the dish, buttered sides against the dish, so that they stand lengthwise and overlap each other slightly. The slices should reach about 1 inch above the rim of the dish.

4. Mix the apples with the bread crumbs. Spoon a 1-inch layer of the apple mix-ture into the dish, and press it with the back of a spoon to pack it down tightly. Arrange some mango slices, slightly overlapping, on top of the apples. Continue to layer the apples and mango until all of the fruit is in the dish. It should come just to the rim of the dish and 1 inch below the bread.

5. Fold the standing bread slices toward the center of the dish. Place a pan that is just a little smaller in diameter than the baking dish on top of the dish to flatten the bread, and press on it to compact the contents. Remove the smaller pan.

6. Bake for 15 minutes. Then loosely tent the charlotte with brown paper so it doesn't burn, and bake until the bread is completely brown, about 30 minutes more. Remove the charlotte from the oven and invert it onto a plate. Slowly lift the dish to check on the color of the bread. If it is too pale, put the dish back in the oven for an additional 10 to 15 minutes.

7. Remove the charlotte from the oven and let it cool on a wire rack for 20 minutes. Invert it onto a serving platter, pour the sauce around it, and serve immediately. Or invert the charlotte onto a heatproof serving platter, keeping the baking dish in place, and keep it in a warm (75 degrees) oven for up to 45 minutes. Then remove the dish and garnish with the sauce just before serving.

Two OUT-OF-THE-ORDINARY RECIPES FOR INDIVIDUAL TARTS

These last two recipes don't quite fit into any of the other categories. Since they are both made in individual serving sizes I've decided to group them together here.

The Individual Yogurt Tarts have remarkably light and thin pastry shells that are filled with piquant yogurt cheese and fruit. The crustless tartlets are made by baking a half pear or peach on top of a portion of delicate almond cake. Served in pretty individual portions, each dessert is sure to make your guests feel special, whether they are watching their calories or ready to indulge.

INDIVIDUAL YOGURT TARTS

Serves 12

This was one of my first attempts at a low-calorie dessert. I had just come to the White House, during the Carter administration, and was asked for a light fruit tart. The tart shells are made of a very thin and crisp batter and are filled with a refreshing combination of yogurt cheese and fruit. They taste just as fresh today as they did back then.

Time is of the essence when you are baking and shaping the tart shells, so make sure that you are well organized before you start to bake. As soon as one baking sheet is ready to come out of the oven, have the next one ready to go in. As soon as the pastry rounds come out of the oven, transfer them to the upside-down glasses to shape them before they harden. If they do harden before you get a chance to shape them, return them to the oven for 30 seconds to soften them up.

The yogurt must be drained of excess water so that it is thick enough to become a filling. Dump the whole carton into a strainer set over a bowl, but don't stir the yogurt. If you do, all of it will just drip through the strainer and you won't have anything left.

FOR THE TART SHELLS:
4 tablespoons unsalted butter, softened
½ cup confectioners' sugar
1 teaspoon pure vanilla extract
2 teaspoons grated lemon zest
Pinch salt
2 large egg whites, at room temperature
⅓ cup all-purpose flour

FOR THE FILLING:
One 32-ounce container plain low-fat yogurt
1 pint fresh raspberries, blueberries, or stemmed and sliced strawberries
6 tablespoons honey

Mint sprigs for garnish (optional)

1. Preheat the oven to 375 degrees. Trace a 4-inch-diameter circle centered on a thin (1/16-inch-thick) piece of cardboard measuring approximately 6 x 6 inches. Neatly cut the round away from the cardboard. (You will be using the cardboard frame as a stencil to form the tart shells.) Set 12 glasses upside down on the counter (these will be the molds for the tart shells).

2. Combine the butter, confectioners' sugar, vanilla, lemon zest, and salt in the

bowl of an electric mixer fitted with the paddle attachment. Mix on medium speed until smooth.

3. With the mixer running on medium-high speed, alternately add a tablespoon of egg white and a tablespoon of flour until all of the egg whites and flour are incorporated and the batter is smooth.

4. Line two baking sheets with parchment paper. Place the cardboard square in one corner of one of the baking sheets, and drop a tablespoonful of batter into the cut-out round. Use a small offset spatula to smooth the batter to the edges of the round. Carefully lift the stencil straight up and away from the baking sheet so that you leave a neat round of batter on the parchment. Make 2 more batter rounds on the same sheet.

5. Bake until the edges of the rounds are light brown, 6 to 7 minutes. While the first baking sheet is in the oven, make 3 more batter rounds on the second parchment-lined sheet so that they are ready to bake as soon as the first sheet comes out of the oven. Repeat the forming and baking of the batter rounds until all the batter has been used and you have 12 rounds.

6. When the rounds come out of the oven, immediately lift them from the baking sheet, using an offset spatula and your finger, and drape them over the upside-down glasses. Let them cool completely on the glasses. Cooled tart shells may be stored in an airtight container at room temperature for 3 to 4 days.

7. For the filling: Place a fine-mesh strainer over a bowl and empty the yogurt container into the strainer. Do not stir. Place the bowl and strainer in the refrigerator overnight to allow the excess liquid to drain off.

8. Just before serving, spoon the yogurt cheese into the tart shells. Arrange the berries of your choice on top of the yogurt, and drizzle each tart with ½ tablespoon honey. Garnish each tart with a mint sprig if desired, and serve immediately.

CRUSTLESS ALMOND PEAR OR ALMOND PEACH TARTLETS

Makes 8 tartlets

Frangipane is a fragrant, delicate cake batter made with ground nuts. Conventionally it is used as a tart filling when it is spread over the bottom of a pastry crust and topped with fruit. When baked, the batter rises slightly and puffs around the fruit. I always loved the combination of frangipane and fruit, but I felt that the pastry crust was superfluous when you had the nut batter to support the fruit. So I simply dispensed with it!

I like to bake these in individual-size pans, so each person gets one pretty pear or peach half. Enjoy the tartlets warm with Vanilla Sauce, a small scoop of Vanilla Ice Cream, or a glass of sweet Champagne.

1 recipe Frangipane (page 508)
4 ripe pears, peeled, halved, and cored, or 4 ripe peaches, peeled, halved, and pitted

Vanilla Sauce (page 514) or Vanilla Ice Cream (page 185) for serving

1. Preheat the oven to 375 degrees. Fill eight 3-inch nonstick tartlet pans halfway with Frangipane.
2. Using a sharp paring knife, cut the pear or peach halves into very thin slices at an angle, leaving the slices slightly attached at one end. Place one half on top of each tart, pressing down lightly to fan out the slices so the fruit lies almost flat against the Frangipane.
3. Place the tartlet pans on a baking sheet and bake until the Frangipane is set, about 20 minutes. Place the tartlet pans on a wire rack and allow to cool for 10 minutes. Then run a sharp paring knife around the edge of each tartlet, tilting the tart toward the palm of your hand so it will slip out of the pan. Place each one on a dessert plate and serve warm or at room temperature, with Vanilla Sauce or Vanilla Ice Cream. Crustless almond tarts are best served the day they are made.

TEN

Perfect Cakes for All Occasions

CAKES ARE A WONDERFUL WAY to mark occasions both big and small. Plain cakes like Lemon Pound Cake or Pumpkin Ring Cake make brunch or teatime get-togethers memorable. Serving a layer cake like Island Rum Cake or Chocolate Cherry Cake at the end of a dinner party shows that you have really made an effort for your guests. Birthdays, graduations, weddings, anniversaries, and other personal milestones, as well as holidays throughout the year, traditionally call for a special cake to cap the celebration.

You can always buy a cake—I see them everywhere I go, from the local warehouse club, to the supermarket, to the high-end bakeries in the cosmopolitan neighborhoods of Washington, D.C.—but there is nothing like homemade cake. When you make a cake yourself, you can be sure that the ingredients are of the highest quality and that the cake will be as fresh-tasting as can be. You can choose whatever flavor combinations and finishes you like, whereas with a store-bought cake you are limited by what is offered at the bakery. Even using the most expensive ingredients, a homemade cake will cost less than a store-bought cake. And there is the immeasurable satisfaction of making something yourself, something that is so good and beautiful that it could not be purchased at any bakery for any price.

It is true that in many cases cakes take time and involve several steps: Not only do you have to bake the cake itself, but you have to prepare filling and frosting, put the cake together, and decorate it. Taken by themselves, however, none of these steps is terribly difficult. Very often the different components of a cake can be put together well in advance, so you can spread the work out over several days or even weeks.

I have made hundreds of different cakes over the years, tailoring combinations of cake layers, fillings, and frostings to particular audiences and occasions. When designing a birthday cake for a children's birthday party, I thought about the kinds of things kids like to eat before I decided to spread a roulade cake with grape jelly and peanut butter cream. For a black-tie dinner at the White House, I wanted to use luxury ingredients, and decided on alternating layers of Chocolate Genoise with Chocolate Bavarian and Champagne Mousse.

After deciding on flavors, texture is always a big consideration when I design a cake. There are two directions I can take. Sometimes I like to add a crunchy or crisp component to give the cake some textural variation. Chopped nougat stirred into chocolate glaze gives the Chocolate Bavarian Cake a little crunch. Crisp layers of meringue contrast beautifully with the soft layers of genoise and buttercream in the Island Rum Cake. At other times I will go in the opposite direction, aiming for a cake that completely melts in your mouth. Peach Meringue Cake, Marjolaine, and Low-Calorie Strawberry Cake are all examples of this style, in which the components seem to melt into each other to create a single layer of incredible delicacy and softness. Whatever flavors and textures I choose, I always aim for a finished cake that tastes light and fresh, never heavy or overly rich.

This chapter contains recipes for some of my most successful and popular cakes. Each one has been refined so that the elements are in perfect balance and the finishes and decorations add flavor as well as beauty. Once you study these examples and put together some of the cakes, you may want to make a cake of your own design. Keep in mind the basic rules of proportion and restraint when mixing and matching cake layers, fillings, frostings, and other finishes from various recipes, and you will be able to create a dessert that perfectly suits your taste and the occasion.

A FEW CAKE BASICS

GREASING, FLOURING, AND LINING THE PANS WITH PARCHMENT: There is nothing worse than half a baked cake stuck to the bottom of a cake pan. When this happens, there is not much to do except start over again. But the appropriate combination of greasing, flouring, and lining the pan with parchment will prevent this disaster. In general, I grease cake pans to prevent the cakes from sticking. Butter, vegetable shortening, and cooking spray all work fine, as long as they are liberally applied to the pan. In most cases, I suggest sprinkling a small amount of flour into the pan, tapping and rotating the pan until the bottom and sides are lightly coated, and then tapping the excess flour out of the pan. Occasionally I call for the step of lining the greased and floured pan with parchment and greasing and flouring the parchment in the same manner. This provides extra insurance that the cake won't stick. Pay careful attention to the recipe directions for the combination appropriate to the cake you are baking, and be aware that different cakes require different anti-sticking measures. For example, Cheesecake is baked in an ungreased, unfloured, unlined pan. Angel Food Cake is baked in a parchment-lined but ungreased pan.

TESTING FOR DONENESS: The toothpick test works well for most cakes: Insert a wooden toothpick or skewer into the center of the cake. If the toothpick comes out clean, or with a couple of crumbs attached, the cake is done. For angel food cake and roulade cakes, I prefer to check for doneness by pressing on the cake with my finger. If the cake springs back, it is done. Cheesecake should be judged similarly to a baked pudding: If it is set around the edges but still a little jiggly in the center, it is ready to come out of the oven. It will continue to cook from the residual heat as it cools, becoming completely firm.

COOLING THE CAKE: Unless the recipe specifies otherwise, cakes should be inverted onto a wire rack right away, unmolded, and left there to cool completely. Do not try to split a cake layer in two while it is still warm; it will tear and crumble. Most cooled cakes may be wrapped in plastic wrap and frozen; defrost them in the refrigerator before proceeding with the recipe. Cakes that are chilled or still slightly frozen are easier to slice and work with. Exceptions are noted in individual recipes.

ASSEMBLING LAYER CAKES: Cakes with Bavarian or mousse fillings are usually assembled inside a cake pan, refrigerated or frozen until set, and then inverted onto a platter to be decorated before serving. Specific directions for assembly are given in each recipe. Cakes that are filled with fruit, jam, whipped cream, pastry cream, buttercream, or mousseline are assembled on top of a cardboard cake circle of the same circumference as the cake layers. These cardboard circles can be purchased at pastry supply shops, but you can also cut your own from a clean cardboard box. To hold the cake in place, dab a bit of frosting or filling onto the center of the cardboard before you place the first cake layer on it. Assemble the cake as directed in the recipe, using a small offset spatula to spread the fillings evenly across the layers. Before glazing or frosting the assembled cake, brush the top and sides with a clean pastry brush to remove loose crumbs.

DECORATION: Although I became well known for some of my over-the-top cake decorations during my White House years, for most cakes and occasions I truly believe that simple decorations are the prettiest and most pleasing. When at all possible, I like my decorations to do double duty, adding flavor as well as visual appeal. A dusting of powdered sugar is all that is needed to lightly sweeten and finish Susie's Citrus Angel Food Cake. Island Rum Cake is finished by dusting the top with cocoa powder and pressing sliced almonds onto its sides. I often decorate cakes with fresh fruit. Orange Bavarian Cake is garnished with orange segments, raspberries, and shavings of white chocolate, all of which add flavor as well as color to the dessert. I love to frost cakes with buttercream, but I do not like to overload a cake with piped buttercream decorations, since too much buttercream just doesn't taste good. At the most, I will use a star tip to pipe a shell border. Individual recipes contain suggestions for decorating, many of which are optional.

THE RECIPES

The recipes in this chapter are divided into several categories. To begin there are the **plain cakes,** which require little in the way of finishing. Next come several **cake layer recipes,** used in assembling more complicated **layer cakes.** Layer cake recipes, complete with directions for filling, frosting, and decorating, come next. **Roulade cakes,** which are filled and rolled rather than layered, are treated separately. Finally, two favorite recipes for **cakes made with meringue layers** complete the chapter.

LEMON POUND CAKE

ORANGE SABAYON CAKE

PUMPKIN RING CAKE

SUSIE'S CITRUS ANGEL FOOD CAKE

FRUITCAKE

CHEESECAKE

PEACH MERINGUE CAKE

SPICED APPLE MERINGUE CAKE

GENOISE

CHOCOLATE GENOISE

CHOCOLATE BUTTER CAKE

FRENCH BUTTERCREAM

ITALIAN MERINGUE BUTTERCREAM

ENGLISH CUSTARD COFFEE BUTTERCREAM

LEMON LAYER CAKE

ISLAND RUM CAKE

SURE-TO-PLEASE BIRTHDAY CAKE

ORANGE BAVARIAN CAKE

LOW-CALORIE STRAWBERRY CAKE

CHOCOLATE CHERRY CAKE

CHOCOLATE CHAMPAGNE MOUSSE CAKE

CHOCOLATE BAVARIAN CAKE

CHOCOLATE ROULADE CAKE

PEANUT BUTTER AND JELLY ROULADE CAKE

CHOCOLATE-VANILLA DACQUOISE

MARJOLAINE

PLAIN CAKES

This section contains recipes for cakes that require little or no finishing before serving. There is no mixing and matching of different types of cake layers, no buttercream frostings or mousseline fillings, no chocolate curls, marzipan flowers, or other frills. This is why they are called "plain" cakes.

But something in me rebels at the notion of calling them plain, since not one of them is the least bit ordinary. I prefer to think of them as casual cakes, the ones to serve for brunch or tea or after a simple meal with family and friends. The Lemon Pound Cake has the most delicate crumb of any pound cake I have ever made. I almost hate to call my Fruitcake by that name, since it is much too good to be "re-gifted" (passed along to the next innocent party) in the traditional manner.

Some of my plain cakes are hardly as austere as the name suggests. The Peach Meringue Cake consists of brioche that is sliced in half, soaked with a spiced syrup, filled with peaches, and slathered with meringue. I serve my creamy Cheesecake with fresh fruit and Lemon Cream. These additions push an already good cake over the top in terms of flavor and presentation.

As a pastry chef, I can hardly resist the urge to transform the truly plain cakes into real desserts. Pumpkin Ring Cake, delicious with coffee, becomes a celebratory Thanksgiving dessert when Maple Syrup Bavarian is heaped into its center. Orange Sabayon Cake, served plain, is just right at brunch. When it's covered with Ganache and served with Chocolate Mousse, it is just right after a great dinner. The humble Fruitcake is outrageously delicious when served warm with hot Light Lemon Sauce or Bourbon Sauce and whipped cream or ice cream.

So take these recipes for what they are: the simplest cakes I know how to make. But let your taste and imagination be your guide if you'd like to transform them into special-occasion desserts.

LEMON POUND CAKE

Serves 8

Serve this cake for afternoon teas or other occasions, or serve it for dessert alongside fruit compote or chocolate mousse. This recipe calls for less butter than traditional pound cake recipes, but it makes up in richness with the addition of crème fraîche. For the lightest cake, do not overmix the ingredients. Beating the batter too much will make the cake greasy and heavy.

1 cup plus 2 tablespoons all-purpose
    flour
1 teaspoon baking powder
Pinch salt
2 large eggs, at room temperature
¾ cup sugar

1 tablespoon pure vanilla extract
1 teaspoon grated lemon zest
4 tablespoons unsalted butter, melted
    and cooled
½ cup crème fraîche or sour cream,
    at room temperature

1. Preheat the oven to 400 degrees. Grease an 8 x 4-inch loaf pan. Line the bottom and longer sides with parchment paper.

2. Sift the flour, baking powder, and salt together in a small bowl.

3. In a large bowl, combine the eggs, sugar, vanilla, and lemon zest. Stir until well combined, but do not overmix. Stir the flour mixture into the egg mixture. Then stir in the butter and the crème fraîche.

4. Pour the batter into the prepared pan. Bake until the cake begins to form a crust on top, about 15 minutes. Carefully pull it out of the oven and make a ½-inch-deep cut down the center of the cake to allow it to rise without cracking. Turn the heat down to 350 degrees, return the cake to the oven, and bake until a toothpick inserted into the center comes out clean, 35 to 45 minutes.

5. Invert the cake onto a wire rack and unmold it. Then re-invert it onto another wire rack so it is right side up. Let the cake cool slightly, then remove the parchment. Serve it warm or at room temperature. Lemon Pound Cake will keep, wrapped in plastic wrap, at room temperature for 2 to 3 days.

ORANGE SABAYON CAKE

I call this a sabayon cake because I beat the eggs and sugar together until pale and light, just as in sabayon sauce. The resulting cake is like a pound cake but more delicate and less buttery. It is one of my all-time favorite plain cakes. In fact, I would serve it all the time even if it weren't so simple to make!

1¾ cups plus 2 tablespoons cake flour

1 teaspoon baking soda

Pinch salt

7½ tablespoons unsalted butter, softened

11 tablespoons sugar

2 tablespoons frozen orange juice concentrate

1½ teaspoons grated orange zest

1 large egg

2 large egg yolks

⅓ cup milk

1. Preheat the oven to 375 degrees. Grease and flour a 9-cup bundt pan. Sift 1 cup plus 2 tablespoons of the cake flour, the baking soda, and the salt together in a small bowl. Set aside.

2. Combine the butter, 6 tablespoons of the sugar, the remaining ¾ cup cake flour, the orange juice concentrate, and the orange zest in the bowl of an electric mixer and beat until smooth and well combined.

3. In a clean bowl, combine the egg, yolks, and the remaining 5 tablespoons sugar. Beat with the mixer on high speed until pale yellow and increased in volume, 5 to 7 minutes.

4. Fold the egg mixture into the butter mixture. Mix in one third of the milk until incorporated. Mix in one third of the flour mixture. Repeat 2 more times, ending with the the flour.

5. Scrape the batter into the prepared pan. (It will be just a little more than halfway full.) Bake until a toothpick inserted into the center comes out clean, about 20 minutes.

6. Remove the pan from the oven and immediately invert it onto a wire rack. Unmold the cake and allow it to cool completely. Covered with a cake dome, Orange Sabayon Cake will keep at room temperature for up to 3 days. Wrapped in plastic wrap and then in aluminum foil, it can be frozen for up to 2 months.

VARIATION:

PASSION FRUIT SABAYON CAKE. Substitute 3 tablespoons passion fruit puree for the orange juice concentrate.

GANACHE-COVERED ORANGE CAKE WITH CHOCOLATE MOUSSE. Cool the cake in the pan. (Or freeze it as described and then defrost it on the counter for a couple of hours; return it to the pan before proceeding.) Heat 1½ cups Light Syrup (page 506) in a small saucepan until warm. Stir in ⅓ cup Grand Marnier. Pour the syrup, a little at a time, onto the cake until it is all absorbed. Invert the cake onto a serving platter. Make a double recipe of Ganache (page 513) and let it cool to room temperature. Brush 1 cup of the Ganache over the outside of the cake. Whip 1 cup heavy cream until it holds stiff peaks, and fold in the remaining cooled Ganache to make a chocolate mousse. Pipe the mousse into the center of the cake, and pipe a border of mousse around the cake using a large star tip. Serve immediately, or cover loosely with plastic wrap and refrigerate overnight and then let stand at room temperature for 2 hours before serving. Decorate with fresh raspberries, Chocolate Shavings (page 436), or Marzipan Fruit (page 469) before serving. *Serves 16.*

PUMPKIN RING CAKE

Serves 8

If you like simple cakes and the old-fashioned flavor of pumpkin and spices, this is the dessert for you. Serve it plain, or dress it up for the holidays by filling the center with Maple Syrup Bavarian (page 140).

1 cup all-purpose flour	¼ teaspoon ground nutmeg
1 teaspoon baking soda	2 large eggs
Pinch salt	1 cup sugar
1 teaspoon ground cinnamon	½ cup sunflower oil
¼ teaspoon ground cloves	1 cup fresh or canned pumpkin puree

1. Preheat the oven to 350 degrees. Grease a 10-cup bundt pan and dust it with flour, tapping out any extra.
2. Sift the flour, baking soda, salt, cinnamon, cloves, and nutmeg together in a medium bowl.
3. Place the eggs, sugar, and oil in a large mixing bowl, and beat with an electric mixer on medium-high speed for 5 minutes. Add the flour mixture and mix well, scraping down the sides of the bowl once or twice as necessary. Mix in the pumpkin puree.
4. Scrape the batter into the prepared pan and smooth it with a spatula; the batter should come about halfway up the sides of the pan. Bake until a toothpick inserted into the center comes out clean, about 35 minutes.
5. Remove the pan from the oven and immediately invert it onto a wire rack. Unmold the cake and allow it to cool completely. Covered with a cake dome, Pumpkin Ring Cake will keep at room temperature for up to 3 days. Wrapped in plastic wrap and then in aluminum foil, it can be frozen for up to 3 months.

SUSIE'S CITRUS ANGEL FOOD CAKE

Serves 12

This recipe comes from my longtime assistant at the White House, Susie Morrison. It is the best angel food cake I have baked, always rising nice and high and never deflating, as some do. I think this is because Susie whips the egg whites on medium, not high, speed so that not as much air is beaten in. As a result, the baked cake doesn't have many large air bubbles that could deflate as it cools. Unlike most other cakes, with this one you don't want to grease the pan; you want the batter to stick to the sides so that the finished cake will maintain its height. Brushing water onto the sides of the pan helps the batter cling and rise high. The citrus zest adds flavor without weighting down the batter. This cholesterol-free cake is a good choice for people who are watching their fat intake. Nice and light, it is a terrific cake to serve for tea. Just before serving, top individual slices with fruit compote, fruit salad, or (my favorite) Blueberry Sauce (page 38) to moisten them. This cake travels very well, so it's a good choice for picnics and other outings.

1½ cups confectioners' sugar, plus more for dusting
1 cup cake flour
Pinch salt
12 large egg whites, at room temperature

1½ teaspoons cream of tartar
1 cup granulated sugar
1 teaspoon grated lemon zest
½ teaspoon grated orange zest
1 teaspoon pure vanilla extract
½ teaspoon almond extract

1. Preheat the oven to 350 degrees. Sift the confectioners' sugar, cake flour, and salt together in a medium bowl. Set aside.
2. Place the egg whites and cream of tartar in the bowl of an electric mixer fitted with the whisk attachment, and beat on medium speed until foamy. With the mixer still on medium, very slowly pour in the granulated sugar in a steady stream, and continue to whip until the mixture holds stiff peaks.
3. Sift the confectioners' sugar mixture over the egg white mixture and gently fold to combine. Fold in the lemon zest, orange zest, and vanilla and almond extracts.
4. Brush water over the bottom and sides of an angel food tube pan with removable bottom. Pour the batter into the pan and smooth the top with a rubber

(continued)

spatula. Bake until the top is golden brown and springs back when you touch it, about 1 hour.

5. Remove the pan from the oven. If your pan has feet, invert the pan onto a heat-proof surface and allow the cake to cool. If your pan doesn't have feet, invert four drinking glasses on the counter and rest the inverted pan on top of the glasses (to allow air to circulate around the cake while it cools). Let the cake cool in the pan for at least 1 hour and up to 6 hours.

6. Run a sharp paring knife around the edge of the pan. Invert the cake onto a serving platter and lift off the ring. Run the paring knife under the removable bottom and lift it off the cake. Dust the cake with confectioners' sugar before serving. Susie's Citrus Angel Food Cake will keep under a cake dome at room temperature for 2 to 3 days.

FRUITCAKE

Serves 20

Why am I including a recipe for probably the most detested cake in the world? Because my version is fabulous, if I do say so myself. To disarm people, I've often presented it as "plum pudding" at Christmastime. When I don't call it fruitcake, they beg for seconds and thirds! To serve it as a dessert, cut the chilled cake into 1-inch slices and heat each slice in the microwave until warmed through (30 seconds to 1 minute, depending on the strength of your microwave). Cut each slice in half. Place each warmed half-slice on a dessert plate, pour hot Light Lemon Sauce (page 515) or Bourbon Sauce (page 516) over it, and add a dollop of whipped cream or a spoonful of softened vanilla ice cream on the side.

Of course, like any other fruitcake, this one will keep, well wrapped and refrigerated, for up to 1 year. Give it as a gift and I promise that the recipient will enjoy it and not use it as a doorstop!

3 tablespoons dry sherry

3 tablespoons brandy

2 tablespoons diced dried pears

⅓ cup diced glazed fruit

⅓ cup dark raisins

⅓ cup golden raisins

⅓ cup dried currants

3 tablespoons dried cranberries

3 tablespoons dried cherries

2 tablespoons dried blueberries

1½ tablespoons chopped candied lemon peel (see Note, page 390)

1½ tablespoons chopped candied orange peel

3½ tablespoons all-purpose flour

1 teaspoon baking powder

8 tablespoons (1 stick) unsalted butter, softened

¼ cup granulated sugar

¼ cup packed light brown sugar

¾ cup cake flour

½ tablespoon pure vanilla extract

1 teaspoon almond extract

1 teaspoon lemon extract

1 teaspoon ground cinnamon

¼ teaspoon ground nutmeg

Pinch salt

1 tablespoon plus 1 teaspoon honey

2 eggs

⅓ cup coarsely chopped pecans

⅓ cup dark rum

¼ cup apricot jam

½ recipe Rum Glaze (page 520)

1. Combine the sherry, brandy, pears, glazed fruit, dark and golden raisins, currants, cranberries, cherries, blueberries, lemon peel, and orange peel in a large bowl. Stir together, then cover the bowl with plastic wrap and let it stand overnight.

2. Preheat the oven to 400 degrees. Line the bottom of a 10 x 4-inch loaf pan with parchment paper. Sift the all-purpose flour and baking powder together in a medium bowl.

3. Combine the butter, granulated sugar, and brown sugar in the bowl of an electric mixer fitted with a paddle attachment, and cream together until smooth. Stir in the cake flour until just combined. With the mixer on low speed, add, one at a time, the vanilla extract, almond extract, lemon extract, cinnamon, nutmeg, and salt, stirring after each addition. Stir in the honey and then the eggs, one by one. Stir in the flour mixture, scraping down the sides of the bowl several times as necessary. Stir in the pecans. Remove the bowl from the mixer and stir in the soaked fruit by hand.

(continued)

4. Scrape the batter into the prepared pan. Turn the oven heat down to 350 degrees, and bake until a toothpick inserted into the center comes out clean, about 1¼ hours.

5. Transfer the cake, still in the pan, to a wire rack. Sprinkle the top of the hot cake with the rum. Bring the apricot jam to a boil in a small pan. Strain the hot jam, and brush it over the top of the cake. Brush on the Rum Glaze. Allow the cake to cool completely in the pan before unmolding. Wrap the cake in plastic wrap and refrigerate it for at least 2 weeks before serving. Fruitcake will keep in the refrigerator, wrapped tightly in plastic wrap, for up to 1 year.

NOTE: Candied citrus peel is available at specialty food stores and by mail order from the Baker's Catalogue (see Resources, page 523).

CHEESECAKE

Serves 10

For the smoothest batter, make sure that all the ingredients for this cake—except the Pâte Sucrée—are at room temperature. I bake my cheesecake in a cake pan rather than a springform pan because the batter is very liquid, and only a regular cake pan can contain it. Most recipes call for chilling cheesecake in the refrigerator before serving it. I prefer to actually freeze the cake because frozen cheesecake is easier to unmold. Partially defrosted on the counter, very cold cake is also easier to slice, and the individual slices will finish thawing almost as soon as they are cut. This cake may be served plain but is even better garnished with fresh seasonal fruit and Lime or Lemon Cream on the side.

1 recipe Pâte Sucrée (page 267), chilled	2 large egg yolks, at room temperature
Four 8-ounce packages cream cheese, softened	½ tablespoon pure vanilla extract
1¼ cups sugar	1 cup heavy cream
1 teaspoon grated lemon zest	
½ teaspoon grated orange zest	Fresh fruit of your choice (optional)
5 large eggs, at room temperature	1 recipe Lime Cream or Lemon Cream (pages 510 or 511, optional)

1. Preheat the oven to 400 degrees. Position an oven rack in the middle of the oven. Turn the chilled dough out onto a lightly floured work surface and sprinkle it with a little flour. With a lightly floured rolling pin, roll the dough out to form an 11-inch round about ⅛ inch thick, rotating the dough as you roll it and occasionally sliding a flat metal spatula underneath to make sure that it does not stick to the work surface. Place a 10-inch round cake pan on top of the rolled dough, and use a sharp paring knife to trim the dough to fit exactly inside the pan. Place it in the bottom of the pan, prick it all over with a fork, and bake until golden, 15 to 20 minutes. Remove the pan from the oven and let it cool on a wire rack. Turn the oven heat down to 350 degrees.

2. Combine the cream cheese, sugar, lemon zest, and orange zest in the bowl of an electric mixer fitted with the paddle attachment, and mix on low speed until smooth. Add the eggs and then the yolks, one at a time, scraping down the sides of the bowl after each addition. Mix in the vanilla. Then mix in the heavy cream, ½ cup at a time, scraping down the sides of the bowl after each addition. The mixture should be very smooth.

3. Place the pastry-lined cake pan on a rimmed baking sheet, and pour the filling into the pan. Place the baking sheet in the oven and carefully pour ½ inch of very hot tap water into it. Bake until the cake is set around the edges but still jiggly in the center, about 1 hour. Remove it from the oven and allow it to cool completely in the pan on a wire rack.

4. When the cake has cooled completely, place it in the freezer overnight. (Cheesecake, still in the pan, can be wrapped in plastic wrap and then in aluminum foil and frozen for up to 2 months.)

5. To unmold and serve: Remove the cake from the freezer. Hold the bottom of the pan over a gas or electric burner for several seconds to loosen the cake from the pan. Run a sharp paring knife around the edge of the pan. Cover the top of the pan with plastic wrap and invert a plate over the plastic. Invert the pan and plate together, and gently shake to release the cake. Invert a serving platter over the released cake and invert again so that the cake is right side up. Allow the cheesecake to defrost for about 30 minutes. Then slice the cake. Garnish individual slices with fresh fruit and Lime or Lemon Cream if desired, and serve immediately.

PEACH MERINGUE CAKE

Serves 12

People are pleasantly surprised when they taste this cake, which is made with brioche layers instead of sponge cake or meringue. Although the brioche is soaked in a flavorful syrup, which makes it soft and delicious, it maintains its yeasty flavor. To smash the cinnamon sticks, wrap them in a kitchen towel, place the towel on a work surface, and pound them with a rolling pin. They will release much more flavor into the syrup this way. I like soft Honey Vanilla Ice Cream (page 187) as an accompaniment. Champagne is a must.

1 pound Brioche Dough (page 293), ready to rise in the baking pan
5 large ripe peaches, peeled and pitted, or 3 Poached Peaches (page 59), canned peaches, or defrosted frozen peaches

FOR THE SYRUP:
1 quart water
2 cups sugar
2 oranges, halved
1 lemon, halved

Six 3-inch cinnamon sticks, smashed
⅓ cup Amaretto or other almond liqueur

½ recipe Pastry Cream (page 509)

FOR THE SWISS MERINGUE:
8 large egg whites
1¼ cups granulated sugar
Confectioners' sugar for dusting

2 cups Raspberry Sauce (page 516)

1. Grease a 9 x 2-inch-deep round cake pan. Flatten the brioche dough and fit it into the prepared pan. Lightly drape the pan with plastic wrap and let it stand in a warm, draft-free place until the dough has doubled in size, about 1½ hours.
2. Preheat the oven to 400 degrees.
3. Bake the brioche for 10 minutes. Then reduce the heat to 375 degrees and bake until golden and fully risen, another 45 to 50 minutes. Let the brioche cool in the pan on a wire rack for 5 minutes. Then turn it out of the pan and let it cool completely. Leave the oven on.
4. If using poached, canned, or defrosted frozen peaches, drain them well and pat dry with paper towels. Set aside one peach half for the top of the cake. Slice the remaining peaches into pieces measuring approximately ½ x 1 inch.

5. Cut the cooled brioche in half horizontally. Place the 2 layers on a rimmed baking sheet.

6. Prepare the syrup: Combine the water, sugar, orange and lemon halves, and the smashed cinnamon sticks in a large saucepan and bring to a boil. Strain the syrup into a measuring cup or bowl. Stir in the Amaretto.

7. Brush both sides of each brioche layer with the hot syrup, soaking them completely. (To turn the layers over without breaking them, slide them onto a cardboard cake circle or the bottom of a cake pan.)

8. Using a cardboard cake circle or the bottom of a cake pan, transfer one of the soaked brioche layers to a heatproof or silver serving tray. Use a pastry bag fitted with a large flat tip to pipe half of the Pastry Cream over this layer. Arrange the peaches on top of the Pastry Cream. Pipe the remaining Pastry Cream over the peaches. Place the second brioche layer on top and press down gently so the cake is level. If some of the syrup releases from the cake at this point, tip the serving tray a little bit to one side and soak up the excess syrup with a clean paper towel.

9. Make the meringue: Pour 1 inch of water into a large saucepan and bring to a bare simmer. Combine the egg whites and granulated sugar in a large stainless steel mixing bowl, and set it over the simmering water, making sure that the water doesn't touch the bowl. Heat, whisking slowly but constantly, until the egg whites are warm (about 125 degrees on an instant-read thermometer) and the sugar has dissolved. Remove the bowl from the heat and beat with an electric mixer on high speed until the meringue is cool and stiff.

10. Raise the oven heat to 450 degrees. Use an offset spatula to cover the top and sides of the cake evenly with the meringue. If desired, place any extra meringue in a pastry bag fitted with a #6 plain tip and pipe a design on the top of the cake. Use a star tip to pipe a shell border around the top and bottom edges. Dust the meringue generously with confectioners' sugar. Place the cake in the oven and bake until golden all over, 1 to 2 minutes. Turn the cake once or twice if necessary for even browning.

11. Let the cake cool. If desired, fill in your design with colored piping jelly, or with strained apricot jam with a little bit of food coloring. Keep the cake, uncovered, at room temperature for up to 8 hours.

12. Just before serving, place the reserved peach half on top of the cake. Slice the cake, and serve it with Raspberry Sauce on the side.

SPICED APPLE MERINGUE CAKE

Serves 10

This rustic, comforting cake tastes old-fashioned, like something your grandmother would have made. But like a good family heirloom, it's a recipe you'll want to use today and pass on to your children. Even though it is baked in two layers and frosted (with a delicious Honey Meringue), I include it with the "plain cakes" because it has more in common with Lemon Pound Cake or Pumpkin Ring Cake than with Marjolaine or Chocolate-Vanilla Dacquoise. Serve it warm from the oven or at room temperature, with or without ice cream, for a classic dessert that everyone will appreciate.

⅓ cup plus 3 tablespoons chopped raisins
4½ tablespoons candied orange peel
1 teaspoon grated lemon zest
1 teaspoon grated orange zest
1¾ cups plus 2 teaspoons cake flour
1¾ teaspoons baking powder
1 teaspoon baking soda
2 teaspoons ground cinnamon
2 teaspoons ground ginger
1 teaspoon ground cloves
1 teaspoon ground allspice
Pinch ground nutmeg
10 tablespoons unsalted butter, softened

½ cup plus 2 tablespoons granulated sugar
½ cup plus 2 tablespoons packed light brown sugar
3 large eggs, at room temperature
3 large egg yolks, at room temperature
¾ cup buttermilk, at room temperature
2½ cups Prebaked Apple Chunks (page 27)
1 recipe Honey Meringue (page 209)
Confectioners' sugar for dusting

1. Preheat the oven to 375 degrees. Grease two 9-inch round cake pans, and line them with parchment paper. Grease the paper. Dust the bottoms and sides of the pans with flour, tapping out any extra flour.
2. Stir the raisins, candied orange peel, lemon zest, orange zest, and the 2 teaspoons cake flour together in a medium bowl. Set it aside.
3. Sift the remaining 1¾ cups cake flour with the baking powder, baking soda, cinnamon, ginger, cloves, allspice, and nutmeg in a medium bowl.
4. Combine the butter, granulated sugar, and brown sugar in the bowl of an elec-

tric mixer fitted with the paddle attachment. Beat on medium-high speed until smooth. Do not overbeat. Add the eggs and then the yolks, one at a time, scraping down the sides of the bowl after each addition.

5. Add one fourth of the flour mixture to the bowl and mix to combine, then add ¼ cup of the buttermilk and mix to combine. Repeat, ending with the flour mixture, mixing until smooth after each addition. Scrape down the sides of the bowl after each addition. Stir in the raisin mixture.

6. Divide the batter between the two prepared pans and smooth the tops with a spatula. Bake until a toothpick inserted into the center of the cake comes out clean, 20 to 25 minutes. Cool the pans on wire racks for 5 minutes. Then invert the cakes onto the racks, peel off the parchment, and let the cake layers cool completely.

7. Preheat the oven to 450 degrees. Place 1 layer on a 9-inch round cardboard cake circle. Spread the apples over the cake layer. Place the second layer on top of the apples. Cover the top and sides of the cake with the meringue, and dust it heavily with confectioners' sugar. Place the cake in the oven and bake until golden all over, 1 to 2 minutes. Serve immediately, or let stand at room temperature for up to 8 hours before serving.

VARIATION:

PEACH, APRICOT, APPLE, OR PINEAPPLE UPSIDE-DOWN CAKE. One layer of this cake batter can be used to make a fruit upside-down cake: Preheat the oven to 375 degrees and grease a 9-inch round cake pan. Line the pan with parchment paper. Spread 3 tablespoons softened unsalted butter across the parchment paper in a thin layer. Sprinkle ½ cup light brown sugar over the butter. Arrange sliced peeled peaches or apricots, or pineapple rings, on top of the brown sugar. For an apple upside-down cake, use Prebaked Apple Slices (page 28). Pour half a recipe of Spiced Apple Meringue Cake batter on top of the fruit, and bake until a toothpick inserted into the center of the cake comes out clean, 30 to 40 minutes. Run a sharp paring knife around the edge of the pan and invert the cake onto a serving plate. Carefully peel away the parchment paper. Serve warm, or let stand at room temperature for up to 8 hours before serving. Serve with Vanilla Ice Cream (page 185) or Vanilla Sauce (page 514).

CAKE LAYERS

Because plain cakes are usually unadorned, they must be extremely flavorful and completely satisfying all by themselves. A plain cake is the star of its own show. On the other hand, cakes that are to be filled and frosted have to be supporting players, not stars. The three recipes that follow are for cakes with the qualities you want in a supporting player. They have enough character so that they add something to the production, but none of them will hog the stage.

Genoise, Chocolate Genoise, and Chocolate Butter Cake all taste good alone, but you would never serve them that way. They are destined to become part of a layer cake. They taste so much better when sprinkled with syrup, filled with jam or fruit, and frosted with rich buttercream or ganache. These cakes actually improve when embellished.

Genoise and Chocolate Genoise are sponge cakes, so named because they are dry enough to soak up whatever flavorful syrup you choose to brush on them. Either one can be made with or without butter. The choice is yours. There's no doubt that butter adds rich flavor, but cakes made without butter absorb the flavors of syrups, fillings, and frostings more efficiently. If you are going to make a relatively spare layer cake without a lot of juicy filling, syrup, and moist frosting, then you might want to use butter in your genoise. If the cake you are designing has a lot of rich add-ons and needs to soak up a lot of syrup, you might want to skip it.

Chocolate Genoise, made with cocoa powder, has a pleasant but light chocolate flavor. I turn to Chocolate Butter Cake when I want a richer chocolate flavor in my cake layers. This cake is made with semisweet chocolate chips rather than cocoa powder. It also contains twice as much butter as the Genoise. Chocolate Butter Cake stands up well to very rich fillings and frostings, like Chocolate Bavarian or Sweetened Whipped Cream.

GENOISE

Makes one 9-inch round cake

In this recipe, take care when you are whipping the eggs to reduce the speed to medium after 5 minutes. Lengthy whipping at a high speed will produce large air bubbles in the batter, which will pop during baking and result in a flat, heavy cake. If your genoise batter looks very fluffy and light and you are afraid that you have overwhipped it, tap the cake pan on the counter a couple of times to burst some of the bubbles before putting it in the oven. Don't worry if the batter looks a little heavy. It still contains a lot of little air bubbles that will give the cake a nice rise in the oven.

Adding butter to genoise batter is optional. Leave it out if you want a lighter cake that's lower in fat. If you are going to soak a cake heavily with syrup, use genoise made without butter. The drier genoise will absorb syrup better. Butter in genoise makes the cake a little heavier but gives it a wonderful buttery taste.

This recipe makes one 2-inch-thick cake. This amount of batter can also be baked in a 12 x 16-inch jelly roll pan. If you use the jelly roll pan, you will have a thinner cake that will bake more quickly. Genoise freezes very well, so if you are going to use only one layer, wrap the other one tightly in plastic wrap and then in aluminum foil, and freeze it for up to 1 month.

4 large eggs
½ cup sugar
¾ cup plus 1½ tablespoons all-purpose flour

Pinch salt
1 teaspoon pure vanilla extract
4 tablespoons unsalted butter, melted and cooled (optional)

1. Preheat the oven to 375 degrees. Grease a 9 x 2-inch-deep round cake pan. Line the bottom of the pan with parchment paper, and grease the paper. Dust the pan with flour, tapping out any excess flour.

2. Pour 2 inches of water into a medium saucepan, and bring to a bare simmer. Combine the eggs and sugar in the bowl of an electric mixer fitted with the whisk attachment. Place the bowl over the simmering water and whisk constantly until the egg mixture is just lukewarm to the touch, 86 to 90 degrees on an instant-read thermometer.

(continued)

3. Return the bowl to the mixer and whisk on high speed for 5 minutes. Then reduce the speed to medium and whisk until the mixture is completely cool, thick, and shiny, another 12 minutes.

4. Using a rubber spatula, fold in the flour, salt, and vanilla. If you are using the melted butter, spoon about 1 cup of the batter into a small mixing bowl and stir in the butter; then carefully fold the batter-and-butter mixture back into the larger bowl of batter.

5. Pour the batter into the prepared pan and bake for 10 minutes. Without opening the oven door, lower the heat to 375 degrees. Bake until a toothpick inserted into the center comes out clean, about 20 minutes more.

6. Remove the pan from the oven and immediately turn the cake out onto a cardboard cake circle. Place the circle on a wire rack and allow the cake to cool completely. When served with mousses, fruit compotes, and fruit salads, genoise is best used on the day it is baked. For layered cakes, wrap the genoise in plastic wrap and refrigerate it overnight before using. Genoise can be wrapped in plastic wrap and then in aluminum foil and frozen for up to 1 month; defrost it overnight in the refrigerator before using.

CHOCOLATE GENOISE

Makes one 9-inch round cake

¾ cup all-purpose flour
2 tablespoons plus 2 teaspoons
   unsweetened cocoa powder
4 large eggs
½ cup sugar

Pinch salt
1 teaspoon pure vanilla extract
4 tablespoons unsalted butter, melted
   and cooled (optional)

1. Preheat the oven to 375 degrees. Grease a 9 x 2-inch-deep round cake pan. Line the bottom of the pan with parchment paper, and grease the paper. Dust the pan with flour, and tap out any excess flour.

2. Sift the flour and cocoa powder together into a small bowl. Set aside.

3. Pour 2 inches of water into a medium saucepan, and bring to a bare simmer. Combine the eggs and sugar in the bowl of an electric mixer fitted with the whisk attachment. Place the bowl over the simmering water and whisk constantly until the egg mixture is just lukewarm to the touch, 86 to 90 degrees on an instant-read thermometer.

4. Return the bowl to the mixer and whisk on high speed for 5 minutes. Then reduce the speed to medium and whisk until the mixture is completely cool, thick, and shiny, another 12 minutes.

5. Using a rubber spatula, fold in the flour mixture, salt, and vanilla. If you are using the melted butter, spoon about 1 cup of the batter into a small mixing bowl and stir in the butter; then carefully fold the batter-and-butter mixture back into the larger bowl of batter.

6. Pour the batter into the prepared pan and bake for 10 minutes. Without opening the oven door, lower the heat to 375 degrees. Bake until a toothpick inserted into the center of the cake comes out clean, about 20 minutes more.

7. Remove the pan from the oven and immediately turn the cake over onto a cardboard cake circle. Place the circle on a wire rack and allow to cool completely. When served with mousses, fruit compotes, and fruit salads, genoise is best used on the day it is baked. For layered cakes, wrap it in plastic wrap and refrigerate it overnight before using. Genoise can be wrapped in plastic wrap and then in aluminum foil and frozen for up to 1 month; defrost it overnight in the refrigerator before using.

CHOCOLATE BUTTER CAKE

Makes one 9-inch round cake

This simple chocolate cake can be used wherever Chocolate Genoise is called for. It is not quite as dry as a genoise and will soak up less syrup.

6 tablespoons all-purpose flour
6 tablespoons cornstarch
1 teaspoon baking powder
6 ounces semisweet chocolate chips
8 tablespoons (1 stick) unsalted
    butter, softened

½ cup plus 2 tablespoons sugar
4 large eggs, separated, at room
   temperature

1. Preheat the oven to 375 degrees. Grease a 9 x 2-inch-deep round cake pan. Line the bottom of the pan with parchment paper, and grease the paper. Dust the pan with flour, tapping out any excess flour.

2. Sift the flour, cornstarch, and baking powder together into a small bowl. Set aside.

3. Pour 2 inches of water into a small saucepan and bring to a bare simmer. Place the chocolate chips in a stainless steel bowl that is big enough to rest on top of the saucepan, and place it over the simmering water, making sure that the bowl doesn't touch the water. Heat, whisking occasionally, until the chocolate is completely melted. Set it aside to cool.

4. Combine the butter and the ½ cup sugar in the bowl of an electric mixer fitted with the paddle attachment. Cream on medium-high speed until smooth but not fluffy, about 3 minutes. Do not overmix. Add the egg yolks, one at a time, scraping down the sides of the bowl after each addition. Stir in the cooled chocolate. Stir in the flour mixture. The mixture should resemble chocolate buttercream.

5. Place the egg whites in a clean bowl and fit the mixer with the whisk attachment. Whip on high speed until just about to hold soft peaks. With the mixer still on high, pour in the remaining 2 tablespoons sugar in a slow, steady stream. Whip until the whites hold stiff peaks.

6. Using a rubber spatula, fold half of the egg whites into the chocolate batter; then fold in the remaining half. At this point, the batter will look like chocolate

mousse. Pour the batter into the prepared pan and bake until a toothpick inserted in the center comes out clean, about 25 minutes.

7. Remove the pan from the oven and let the cake rest in the pan on a wire rack for 5 minutes. Then invert the cake onto a wire rack, turn it right side up, and allow it to cool completely on the rack. Chocolate Butter Cake may be wrapped in plastic wrap and then in aluminum foil and frozen for up to 1 month; defrost it overnight in the refrigerator before using.

BUTTERCREAM FROSTING AND FILLING

If I am not going to cover a cake with whipped cream or ganache, chances are I'll cover it with buttercream. I use one of three different types of buttercream, depending on the type of cake I'm filling and frosting and on how and when it is going to be served.

If I am going to put together a cake more than a day in advance, I choose French Buttercream, since it keeps better than Italian Buttercream. It is also simpler to make, so when I need a large quantity for a big cake or several cakes at once, it saves me time.

I prefer the flavor and texture of Italian Buttercream, which has the consistency of a mousse and tastes less rich and buttery than French Buttercream. When I am making a cake and serving it the same day, this is the buttercream I usually choose.

English Custard Coffee Buttercream is a more delicate version of French Buttercream, smoother and richer in taste. The eggs are cooked as in a custard or crème brûlée, so the flavor is more creamy than buttery. Because the milk for the custard has to be heated anyway, it is easy and very effective to infuse the milk with ground coffee. (For a plain vanilla custard buttercream, substitute a split vanilla bean for the coffee.)

FRENCH BUTTERCREAM

Makes about 7 cups, enough to fill and frost one 9-inch round 2-layer cake

5 large eggs, at room temperature
2 cups sugar
½ cup water
1 tablespoon light corn syrup

2½ cups (5 sticks) unsalted butter, softened
1 tablespoon pure vanilla extract
Pinch salt

1. Place the eggs in the bowl of an electric mixer fitted with the whisk attachment.
2. Combine the sugar, water, and corn syrup in a small saucepan and cook until the mixture reaches the soft ball stage (235 degrees on a candy thermometer).
3. Turn the mixer on high speed and pour the syrup into the bowl in a slow, steady stream, making sure that none of it falls on the whisk. Continue to whip on high speed until the mixture is fluffy and warm room temperature.
4. Beat in the butter until smooth, about 2 minutes. Stir in the vanilla and salt.
5. If the buttercream separates during beating, your ingredients were probably too cold. Place the bowl over a pot of barely simmering water to warm it up. Do not overheat—you don't want the butter to begin to melt. Return it to the mixer and beat until smooth. The buttercream should be silky, with the consistency of thick mayonnaise. Use immediately, or cover with plastic wrap and refrigerate for up to 4 days. French Buttercream may be frozen in an airtight container for up to 1 month; defrost it in the refrigerator overnight. Chilled buttercream must be brought to room temperature and rewhipped before using.

Flavoring French Buttercream

It is simple enough to flavor the basic recipe for French Buttercream with coffee, chocolate, citrus, or a liqueur. I do not like to add fruit purees or jams to buttercream. Fruit purees contain too much liquid and will make the buttercream runny. Jams are too sweet; I'd rather spread jam on top of a cake layer, and then spread a layer of buttercream on top of the jam.

CHOCOLATE BUTTERCREAM: To flavor 1 cup buttercream, beat in 2 tablespoons unsweetened cocoa powder or 3½ tablespoons melted and cooled bittersweet or semisweet chocolate.

COFFEE BUTTERCREAM: To flavor 1 cup buttercream, make a paste of 2 teaspoons instant espresso powder and ½ teaspoon hot water, and beat it into the buttercream.

LEMON OR LIME BUTTERCREAM: To flavor 1 cup buttercream, beat in ½ cup either Lemon Cream or Lime Cream (pages 510 or 511).

ORANGE BUTTERCREAM: To flavor 1 cup buttercream, beat in ¼ cup pureed Glazed Kumquats (page 49) or 1 tablespoon finely grated orange zest.

PRALINE BUTTERCREAM: To flavor 1 cup buttercream, beat in ¼ cup praline paste and either ¼ cup crushed Nougat (page 502) or ¼ cup crushed Caramelized Almonds (page 503).

HAZELNUT BUTTERCREAM: To flavor 1 cup buttercream, beat in ¼ cup unsweetened hazelnut paste.

HAZELNUT-ORANGE BUTTERCREAM: To flavor 1 cup buttercream, beat in ¼ cup unsweetened hazelnut paste and ¼ cup pureed Glazed Kumquats (page 49).

RUM, GRAND MARNIER, PEAR BRANDY, OR RASPBERRY BRANDY BUTTERCREAM: To flavor 1 cup buttercream, beat in 1½ tablespoons of the liquor or liqueur, or a little more to taste. Don't add too much liquid to the buttercream or it will break.

ITALIAN MERINGUE BUTTERCREAM

Makes enough to fill and frost one 9-inch round 2-layer cake

This is my favorite type of buttercream because it is the lightest and the least rich. There are no egg yolks in it and a relatively small amount of butter. It has a mousselike consistency and melts in your mouth.

This buttercream can't be rewhipped or it will collapse. Use it on your cake right away, and then refrigerate the cake.

2 cups (4 sticks) unsalted butter, softened

2 tablespoons pure vanilla extract, or 1 tablespoon espresso powder dissolved in a few drops of warm water, or 1 cup semisweet chocolate chips, melted and cooled (optional)

1 recipe Italian Meringue (page 207), completely cooled

1. Place the butter and the vanilla extract or other flavoring if desired in the bowl of an electric mixer fitted with the paddle attachment. Mix on medium-high speed until very light and fluffy, almost the consistency of mayonnaise.

2. Fold the meringue into the butter by hand using a rubber spatula, until it is thoroughly incorporated, taking care not to deflate the meringue.

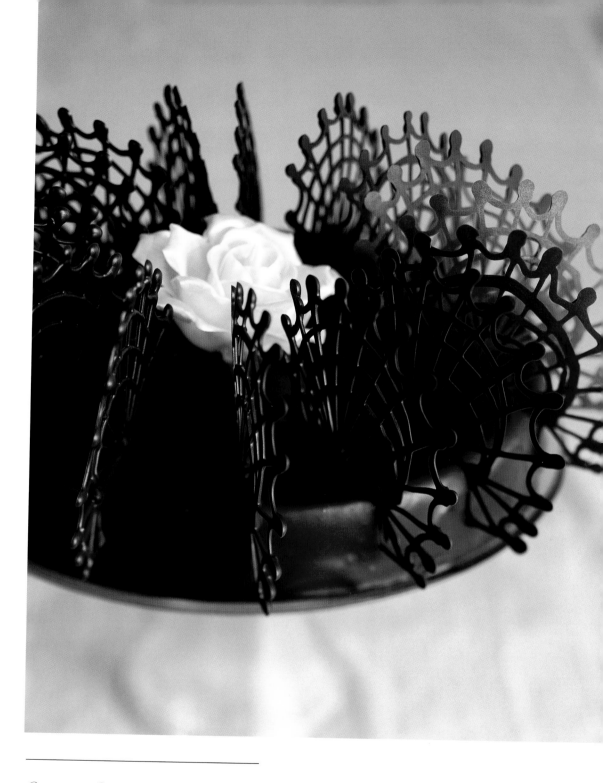

 Chocolate Cherry Cake (PAGE 414)

Banana Strawberry Tart (PAGE 365)

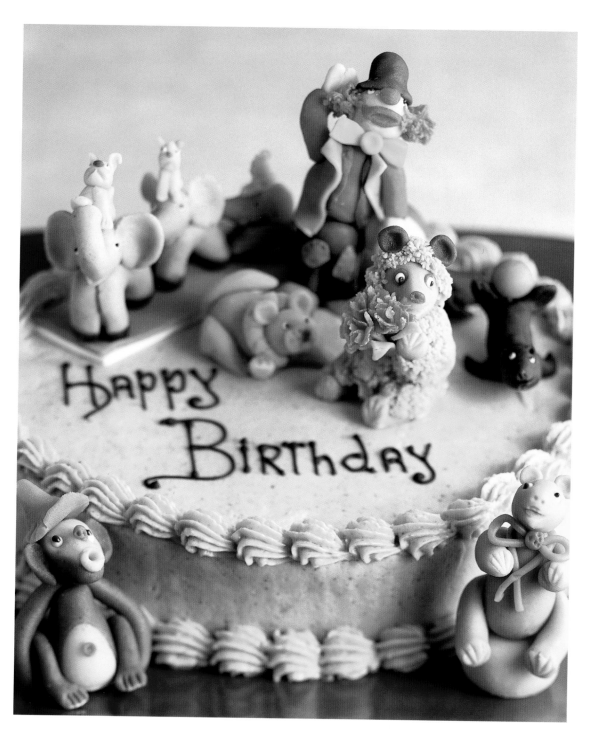

Floating Hearts (PAGE 226)

Apricot Sunburst (PAGE 109)

Pumpkin Ice Cream and Maple Syrup Parfait (PAGE 173)

ENGLISH CUSTARD COFFEE BUTTERCREAM

Makes enough to fill and frost one 9-inch round 2-layer cake

I am including this recipe because I have received so many requests for it over the years. I always flavor it with coffee, but if you'd like to experiment with a vanilla version, replace the coffee with a vanilla bean. For other flavor variations, skip the coffee-steeping step and follow the directions for flavoring French Buttercream (page 402).

2 cups whole milk, or more as needed	2 cups sugar
¾ cup freshly ground coffee beans	3 cups (6 sticks) unsalted butter, at
8 large egg yolks	room temperature

1. Combine the 2 cups milk and the ground coffee in a medium saucepan and bring to a boil. Remove from the heat and allow to steep for 4 minutes. Then strain the milk mixture through a fine-mesh strainer into a large measuring cup. If it falls a little short of 2 cups, add enough extra milk to make an even 2 cups.

2. Return the milk mixture to the saucepan and bring to a boil. Remove the pan from the heat. Whisk the egg yolks and sugar together in a medium bowl. Very slowly dribble 2 tablespoons of the hot milk into the egg yolk mixture, whisking constantly. Dribble another ¼ cup hot milk into the egg yolk mixture, again whisking contantly.

3. Whisk the egg yolk mixture back into the milk mixture and return the pan to the heat. Cook on medium heat, stirring with a wooden spoon or rubber spatula, until the mixture is just about to boil. Then strain the mixture into a clean bowl and let it cool to room temperature.

4. Place the butter in the bowl of an electric mixer fitted with the whisk attachment, and whisk until light and fluffy. Slowly whisk in the cool custard, and beat until light and creamy. Use immediately or cover with plastic wrap and refrigerate for up to 3 days before using. Chilled English Custard Coffee Buttercream must be brought to room temperature and rewhipped before using.

$\mathcal{L}$AYER CAKES

Truly one of the biggest challenges and joys in the life of a pastry chef is creating a great layer cake, one in which the elements come together to form a perfectly balanced dessert.

Layer cakes give you the opportunity to show off your skills. In one cake you can have genoise layers, meringue layers, pastry cream filling, and buttercream frosting. But the point isn't to make the most difficult cake you can—it is to make the best-tasting and most beautiful cake. When designing a layer cake, think about whether or not a particular element is truly necessary. Will it enhance the other elements, or will it add a jarring note?

Take, for example, the recipe for Sure-to-Please Birthday Cake. Each element is absolutely necessary to achieve the overall effect, which is to make a crowd-pleasing cake that is also really special. Plain genoise is moistened with Grand Marnier Syrup so that the cake layers are not too dry and have a bit of citrus flavor. French Buttercream, flavored with vanilla, is a safe choice for frosting when you are serving cake to a lot of people at a birthday party. But when there is nothing to counterbalance the richness of this frosting; people tend to scrape it away. So I add tart apricots sprinkled with crunchy toasted almond meringue as a filling. The fruit and meringue contrast so beautifully with the smooth buttercream that you want to eat every bite. A simple decoration of chopped nuts pressed into the sides of the cake adds flavor and texture as well as beauty, without a lot of fuss.

These recipes are certainly more complicated than the ones for plain cakes, but when you take them step by step they are not difficult—and the results are well worth the time and effort.

LEMON LAYER CAKE

Serves 10

This is a simple, refreshing cake that will stay moist for several days. It is good for after-noon tea at home and travels well if you want to bring along a dessert. To dress it up, decorate the cake with marzipan lemons and leaves (page 469). Or simply serve it with fresh berries and whipped cream.

½ cup Heavy Syrup (page 506)
¼ cup plus 2 tablespoons fresh
    lemon juice
1 tablespoon water
1 recipe Genoise (page 397) made
    with butter

2 cups Lemon Cream (page 510)
2 cups confectioners' sugar
1 teaspoon grated lemon zest
2 cups apricot jam

1. Combine the Heavy Syrup, the 2 tablespoons lemon juice, and the water in a small bowl.
2. Using a sharp serrated knife, slice the Genoise into 5 very thin layers.
3. Place 1 layer on a cardboard cake circle, and sprinkle it with some of the lemon syrup. Spread ½ cup of the Lemon Cream over the cake. Repeat with the next 3 cake layers, syrup, and Lemon Cream. Top with the remaining cake layer. Press the top of the cake lightly with the bottom of a cake pan to make it level.
4. Whisk the confectioners' sugar, the remaining ¼ cup lemon juice, and the lemon zest together in a medium bowl until smooth.
5. Bring the apricot jam to a boil. Strain the hot jam, and brush it over the top and sides of the cake. Immediately brush the confectioners' sugar mixture over the jam. Let the glaze dry completely. Covered with a cake dome, Lemon Layer Cake will keep at room temperature for up to 3 days.

ISLAND RUM CAKE

Serves 12

If you'd prefer a nonalcoholic version of this cake, you can soak the genoise layer with 1¾ cups orange juice mixed with ¼ cup lemon juice. In that case, dust the frosted cake with confectioners' sugar instead of cocoa powder.

1 recipe Genoise (page 397)
1½ cups Light Syrup (page 506)
½ cup dark rum
Two 10-inch layers Japonaise
   Meringue (page 216)

3 cups French Buttercream
   (page 402)
1 cup sliced almonds, toasted
Unsweetened cocoa powder for
   dusting

1. Trim the top and bottom of the Genoise so that you have a cake layer about 1 inch thick with no browned crust on either side. Trim the sides so that the layer measures 8½ inches in diameter. Combine the Light Syrup and the rum in a small bowl. Place the Genoise on a rimmed baking sheet. Brush both sides of the layer with the syrup, soaking it completely. (To turn the layer over without breaking it, slide it onto a cardboard cake circle or the bottom of a cake pan.)

2. Trim the Japonaise layers so that they measure 9 inches in diameter. Reserve the scraps for another use.

3. Place 1 layer of the Japonaise on a 10-inch cardboard cake round. Spread a ¼-inch-thick layer of the buttercream over the Japonaise. Using another cardboard cake round or a large spatula, carefully lift the soaked Genoise and place it on top of the frosted Japonaise layer. Spread ¼ inch of buttercream over the Genoise. Place the remaining Japonaise on top of the Genoise layer.

4. Evenly coat the sides of the cake with the remaining buttercream. Press the sliced almonds into the sides. Heavily dust the top with cocoa powder, and refrigerate for at least 2 hours or up to 1 day. Slice the cake as soon as you take it out of the refrigerator. Let the slices stand at room temperature for 1 hour before serving.

SURE-TO-PLEASE BIRTHDAY CAKE

Serves 12

When you make a lot of birthday cakes for people you don't know very well, you have to have a recipe that you are sure will please anyone. Over the years, I found this flavor combination to be universally popular. Apricots are my choice here because their slightly acidic flavor cuts the sweetness of the buttercream. The toasted meringue lends its rich caramel flavor as well as a nice crunchy texture to the cake.

For a super-smooth finish, give the cake a third coating of buttercream: Place it in the freezer again after spreading the second layer of buttercream, and heat the leftover buttercream in a double boiler over simmering water, stirring constantly, until it is just pourable but not yet runny. Place the chilled cake on a wire rack over a rimmed baking sheet, and pour the buttercream over the cake, using a large offset spatula to smooth the top as you pour and to push the buttercream over the sides. Tilt and gently shake the wire rack so that the runny buttercream covers the sides.

½ cup Light Syrup (page 506), plus
   ¼ cup if not using Grand Marnier
¼ cup Grand Marnier (optional)
1 recipe Genoise (page 397)
1 recipe French Buttercream
   (page 402)

Two 15-ounce cans apricot halves in
   syrup, drained and patted dry
2 cups coarsely crumbled Almond or
   Swiss Meringue (pages 204, 215)
1 cup toasted, sliced almonds

1. Combine the Light Syrup and Grand Marnier, if using, in a small bowl. If not using Grand Marnier, add the extra ¼ cup Light Syrup.

2. Slice the Genoise horizontally into 3 equal layers. Place the bottom layer on a 9-inch cardboard cake round. Sprinkle with ¼ cup of the syrup mixture. Spread a ⁵⁄₁₆-inch-thick layer of buttercream over the cake layer. Arrange a layer of apricots on top of the buttercream. Sprinkle a layer of crumbled meringue over the apricots. Press lightly with a spatula so that the apricots and meringue will adhere. Spread another thin layer of buttercream over the apricots and meringue. Repeat the layers of cake, syrup, buttercream, apricots, meringue, and buttercream. Place the third cake layer on top, soak it with the remaining ¼ cup syrup; smooth some of the remaining buttercream over the top and sides of the cake.

(continued)

3.   Chill the cake in the freezer for 30 minutes. Then smooth another thin layer of buttercream over the top and sides to cover any brown spots or imperfections. (At this point you can return the cake to the freezer until the frosting is hardened, wrap it in plastic wrap, and freeze it for up to 1 month. Let the cake defrost in the refrigerator overnight before serving.) Press the sliced almonds onto the sides of the cake if desired, and refrigerate for up to 1 day before serving. Let the cake stand at room temperature for 1 hour (or 4 hours if it was frozen) before slicing and serving.

ORANGE BAVARIAN CAKE

Serves 10

If you prefer a nonalcoholic flavor, replace the Grand Marnier and Light Syrup in this recipe with 1 cup orange juice mixed with 1 tablespoon lemon juice.

1 recipe Genoise (page 397)
⅓ cup Grand Marnier or other
   orange-flavored liqueur
½ cup Light Syrup (page 506)
1 recipe Orange Bavarian (page 129),
   freshly made and still soft

3 to 4 navel oranges, peeled and
   segmented
1 cup fresh raspberries
White Chocolate Shavings (page 436)

1.   Trim the top and bottom of the Genoise so that you have a cake layer about 1 inch thick with no browned crust on either side. Trim ½ inch from the sides all the way around, so that the layer measures 8 inches across. Place the cake on a rimmed baking sheet.

2.   Combine the Grand Marnier and Light Syrup in a small bowl. Brush most of this syrup over both sides of the cake, soaking it completely. (To turn the cake over without breaking it, slide it onto a cardboard cake circle or the bottom of a cake pan.) To check that the cake is soaked through, cut a small plug from the

center of the cake with a paring knife. If the cake is still dry, sprinkle on the remaining syrup. Replace the plug.

3. Line a 10-inch round cake pan with parchment paper. Fill the pan three-fourths full with the soft Bavarian. Place the soaked Genoise in the center of the pan (there should be about ½ inch between the edge of the cake and the edge of the pan), pushing it down so that it is level and fully in contact with the Bavarian. Wrap the pan in plastic wrap and freeze it overnight or for up to 3 weeks.

4. To serve: Remove the cake from the freezer and unwrap it. Run a sharp knife around the edge of the pan. Hold the bottom of the pan over a gas or electric burner for several seconds to loosen the cake from the pan. Invert a serving plate over the top of the pan. Invert the two together, and gently shake to release the cake. Gently peel off the paper. Let the cake defrost on the counter until it reaches room temperature, 2 to 3 hours. Just before serving, arrange the orange segments and raspberries around the base of the cake. Cover the top of the cake with White Chocolate Shavings.

LOW-CALORIE STRAWBERRY CAKE

Serves 10

This is an unusual and absolutely beautiful cake, wonderful in late spring and summer, when local strawberries are in season. Made with butter-free genoise, strawberry gelatin, and tons of fruit, it is also among the lightest desserts in my repertoire. Butter-free genoise, in addition to being less caloric, absorbs liquid better than genoise made with butter. Melon balls and sliced strawberries are pretty and simple garnishes. In addition, any extra gelée can be poured on the platter around the cake or served on the side as a sauce. For extra-special occasions, decorate the top of the cake with a white pulled sugar rose (page 489) or white marzipan rose (page 471) with green leaves.

¾ cup cold water
2¼ cups sugar
3 pints fresh strawberries, washed
   and stemmed (about 2 pounds,
   6 ounces without the stems)
Red food coloring
3 tablespoons fresh lemon juice
1 envelope unflavored gelatin
   (or 7 sheets; see page 119)

1 recipe Genoise (page 397), made
   without butter
Melon balls and sliced strawberries
   for garnish
Sweetened Whipped Cream
   (page 521) or Vanilla Ice
   Cream (page 185, optional)

1. Combine ½ cup of the water and 1½ cups of the sugar in a large saucepan and bring to a boil, stirring occasionally to dissolve the sugar. Lower the heat, add 1 pint plus ½ cup strawberries and a few drops of red food coloring, and cook at a bare simmer until softened, about 15 minutes. Remove the pan from the heat, transfer the berries and syrup to a bowl, and let cool completely.

2. Place the remaining 1 pint plus 1½ cups strawberries, the remaining ¾ cup sugar, and the lemon juice in a blender and blend until smooth. Stir in a few drops of red food coloring to brighten the puree. You should have about 3½ cups of strawberry puree.

3. Place 2½ cups of the puree in a medium bowl. Pour 1 inch of water into a small saucepan and bring to a bare simmer. Place the remaining ¼ cup cold water in a small heatproof bowl and sprinkle the gelatin on top. Let stand to dissolve. Then place the bowl over the simmering water and heat, whisking constantly,

just until the gelatin melts, 30 seconds to 1 minute. Mix the melted gelatin into the 2½ cups of puree, working quickly so that no rubbery strands form.

4. Trim away ⅛ inch of the Genoise all the way around the sides. Slice the cake horizontally into 2 layers, and place them on a rimmed baking sheet.

5. Drain the poached strawberries thoroughly, reserving the poaching liquid.

6. Combine the remaining 1 cup strawberry puree with ½ cup of the cooled poaching liquid. Soak both sides of both cake layers with this mixture. (To turn the layers over without breaking them, slide each onto a cardboard cake circle or the bottom of a cake pan.)

7. Pour ½ inch of the strawberry gelée into a 9 x 2-inch-deep round cake pan. Place it in the freezer until the gelée is set, about 30 minutes.

8. Place 1 layer of the soaked genoise on top of the gelée. Arrange the poached strawberries on top of the Genoise, making sure that neither the cake nor the berries are touching the sides of the pan. Place the remaining Genoise layer on top of the poached strawberries. Pour the remaining gelée over the cake so that it runs over the sides and fills up the space between the cake and the pan and comes just to the top of the second cake layer without covering it. Set aside any extra gelée and keep at room temperature.

9. Place the cake in the freezer until completely set, about 1 hour. If at this point the gelée has settled and no longer reaches the top of the second layer, pour additional gelée into the pan so that it is once again even with the top of the cake. (If the extra gelée has become too thick to pour, heat it gently over a pot of barely simmering water until it is just pourable. Do not overheat.) Freeze until well set, 1 hour. The cake can be refrigerated at this point for up to 1 day before unmolding and serving.

10. To unmold and serve: Dip the bottom of the cake pan in hot water for 10 to 15 seconds. Invert a serving platter over the pan, invert the two together, and tap gently to unmold. Let the cake come to room temperature, about 30 minutes. Just before serving, spoon any remaining gelée around the edges of the cake. Garnish the plate with melon balls and sliced strawberries, placing some sliced strawberries on the center of the cake as well. Slice, and serve with whipped cream or ice cream if desired.

CHOCOLATE CHERRY CAKE

Serves 10

Here is a very simple and tasty way to dress up the Chocolate Butter Cake layers. Fresh raspberries may be substituted for the cherries if you like.

¼ cup cold water
1 envelope unflavored gelatin
   (or 5 sheets; see page 119)
3 cups heavy cream, chilled
½ cup confectioners' sugar
½ tablespoon pure vanilla extract
1 recipe Chocolate Butter Cake
   (page 400), split into 2 layers

3 tablespoons seedless raspberry jam
Two 14-ounce cans dark pitted
   cherries, drained and patted dry
1 recipe Semisweet Chocolate Glaze
   (page 512), cooled but still liquid
Chocolate Shavings (page 436,
   optional)

1. Pour 1 inch of water into a small saucepan and bring to a bare simmer. Place the cold water in a small heatproof bowl and sprinkle the gelatin on top. Let stand to dissolve. Then place the bowl over the simmering water and heat, whisking constantly, just until the gelatin melts, 30 seconds to 1 minute.

2. Whip the heavy cream in an electric mixer until it just begins to hold soft peaks. Add the confectioners' sugar and vanilla, and whip until it holds stiff peaks. With the mixer on high speed mix in the melted gelatin, working quickly so that no rubbery strands form.

3. Place 1 cake layer on a 9-inch cardboard cake round. Spread the jam over the cake layer. Spread a ¼-inch-thick layer of whipped cream over the jam, smoothing it with a spatula. Arrange the cherries over the whipped cream, and cover the cherries with another layer of whipped cream. Place the second cake layer on top. Cover it with the remaining whipped cream and smooth the top with a spatula. Place the cake in the freezer and leave it until the whipped cream is firm, about 30 minutes.

4. Place the cake on a wire rack set in a rimmed baking sheet. Pour the glaze all over the cake, smoothing it with a small offset spatula. Gently tap and tilt the cake so that the glaze runs down and completely coats the sides. Work quickly so that the glaze covers the cake before it has a chance to harden. Place the covered cake on a serving platter, and arrange Chocolate Shavings on the cake if

desired. Serve immediately, or let stand under a cake dome at room temperature for up to 8 hours before serving.

CHOCOLATE CHAMPAGNE MOUSSE CAKE

Serves 10

This is a chic dessert for a special occasion. Chocolate and Champagne are a surprisingly delicious combination. You'll need a cake ring, available at baking supply and housewares shops, because the cake is too delicate to assemble in a pan and then remove. The decorative chocolate ribbon sounds tricky, but once you get the hang of it, it's really quite easy to make.

¼ cup fresh orange juice
¼ cup Heavy Syrup (page 506)
One ½-inch-thick layer Genoise (page 397)
1 cup Chocolate Bavarian (page 129), freshly made and still soft
One ½-inch-thick layer Chocolate Genoise (page 399)
1 cup Champagne Mousse (page 126), freshly made and still soft

Decorative chocolate ribbon (page 438)
Chocolate Shavings (page 436) for garnish (optional)
Frosted Grapes (page 47) for garnish (optional)
Raspberry Sauce (page 516) for garnish (optional)

1. Combine the orange juice and Heavy Syrup in a small bowl and set aside.
2. Place a 9-inch cake ring on a 10-inch cardboard cake round. Place the Genoise in the center of the ring. Pour the Chocolate Bavarian over the Genoise and let it run down the sides so that the cake is completely covered and the space between the cake and the sides of the ring is filled. The cake ring should be about one-third full. Refrigerate until the Bavarian has begun to set, about 30 minutes.
3. Place the Chocolate Genoise in the center of the cake ring. Brush the chocolate layer with the orange juice mixture. Pour the Champagne Mousse over the

(continued)

chocolate layer, filling the ring to the top. Refrigerate until completely set, at least 1 hour and up to 1 day.

4. To unmold, run a sharp paring knife around the ring and carefully lift the ring up from the cake. (If you have a small kitchen torch, you can briefly warm the outside of the ring and then lift it off, instead of using the knife.) Wrap the chocolate band, still on the plastic, around the cake (see page 439). Refrigerate the cake for 20 minutes.

5. Peel away the plastic and decorate the top of the cake with chocolate shavings if desired. Serve immediately, or refrigerate for up to 1 day before serving; garnish the cake with Frosted Grapes and Raspberry Sauce if desired.

CHOCOLATE BAVARIAN CAKE

Serves 16

Chocolate Bavarian Cake is a wonderful special-occasion dessert consisting of several components, none of which is terribly difficult to make.

Why cut the cake into slices before glazing them, rather than just glaze the entire cake? Because if you are going to make the effort to put together a Bavarian cake, you want it to look good when it finally reaches the table. Cutting the cake into slices before glazing it allows you to serve what look like beautiful individual desserts rather than messy, falling-apart pieces of cake. Freezing the cake before glazing it allows you to make perfect slices, and frozen slices of cake hold their perfect shape while being glazed. Let the slices come to room temperature before serving.

If you are serving this dessert in the summer, consider this option: Insert a popsicle stick into the wider side of each slice and dip each slice completely in the glaze. Let the excess glaze drip back into the bowl. Place the glazed slices on a parchment-lined baking sheet and freeze them until the glaze is completely hardened, or for up to 1 month. Serve the cake frozen, as you would ice cream pops. I like to stick the popsicle sticks into a halved watermelon just before serving, so that the pops look like chocolate flowers sprouting from the melon.

1 recipe Chocolate Butter Cake
(page 400) or Chocolate Genoise
(page 399)
½ recipe Chocolate Bavarian
(page 129)
2 pounds semisweet chocolate

⅔ cup vegetable oil
1½ cups finely chopped Nougat
(page 502)
Chocolate Fountain decoration
for garnish (page 441, optional)

1. Slice the chocolate cake into 2 equal layers. Wrap 1 layer in plastic wrap and freeze it, reserving it for another use.
2. Line a 9-inch round cake pan with a circle of parchment paper, and place the remaining cake layer inside.
3. Scrape the Bavarian into the cake pan and smooth it with a spatula. Cover with plastic wrap and freeze until hard, at least 24 hours and up to 2 weeks.
4. Prepare the glaze: Pour 2 inches of water into a medium saucepan and bring it to a bare simmer. Combine the chocolate and oil in a stainless steel bowl that is big enough to rest on top of the saucepan, and place it over the simmering water, making sure that the bowl doesn't touch the water. Heat, whisking occasionally, until the chocolate is completely melted. Remove the bowl from the heat and stir in the chopped Nougat.
5. Remove the cake from the freezer and run a sharp knife around the edge of the pan. Hold the bottom of the pan over a gas or electric burner for several seconds to loosen the cake from the pan. Cover the top of the pan with plastic wrap and invert a plate over the plastic wrap. Invert the pan and plate together, and gently shake to release the cake. Place a cutting board on top of the released cake and invert it again so that the cake is right side up. Remove the plastic.
6. Place a wire rack on a rimmed baking sheet. With a sharp chef's knife, cut the frozen cake into 16 wedges. While the wedges are still frozen, glaze them: Holding a slice between two fingers, dip it into the lukewarm glaze to cover the top and sides completely. Quickly set it down, right side up, on the wire rack, so that the glaze runs down and covers the spots where you were holding the cake and the excess glaze drips off. Repeat with the remaining slices. Let them stand at room temperature until the glaze hardens and the cake thaws, 2 to 3 hours.
7. To serve, place the glazed slices on individual dessert dishes or arrange them in a circle on a large platter, with a Chocolate Fountain decoration in the middle of the platter if desired.

Two Roulade Recipes

Cakes baked in 16 x 12-inch jelly roll pans can be spread with a variety of fillings and rolled up. They make a beautiful presentation when they are sliced into rounds, each piece with a swirl of filling. Or the slices can be arranged in a cake pan, unmolded, and then frosted.

Many recipes call for rolling the still-warm cake to keep it pliable, then unrolling it, filling it, and re-rolling it. But my roulade cakes remain pliable without the need for this extra step.

Chocolate Roulade Cake

Serves 12

Depending on my mood or the occasion, I make this dessert in one of two shapes: The cake can be cut into pieces and layered with whipped cream and fresh raspberries, as described on page 420, or the cream and berries can be spread on the uncut cake before it is rolled up in a traditional roulade. In both cases, a covering of ganache completes the picture. This is a very simple recipe, but the results are great. The combination of chocolate, whipped cream, and raspberries is straightforward and universally popular.

6 ounces semisweet chocolate, finely chopped, or 6 ounces (1 cup) semisweet chocolate chips
8 large egg whites
¾ cup granulated sugar
6 tablespoons all-purpose flour
¼ cup seedless raspberry jam
2 cups heavy cream

3 tablespoons confectioners' sugar
1 pint fresh raspberries, plus more for garnish
1 recipe Semisweet Chocolate Glaze (page 512), cooled but still pourable
Molded Chocolate Leaves (page 437, optional)

1. Preheat the oven to 425 degrees. Line a 16 x 12-inch jelly roll pan with parchment paper.

2. Pour 2 inches of water into a small saucepan and bring it to a bare simmer. Place the chocolate in a stainless steel bowl that is big enough to rest on top of the saucepan, and place it over the simmering water, making sure that the bowl doesn't touch the water. Heat, whisking occasionally, until the chocolate is completely melted. Set aside to cool.

3. Place the egg whites in the bowl of an electric mixer fitted with the whisk attachment, and whip on high speed until just about to hold soft peaks. With the mixer still on high, pour in the sugar in a slow, steady stream. Whip until the whites hold stiff peaks. Turn the mixer to low speed and add the flour. When it has just been incorporated, turn the mixer to high speed and whip for 10 seconds. Fold in the cooled chocolate by hand, using a rubber spatula, taking care not to deflate the egg whites.

4. Fit a pastry bag with a ⅝-inch plain tip, and fill the bag with the batter. Starting in one corner, pipe back and forth the long way across the prepared pan until about half of the pan is covered with a 16 x 6-inch rectangle of batter. Bake until it is firm to the touch, 12 to 15 minutes. Place the pan on a wire rack and allow the cake to cool completely in the pan. The cooled cake, still in the pan, can be wrapped in plastic and kept at room temperature for up to 1 day or frozen for up to 1 month.

5. Invert the cooled cake onto a piece of parchment paper that has been sprinkled with granulated sugar (to prevent sticking). Peel off the other piece of parchment paper.

6. Spread the raspberry jam over the cake. Whip the heavy cream with the confectioners' sugar in an electric mixer until it holds stiff peaks. Spread the whipped cream over the jam. Arrange the raspberries over the whipped cream.

7. Position the cake with a long edge facing you. Fold over 1 inch of the edge closest to you. Slide a long ruler under the parchment, parallel to the folded edge. Use the ruler, pressed against the parchment and the cake, to help you roll the cake away from you into a tight roll. When the cake is rolled up, roll it back to the middle of the parchment and wrap the parchment tightly around the roll, twisting the ends of the paper to seal. Refrigerate until firm, about 1 hour.

8. Place the chilled roulade on a wire rack set on top of a rimmed baking sheet. Brush the glaze over the roll with a pastry brush until it is completely covered.

(continued)

Transfer the roulade to a serving platter, garnish with raspberries and Chocolate Leaves as desired, and serve. (For a Yule Log, use the tines of a fork on the cooled ganache to make lines of "bark." Decorate the log with Meringue Mushrooms, page 203, and marzipan holly berries and leaves, page 469.)

VARIATION:

CHOCOLATE SOUFFLÉ LAYER CAKE. To make the layer cake version of this recipe, you'll need an additional cup of heavy cream and a little more confectioners' sugar.

1. Invert the cooled cake onto a work surface and peel away the parchment paper. The cake should measure about 16 x 8 inches. Cut the cake crosswise into 3 equal pieces, each measuring about 5⅓ x 8 inches.

2. Whip 3 cups heavy cream with ¼ cup confectioners' sugar until it holds stiff peaks.

3. Spread 2 tablespoons of the jam on one of the cake layers. Cover the jam with a ⅜-inch-thick layer of whipped cream. Arrange ½ pint of raspberries on top of the cream. Place the second cake layer on top of the raspberries and press down gently. Spread the remaining 2 tablespoons jam on top of this layer, spread another ⅜-inch-layer of whipped cream on top of the jam, and arrange the remaining ½ pint raspberries on top of the cream. Place the third cake layer on top of the raspberries and press down gently to level the cake. Use an offset spatula to cover the top and sides of the cake with the remaining whipped cream. Place the cake in the freezer until the cream has hardened but the cake has not yet started to freeze through, about 30 minutes.

4. Place the cake on a wire rack set on a rimmed baking sheet. Pour the glaze over the cake, using a small metal spatula to smooth it over the top and sides. Allow the glaze to set, 1 to 2 minutes, and then carefully transfer the cake to a serving platter. Serve immediately or let stand at room temperature for up to 8 hours. Scatter fresh raspberries around the base of the cake and garnish with Chocolate Leaves, if desired, before serving.

PEANUT BUTTER AND JELLY ROULADE CAKE

Serves 12

I have baked a surprising number of children's birthday cakes during the past twenty-five years. This one was always a favorite, for obvious reasons. Since elephants are fond of peanuts, I often decorated the cake with tiny marzipan elephants, although when the administration was Democratic, donkeys would do just as well! I don't like to add sugar to the peanut butter cream because the grape jelly is so sweet, but if you like a sweeter filling and frosting, add confectioners' sugar to taste.

I often simply fill this vanilla roulade with Lime Cream or Lemon Cream (pages 511 or 510), and then top it with a layer of raspberries or blueberries before rolling it up. I don't even bother frosting the cake, since it's so pretty as is, served with just a little fruit sauce or Vanilla Sauce (page 514) on the side.

1 recipe Pâte Sucrée (page 267), chilled

FOR THE ROULADE:
5 large eggs, separated
½ cup sugar
1 tablespoon very hot tap water
¾ cup all-purpose flour
1 tablespoon finely grated lemon zest

FOR THE PEANUT BUTTER CREAM:
14 tablespoons unsalted butter, softened
1½ cups smooth peanut butter
Pinch salt
3 cups heavy cream, chilled

1 cup Welch's Concord grape jelly
Marzipan Figurines (page 474, optional)

1. Preheat the oven to 375 degrees. Turn the chilled dough out onto a lightly floured work surface and sprinkle it with a little flour. With a lightly floured rolling pin, roll the dough out to form a 10-inch round about ⅛ inch thick, rotating the dough as you roll it and occasionally sliding a flat metal spatula underneath to make sure that the dough does not stick to the work surface. Place a 9-inch round cake pan on top of the rolled dough, and use a sharp paring knife to trim the dough to fit exactly inside the pan. Place the dough in the bottom of the pan, prick it all over with a fork, and bake until golden, 15 to 20 minutes. Remove the pan from the oven and let it cool on a wire rack.

(continued)

2. Turn the oven heat up to 425 degrees. Grease the bottom of a 16 x 12-inch jelly roll pan and line it with parchment. Grease the parchment and dust it with flour.

3. Make the roulade: Combine the egg yolks, 6 tablespoons of the sugar, and the hot water in the bowl of an electric mixer fitted with the whisk attachment. Whisk on high speed until the mixture is pale yellow and has increased in volume, 5 to 7 minutes.

4. Place the egg whites in a clean bowl of an electric mixer fitted with the whisk attachment, and whip on high speed until just about to hold soft peaks. With the mixer still on high, pour in the remaining 2 tablespoons sugar in a slow, steady stream. Whip until the whites hold stiff peaks.

5. Fold the flour and lemon zest into the egg yolk mixture. Fold a little of the whites into the yolk mixture to lighten it. Then fold the lightened egg yolk mixture into the remaining egg whites, being careful not to deflate the whites.

6. Spread the mixture evenly on the prepared sheet pan, smoothing it with a spatula. Bake until just firm to the touch, 5 to 6 minutes. Do not overbake or the cake will be difficult to roll. Remove the cake from the oven and allow it to cool completely in the pan.

7. Prepare the peanut butter cream: Place the butter in the bowl of an electric mixer fitted with the paddle attachment, and beat until light and fluffy. Add the peanut butter and salt, and beat until smooth and well incorporated, 3 to 4 minutes.

8. Whip the heavy cream in an electric mixer until it holds stiff peaks. Fold the whipped cream into the peanut butter mixture, taking care not to deflate the cream.

9. Sprinkle a work surface with granulated sugar. Invert the sheet pan onto the work surface and peel away the parchment paper. Spread the grape jelly evenly over the cake. Reserving 2 cups of the peanut butter cream, spread the remainder over the jelly. Cut the cake crosswise into six 16 x 2-inch strips. Roll up one strip and place it, cut side down, in the center of the pâte sucrée in its pan. Continue to roll the strips, and place them in a circle around the first strip, so that their edges touch the sides of the pan. Place the pan in the freezer for 45 minutes.

10. Invert the cake onto a serving platter. Frost with the remaining 2 cups peanut butter cream. Decorate with Marzipan Figurines, if desired. Peanut Butter and Jelly Roulade Cake will keep at room temperature for up to 8 hours, or refrigerated for up to 2 days. Wrapped in plastic wrap and then aluminum foil, it will keep in the freezer for up to 2 months.

MERINGUE LAYER CAKES

Cakes made with meringue layers are a special favorite of mine. When first put together, the meringue layers are slightly crunchy, a nice contrast with the smooth fillings and frostings. As time passes (conveniently, these cakes can be made up to 3 days before serving), the meringue, filling, and frosting seem to melt into each other. The two experiences are different but equally pleasing.

For more suggestions about how to make simple layer cakes with meringue layers, see the meringue cake layer recipes in Chapter 5.

CHOCOLATE-VANILLA DACQUOISE

Serves 8

This is one of my favorite uses for Meringue Dacquoise. The mousseline filling is simply a combination of two of the best cake fillings ever—French Buttercream and Pastry Cream. Depending on your taste, you may cover the sides with either crushed sliced almonds or crushed Nougat. You could also add an extra 2 tablespoons melted chocolate for a stronger chocolate taste, and/or stir ½ cup additional crushed Nougat into the chocolate mousseline for more crunch.

1½ cups French Buttercream (page 402)
1½ cups Pastry Cream (page 509)
3½ tablespoons semisweet or bittersweet chocolate, melted and cooled
Three 10-inch layers Meringue Dacquoise (page 214), baked and cooled

1½ cups crushed Nougat (page 502), or 1½ cups sliced almonds, toasted
Confectioners' sugar for dusting

(continued)

1. Make the chocolate mousseline: Stir ¾ cup of the buttercream, ¾ cup of the Pastry Cream, and the melted chocolate together in a bowl. Reserve ½ cup of the mousseline for the sides of the cake.
2. Make the vanilla mousseline: Stir the remaining ¾ cup buttercream and the remaining ¾ cup Pastry Cream together in a bowl. Reserve ½ cup of the mousseline for the sides of the cake.
3. Place an 8-inch cardboard cake round on top of one of the Meringue Dacquoise layers, and trim the meringue with a sharp paring knife so it is perfectly round. Repeat with the remaining 2 layers. (Use the best-looking layer for the top. If you have a layer that is especially misshapen or uneven, reserve it for the middle.)
4. Dab a bit of the buttercream mixture on the cardboard cake round and place one of the meringue layers on the round. Spread the chocolate mousseline (minus the reserved ½ cup) across the top. Place the second meringue layer on top of the chocolate mousseline. Spread the vanilla mousseline (minus the reserved ½ cup) across the top of the second layer. Place the third cake layer, top side up, on top of the vanilla mousseline. Press the top of the cake gently with another cardboard cake round or a baking sheet to level it out.
5. Combine the reserved ½ cup chocolate mousseline and ½ cup vanilla mousseline in a small bowl. Coat the sides of the cake with the mousseline mixture, spreading it evenly with a small offset spatula.
6. If you are using sliced almonds, crush them slightly by placing them in a zipper-lock bag and rolling over the bag once or twice with a rolling pin. Holding the cake in the palm of one hand, press the crushed Nougat or almonds onto the sides of the cake with the other hand. Dust the top of the cake with confectioners' sugar. Serve immediately, or lightly drape the cake in plastic wrap and refrigerate it for up to 2 days. Let it come to room temperature before serving.

Mousseline

Mousseline filling is simply a mixture of half French Buttercream and half Pastry Cream. Because it contains such a large proportion of pastry cream to buttercream, it never sets up and hardens like buttercream.

To make enough Vanilla Mousseline to fill a 3-layer cake, combine 1½ cups French Buttercream (page 402) with 1½ cups Pastry Cream (page 509).

For Chocolate Mousseline, stir together ¾ cup French Buttercream, ¾ cup Pastry Cream, and 3½ tablespoons melted and cooled semisweet or bittersweet chocolate (or more if you like).

Use Mousseline immediately or cover and refrigerate it for up to 2 days. Let it come to room temperature before using.

MARJOLAINE

Serves 15

Long, rectangular layers of thin Almond Meringue sandwiched with three different fillings make a spectacular special-occasion cake. I like it for birthdays—its straightforward, robust flavors are perfect for such a celebration. Either Light Chocolate Sauce (page 512) or Vanilla Sauce (page 514) is good on the side. This cake is simple to put together, but make sure that your ingredients are all at room temperature so that they fold smoothly together without deflating. Peanut butter can be substituted for the hazelnut butter (available at natural-foods stores and many supermarkets) if you like.

If you serve it right away, the meringue layers will still have a lot of crunch. Be aware that the cake will change character as it sits in the refrigerator, becoming softer. Some people prefer it one way, others the other. I think it tastes very good in all of its forms.

One 12 x 16-inch layer Almond
    Meringue (page 215)

FOR THE VANILLA CREAM:
½ cup heavy cream, chilled
2 tablespoons unsalted butter,
    softened
2 tablespoons confectioners' sugar
1 teaspoon pure vanilla extract

FOR THE HAZELNUT CREAM:
½ cup heavy cream, chilled
2 tablespoons unsalted butter,
    softened
2 tablespoons confectioners' sugar
¼ cup unsweetened hazelnut paste,
    at room temperature

½ recipe Ganache (page 513),
    whipped
½ cup sliced almonds, toasted
Confectioners' sugar for dusting

1. Cut the Almond Meringue into 4 equal pieces, each measuring 4 x 12 inches.
2. Make the vanilla cream: Whip the heavy cream in an electric mixer until it holds soft peaks. Place the butter in a clean mixing bowl and beat until it is light and fluffy. Add the confectioners' sugar and vanilla, and beat until smooth. Fold the whipped cream into the butter mixture.

3. Make the hazelnut cream: Whip the heavy cream in an electric mixer until it holds soft peaks. Place the butter in a clean mixing bowl and beat until it is light and fluffy. Add the confectioners' sugar and hazelnut paste, and beat until smooth. Fold the whipped cream into the butter mixture.

4. To assemble the marjolaine: Place 1 cake layer on a long serving platter and spread the whipped Ganache over it. Top with the second layer and spread the vanilla cream over it. Top with the third layer and spread the hazelnut cream over it. Place the fourth layer on top and press the assembled cake gently with a sheet pan to level it out.

5. Smooth any of the fillings that have oozed out of the sides of the cake with a small offset spatula. Press the toasted almonds against the sides of the cake, and dust the top of the cake with confectioners' sugar. Refrigerate for at least 3 hours and up to 3 days before serving (as the days go by, the cake will become softer).

ELEVEN

Chocolate Candy and Decorations at Home

CHOCOLATE WORK is a vast and fascinating area of pastry making, dominated by specialists who have devoted their careers to creating beautiful, luscious truffles and glossy filled chocolates as well as elaborate showpieces and decorations. You might wonder why a home cook would want to attempt homemade chocolate candy and decorations when some of the world's greatest pastry chefs have made it their life's work. I guess I would answer that in making something wonderful to eat, the greater the challenge, the greater the satisfaction.

I don't recommend that home cooks try to hand-paint miniature Mona Lisas on the tops of their filled candies or to construct scale models of the Lincoln Memorial in chocolate. But with some good advice and some practice, simpler projects like Chocolate Pear Brandy Truffles, Chocolate-Covered Caramel Walnut Candy, and even a three-foot-tall chocolate bunny are well within the reach of anyone with a block of chocolate, an instant-read thermometer, and a generous dose of patience.

In this chapter, I will explain how to temper chocolate so that it dries and hardens to a beautiful sheen. I will then show you some things to do with tempered chocolate: How to make simple decorations like leaves, ribbons, and bows to adorn special cakes; how to make chocolate containers to hold ice cream and sorbet; and how to mold tempered chocolate both freehand and using a special mold. For the recipe section, I've chosen relatively uncomplicated candies that nonetheless make a big impact when presented at the end of a meal or as a special gift at holiday time.

If you love chocolate and want to learn how to use it in this way, read on.

THE RECIPES

$\mathcal{C}$OUVERTURE CHOCOLATE

All chocolate products originate with cocoa beans harvested from cacao trees, which grow in tropical areas around the world. These beans are removed from their pods and then dried, roasted, and ground into a smooth paste, which is then cooled and hardened. This processed cocoa bean product is called "chocolate liquor" in the industry.

Some chocolate liquor is packaged without further processing and sold as unsweetened chocolate. In this form, it is used with sugar in baked goods like brownies and cakes. Chocolate liquor can also be further processed to separate it into cocoa butter and cocoa solids. The solids are ground and sold as unsweetened cocoa powder, which is also used in baking.

Before chocolate liquor can be eaten out of hand, it must be processed further. Semisweet and bittersweet chocolate are made by combining chocolate liquor, sugar, and powdered milk. Milk chocolate has added butterfat and a higher percentage of milk solids, which make it milder and lighter in flavor than semisweet and bittersweet chocolate. White chocolate doesn't actually contain chocolate liquor; it is made from sugar, powdered milk, cocoa butter, and vanilla flavoring.

Chocolate and white chocolate to be used in candy making are designated "couverture" chocolate. Couverture chocolate contains a relatively high proportion of cocoa solids and cocoa butter as compared with the other ingredients. The extra cocoa solids give couverture chocolate a rich flavor. The extra cocoa butter makes the melted couverture chocolate very fluid and easy to work with. Cocoa butter also lends a beautiful sheen to tempered chocolate.

Although you may not have heard this term, you have undoubtedly seen couverture chocolate in a supermarket or gourmet shop. Fine chocolate that has been molded into shiny bars, wrapped in foil, and sold for eating out of hand is couverture chocolate. It is represented by brands such as Lindt, Valrhona, and Callebaut. Baking squares wrapped in paper and sold next to the flour and sugar at the supermarket have a relatively low amount of cocoa solids and cocoa butter and are not couverture. Nor are the less expensive American brands like Hershey, which is sold in bars in the candy aisle. You may of course buy small bars of good chocolate to use in the recipes in this chapter, but it is more practical and cheaper to buy larger quantities by mail. Purveyors like The Baker's Catalogue (page 523) offer couverture chocolate in 1-pound, 5-pound, and 10-pound blocks at a good discount. If you purchase chocolate this way, you will always have enough on hand for whatever project you may choose. Just wrap the chocolate tightly in plastic wrap, then in aluminum foil, and store it in a cool, dry place for up to 1 year.

$\mathcal{T}$EMPERING CHOCOLATE

Even the most avid chocoholics—the people who bake brownies, devil's food cake, chocolate cheesecake, and chocolate chocolate chip cookies at the drop of a hat—often avoid making chocolate candy and decorating with chocolate. There is a lot of mystery surrounding chocolate work, and especially the process of "tempering" chocolate. But once you understand how chocolate reacts to heat, tempering becomes less scary and even kind of fun.

When chocolate is melted, the fat crystals in the cocoa butter become unstable. If simply left to harden, these unstable crystals will separate from the cocoa solids and form an unattractive gray "bloom" on the surface of the chocolate. The crystals must be reincorporated into the melted chocolate so that they will arrange themselves in a stable, orderly pattern. For this, the chocolate is brought to a temperature of between 100 and 105 degrees and then cooled to a temperature of 75 to 80 degrees. It is then slowly and carefully brought to a temperature of about 88 degrees (85 or 86 degrees for milk or white chocolate) but not exceeding this, so that it is fluid enough to work with but not so hot that the crystals become unruly again. Depending on the brand, temperatures for tempering will vary. If you buy a big block of chocolate from a professional source, look on the back of the wrapping. There will probably be a chart giving exact temperatures for the particular chocolate.

But the work doesn't end once you've reached this stage. As you are using your tempered chocolate, it will cool in the bowl, becoming too thick to pipe or to use as a covering for truffles. You will have to rewarm it over barely simmering water so that it is fluid enough to use. Whisk it very briefly; 2 to 3 seconds will probably do. Be careful not to overheat your chocolate once you have tempered it. If it goes above 88 degrees, chances are good that those crystals will have to be tamed again and you will have to start all over.

Don't let the numbers confuse or intimidate you. The bottom line is that if you start with a block of chocolate that is already in temper (one that doesn't show any gray spots or streaks) and heat it so it is just liquid enough to work with but not too hot, you won't have a problem. To quickly test whether or not your chocolate is in temper, dip the end of a knife into the melted chocolate. If it sets up hard and shiny within a minute, it's fine.

There is no doubt that tempering is a process that requires strict attention and a little practice, but there is nothing inherently difficult about it.

NOTE: Make sure that your kitchen is dry and no warmer than 70 degrees before proceeding with any recipe using tempered chocolate.

SIMPLEST TEMPERED CHOCOLATE

Makes 1 pound (about 2 cups)

As a professional pastry chef, I have come across many complicated and time-consuming ways to temper chocolate. But because I had to produce glossy, smooth chocolate confections on an almost daily basis at the White House, I needed to find the simplest way. Here is the method I have relied on for over twenty-five years to temper chocolate for candies, coatings, and decorations. Follow these instructions carefully and you will be able to produce beautiful homemade chocolate candy, too. If you are unsure about how hot the inside of your gas oven is, check the temperature with an oven thermometer. If you don't have a gas oven, or if your gas oven is ignition-lit, use the stovetop method for tempering (page 435).

The minimum amount of chocolate that you can temper easily is 1 pound. It is easier to work with larger quantities, because the chocolate, once tempered, won't start to thicken in the bowl so quickly. If you need only a little bit of tempered chocolate, still temper this amount. Then let the leftover chocolate solidify, wrap it in plastic wrap, and use the leftover chocolate, along with fresh chocolate, the next time you temper a batch.

> **1 pound bittersweet, semisweet, milk, or white chocolate, coarsely chopped**

(continued)

1. Place the chocolate in a large stainless steel bowl and place the bowl in a gas oven with the pilot lit. The temperature inside the oven should be 85 to 90 degrees. Close the oven door and let the chocolate stand overnight in the oven.

2. Pour 2 inches of water into a large saucepan and bring it to a bare simmer. Remove the chocolate from the oven. It should be melted but still very thick on top. Place the bowl over the simmering water and stir often until the chocolate is just warm and liquid enough to work with, no higher than 88 degrees on an instant-read thermometer.

3. To make sure the chocolate is properly tempered, test it before you begin to use it: Dip the tip of a knife into the chocolate. It should set evenly on the knife within 1 minute. As you work, make sure to stir the chocolate frequently so that its temperature is even and it doesn't begin to separate. If it starts to get too thick to work with, place the bowl over the barely simmering water very briefly, stirring constantly until the chocolate is just warm enough to work with again but no warmer than 88 degrees. Shift the bowl between the counter and the pot to maintain the right temperature and consistency.

STOVETOP TEMPERED CHOCOLATE

Makes 1 pound (about 2 cups)

**1 pound bittersweet, semisweet, milk,
or white chocolate, coarsely
chopped**

1. Pour 2 inches of water into a medium-size saucepan and bring it to a bare simmer. Place the chocolate in a stainless steel bowl that is big enough to rest on top of the saucepan and place it on top of the simmering water, making sure that the bowl doesn't touch the water. Heat, whisking occasionally, until the chocolate is completely melted.
2. Meanwhile, prepare a large bowl of ice water.
3. Remove the bowl from the saucepan and let the chocolate cool slightly until it is just warmer than body temperature, about 100 degrees on an instant-read thermometer (return the saucepan to the heat). Set the bowl into the bowl of ice water and stir constantly just until the chocolate turns into a paste, less than 1 minute.
4. Place the bowl over the barely simmering water very briefly, stirring constantly until it is just warm enough to work with again but no warmer than 88 degrees.
5. To make sure the chocolate is properly tempered, test it before you begin to use it: Dip the tip of a knife into the chocolate. It should set evenly on the knife within 1 minute. As you work, make sure to stir the chocolate frequently so that its temperature is even and it doesn't begin to separate. If it starts to get too thick to work with, place the bowl over the barely simmering water very briefly, stirring constantly until it is just warm enough to work with again but no warmer than 88 degrees. Shift the bowl between the counter and the pot to maintain the right temperature and consistency.

$\mathcal{S}$IMPLE CHOCOLATE DECORATIONS

Tempered Chocolate (pages 433, 435) is an ideal medium for a variety of decorations. Not only is it very pretty when hardened but it tastes great!

CHOCOLATE SHAVINGS

Makes enough to decorate 1 cake

> *At the end of any job requiring tempered chocolate, you are sure to have some left over. Here is a good way to use it up. Chocolate shavings are a simple but pretty decoration. Make them when you can and save them for later use.*

½ cup tempered bittersweet, semi-sweet, milk, or white chocolate

Using an offset spatula, spread the tempered chocolate in a paper-thin layer on a marble work surface. Start shaving as soon as the chocolate begins to set: Holding a heavy, sharp chef's knife horizontally in front of you, with one hand on the handle and the other hand holding the dull side of the tip, place the sharp edge of the knife at a 45-degree angle about 1½ inches from the far right edge of the chocolate. Push the blade away from you, shaving bits of chocolate as you go. Rapidly continue to shave, moving the knife closer and closer to you until all of the chocolate has been shaped into shavings. Quickly gather them onto a sheet pan, lightly drape it with plastic wrap, and keep at cool room temperature until ready to use. Or carefully transfer the shavings to an airtight container and keep at a cool room temperature for up to 2 months.

MOLDED CHOCOLATE LEAVES

Chocolate leaves are among the simplest and most attractive ways to decorate almost any chocolate dessert. For the easiest and most realistic leaves, use real (washed and thoroughly dried, of course) or plastic leaves and brush the chocolate on the shiny side of the leaf. Or make them freehand by piping chocolate teardrop shapes onto parchment and sculpting veins with a paring knife when the chocolate has begun to set (see the variation below).

1 recipe Tempered Chocolate
(pages 433, 435)

Smooth ivy, magnolia, or holly
leaves, washed and thoroughly
dried, or plastic leaves (available
at crafts stores)

Line a baking sheet with parchment paper. Use a small pastry brush or the tip of your finger to spread the tempered chocolate in a thin layer onto the leaves. Place the leaves, chocolate side up, on the prepared baking sheet and refrigerate for 20 minutes. Carefully peel the leaves away from the chocolate. Store in an airtight container at room temperature for up to 1 month.

VARIATIONS:

WHITE CHOCOLATE-EDGED LEAVES. Paint just the edges of each leaf with a thin layer of tempered white chocolate. Then brush the entire leaf with the tempered dark chocolate. Finish and store as above.

FREEHAND CHOCOLATE LEAVES. Line a sheet pan with parchment paper. Pipe 1½-inch-long teardrop shapes on the parchment, tapping the pan a little bit to spread and flatten the chocolate. While the chocolate is still soft, drag the tip of a paring knife down the center of each leaf to create a vein. Drag the tip of the knife from the center vein toward the edges on both sides for the secondary veins. Refrigerate for 20 minutes. Carefully peel the chocolate away from the parchment. Store in an airtight container at room temperature for up to 1 month.

FREEHAND TWO-TONED LEAVES. Line a sheet pan with parchment paper. Pipe 1½-inch-long teardrop shapes on the parchment, tapping the pan a little bit to spread and flatten the chocolate. Pipe a smaller teardrop of white chocolate (or any other color chocolate) inside the dark chocolate teardrop. Sculpt veins as described for Freehand Chocolate Leaves. Refrigerate for 20 minutes. Carefully peel the chocolate away from the parchment. Store in an airtight container at room temperature for up to 1 month.

CHOCOLATE RIBBONS AND BOWS

I like to wrap cakes with chocolate bows or to put a large bow on top of a cake. Sometimes I'll make a square cake and wrap it with chocolate ribbon so it looks like a box. Chocolate ribbons and bows are also pretty when wrapped around chocolate Easter eggs. The plastic sheeting that I use to form the chocolate is available in any art supply shop, and precut plastic can also be purchased at pastry supply shops. It is usually labeled "medium-weight acetate." Use several strips of sheet plastic at a time. To make a very long ribbon, tape shorter pieces of sheet plastic together.

Chocolate ribbons and bows, kept on top of the sheet plastic, will keep at room temperature, loosely covered with plastic wrap, for up to 1 month. Colored chocolate confection, available in pastry supply shops, does not have to be tempered and may be substituted for chocolate. It doesn't taste great, and I wouldn't recommend it for molding chocolate that you are going to eat, but for ribbons and bows it's convenient.

1. Use a small offset spatula to spread a thin coat of tempered white chocolate on a band of plastic sheeting approximately 2 inches wide and 20 inches long.

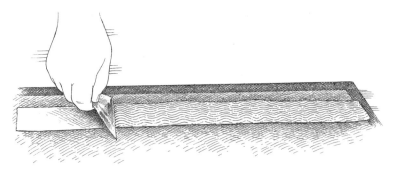

Use a small offset spatula to spread a thin coat of tempered white chocolate on a band of plastic approximately 2 inches wide and 5 inches long. Use a cake comb to imprint the chocolate with either vertical or horizontal stripes.

2. Use a cake comb to imprint the chocolate with either lengthwise or crosswise ridges. Let the chocolate stand until set, about 2 minutes.

3. Spread a thin layer of tempered dark chocolate on top of the white chocolate, allowing the white stripes to show through. When the chocolate is beginning to set but has not yet completely hardened, pick up one corner of the chocolate (with the sheet plastic) with your thumb and index finger. With your other thumb and index finger, wipe the edges of the chocolate strip so that they are smooth.

4. Fold the chocolate band into a loop, plastic side facing out, and press the ends together to seal. Let stand to set completely. The sheet plastic should be ready to peel off in about 15 minutes. I prefer to store the chocolate ribbons and bows with the plastic on to protect them. Remove the plastic just before using.

To make a chocolate bow, use two or more loops of chocolate ribbon and two or more ribbons that you've left straight. When the chocolate is set, peel away the plastic. Use ½ cup melted tempered chocolate mixed with ¼ teaspoon warm water to "glue" the pieces together.

To make a ribbon to wrap around a cake, use a sheet plastic strip that measures ½ inch longer than the circumference of the cake pan or ring you've baked the cake in, and bend the ribbon before it has completely hardened so that it fits snugly around the outside of the cake. Glue the ends where they overlap with the melted chocolate. Let it harden for 15 minutes and then peel away the plastic. Attach a chocolate bow to the side if desired.

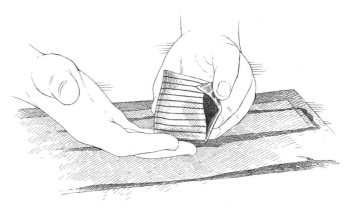

Fold the chocolate band into a loop, plastic side facing out, and press the ends together to seal.

To make a chocolate bow, use two or more loops of chocolate ribbon and two or more ribbons that you've left straight. Use ½ cup melted chocolate mixed with ¼ teaspoon warm water to glue the pieces together.

FINE PIPING WITH CHOCOLATE

Melted chocolate can be finely piped through a cornet, a small cone made of parchment. (A cornet is a handy thing to know how to make. You can also use one to finely pipe ganache, buttercream, and royal icing when even the smallest pastry bag tip is not fine enough for your project.)

It is not necessary to temper the chocolate before piping. Do add a few drops of warm water to the hot chocolate (2 drops of water for about 4 tablespoons melted chocolate should be about right). This will thicken it so it will run less quickly from the cornet, making it easier to work with. To make sure your chocolate is completely lump-free and smooth, pour it through a fine-mesh strainer before pouring it into the cone. Even tiny lumps will clog the opening of the cornet and prevent you from piping smoothly and evenly.

To make and fill a cornet:

1. Cut a triangle with one side measuring 12 inches and the other two sides measuring 7 inches from a piece of parchment paper.

2. Place the triangle on the counter with the shortest point facing you. Bring the far right point up to meet the middle point, curling it under as you bring it up to form a cone shape.

3. Hold the two points tightly together with the thumb and index finger of your right hand. With your left hand, bring the far left point up and around as you did the far right point. All three points should meet at the wide opening of the cone.

4. Close the bottom of the cone tightly by sliding the right and left points in opposite directions. The bottom of the cone should be completely closed.

5. Fill the cone no more than halfway with warm melted chocolate. Roll the top of the cone toward the bottom to seal it and to push the chocolate toward the tip.

6. Cut a pinhole-size opening in the bottom of the tip with sharp scissors. (If you are using the cone for buttercream or ganache, you'll have to cut a larger opening.) Test by writing on a piece of parchment. If the chocolate does not flow freely enough, enlarge the hole slightly and test it again.

There are two ways to pipe chocolate, depending on whether you are writing or making borders and decorations. For writing, hold the cone at a 45-degree angle so that it touches the surface of the cake. Drag the cone over the cake as you would a pencil, applying even pressure to the cone to squeeze out the chocolate, forming letters as you go.

For borders and decorations I prefer to hold the cone at a 90-degree angle, about 1 inch above the cake, and let the chocolate drop onto its surface as I move it to form the desired shapes.

It can be nerve-wracking to pipe hot chocolate directly onto the surface of a finished cake. What if you make a mistake? If you do not trust yourself to pipe neatly and flawlessly, there is an alternative: Pipe your writing or decorations onto a sheet of clear plastic on a flat pan, using the drop technique. (Make sure the plastic is clean and dry so that the chocolate will lift off easily.) After piping, transfer the pan and plastic to the refrigerator until the chocolate is hardened, about 10 minutes. Remove the writing or decoration by sliding a small offset spatula underneath it, and slide it onto the cake. Or store the piped and hardened chocolate in an airtight container for up to 1 month.

CHOCOLATE FOUNTAIN

Makes one 8-inch-high fountain

This is one of the prettiest piped-chocolate decorations that I routinely use.

3 cups Tempered Chocolate
(pages 433, 435)

1. Arrange two pieces of parchment paper on a work surface. Fill a parchment paper cone halfway with tempered chocolate. Cut an opening a little larger than one you would use for writing, about the size of the tip of a ballpoint pen, in the tip of the cone.
2. Pipe a bent teardrop shape that measures about 8 inches long and about 2 inches across at its widest point. Pipe another teardrop, beginning at the same point and overlapping by 1 inch. Repeat, so that you have four overlapping teardrops that connect at their ends. The entire piece should measure about 4 inches across at its widest point. Repeat, making a total of eight of these overlapping teardrop pieces. To the final piece, pipe six curving lines, about 9 inches tall, to form the central spray of the decoration.

(continued)

Pipe a bent teardrop shape that measures about 8 inches long and about 2 inches across at its widest point. Pipe another teardrop, beginning at the same point and overlapping by 1 inch. Repeat, so that you have four overlapping teardrops that connect at their ends. The entire piece should measure about 4 inches across at its widest point. Repeat, making eight of these overlapping teardrop pieces.

Attach the remaining pieces in the spaces between the first four.

3. For the base, pipe a round measuring 3 inches across. Let the teardrop pieces and the base rest to set, about 15 minutes.

4. To assemble, stand 2 teardrop pieces upright on a fresh piece of parchment so that they touch, mirroring each other. Pipe a little chocolate between the pieces to glue them together. Place a third piece at a 90-degree angle, and press it lightly into the melted chocolate to secure it. Let stand until dry, 4 to 5 minutes. Pipe a little melted chocolate on the bottom, and then stand the assembly upright on the chocolate base. Make sure it is standing straight. Allow to set, 4 to 5 minutes. Attach a fourth fountain piece across from the third one. Attach the remaining four pieces in the spaces between the first four. Let set completely before placing on your cake.

PLASTIC CHOCOLATE RIBBONS AND ROSES

Plastic, or decor, chocolate is a moldable chocolate confection similar in use to marzipan. It is made with either white or dark chocolate and corn syrup. You can purchase it ready-made from a pastry supply shop, or if this is inconvenient you can make your own (see page 452).

Plastic chocolate can be rolled into ribbons, shaped into flowers, or used to cover entire cakes. I use it sparingly for decoration. It is not the best-tasting type of chocolate candy, but it is wonderfully easy to work with and produces beautiful results.

Roll small pieces of plastic chocolate into marble-size balls. Place each ball between two sheets of plastic. Push down on a ball with your thumb to flatten, and then move your thumb in a circular motion outward toward the edges to create petal shapes that are thinner at the edges.

- To make very fine plastic chocolate ribbons, run pieces of plastic chocolate through a pasta machine until it is very thin, as if you were making fettuccine.
- To make a ribbon to wrap a cake, run the plastic chocolate through a pasta machine to make a wide, long strip and then cut it to the desired width.

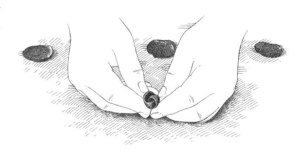

Pinch two petals together at their bases, curving their tops inward toward each other to resemble the still-closed center of the flower.

- For large, thin sheets to cover a cake or to drape decoratively to look like fabric, roll plastic chocolate between two layers of plastic wrap with a rolling pin until it is very thin.
- To make plastic chocolate rose petals: Roll small pieces of plastic chocolate into marble-size balls. Place each ball between two sheets of plastic wrap. Push down on a ball with your thumb to flatten it, and then move your thumb in a circular motion outward toward the edges to create petal shapes that are thinner at the edges.

Arrange three more petals around the inner two, pinching their bases in and against the inner two petal bases. If a larger rose is desired, arrange another ring of four petals around the flower, pinching the bottoms together. The center rose petals should be more tightly closed than the outer petals, which should open more, as with a real rose.

- To make plastic chocolate roses: Pinch two petals together at their bases, curving their tops inward toward each other to resemble the still-closed center of the flower. Arrange three more petals around the inner two, pinching their bases in and against the inner two bases. If a larger rose is desired, arrange another ring of four petals around the flower, pinching the bottoms together. The center rose petals should be more tightly closed than the outer petals, which should open more, as with a real rose. Each of your rose petals and roses should be a little bit different, bending this way and that, the way Mother Nature has fashioned hers.

Spraying Chocolate with a Spray Gun

Using a regular paint sprayer available at any hardware store, it is possible to spray a thin coat of dark or milk chocolate onto a cake, showpiece, candies, or any dessert that you choose. This method gives a dessert an attractive velvety finish.

Spraying is not for everyone. But for the ambitious or advanced home pastry chef, it is a fun and satisfying way to finish desserts. It can be messy and requires special equipment and ingredients. In addition to the sprayer, you'll need a plastic drop cloth to protect your walls and work surface, and cocoa butter, which can be purchased at a pastry supply shop or by mail order (see page 523 for sources). Wear old clothes, as you will probably spray yourself with some chocolate too.

1. Place the piece you are going to spray in the freezer for 40 minutes to chill its surface. Cover your work surface and the walls and floor surrounding it with a drop cloth. Make sure the spray gun is at room temperature.

2. To make the chocolate coating, use 50 percent melted chocolate and 50 percent cocoa butter. Melt the cocoa butter in a saucepan and heat it to a temperature of 95 degrees. Mix the melted cocoa butter with the warm chocolate. Strain to remove any lumps. The ideal temperature of chocolate for spraying is 95 degrees. For a finer spray, heat the mixture to about 100 degrees.

3. Pour the chocolate into the spray gun container. Test the spray gun on a small section of the drop cloth. Adjust the nozzle for a thicker or thinner spray. Remove the dessert from the freezer and place it on a turntable or lazy susan. Keeping the gun constantly in motion, spray the entire piece, rotating it as you spray, until it is finely but completely coated. Let the chocolate set, 10 to 20 minutes, before handling. Pour any leftover chocolate mixture into a container and let it harden; it will keep at room temperature for 3 months. Reheat to reuse.

CHOCOLATE CONTAINERS AND LARGE MOLDED CHOCOLATE PIECES

For me, the ultimate decorated dessert is one that is 100 percent edible. I am never happier than when I can serve ice cream in a chocolate cup that can then be nibbled when the ice cream is gone. I also love to mold chocolate into all kinds of unexpected shapes, to surprise people and make them smile. Here are some of the techniques I have used over the years to mold chocolate into both useful containers and whimsical decorative objects.

FREE-FORM CHOCOLATE CUPS

I love to serve ice cream, Bavarians, and mousses with fresh fruit in edible cups made of chocolate. There are a couple of different ways to mold the cups, depending on the size I need, how many I need, and the materials I happen to have on hand. The simplest chocolate cups are made of a single type of tempered chocolate, but you can also get creative and use several types of chocolate and/or colored chocolate for each cup.

Using a dowel as the mold: Use a wooden dowel or a rolling pin without handles, 1½ to 2 inches in diameter. Wrap one end of the dowel tightly with aluminum foil, covering 2 to 2½ inches of the length. Dip the foil-covered end in tempered chocolate, covering all but ½ inch of the foil. Lift the dowel from the chocolate and let the excess drip back into the bowl. Scrape the bottom of the cup against the edge of the bowl so it won't be too thick, but be careful not to scrape off too much of the chocolate. Slide the chocolate-covered foil cup from the dowel onto a piece of parchment paper, and allow the chocolate to harden in a cool place for about 30 minutes. Then carefully remove the foil by twisting it away from the chocolate.

Using a sponge as a mold: Use a round biscuit cutter to cut a piece of dry, clean kitchen sponge 1½ to 2 inches in diameter and 2 inches thick. Wrap the sponge tightly in plastic wrap, twisting the ends of the plastic wrap tightly on top to form a little knob for gripping. Holding the plastic wrap knob, dip the plastic-covered sponge in the tempered chocolate almost to the top. Let the excess drip back into the bowl. Scrape the bottom of the cup against the edge of the bowl so it won't be too thick, but be careful not to scrape off too much of the chocolate. Transfer the sponge to a piece of parchment paper, knob side up,

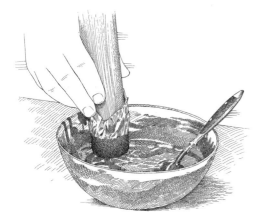

Dip the foil-covered end in tempered chocolate, covering all but ½ inch of the foil.

Use a round biscuit cutter to cut a piece of sponge 1½ to 2 inches in diameter and 2 inches thick. Wrap the sponge tightly in plastic wrap, twisting the ends of the plastic wrap tightly on top to form a little knob for gripping. Holding the plastic wrap knob, dip the plastic-covered sponge in the tempered chocolate almost to the top. Let the excess drip back into the bowl. Scrape the bottom of the cup against the edge of the bowl so it won't be too thick, but be careful not to scrape off too much of the chocolate.

and allow the chocolate to harden in a cool place for about 30 minutes. Then squeeze and twist the plastic-covered sponge to release the chocolate. The plastic-covered sponge can now be used again.

Molding with balloons: If you like a more free-form shape, use balloons to mold chocolate cups. Blow up a small balloon (or any size balloon you like). Dip the balloon into the tempered chocolate as far as you wish to create the desired bowl shape. Lift the balloon from the chocolate and set it on parchment paper to allow the excess chocolate to drip down and form a base for the cup. Alternatively, place a balloon right side up in a glass to hold it steady. Pour several different colored chocolates, unmixed, over the top of the balloon and let them drip down the sides unevenly. Refrigerate until fully set, about 30 minutes. Pour a little leftover chocolate into a puddle shape 6 to 8 inches in diameter. Overturn the chocolate-covered balloon onto this base and hold it in place until it is set and stable. Prick the balloon with a pin to release the air, and peel it away from the chocolate.

Dip the balloon into the tempered chocolate as far as you wish to create the desired bowl shape.

Place a balloon right side up in a glass to hold it steady. Pour chocolate over the top of the balloon and let it drip down the sides unevenly.

MOLDING CHOCOLATE IN COCOA POWDER, CONFECTIONERS' SUGAR, OR CORNSTARCH

It's fun and not too difficult to make one-sided chocolate decorations by making an impression of a toy, tool, fruit, medal, or any object you wish in a pan of cocoa powder, confectioners' sugar, or cornstarch and then piping Tempered Chocolate (pages 433, 435) into the impression.

1. Sift cocoa powder, confectioners' sugar, or cornstarch into a cake pan that is large enough to contain the impression of the object you'd like to mold. When the pan is full, even out the cocoa, sugar, or cornstarch by scraping away the excess with a flat metal spatula or ruler so that it is flush with the top of the pan.

2. Press the object to be molded into the pan. Carefully remove it, leaving the impression.

3. Use a parchment cone to pipe tempered chocolate into the impression (see page 440). Allow the chocolate to firm up completely.

4. Remove the chocolate form from the pan and brush off any cocoa, sugar, or cornstarch with a clean, dry pastry brush.

Resourceful Freehand Molding

Over the past twenty-five years at the White House, I've made everything from baseball bats to elephants out of chocolate. Needless to say, I don't always (or even often) have molds on hand to make the chocolate objects I need. So I improvise. As long as I'm molding only one or three sides, I can usually figure out a way to make anything out of chocolate without a mold.

Several years ago, I was asked to make twenty-four Big Bens out of chocolate for a dinner in honor of Tony Blair. I promptly got on the phone with a friend in London, who promised to send a replica of the landmark in plastic so I could fabricate my own silicone mold. But overseas shipping being what it is, the miniature Big Ben didn't arrive until the day of the dinner—not enough time to make the mold I had planned.

In my pastry kitchen, there is no such thing as defeat. Instead of panicking, I determined to use this plastic Big Ben somehow to get the job done. Casting my eye around the kitchen for inspiration, I spotted a large block of pâte sucrée in the refrigerator. It has the same consistency as modeling clay, so I thought I'd try to use it to make a mold for my chocolate Big Bens.

I decided to do a three-sided tower that would be placed against a background made of white chocolate with a blue sky and painted clouds. With the chocolate tempered, I laid a piece of plastic wrap over the dough. I took the plastic Big Ben and pushed it, front side down, into the plastic wrap and dough so that they covered three sides of the tower. Working quickly, I removed the plastic Big Ben and filled the cavity with tempered chocolate. I placed the filled mold in the refrigerator for an hour. When the chocolate had set, I removed the dough from around the plastic wrap, peeled away the plastic wrap from the chocolate, and voilà, three sides of Big Ben in chocolate!

Exhilarated, I produced twenty-three more chocolate clocktowers just like this one in record time. Everyone marveled at the towers against their beautiful backgrounds, and no one asked why they were three-sided. My dilemma and my solution remained my secret until this day.

LARGE MOLDED CHOCOLATE PIECES

Once you have gained a little confidence in working with chocolate, you might want to attempt molding a large chocolate Easter egg, bunny, Santa figure, or any other shape for a holiday or special occasion. Large molded chocolate figures make impressive centerpieces; nothing delights both children and adults like a larger-than-life chocolate bunny surrounded by chocolate Easter eggs decorated with royal icing and marzipan flowers and carrots.

Large chocolate molds made of plastic, metal, or silicone are available in pastry supply shops and by mail order (see page 523), and they aren't really any more difficult to work with than small molds. (While vintage molds, which are abundant at flea markets and antique stores, are charming for decorating your kitchen or even molding marzipan, I don't recommend them for chocolate work. Their scratched surfaces won't give you the shiny results that you want and may even make the chocolate difficult to unmold.)

As with small molds, your chocolate must be perfectly tempered and the molds perfectly clean and dry. Make sure that all ladles, spatulas, and any other utensils that come into contact with the tempered chocolate are also free of water, dust, and dirt. The least bit of water or dirt may cause your chocolate to seize and may mar the shiny surface of the finished figure. Ideally, your kitchen should be cool (not above 70 degrees) and dry.

Large molds are perfect canvases for colored chocolate. To make colored chocolate, stir coloring oil made especially for chocolate (see page 524) into tempered white chocolate as you need it. Say you have a large rooster mold. You might brush some yellow chocolate on the beak, red on the comb, black on the feathers, orange on the chest. You'd let the colored chocolate set and then you'd brush the entire surface of the mold with dark chocolate, and let that set. Proceed with the molding, with dark or white chocolate, as described below.

1. Set wire racks over a rimmed baking sheet that is large enough to hold the mold when it is standing upright. Open the mold, and holding it by its edges, brush a thin layer of tempered chocolate inside each half. (Avoid holding the mold in the palm of your hand, as this might warm it up and cause problems when it's time to unmold the chocolate.)

2. Place the two halves of the mold together and secure them with clamps. Let it stand

until firm, 15 to 20 minutes. (Don't let it stand too long or this thin layer might become brittle and crack when you unmold it.)

3. When the thin layer of chocolate is firm, turn the mold upside down, rest the top on the table, and hold it steady with one hand. Use a ladle to fill the mold to the top with tempered chocolate. Tap the sides of the mold gently with a wooden spoon to allow air bubbles to escape. Turn the mold upside down over the bowl to allow excess chocolate to run off.

4. Place the mold right side up on the wire rack and let any remaining loose chocolate drip onto the baking sheet. As the chocolate starts to firm up, scrape away any excess chocolate from the edges of the mold, using a plastic scraper or metal spatula. After the mold has been neatly trimmed, place it in the refrigerator for 30 minutes.

5. As the chocolate cools, it will pull away from the mold slightly. When it is ready to be unmolded, you will be able to see a gap of approximately 1 millimeter between the chocolate and the mold. To unmold the chocolate figure, remove the clamps and carefully insert a paring knife into the crack between the two sides of the mold. Slowly twist the knife back and forth until the mold pulls away from the chocolate. (If you are using a one-sided mold, simply turn the chocolate-coated side of the mold down. Position one hand underneath the chocolate. With the other hand, gently tap the corner of the mold against the work surface. The molded chocolate should come right out onto your other hand.)

HOMEMADE PLASTIC CHOCOLATE

Makes 1⅓ pounds

There is no need to temper the chocolate you use for this decorating confection. If you store plastic chocolate for any length of time, it may harden slightly and become difficult to work with. To soften it, place it in the microwave and heat it for just 2 seconds. Remove it from the oven, test it, and if it is still too hard, microwave for 2 more seconds. Continue in this manner until the plastic chocolate is soft enough to work with, but be careful not to overheat or it will begin to separate and become unusable.

1 pound dark or white chocolate, melted and cooled to lukewarm	6 ounces light corn syrup

Mix the melted chocolate and corn syrup in a bowl by hand with a wooden spoon or spatula until well combined. Work the mixture through a pasta machine from the thickest setting gradually going down to the thinnest setting, according to the manufacturer's instructions, until it is completely smooth and uniform in texture. Use immediately, or store at room temperature, wrapped in a double layer of plastic wrap and put in an airtight container, for up to 2 months.

CHOCOLATE GALETTE

Makes about 100 candies

This is a very easy candy to make, and a fun one to eat. Once it is piped, the chocolate will set quickly, so it's helpful to have another pair of hands to place the topping on each disk as you pipe. If you have children who like to cook, give them this job—kids love to place the pretty nuts, raisins, and violets on each candy. Vary the toppings according to your preference and what you have on hand.

1 pound Tempered Chocolate (pages 433, 435)
Walnut halves
Large golden raisins
Shelled pistachio nuts
Candied violets (see page 524)

1. Line a baking sheet with aluminum foil, letting an inch or two hang over the edges of the sheet. Wrap the overhanging foil tightly under the sheet to secure it.
2. Using a paper cone, pipe the chocolate in quarter-size disks onto the foil-lined pan, tapping the pan lightly on the counter as you pipe so that the chocolate spreads evenly. Before the chocolate sets, place a walnut half, a raisin, a pistachio, and a violet on top of each piece. Let the chocolate cool and harden completely, a minute or two. Chocolate Galette will keep in an airtight container at room temperature for 1 month.

CHOCOLATE KISSES

Makes 25 pieces

Make sure that all of the filling ingredients are at room temperature or your filling will be lumpy.

1 recipe Tempered Chocolate
   (pages 433, 435)
4 tablespoons unsalted butter,
   softened

6 tablespoons confectioners' sugar
2 tablespoons Kirsch or brandy

1. Pour ¾ cup of the Tempered Chocolate into a shallow bowl and let it cool slightly for use in the filling.
2. Line a baking sheet with aluminum foil, letting an inch or two hang over the edges of the sheet. Wrap the overhanging foil tightly under the sheet to secure it. Using a paper cone filled with some of the Tempered Chocolate, pipe 25 nickel-size chocolate disks onto the foil-lined pan, tapping the pan lightly on the counter as you pipe so the chocolate spreads evenly. Let stand at cool room temperature (no warmer than 70 degrees) to set.
3. Combine the butter and confectioners' sugar in the bowl of an electric mixer fitted with the paddle attachment, and beat until light and fluffy. Beat in the reserved chocolate and then the Kirsch.
4. Scrape the filling into a pastry bag fitted with a large star or plain tip measuring about ½ inch in diameter. Pipe the filling onto the chocolate disks in the shape of chocolate kisses. Refrigerate to harden, about 5 minutes.
5. Use a dipping fork (see page 462) to dip each piece into the remaining Tempered Chocolate, and place the candies, flat side down, on the foil-lined baking sheet to set. Chocolate Kisses will keep in an airtight container at room temperature for up to 3 weeks.

Molded Chocolates

Chocolate molds are a relatively quick and simple way to make a large quantity of good-looking candies. Most molds have twelve or more impressions of everything from hearts, to Santas, to shamrocks. Whatever the season or occasion, you will probably be able to find a mold to match it.

The best molds are made of rigid plastic. Metal molds are more temperamental, more difficult to clean and dry, and more easily scratched. Before beginning, be sure your molds are clean, dust-free, and at room temperature. Remove dust and moisture from less intricate molds with a cotton ball. For more intricate designs, wash the molds in hot water and soap, being careful not to scrub too hard lest you mar the polished surface of the plastic. Rinse well and place the molds in a barely warm oven (about 90 degrees) to allow any water to evaporate. Remove the molds from the oven and let stand until cooled to room temperature.

Use dark, milk, or white chocolate and the filling of your choice for professional-looking candies:

1. Ladle the Tempered Chocolate into the molds. Tap the side of each mold with the wooden handle of a spatula to eliminate any air bubbles and ensure even coverage.
2. Turn the molds upside down over the bowl of Tempered Chocolate and again tap gently on the sides of the molds to encourage excess chocolate to drip back into the bowl.
3. Turn the molds right side up, and scrape the excess chocolate from the top of the molds with a small metal spatula.
4. Turn the molds upside down again, and place them on a wire rack set over a parchment-lined baking sheet. Let stand until the chocolate has begun to set but is still soft, about 1 minute. Scrape the tops of the molds again, and let them stand until completely set, another minute.
5. Scrape the filling of your choice into a pastry bag fitted with a #3 plain tip. Be

(continued)

sure that the filling is not warm or it will melt the chocolate underneath. Pipe a small amount of the filling into each impression, leaving ⅛ inch between the top of the filling and the top of the mold. Be careful not to pipe in too much filling; you don't want it peeking or oozing out of the finished candy. Let stand until the filling is firm to the touch.

6. Smooth a layer of Tempered Chocolate over the filling with a small metal spatula, making sure that the chocolates are completely sealed and that no filling is visible.

7. Scrape away the excess chocolate so that the candies will not be attached to each other and their edges will be clean when removed from the molds.

8. Refrigerate the molds until hardened, about 1 hour. To unmold, turn the molds upside down over a sheet of parchment paper. Tap the molds at an angle against the tabletop and the chocolate candies should fall right out. If your chocolate was properly tempered and your molds clean, your candies will pop out easily and have a beautiful shine.

GIANDUJA FILLING

Makes enough for 36 small molded chocolates

Molded chocolates can be filled with Ganache (page 513) or any of the other truffle fillings in this chapter. This gianduja filling is one of my favorites. Whatever filling you choose, make sure it is soft enough to pipe but cooled to room temperature so it won't melt the chocolate underneath. Unsweetened hazelnut paste is available in natural foods stores and many supermarkets.

6 ounces unsweetened hazelnut paste
1 cup plus 2 tablespoons
   confectioners' sugar

4 ounces milk chocolate, melted and
   cooled

Stir the hazelnut paste and confectioners' sugar together in a bowl until well combined. Stir in the chocolate.

CHOCOLATE PEAR BRANDY TRUFFLES

Makes 35 pieces

These delicately flavored but rich truffles are best appreciated when made small. I don't like the centers to be any bigger than the size of a marble. For a more robust truffle, add another 1½ ounces of chocolate; the mixture will be firmer and easier to work with. If you want to keep these truffles on hand for more than 3 or 4 days, I recommend coating them twice in Tempered Chocolate and cocoa powder: Let the truffles stand on parchment paper until the chocolate coating has completely hardened and then repeat the process of coating with Tempered Chocolate and cocoa. You may be wondering why the chocolate has to be tempered, since the truffles will be coated in cocoa powder. Even though you won't see the shiny surface of the Tempered Chocolate, tempering ensures that the coating will dry evenly and won't crack.

(continued)

4 ounces semisweet or bittersweet chocolate, finely chopped

½ cup heavy cream or crème fraîche

2 tablespoons unsalted butter, softened

1 tablespoon pear brandy (Poire Williams)

2 cups unsweetened cocoa powder, plus a little more for dusting your hands

1 recipe Tempered Chocolate (pages 433, 435)

1. Place the chopped chocolate in a mixing bowl. Bring the cream almost, but not quite, to a boil in a small saucepan. Whisk the hot cream into the chocolate until smooth. Beat in the butter and then beat in the brandy. Let stand at room temperature until the mixture is thick enough to hold its shape when piped, about 2 hours.

2. Scrape the filling into a pastry bag fitted with a #6 or #7 plain tip measuring ⅜ inch in diameter. Pipe nickel-size balls onto parchment paper and refrigerate to chill, about 30 minutes.

3. Line a rimmed baking sheet with parchment paper. Spread the 2 cups cocoa powder over the parchment in a ½-inch-thick layer.

4. Dust your hands lightly with cocoa powder. Spoon about 2 tablespoons of the Tempered Chocolate into the palm of your left hand (assuming you are right-handed). Place a filling ball in the middle of your left palm and roll with your right hand until coated with the chocolate. Deposit the coated truffle onto the cocoa-covered parchment and use a fork to roll it in the cocoa powder until completely coated. Repeat with the remaining truffles, dusting your hands with cocoa powder and rolling each ball in the Tempered Chocolate, then in cocoa powder.

5. Let the truffles stand until the Tempered Chocolate has set, 2 to 3 minutes. Place the truffles in a sieve and shake gently to remove any excess cocoa powder. Chocolate Pear Brandy Truffles will keep in an airtight container at room temperature for 3 to 4 days.

CHOCOLATE ROCHER

Makes 40 pieces

These truffles use praline paste, which is a thick, creamy mixture made with ground almonds or hazelnuts (not to be confused with nut butters, which are unsweetened). It resembles peanut butter in texture, and the flavor of the nuts is extremely concentrated. It is available at baking and pastry supply stores or by mail order (see page 523).

1 recipe Tempered Chocolate
   (pages 433, 435)
½ cup plus 3 tablespoons praline
   paste

½ cup Caramelized Almonds
   (page 503)
1½ cups sliced almonds, toasted and
   lightly crushed

1. Pour 3 ounces of the tempered chocolate into a medium bowl. Mix in the praline paste until well combined. Stir in the Caramelized Almonds. Let the mixture stand until firm enough to hold its shape, about 30 minutes.

2. Roll the praline mixture between the palms of your hands to form marble-size balls. Alternatively, use a very small (#100) ice cream scoop to scoop out balls. Refrigerate until hard, about 30 minutes.

3. Line a rimmed baking sheet with parchment paper. Spread the lightly crushed toasted almonds over the parchment.

4. Spoon about 2 tablespoons Tempered Chocolate into the palm of your left hand (assuming you are right-handed). Place a praline ball in the middle of your left palm and roll with your right hand until coated with the chocolate. Deposit the coated truffle onto the nut-covered parchment and roll it in the nuts until completely coated. Repeat with the remaining truffles, rolling each one in Tempered Chocolate and then in the nuts. Let the truffles stand until the chocolate has set, about 10 minutes.

5. Line another baking sheet with aluminum foil. Using a dipping fork (see page 462), coat the truffles in the remaining Tempered Chocolate. Place the coated truffles on the foil-lined baking sheet and let stand until completely set, about 5 minutes. Chocolate Rocher will keep in an airtight container at room temperature for up to 1 month.

RASPBERRY CHOCOLATE CUPS

Makes 45 pieces

This is a very festive candy with tremendous flavor.

1 recipe Tempered Chocolate
  (pages 433, 435)
7 ounces semisweet or bittersweet
  chocolate, finely chopped
5 tablespoons strained pureed
  raspberries, fresh or frozen
1 tablespoon seedless raspberry jam

½ cup plus 1 tablespoon heavy cream
  or crème fraîche
2 tablespoons light corn syrup
2 tablespoons good-quality
  raspberry brandy
45 fresh raspberries (optional)

1. Coat 45 petit four paper cups with Tempered Chocolate: Hold a paper cup in the palm of your left hand (if you are right-handed). Dip your right index finger into the chocolate and spread the chocolate evenly over the bottom and up the sides of the interior of the cup. Place the cups on a baking sheet and let stand until set, 15 minutes.

2. Place the chopped chocolate in a medium-size heatproof bowl. Combine the raspberry puree and raspberry jam in a small saucepan and bring almost, but not quite, to a boil. In another saucepan, bring the cream almost, but not quite, to a boil. Pour the hot raspberry mixture and the hot cream over the chopped chocolate and whisk until smooth. Whisk in the corn syrup. Then whisk in the brandy. Let stand at room temperature until stiff enough to pipe, 45 minutes to 1 hour.

3. Scrape the ganache into a pastry bag fitted with a #4 star tip, and pipe it into the chocolate cups. With the help of a small paring knife, remove the paper from around the cups. If serving immediately, place a fresh raspberry on top of each cup. (If keeping for more than 1 day, omit the raspberries.) Raspberry Chocolate Cups, without the fresh raspberries, will keep in an airtight container at room temperature for up to 1 week.

ORANGE PALAIS

Makes 25 pieces

When making Orange Palais, it is important to roll the ganache into a very even sheet before cutting it into rounds. My method, described below, does the trick.

8 ounces bittersweet or semisweet
    chocolate, finely chopped
½ cup crème fraîche
1 teaspoon grated orange zest

Confectioners' sugar for dusting
Edible gold foil (optional; see Note)
1 recipe Tempered Chocolate
    (pages 433, 435)

1. Make ganache: Place the chopped chocolate in a heatproof bowl. Bring the crème fraîche almost, but not quite, to a boil in a small saucepan. Whisk the hot crème fraîche into the chocolate until smooth. Stir in the orange zest. Refrigerate until completely firm, about 15 minutes.

2. Lightly dust a work surface with confectioners' sugar. Place the chilled ganache on the work surface. Place two ⅜-inch-thick strips of wood on either side of the ganache. Roll a rolling pin on top of the wood pieces to roll the ganache out to an even ⅜-inch thickness. Use a small round cutter, ½ inch to 1 inch in diameter, to cut the ganache into rounds. Reroll and cut the ganache scraps until there is no more left.

3. Line a baking sheet with aluminum foil. Sprinkle the foil with the gold if desired. Use a dipping fork (see page 462) to dip the ganache rounds into the Tempered Chocolate. Place the dipped chocolates on the foil-lined baking sheet and let set, about 1 minute. Orange Palais will keep in an airtight container at room temperature for 3 weeks.

NOTE: Edible gold foil is available at bakery supply shops and by mail order (see page 523).

Dipping Candy into Chocolate

In some cases, the simplest way to dip candy into chocolate is by hand. But for the most part, the best way to dip pieces of candy—caramels, truffles, or any other center—into tempered chocolate is with a dipping fork, available in better cookware shops and by mail (see page 524). Dipping forks come with 2, 3, or 4 prongs. Narrow chocolates require 2-prong forks; wider pieces need a 3- or 4-prong fork. The prongs allow you to transfer the dipped candies from the bowl of chocolate to a foil-lined baking sheet. They are also handy for decorating the tops of the candies with drizzled chocolate or for making decorative patterns in the still-soft chocolate.

Although it is possible to dip with just 1 pound of Tempered Chocolate, I always temper at least 2 to 3 pounds to make the dipping go faster and to ensure that I'll have enough chocolate to cover my candy comfortably. Leftover tempered chocolate can always be allowed to solidify and then tempered again the next time you need it.

With a dipping fork, the process is simple:

1. Place the candies to be dipped to one side (your left if you are right-handed). Place the bowl of tempered chocolate in front of you. Place a foil-lined baking sheet to the other side. With your fingers, place a candy in the tempered chocolate. Use the back of the fork to completely submerge it in the chocolate.
2. Position the tines of the fork beneath the candy and lift it out of the chocolate. Wave the fork up and down to allow the excess chocolate to drip back into the bowl.
3. Carefully move the fork to the edge of the bowl and gently tap it. Then scrape the underside of the fork against the rim of the bowl, allowing any remaining excess chocolate to run back into the bowl.

4. Holding the fork at a slight angle against the bottom of the foil-lined baking sheet, let the candy slide off the fork and onto the foil. Quickly pull the fork away from the candy. Repeat with the remaining candies and chocolate.

5. Decorate the tops of flat candies by pressing the tines of the dipping fork lightly into the still-soft chocolate. Alternatively, place a nut or candy decoration on top of the candies before the chocolate has set.

CHOCOLATE-COVERED CARAMEL WALNUT CANDY

Makes 64 pieces

This is a very good caramel recipe. Although your dentist probably won't believe it, this caramel doesn't even stick to your teeth! To simplify the recipe, serve the caramel squares plain, without the chocolate.

½ cup plus 1 tablespoon honey
  (preferably clover)
6 tablespoons sugar
¾ cup light corn syrup
¾ cup heavy cream

¾ cup whole or 2 percent milk
1¾ cups chopped walnuts
1 pound Tempered Chocolate
  (pages 433, 435)

1. Line an 8 x 8-inch baking pan with aluminum foil. Combine the honey, sugar, corn syrup, heavy cream, and milk in a heavy saucepan. Cook over medium-high heat, stirring occasionally with a wooden spoon, until the mixture reaches the hard ball stage (255 degrees on a candy thermometer). Remove the pan from the heat and stir in the nuts. Spread the mixture onto the prepared baking pan, making a ½-inch-thick layer. Allow it to cool completely, overnight.
2. Use a clean, dry pastry brush to brush a thin layer of Tempered Chocolate on top of the caramel (this will be the bottom). Let the chocolate harden, about 15 minutes.
3. Invert the caramel onto a cutting board and peel away the foil. Use a sharp chef's knife to cut it into 1-inch squares.
4. Use a dipping fork (see page 462) to dip the caramels partway into the chocolate, leaving the caramel tops uncovered.

TWELVE

Sugar Decorations for Passionate Cooks

SUGAR WORK has been my passion for almost the entire length of my career. As one of many assistant pastry chefs at the Savoy Hotel in London, I decided to distinguish myself by learning the art of pulled and blown sugar decorations. After a shift that began at 12 noon and ended at midnight, I would stay in the hotel's pastry kitchen and practice my ribbons, roses, and fruit until the wee hours of the morning. When I arrived at work the next day, I would ask the chef to critique my work, and that night I'd try to improve on what I'd done the night before. After I had practiced for months, the chef began to use my decorations on the elaborate petit four trays that went out to diners at the end of the meal. After a certain point, the sugar work on view in the dining room was exclusively mine.

When the Princess Hotel hired me away from the Savoy, it was in part because of my prize-winning sugar pieces. Eager to impress my new employers when I arrived in Bermuda, I was horrified to discover that my sugar recipes and techniques—the ones I had perfected to the point that I had begun to take them for granted—just didn't work in the humid climate. My sugar refused to harden, remaining a sticky, soft mass that was impossible to mold. Instead of turning tail, I swore to figure out a way to work with sugar in that locale. Alone in my kitchen, I experimented with my formula for cooked sugar. Gradually I eliminated most of the corn syrup from my recipe, hoping that an almost pure cooked sugar would set up. I was left with sugar that was so hot that I must have been crazy to touch it with my bare hands. But such was my determination that I managed to pull sugar in a place where no one had done it before, without too much damage to my fingertips.

During my years at the White House, I continued to challenge myself to create new decorations made out of sugar. This humble material, really one of the cheapest ingredients you can buy, is capable of so much if you practice with it and use your imagination. Inspired by the fascinating people passing through the White House dining room—with their various holidays, histories, and cultures—I created hundreds if not thousands of decorations that I hoped would surprise and delight them. My job at the White House offered almost daily opportunities to be creative and to improve my skills as a sugar artist. For this I am grateful beyond words.

I wanted to include a chapter on sugar work in this book for those of you who have the desire and skill to try something more challenging than what is offered in most dessert cookbooks today. Here are the recipes, techniques, and step-by-step instructions for basic decorations that I have tested and perfected over the years. But sugar work takes effort and tenacity. Simply following a recipe is not enough. You have to practice and experiment until you feel comfortable with the materials, and then you have to practice and experiment some more to develop your own style and express yourself creatively. There is nothing more difficult than beautiful sugar work, but there is also nothing more rewarding. When you are able to create something really unique with sugar, you will feel thrilled and proud.

I don't want to make sugar work sound scary or impossible. Although the more difficult recipes in this chapter are best attempted by the very dedicated amateur and the professional pastry chef and baker who wants to expand his or her repertoire of decorations, the approach is the same as in the rest of this book. I try wherever possible to demystify the process. I don't use expensive equipment or complicated techniques. Instead, I use a lot of common sense and tools available to anyone. I stay away from the complicated terms often used in reference to cooking sugar. If you want to find a chart that lists the different stages and temperatures of cooking sugar, you will have to look elsewhere. I don't use a candy thermometer to judge my sugar; rather, I judge when it is ready by how it looks and feels.

I begin with some of the simpler things you can do with sugar. Working with marzipan, a confection made of sugar and ground almonds, provides a similar satisfaction to molding modeling clay. If you have rolled and cut cookie dough, you can make marzipan leaves, stars, or any other cutout shape you desire. Working in three dimensions, you can mold pretty flowers and fanciful figurines without too much practice.

Royal Icing, made from sugar, egg whites, and a little bit of lemon juice, is the perfect consistency for fine piping. When I have to make a lot of fine decorations for a large cake, I pipe them on parchment with Royal Icing, let them harden, and then just place them on the cake before serving.

Pastillage is a modeling sugar, wonderful for forming heavier objects—cake stands, sturdy boxes, even architectural models.

The final recipe, for cooked sugar, is the trickiest but the most versatile. This single recipe can be used to make spun sugar, pulled sugar, and blown sugar decorations.

HE RECIPES

The following list is deceptively short. There is no recipe for marzipan here, since I use commercial marzipan exclusively. But with these recipes and the instructions below, there is no limit to the number of decorations you can make. My advice is to start small and simple, and as your skill and confidence increase, to take on bigger and more difficult projects. I remember with fondness the first small pulled sugar bow I was able to manage my first week in Bermuda. It was almost as great an accomplishment as the scale model of the Bermuda House of Parliament that I sculpted from pastillage several years later.

ROYAL ICING

PASTILLAGE

COOKED SUGAR

GLAZED ORANGE SEGMENTS

MARZIPAN SHAPES

Marzipan is a confection made of ground almonds, sugar, egg whites, and water. It can be colored with food coloring; flavored with chocolate, coffee, or a liqueur; and molded into a variety of decorative shapes. These shapes can be served as individual candies, but more often I use them to decorate cakes and other desserts.

I always buy marzipan from a pastry supplier, since homemade marzipan often has an uneven and grainy texture that compares poorly with the commercially manufactured product. To ensure freshness, take care to buy marzipan from a reputable source. Marzipan that is crusty and granular has probably not been stored properly or has passed its prime and will be difficult to work with.

Commercial marzipan may require some preparation before molding. Marzipan should be pliable but stiff enough to keep its shape. If your marzipan is not ready to go when you open the package, you can try a few things to improve its texture. If it feels too dry and brittle, add a little Heavy Syrup (page 506), drop by drop, until its texture is smooth. If it feels too soft, knead in a little confectioners' sugar. In any case, knead the marzipan a little on the counter before beginning to mold it, to warm it up and make it workable. Take care not to overknead it or you will release the almond oil from the marzipan and it won't be any good for modeling. You want the marzipan to feel smooth but not at all greasy.

Marzipan can be colored before molding: Knead in a little food coloring of your choice, adding just a little at a time, until you get the color you want. Marzipan can also be painted with food coloring after it has been molded and let stand to dry for 2 days.

To flavor marzipan with chocolate, make a paste with some cocoa powder and water and knead some of the paste into the marzipan. For a piece of marzipan the size of an egg, use about 1 teaspoon cocoa powder mixed with a few drops of water. The same thing can be done with espresso powder. To flavor marzipan with liquor or a liqueur, knead 1 teaspoon of the liquid into a piece of marzipan the size of an apple. If the marzipan becomes too soft to work with, knead in some confectioners' sugar until you have returned it to the proper consistency.

Marzipan will dry out quickly and begin to form a crust if left out in the air. While you are working on one piece, lightly drape any other pieces with plastic wrap to keep them moist. Any leftover marzipan can be wrapped in plastic wrap and stored at room temperature for later use. It will last a couple of months, but after this it will start to lose its freshness.

Let shaped marzipan air-dry for 2 days before using it as a decoration. Once dried, marzipan decorations will keep in an airtight container at room temperature for up to 1 week (flowers will keep for up to 1 month). To preserve marzipan for 4 to 6 weeks, brush it with melted cocoa butter (see Resources, page 524).

Molding marzipan into miniature fruit, flowers, and animals takes practice and an artistic eye but is not really that difficult. Special tools for sculpting with marzipan can be purchased at a pastry supply shop (see page 524). They are inexpensive and can be very helpful. If you don't have special tools, however, you can make almost anything using just a paring knife, a small offset spatula, and your fingers.

MARZIPAN CUTOUTS

The simplest way to shape marzipan is to roll it out with a rolling pin and then cut it either with a small cookie cutter or freehand into any shape you like. Lightly dust your work surface with confectioners' sugar before rolling the marzipan out to a ⅛-inch thickness. After cutting the shapes, brush off any excess confectioners' sugar with a clean, dry pastry brush. You can make holly leaves this way to decorate a variety of Christmas desserts; the red berries can be made by rolling tiny balls of colored marzipan to be placed next to the leaves. For golden marzipan stars, cut yellow-tinted marzipan into star shapes, lightly brush one side of each star with water, dip the wet side in granulated sugar, and let dry.

MARZIPAN FRUIT

Forming marzipan into a variety of fruit shapes is simple and fun. A tiny bunch of lemons on the edge of a lemon cake, or a little orange placed aside each serving of an orange cake, is a fresh and unfussy way to decorate desserts. Holly berries can decorate a Yule log, and little cherries look sweet adorning the Chocolate Cherry Cake on page 414.

Begin by coloring a small quantity of marzipan to correspond to the chosen fruit—yellow for lemons, purple for plums, and so on. Don't forget to make a little green for the leaves.

If possible, mold the fruit as if you were a sculptor, looking at a real pear or cherry while you shape one in marzipan. Start by rolling a perfectly round ball between your palms and work from there. Take notice of an individual piece of fruit's deviation from the simple globe shape, and mold it accordingly.

For a pear, hold your hands as if you were praying and roll the ball back and forth so that one end of the ball forms a point. Bend the top of the cone with your fingers to resemble the narrower part of the pear. If the bottom will be visible, make an indentation in it with a marzipan tool or the tip of pencil. Don't fuss with the bottoms of fruits if no one is going to see them.

For cherries, use the back of a paring knife to make the cleft at the top where the stem comes out. Use a piece of spaghetti, browned with a torch or over a gas flame, as a stem. To give marzipan cherries a porcelain finish, let them dry for 2 days and then dip the cherries in the same glaze used for dipping orange segments (page 487).

To give texture to the surface of marzipan oranges and lemons, roll them on a cheese grater.

MARZIPAN MUSHROOMS, MOSS, AND BUSHES

Marzipan mushrooms are very simple to make and very effective when placed around a Yule log cake or gingerbread house. They look even more adorable when set atop marzipan moss and next to marzipan bushes.

Start with a small ball of marzipan and roll it into a cone shape about half the length of your pinkie. Top the cone with half a glazed cherry. Pipe polka dots with royal icing on the cherry.

For the moss, simply push green marzipan through a strainer. To make wintry bushes without leaves, push brown marzipan through a garlic press so that it forms long strings. Lay the strings down flat on a piece of parchment to dry. When dry, bunch them together and stand them upright on disks of tempered chocolate that have not yet set.

MARZIPAN FLOWERS

Plates for molding marzipan and pastillage into flowers and leaves can be purchased at pastry supply shops, but freehand molding results in prettier, more unique flower shapes and allows you to really develop your creativity and skill. Adorn your marzipan flowers with leaves, made either by pressing the marzipan into a mold or by rolling it thin, cutting it into small leaf shapes with a sharp paring knife, and making indentations with the dull side of the knife on the leaf to resemble veins.

Marzipan roses are surprisingly realistic-looking and not difficult to make (see pages 443–44, or illustrations):

1. Color the marzipan as desired and adjust its consistency so it is firm enough that your petals won't droop. Roll 8 pieces of marzipan into balls about the size of large marbles. Roll another piece about 3 times the size of one of these marbles into a larger ball.
2. Form the larger ball into a cone. This will be the center of your rose.
3. Spread a small piece of plastic wrap on your work surface. Drape all of the balls except one with another piece of plastic wrap to keep soft. Place the remaining ball on the small piece of plastic wrap and fold the plastic over so it covers the ball. Rub your thumb in a circular motion over the ball to flatten it into a petal shape. Continue to rub one edge until it is paper-thin, leaving the opposite edge thicker. The petal should gradually increase in thickness from top to bottom. The thick edge will form the stable bottom of the petal.
4. Attach the petals to the cone as you make them, pressing the bottom edge into the bottom of the cone and slightly overlapping them. When you have gone all the way around the cone once, begin with a new layer of petals. The inner petals should be relatively tight and closed, the outer petals more open to resemble a blooming rose. Attach as few or as many layers of petals as you like. When you have attached all of the petals, pinch the base of the rose and cut off the excess marzipan with a sharp paring knife, so that the rose has a flat bottom to rest on. Place the finished rose on a cardboard cake round to dry, 1 to 2 days.

Carnations are also quite simple:

1. To form carnations, roll a 2-ounce piece of marzipan (a piece about the size of half an egg) into a rope about ¼ inch in diameter and about 30 inches long. Place the rope along the edge of the work surface. With the palm of your hand, flatten one edge of the rope along all 30 inches.
2. Use a small offset spatula to go over the flattened edge, using a back-and-forth

(continued)

motion to make the flattened edge paper-thin and ragged. The rope of marzipan should be about ¼ inch thick, with one thick edge and one ragged edge.

3. With the tip of a paring knife, make small cuts along the ragged edge to make it look irregular and torn.

4. Run the offset spatula underneath the marzipan to loosen it from the work surface. Lift one end of the marzipan rope, letting most of the rope rest on the table. With the thin edge facing upward, begin to fold the rope into a ⅓-inch-wide accordion fold. With every fold, rotate the folds a quarter turn, so that the

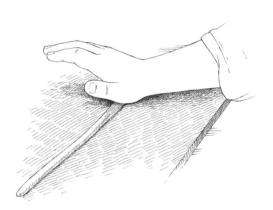

Place the rope along the edge of the work surface. With the palm of your hand, flatten one edge of the rope along all 30 inches.

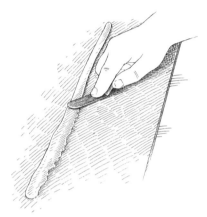

Use a small offset spatula to go over the flattened edge, using a back-and-forth motion to make the flattened edge paper-thin and ragged.

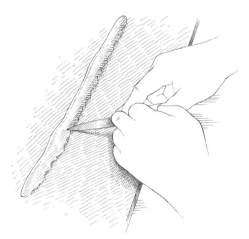

With the tip of a paring knife, make small cuts along the ragged edge to make it look irregular and torn.

With the thin edge facing upward, begin to fold the rope into a ⅓-inch-wide accordion fold. With every fold, rotate the folds a quarter turn, so that the folded marzipan begins to resemble a flower.

Gather the bottom of the flower between your fingers and pinch it together. This should cause the flower to open up. Cut off the excess marzipan with sharp paring knife, so that the carnation has a flat bottom to rest on.

folded marzipan begins to resemble a flower. For larger carnations, continue until you have folded the entire marzipan rope. For smaller carnations, use only one fourth to one half of the rope.

5. When you have finished folding, gather the bottom of the flower between your fingers and pinch it together. This should cause the flower to open up. Cut off the excess marzipan with sharp paring knife, so that the carnation has a flat bottom to rest on. Place the finished carnation on a cardboard cake round to dry, 1 to 2 days.

MARZIPAN FIGURINES

With marzipan figurines, your sculptural talents can really shine. Sculpting figurines is also an area where you can use your sense of humor and have some fun. For a child's birthday party with a zoo theme, a line of tiny marzipan elephants might decorate a cake. Rabbits are a natural at Easter, of course, as are turkeys for Thanksgiving. Santas, snowmen, and elves always populate my holiday dessert table.

No matter what figure you've chosen to shape, the process is the same:

1. Each separate part of the figure begins as a perfectly round ball. To form an elephant, for example, roll a larger ball of marzipan for the body and a smaller one for the head. If you are making more than one elephant and you want to be sure that they turn out to be the same size, weigh your marzipan balls before you begin to shape them so that every piece that is going to be formed into a head is the same size, and so on. Shape the main portion of the figure first. If you are working on an elephant, roll the ball to elongate it slightly, and bend it so that it is an inverted U. Mold each end of the U to form two legs. Shape the head by rolling the smaller ball to lengthen one part of it into the trunk.

Roll the ball to elongate it slightly, and bend it so that it is an inverted U.

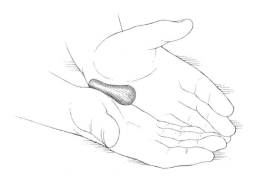

Shape the head by rolling the smaller ball to lengthen one part of it into the trunk.

2. Lightly brush a wash of beaten egg whites over the parts of the figure that you want to attach. It is also a good idea to insert a piece of dry spaghetti into one piece of marzipan so that it partially extends outward, and stick the other piece of marzipan onto it for added stability. For the elephant, push the spaghetti into the body where you want to attach the head, and attach the head to the body so that the spaghetti goes into it and holds it in place until the egg wash has dried. As the marzipan dries, the spaghetti

will absorb some of its moisture, becoming soft and disappearing into the marzipan. This way your figure will remain completely edible. Using toothpicks in place of spaghetti is a bad idea, because chances are that someone will eventually pick up one of your figurines and take a bite out of it!

3. Shape any smaller parts. Elephant ears can be shaped from small round balls, just as you would shape rose petals. A long, thin tail can be rolled from another small ball. Attach these with egg white—very light pieces do not need to be secured with spaghetti.

4. Let your figure dry for 24 hours. Brush it with melted cocoa butter (see Resources, page 523) if the figures are going to be kept for more than 1 week. Pipe eyes by making a larger dot with Royal Icing and then a smaller dot in the middle of the larger one with chocolate. Sometimes I dip the base of a figurine in Tempered Chocolate to give it a nice finish.

Push the spaghetti into the body where you want to attach the head, and attach the head to the body so that the spaghetti goes into it and holds it in place until the egg wash has dried.

Elephant ears can be shaped from small round balls, just as you would shape rose petals.

A tail can be rolled from another small ball.

ROYAL ICING

When I want delicate but durable white sugar decorations for cakes, pastries, and petit fours, I use Royal Icing. Royal Icing is beautiful, pure white, and perfect for wedding cakes and other special-occasion cakes. You can also use a drop or two of food coloring to tint it any color you choose.

ROYAL ICING

Makes 1 cup

1 large egg white	½ teaspoon fresh lemon juice
2 cups confectioners' sugar	Food coloring (optional)

1. Combine half of the egg white and the confectioners' sugar in the bowl of an electric mixer fitted with the paddle attachment. Beat until the egg white is incorporated. Add the remaining egg white and beat until smooth. Stir in the lemon juice. Beat on medium-high speed until the icing is very shiny and smooth and holds stiff peaks, 3 to 4 minutes. (If the icing is too stiff, add a little water, drop by drop, until the proper consistency is achieved. If the icing is too loose, sprinkle in some more confectioners' sugar.) Stir in a few drops of food coloring if desired.

2. Use immediately, or drape a wet kitchen towel over the bowl and let it stand at room temperature for up to 1 hour.

3. To pipe decorations: Draw the desired designs on a piece of parchment paper. Place a piece of wax paper over the parchment, and tape the corners of the wax paper securely to the work surface. Scrape some of the icing into a pastry bag fitted with a fine tip. (Keep the bowl of icing covered with the wet towel while you work so it does not dry out.)

4. Pipe the icing onto the wax paper, following the drawing on the parchment underneath. Let the decorations dry completely, 1 to 2 days (run-out borders will take longer to dry, about 1 week). Dried decorations will keep in an airtight container at room temperature for up to 6 months.

Run-out border

Piping an S for filigree

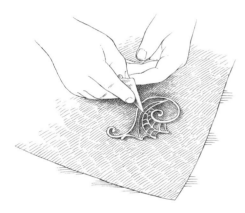

Filigree detail

Hanging border piped onto a disk of chocolate

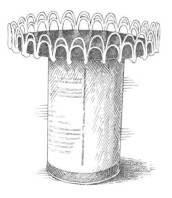

Hanging border, dried and flipped over to show how it would stand on top of a cake

PASTILLAGE

Pastillage can be used to make daisies, poinsettias, roses, and orchids. Purchase special molds from pastry supply shops for this purpose. It can also be modeled into cake stands, decorative boxes for truffles and other chocolate candies, or compote bowls to hold marzipan fruit. I have used pastillage many times to make models of buildings for visiting dignitaries. If you have an architect's eye and hands, you might consider making a more personal model—a childhood home, your church, or your children's school, perhaps.

PASTILLAGE

Makes about 2 pounds

Two 16-ounce boxes confectioners' sugar

⅓ cup plus 2 tablespoons cold water, or more as needed

½ envelope unflavored gelatin (or 3 sheets; see page 119)

1 teaspoon strained fresh lemon juice

Food coloring (optional)

1. Place the confectioners' sugar in the bowl of an electric mixer fitted with the paddle attachment.
2. Place the 2 tablespoons cold water in a small bowl and sprinkle the gelatin on top. Let stand to dissolve. Combine the remaining ⅓ cup water and the dissolved gelatin in a small saucepan and heat over low heat, stirring constantly, until the gelatin is completely melted and the mixture is the temperature of hot soup.
3. Turn the mixer on low speed and pour the gelatin mixture into the bowl. Add the lemon juice. Stop, scrape the sides of the bowl, and then mix on high speed for 30 seconds. Scrape the bowl again, and again mix on high for 30 seconds. Then reduce the speed to low and mix until the pastillage has the consistency of stiff, fluffy royal icing, 2 to 3 minutes. If the mixture is too dry, add more water, ½ teaspoon at a time. At this point the pastillage should be silky, shiny, and soft.

4. Scrape the pastillage out of the bowl and onto a work surface dusted with cornstarch. Gather it together into a smooth ball and place it in a plastic container. Cover the pastillage with plastic wrap and then cover the plastic wrap with a clean, wet kitchen towel. Refrigerate to firm up, overnight or for up to 1 week.

5. Dust a work surface with cornstarch. Turn the pastillage out onto the work surface. Its top will be very wet and gelatinous. Knead it by hand until it has a uniform consistency. It will be very sticky. Continue to dust with cornstarch and knead until it has the consistency of pâte sucrée. If the pastillage becomes too dry or brittle, knead in a few drops of water. If it is too soft, add a little more confectioners' sugar. If you stop kneading it at any point, cover it with a damp kitchen towel so its surface won't dry out. Knead in any food coloring at this point, if desired.

6. Cut off the amount of pastillage you think you will need for your project. Return the rest to the container, cover it with plastic wrap and a wet towel, and refrigerate for later use. Scrape the work surface clean with a bench scraper or spatula, and dust it with cornstarch. Roll the pastillage out ¼ inch thick.

If you are making flat shapes, cut the pastillage into the desired shapes, transfer them to a parchment-lined baking sheet, and let dry on the counter for 12 hours. Flip the shapes and let dry for another 12 hours before assembling. Brush away any excess cornstarch with a clean, dry pastry brush, sand the pieces with fine sandpaper for a very smooth finish if desired, and glue the pieces together with Royal Icing (page 476) or melted white chocolate.

If you are using a mold, sprinkle one side of the pastillage with cornstarch and press this side into the mold. Trim away the excess from the edges of the mold with a sharp paring knife. Allow the pastillage to dry in the mold for 24 hours. Then invert the mold to release the piece and let it dry for an additional 24 hours out of the mold. Brush away any excess cornstarch with a clean, dry pastry brush, sand the piece with fine sandpaper for a very smooth finish if desired, and if necessary use Royal Icing (page 476) or melted white chocolate to glue pieces together.

PULLED, BLOWN, AND SPUN SUGAR DECORATIONS

Beautiful spun, pulled, and blown sugar decorations are among the highest achievements in the pastry arts. If you are looking for a challenge and have mastered other highly prized skills, such as chocolate work and fancy piping, you may want to move on to cooked sugar.

I use the same recipe for making pulled, blown, and spun sugar decorations. The formula is simple: Granulated sugar is dissolved in water and cooked with glucose (available in pastry supply shops) or corn syrup and a little lemon juice. The glucose makes the cooked sugar pliable and silky. The lemon juice prevents the sugar from crystallizing, guaranteeing that your decorations will have a glossy, smooth surface. The hot mixture is poured onto a marble slab and pulled and folded until it is a smooth, elastic mass. While still warm, it can be colored and then shaped any way you like.

Before you attempt any pulled sugar showpieces, test the waters with simpler decorations. Free-form spun sugar and drizzled sugar decorations, made from cooked sugar that does not have to be pulled, are a good place to start. These decorations dry to a clear, bright, brittle finish. Once you are comfortable with cooking sugar, you may want to try more advanced ways of working with it. If you are both an artist and a perfectionist, pulled cooked sugar is the medium in which you can create hyper-realistic and brilliantly colored branches, leaves, and flowers. With the same recipe you can also make incredibly glossy and delicate-looking ribbons and baskets. These decorations require patience and lots of practice. But if you have the time and interest, there is nothing more satisfying.

Because cooked sugar is still very, very hot when it is ready to be pulled or otherwise shaped, wear latex gloves or finger stalls (available in most drugstores) during your first few attempts to prevent blistering. Once your fingers have toughened up and you have learned to work quickly with the sugar, you may want to dispense with the gloves. In my opinion, it is easier to feel the sugar and work with it with bare hands, but only if the experience isn't painful or injurious!

Every utensil and the marble work surface should be absolutely clean before you begin. Lightly oil the marble, knives, and metal scraper to prevent the sugar from sticking.

I prefer to cook sugar in a copper pot, which conducts heat extremely evenly, but stainless steel or anodized aluminum works fine. The size of the pot is very important to the outcome of your sugar work: The bottom of the pot should be slightly smaller than the stove burner so that the heat will reach up the sides of the pot slightly. This will reduce the risk of crystallization during cooking.

You must use clean sugar with no impurities. I suggest opening a new bag each time you want to cook sugar. The glucose or corn syrup should likewise be pure and clean. Cold tap water is fine for this project. Lemon juice should be freshly squeezed and strained. I prefer paste food coloring (see Resources, pages 523–525), although liquid food coloring will work. Make sure that your food coloring is also clean and fresh, with no bits of icing from a previous project mixed in.

To either pull or blow sugar, you have to keep it warm and pliable. Although it is possible to do this by working near an open oven with the heat turned on, this is not terribly efficient or comfortable. The best way to keep your sugar warm is to work with it under a heat lamp. It is not necessary to purchase a special lamp from a restaurant supply store! Any desk lamp fitted with a heat bulb, available at any hardware store, will do the trick. A small electric space heater without a fan, placed on your work surface, will also keep your sugar warm.

Place the sugar on a Silpat pad (see page 17) under a heat lamp, and turn it often so that the parts of the mass that are farther away from the lamp don't begin to cool off and crust over while you work. It is important to keep all parts of the sugar at a uniform temperature. At the White House, I constructed a special piece of equipment to help do this: I made a wood frame measuring 12 x 8 inches with 4-inch-high sides. I stretched a small Silpat over the frame and tacked it to the sides. Then I placed all my different colored cooked sugar pieces on the Silpat and placed the contraption under a heat lamp. Because there was space between the Silpat and the counter, air warmed by the lamp could circulate all around the sugar, keeping it warm so that I didn't have to constantly turn it and worry that the underside was cooling and crusting while I was busy working. If you are going to try to pull sugar once or twice, you can certainly do so without constructing this piece of equipment, but if you find that you would like to do more sugar work, I would certainly recommend that you try my invention. It is easy and inexpensive to construct, and it will take much of the worry out of the process.

Finished sugar pieces should be kept in an airtight container at room temperature. Put a 1½-inch-deep layer of calcium chloride (a substance that is usually used to melt snow and ice and is available at hardware stores) in the bottom of the container and cover it with foil so your sugar pieces won't come in contact with it. The calcium chloride will draw any moisture away from your sugar work and help preserve it for many months.

Let leftover cooked sugar cool in the cake pan, and then place the pan in an airtight container lined with calcium chloride. Reheat in a 325-degree oven until pliable again, and use as needed. With the following recipe and technique, cooked sugar can be reheated as many times as you like.

COOKED SUGAR

Makes 3 cups pulled sugar

I cook sugar differently than most pastry chefs. My method is goof-proof, as long as you follow each step carefully. I wash down the sides of the pot with my hands, not a pastry brush, so I can actually feel that there are no sugar crystals (which will cause crystallization) clinging to the sides. I partially cover the pot so that as the sugar and water cook, the steam will rinse away any sugar that may bubble up. I don't use a candy thermometer. Instead, I look at the sugar periodically and judge by its color whether it is ready to be pulled.

3 cups sugar
½ cup plus ⅓ cup water
½ cup glucose (see Resources,
    page 524), or ½ cup plus
    2 tablespoons light corn syrup

1 tablespoon strained fresh
lemon juice

1. Preheat the oven to the lowest setting possible. Lightly oil a marble slab, a long-handled metal spoon, a metal scraper, and a heavy chef's knife.
2. Place the sugar in a pot that is slightly smaller than the diameter of the burner, and pour in the water. Stir the sugar and water together with your hands until the mixture is homogenous.
3. Bring the pot over to the sink. Holding it by the handle with one hand, hold your other hand under the running water from the faucet. With your wet hand, wipe down the sides of the pot until you can't feel any sugar crystals clinging to the sides, rewetting your hand under the running water as necessary.
4. Place the pot on the stove and turn the heat to high. Partially cover the pot so that just some of the steam will be able to escape during cooking.

5. When the mixture comes just to a boil, uncover the pot. Use a long-handled metal spoon to carefully pour the glucose into the center of the pot. Do not stir, and do not dribble the glucose onto the sides of the pot. Place the spoon in the middle of the sugar, resting the handle against the side of the pot, and leave it there until all of the glucose has dissolved into the sugar mixture, about 1 minute. Remove the spoon and partially cover the pot again. Allow to cook, without stirring, until the mixture just begins to take on a little bit of yellow color and registers 308 to 310 degrees on a candy thermometer, 20 to 25 minutes.

6. Remove the pot from the heat. Pour in the lemon juice and shake the pot back and forth until the juice is incorporated. Return the pot to the stove and bring the mixture back to a boil. Continue to cook until the mixture is a very pale yellow and registers 315 degrees on a candy thermometer, 3 to 4 minutes.

7. Remove the pot from the heat again and let it stand until the mixture stops bubbling. Then pour the sugar onto the oiled marble slab and allow it to cool for 10 to 15 seconds. With the oiled metal scraper or heavy knife, fold the hot sugar back onto itself two to three times, until it is thick enough to be pulled.

8. To pull the sugar: The sugar will be very hot, so put on latex gloves if you want. Lightly grasping one end of the sugar mass with one hand, lightly pull the other end with the other hand until the sugar is 12 to 18 inches long. Fold the end that you've pulled back toward the end that you are holding down on the marble, and pull again. Repeat several times and then switch sides so you are now pulling the other end. Keep pulling and switching sides until the mixture is very white, glossy, and smooth, 25 to 35 more times. Every five or so pulls, give the sugar rope a twist to ensure that the outside surface doesn't cool off too quickly and the temperature of the mass stays uniform.

9. Place the pulled sugar in a nonstick cake pan under a heat lamp or in front of a warm oven with the oven door open. Keep it warm until ready to use, for several hours if necessary.

Coloring Cooked Sugar

Many pastry chefs add food coloring to cooked sugar when it is still in the pot. The danger of doing it this way is that the sugar is still cooking, and if you introduce any impurities with the coloring, the whole mass might crystallize. In addition, it is hard to tell if you are adding too much or too little food coloring while the sugar is bubbling. At this point, too, the sugar has a slight yellow cast to it, which will alter the brightness of the color that you are adding. Instead of pure blue, you'll get a greenish blue and instead of pure pink, your pink will be slightly orange.

If I need only one color for a cooked sugar project, I place a little food coloring on the tip of a paring knife and stir it into the sugar as soon as it has finished resting on the marble slab for 10 or 15 seconds. This way the sugar has already cooked and there is no danger of crystallization. Also, it is so hot that when it comes in contact with the food coloring, any moisture in the food coloring immediately evaporates, leaving the sugar with just pure, vibrant color.

If I need more than one color, I wait until the sugar is pulled and in the cake pan, keeping warm under the heat lamp or in the oven. I cut off as much sugar as I need, and working near the heat, I knead some color into the piece of sugar. This way, I can make as many different colors as I like from one batch.

To get a marbled or variegated effect, I only partially knead the coloring into the sugar, until I see the mixture of shades that I'm looking for. To make beautiful autumn leaves, I use a white sugar base, dab a little green, a little red, a little orange, a little yellow in different spots, let it stand for 30 seconds, and then begin to pull it into leaf shapes. The food coloring dots will stretch into beautiful autumn colors as you pull.

Sometimes I place several different-colored pieces of sugar side by side and pull them together, creating ribbons with beautiful color combinations. It is fun to experiment with different colors to see how they look when pulled. A warning: Coloring the sugar after you have already pulled it can be a little messy, so wear gloves.

DRIZZLED SUGAR DECORATIONS

The simplest way to work with cooked sugar is to drizzle it in abstract or stylized designs onto a Silpat pad or a sheet of aluminum foil. To do so, cook the sugar as directed but instead of pouring it onto the marble slab and pulling it, remove it from the heat and dip the bottom of the pot in a large bowl of cool water to stop the cooking process. (If adding food coloring, do so before you dip the bottom of the pot in the water.) Let the pot

Drizzled sugar decorations

stand on a cool burner or surface until the sugar is slightly thickened. Dip a spoon into the pot and drizzle any decorations you like onto the Silpat or foil. Let it stand until cool, about 1 minute. Use the decorations immediately to garnish your dessert, or store them in an airtight container lined with calcium chloride and foil (see page 481) at room temperature for up to 3 months.

SPUN SUGAR

Delicate spun sugar decorations are also made with cooked sugar that has not yet been pulled. Instead of drizzling it on a foil-covered countertop, the cooked sugar is quickly waved over a few spoon handles that extend from the counter. The resulting strands are delicate in the extreme and make the most ethereal dessert decorations possible.

1. Take an old, clean metal whisk and using wire snips, cut the rounded tip off so the wires stick out from the handle like the bristles of a broom. Set it aside.
2. Cook and color the sugar as directed, but instead of pouring it onto the marble slab, remove it from the heat and dip the bottom of the pot in a large bowl of

(continued)

cool water to stop the cooking process. Let the pot stand on a cool burner or surface until the sugar is slightly thickened.

3. While the sugar is cooling, cover the floor next to your work surface with paper or a plastic sheet. Oil the handles of three or four wooden spoons. Place the spoons on the counter, spaced 10 to 12 inches apart, so the handles extend outward over the floor; weight the spoons down with a heavy pot or pan. Dip the cut end of the whisk into the cooked sugar, and swing it back and forth over the bars. Let the spun sugar sit until cooled, just a few seconds. Carefully, lift it away from the bars and use it immediately, or store it in an airtight container lined with calcium chloride and foil (see page 481) at room temperature for up to 8 hours.

SPUN SUGAR SUNBURST

This beautiful red sunburst is one of my favorite spun sugar decorations. I use it to top desserts like Apricot Sunburst (page 109).

1. Once you have removed the pot of cooked sugar from the heat, color it red. Follow the directions for spun sugar, opposite, folding the strands that dangle from the wooden spoon handles up onto the horizontal strands. Transfer the batch of folded spun sugar to a parchment-covered work surface. Continue to spin and fold batches of sugar, lightly piling the folded strands from each batch on top of each other until you have a cylinder of spun sugar strands about 6 inches in diameter.

2. Stand the cylinder upright and trim the tops of the strands so the cylinder is about 5 inches tall. Fan out the tops of the spun sugar strands. Place the sunburst on top of your dessert and serve, or place it upright in a container lined with calcium chloride and foil (page 481) for a couple of hours before using.

GLAZED ORANGE SEGMENTS

Makes about 16 segments

Cooked sugar makes a beautiful glaze for orange segments. The segments can be used to decorate a variety of orange-flavored desserts and are also delicious on their own or as part of a tray of petit fours.

The segments must be left out to dry overnight so that the sugar will dry and set properly. The same technique can be used for grapes, which should also be left out overnight to dry out a bit. Strawberries and cherries can be dipped in sugar as well. Just wipe them clean (don't wash them), and bring them to room temperature before dipping.

2 navel oranges

2 cups sugar

½ cup water

2 tablespoons corn syrup

¼ teaspoon fresh lemon juice

1. One day before you plan to dip the orange segments, line a baking sheet with a clean kitchen towel. Peel the oranges and pull the segments apart without breaking the membranes. Place the segments on the towel and let them stand overnight. The next day they should have a hard, dry skin.

2. Stir the sugar and water together in a pot with your hands until the mixture is homogenous. Bring the pot over to the sink. Holding it by the handle with one hand, hold your other hand under the running water from the faucet. With your wet hand, wipe down the sides of the pot until you can't feel any sugar crystals clinging to the sides, rewetting your hand under the running water as necessary.

3. Oil a baking sheet, and fill a large bowl with ice water.

4. Place the pot on the stove and turn the heat to high. Partially cover the pot so that just some of the steam will be able to escape during cooking. When the mixture comes just to a boil, uncover the pot. Use a long-handled metal spoon to carefully pour the corn syrup into the center of the pot. Do not stir, and do not dribble the syrup onto the sides of the pot. Place the spoon in the center of the sugar, resting the handle against the side of the pot, and leave it there until all of the corn syrup has dissolved into the sugar mixture, about 1 minute. Remove the spoon and partially cover the pot again. Allow the mixture to cook,

(continued)

without stirring, until it just begins to take on a little bit of yellow color and registers 308 to 310 degrees on a candy thermometer, 10 to 12 minutes.

5. Remove the pot from the heat. Pour in the lemon juice and shake the pot back and forth until the juice is incorporated. Return the pot to the stove and bring it back to a boil. Continue to cook until the mixture is a very pale yellow and registers 315 degrees on a candy thermometer, about 2 minutes.

6. Remove the pot from the heat and dip the bottom in the ice water to stop the cooking process. Let the sugar stand in the pot for 1 minute to thicken.

7. Put a folded kitchen towel under one side of the pot so it tilts a bit and the sugar pools in the lower portion.

8. Dip an orange segment halfway into the sugar. Scrape the bottom of the segment on the edge of the pot to remove excess sugar. Place the dipped segment on the prepared baking sheet. Repeat with the remaining segments. If the sugar becomes too thick, rewarm it on the stove by moving the pot quickly back and forth across the heat, or put the pot in a 375-degree oven for 5 minutes.

9. When all the segments have been dipped halfway, stir a few drops of red food coloring into the remaining sugar mixture. Dip the uncoated half of each segment in the red sugar, scraping them on the edge of the pot as before. Let the orange segments cool on the baking sheet. Use immediately, or let stand (uncovered) for up to 8 hours on a dry day. On a humid day, the sugar will begin to dissolve more quickly.

PULLED SUGAR ROSES AND LEAVES

Pulled sugar flowers are the most delicate and realistic candy flowers you can make. While pulled sugar is still pliable, it can be shaped into very thin, almost translucent petals. The light comes through them just as it does real flower petals. Before you start, take some time to study a fresh rose. Look at pictures in a book or go into the garden or flower shop and observe how each petal is differently shaped and bent and how a single rose can contain so many shades of pink, for example. Include as few or as many petals on your flowers as you like. Make both large and small flowers; make some that are still slightly closed and some that are full-blown. Be sure to play with color, using different shades of the same color in one flower.

1. Place a ball of cooked and pulled sugar on a Silpat pad or in a baking pan under a heat lamp. With two hands, pull it in opposite directions to lengthen it slightly into a thick tube shape.

2. With the thumb and index finger of both hands, work from the center to the ends, forming a 1-inch-high horizontal ridge across the top of the sugar mass.

3. With one hand holding the piece of sugar to the table, use the thumb and index finger of the other hand to stretch

(continued)

With the thumb and index finger of both hands, work from the center to the ends, forming a 1-inch-high horizontal ridge across the top of the sugar mass.

With one hand holding the piece of sugar to the table, use the thumb and index finger of the other hand to stretch and pull a piece of sugar away from the middle of the ridge, massaging it between your fingers to thin it. Bend it around your thumb to form the unfurled inner petal of the rose.

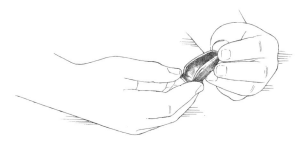

Roll the piece back and forth between your thumb and index finger until it is a tight cone shape.

Place it upright on top of a small round cookie cutter measuring 1" to 1½" in diameter.

While the petal is still warm, shape it around the inner cone, pressing the bottom against the base of the cone to attach it. The sugar should be warm enough so that the two pieces will stick together with no problem. Repeat with two or three more petals, overlapping them slightly, to form the inner portion of the rose.

Form the remaining petals and let them harden on another Silpat pad away from the heat lamp. Once they are completely cool, use a small gas torch or a gas burner to warm the bottom of each petal and attach it to the base of the flower, overlapping them slightly and arranging them in rings.

and pull a piece of sugar away from the middle of the ridge, massaging it between your fingers to thin it. Bend it around your thumb to form the unfurled inner petal of the rose.

4. Pinch the pulled piece of sugar where it is attached to the ridge, and quickly snap it off the larger piece.

5. Roll the piece back and forth between your thumb and index finger until it is a tight cone shape. Place it upright on top of a thimble measuring 1 to 1½ inches in diameter.

6. Pull another piece of sugar from the middle of the ridge, again massaging it between your fingers to thin it. Without wrapping it around your thumb, pinch the piece of sugar where it is attached to the ridge and quickly snap it off the larger piece. Still working under the heat lamp, thin the edges of the piece with your thumb and index finger, shaping it into a petal.

7. While the petal is still warm, shape it around the inner cone, pressing the bottom against the base of the cone to attach it. The sugar should be warm enough so that the two pieces will stick together with no problem. Repeat with two or three more petals, overlapping them slightly, to form the inner portion of the rose.

8. Form the remaining petals and let them harden on another Silpat pad away from the heat lamp. Once they are completely cool, use a small gas torch or a gas burner to warm the bottom of each petal and attach it to the base of the flower, overlapping them slightly and arranging them in rings.

9. To form the leaves, pull small pieces of sugar

from the ridge, as with the petals, making a point at the tip as you pull. Snap each piece off the larger piece and press it into a leaf impression mold, or make vein impressions using the tip of a hot paring knife. Let harden and set aside.

To form the leaves, pull small pieces of sugar from the ridge, as with the petals, making a point at the tip as you pull. Snap each piece off the larger piece and press it into a leaf impression mold. Let harden and set aside.

PULLED SUGAR RIBBONS

Properly made sugar ribbons should be very thin, with some lighter and darker colors for contrast. Start with newly cooked sugar that you are keeping warm in the cake pan, or with reheated cooked sugar. All of the colors that you will be using should be at the same temperature. If they aren't, they will pull differently and will result in an irregular ribbon.

Leftover pieces of ribbons can be placed in a nonstick cake pan and melted slowly in the oven at low temperature. When the sugar has cooled, pop it out of the cake pan and you have a colored sugar plate on which to display candy or cookies.

1. Cut pieces of colored pulled sugar 3 inches long and 1½ inches wide. Arrange the warm, soft pieces side by side, pressing them against each other and making sure the right colors are in the right places.

2. As you press the colors against each other, rub the top of the combined cooked sugar block with a dry, clean kitchen towel to make it shine and to make certain that all the colors are sticking together properly. Use both hands to pull the sugar to about an 8-inch length.

3. With sharp scissors, cut the piece into two 4-inch lengths. Place the lengths side by side, making sure that the colors are arranged the way you want them. Repeat this pulling and recombining several times as desired. The more times you recombine, the wider the ribbon will be. For a very thin ribbon, fold just once. For a very wide one, fold up to four times.

4. Holding one end of the ribbon down on the work surface with one hand, pull

(continued)

on the other end with the other hand. Stretch the ribbon as long as you can. If you have someone else in the kitchen, ask for help—with two people pulling, the ribbon can be stretched that much longer. Pull the ribbon to as long a length as you can.

5. Cut the pulled ribbon away from the thicker mass. Place the ribbon on a clean, dry table. Pull the thicker mass into another long ribbon, cut the end, and repeat until you can't pull any more ribbon from the mass.

6. Warm the tip of a small, heavy knife with a gas torch or on a gas burner. With the heated knife, cut the ribbons into pieces approximately 5 inches long, wiping the knife with a damp kitchen towel between cuts. Reheat the pieces on top of the Silpat pad under the heat lamp or in the oven. When the pieces are just soft enough to bend, shape them into bow loops, pressing the ends together. Reheat the ends of the loops with the torch or over the gas flame, and push the heated ends together to make the two sides of the bow. Use as many loops as you want to make whatever size bow you want. Heat one end of a 6-inch piece of ribbon and press it into the middle of the back of the bow, to resemble the ribbon that hangs down. Repeat with another 6-inch piece for the second ribbon.

PULLED SUGAR BASKETS

When designing desserts at the White House, beautiful presentation was always part of my plan. Of course they had to taste great, but because many of my desserts were to be presented on a very public stage, they had to look incredible too. Arranging homemade sorbets, ice creams, chocolate candies, or cookies in a pulled sugar basket always succeeded in amazing my audience.

Because I have had more experience than most chefs with creating these beautiful containers, I've discovered a few tricks and come up with some new ways to make them as pretty, and with as little fuss, as possible.

Most pastry chefs use a wooden board fitted with removable metal pegs, weaving the pulled sugar around the pegs and then removing the pegs and replacing them with pieces of pulled sugar. There is nothing wrong with relying on this equipment, but you wind up making the same basket every time.

I have developed a method of free-form weaving that allows me to make any shape basket I like. I have woven hearts, octagons, teardrops, figure-eights, and triangles. The instructions here are for an oval basket, but once you have woven this basic shape, you'll be able to vary it. Occasionally I use colored sugar, but I think that white or golden baskets are the most attractive containers for a wide variety of little goodies.

The basket can be woven in stages, at your convenience. Just stop when you have to and then rewarm the sugar to begin again.

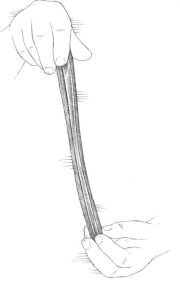

Keep pulling slowly with two hands, stretching the sugar evenly until it is the circumference of your middle finger. Fold in half, pull to the same length, and fold again.

1. Prepare the cooked sugar as described on page 482, but pour only 80 percent of the cooked sugar onto the oiled marble slab to be cooled and pulled. Keep the remaining 20 percent in the pot. After pulling the sugar, place it on a Silpat pad under a heat lamp, and cut off a piece about the size of two eggs.

2. Working under another heat lamp, form the piece into a ball. Start pulling both ends of the ball into a dowel shape. Keep pulling slowly with both hands, stretching the sugar evenly until it is the circumference of your middle finger. Fold it in half, pull it to the same length, and fold again. Pull once more so the sugar is again about the circumference of your finger. The piece should be about 18 inches long.

3. Twist the piece along its length to form a rope. Cut both ends at an angle, using the natural contour of the rope so that when you connect them they will match.

4. While the sugar is still pliable, arrange the rope in an oval shape on a piece of foil, connecting the ends and lightly pushing them together. Let it cool on a piece of aluminum foil. This rope will form the edge of the basket base.

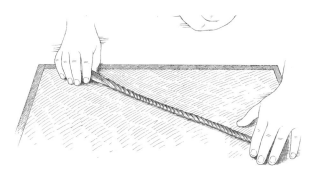

Twist the piece to form a rope.

5. Cut off another piece of the warm cooked sugar and pull it until it is the thickness of a pencil. Cut this piece into 4-inch lengths (or however tall you want the

(continued)

While the sugar is still pliable, arrange the rope in an oval shape on a piece of foil, connecting the ends and lightly pushing them together. This rope will form the edge of the basket base.

Cut off another piece of the warm cooked sugar and pull it until it is the thickness of a pencil. Cut this piece into 4-inch lengths.

When the sugar has become fluid again, pour enough into the base of the basket so that it reaches about three-fourths of the way up to the top of the base rope.

basket to be). Continue to pull and cut 4-inch lengths until you have enough to arrange them every ½ inch around the base of your basket. You will need an uneven number of these pegs. Set them on another piece of foil to cool.

6. When the base of the basket and all the pegs have cooled, place the pot with the reserved sugar in a 350-degree oven. When the sugar has become fluid again, pour enough into the base of the basket to reach about three-fourths of the way up to the top of the base rope.

7. Let the basket bottom cool for 3 to 5 minutes. Before it has set, push the pegs into it, on the inside edge of the rope, at ½-inch intervals all around, making sure that you use an uneven number of pegs. The pegs will not stay in place immediately—you will have to keep pushing them into place and holding them where you want them until the basket base has set. The sugar will harden faster if you slide the piece of foil every minute or two to a cool spot on your work surface. If you happen to break a peg, just reheat the ends with a torch and push the broken pieces together.

8. Once the base is firm and cool and the pegs are properly positioned, begin to weave the basket: Reheat the remaining pulled sugar in a nonstick cake pan in a 325-degree oven until soft and pliable. Cut off an egg-size piece of sugar. Working under a heat lamp, pull on one end of the egg to create a ⅛-inch-thick string. Attach the end of the string to the base of the basket, pressing it into the base with your thumb, behind one of the pegs.

9. Pull gently on the ball so that it releases a long, even string. Holding the egg in your right hand

(assuming you're right-handed), use your left hand to guide the sugar string in and out of the pegs, around and around. Keep pulling on the ball very slowly and weaving the string until you can no longer do so easily. Cut the string, making sure that the cut end will be positioned inside one of the pegs. Repeat with another piece of sugar, weaving until you no longer can, and cutting off the string so that the end is concealed behind a peg. Repeat until you have woven sugar string all the way to the top of the pegs. Let the sugar set completely, 5 to 10 minutes.

10. To even out the top of the basket, warm a baking sheet over a burner until it is very hot. Turn the basket upside down and rub the top edge of the basket back and forth on the cookie sheet until it is smooth and even, 5 to 8 seconds.

11. Make another oval rope slightly larger than the one around the basket base, as described in Steps 1 through 4. While it is still pliable, attach the rope to the top edge of the basket with some warm sugar.

12. To make a handle, cut and bend a piece of a white metal coat hanger into the shape you'd like. Cut off another piece of sugar about the size of an egg, and pull it into a small rope. Press one end of the rope into the end of the wire and wind it around the wire as tightly and evenly as possible. Let the handle set on a piece of foil. Attach the cooled handle to the basket with small balls of warm sugar. Decorate with ribbons, roses, and leaves as desired.

Let the basket bottom cool for 3 to 5 minutes. Before it has set, push the pegs into it, on the inside edge of the rope, at ½-inch intervals all around, making sure that you use an uneven number of pegs.

Holding the egg in your right hand, use your left hand to guide the sugar string in and out of the pegs, around and around.

To make a handle, cut and bend a piece of a white metal coat hanger into the shape you'd like. Cut off another piece of sugar about the size of an egg, and pull it into a small rounded rope. Press one end of the rope into the end of the wire and wind it around the wire as tightly and evenly as possible.

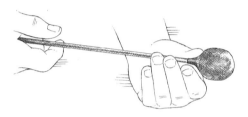

Pinch the cut ends together, shaping the sugar piece into a smooth round ball. At the point where you have pinched the sugar together, make an indentation about 1 inch deep.

Insert the warmed end of the metal tube about ½ inch into the indentation, so that there is about ½ inch of air space between the end of the tube and the sugar. Pinch the sugar together around the tube to enclose the tip.

Slowly begin to blow into the tube. As the sugar expands, shape it with your hand.

BLOWN SUGAR

Cooked sugar can be blown, just like molten glass, to create balls, fruit, birds, swans, and many other shapes. There are pumps you can purchase to blow sugar, but they are hard to find, expensive, and don't work particularly well. I have found that simply blowing air through a metal tube about the size of a drinking straw produces the best results. Searching for just the right kind of tubing for blowing sugar, I experimented with an automobile brake line, which I purchased for pennies at an auto supply shop. It worked perfectly and I've never used anything else since!

1. Color a ball of cooked and pulled sugar as desired, and place it on a Silpat pad under a heat lamp. Warm the tip of a metal tube measuring approximately 8 inches long and ⅜ inch in diameter over a gas burner or with a small gas torch. (It doesn't have to be white-hot, just very warm.)

2. To blow an apple shape, for example, cut off a piece of sugar about the size of a fig. Pinch the cut ends together, shaping the sugar piece into a smooth round.

3. At the point where you have pinched the sugar together, make an indentation about 1 inch deep into the ball. Insert the warmed end of the metal tube about ½ inch into the indentation, so there is about ½ inch of air space between the end of the tube and the sugar. Pinch the sugar together around the tube to enclose the tip.

4. Slowly begin to blow into the tube. As the sugar expands, shape it with your hand. Stop blowing, move the sugar under a heat lamp to warm it, and then shape it some more if necessary. If

some areas are getting too thin, hold those spots in the palm of your hand so they don't expand any further as you continue to blow.

5. When you have blown the sugar to the desired size and shape, it should have the texture of fine glass. Gradually push the sugar off the tube, and pinch it at the opening to seal it. Snip the blown piece away from the excess sugar with scissors. Working under a heat lamp, warm the snipped end and pull it to make a stem. Holding the blown sugar piece in your hand, cool it off in front of a fan until it has hardened completely, 5 to 10 minutes. (If you put it down when it is still warm, it might lose its shape.) Let the excess harden so that you can remove it from the tube, and discard it.

6. Once a piece of blown sugar has cooled completely, it can be painted with food coloring. Store it in an airtight container lined with calcium chloride and foil (see page 481), making sure that the sugar doesn't come into contact with the calcium chloride, for 6 months to 1 year, depending on the humidity.

THIRTEEN

Syrups, Sauces, Glazes, and Other Dessert Essentials

IN THIS CHAPTER I have gathered the recipes I use over and over in putting together or finishing the desserts in this book.

I sprinkle Cinnamon Sugar and Vanilla Sugar on everything from shortbread cookies to pie crusts to add flavor as well as sweetness.

I use candied nuts to give cake fillings some crunch. I also use them often in ice cream desserts for flavor and texture. A sprinkling of sugared nuts and a drizzle of chocolate sauce transforms a molded Maple Syrup Bavarian into a complete and impressive dessert.

Sugar syrups do everything from moistening cakes to sweetening sorbets to gluing together marzipan figures.

Nut fillings can be used with brioche and Danish dough to create a number of different pastries. Frangipane makes a rich tart filling.

Pastry Cream, Lemon Cream, and Lime Cream fill crêpes, flavor buttercream frostings, and make mousseline fillings. Lemon Cream folded with Sweetened Whipped Cream makes a perfect mousse.

Most sauces are very simple to make, and they add another dimension to desserts. Three different chocolate sauces see me through any occasion where I might need one. Vanilla Sauce, Light Lemon Sauce, and Praline Sauce moisten crêpes, cakes, and floating island desserts, to name just a few. There is hardly a dessert in this book that couldn't be paired with a fruit sauce to great advantage.

Glazes add moisture or shine to many baked goods and desserts. Rum Glaze is used on simple cookies like Palais Raisin to give them depth of flavor. It is brushed onto fruitcake to preserve the cake and spike it with flavor. Jelly glazes, like the Cranberry Jelly Glaze that covers Blancmange with Poached Pears (page 143), add beautiful sparkle.

Finally, nothing finishes a dessert as simply and richly as sweetened, perfectly whipped cream. It is almost a dessert all by itself.

THE RECIPES

CINNAMON SUGAR

VANILLA SUGAR

NOUGAT

CARAMELIZED ALMONDS

CARAMELIZED PECANS

CARAMELIZED PUMPKIN SEEDS

CANDIED CITRUS ZEST

LIGHT SYRUP

HEAVY SYRUP

ALMOND PASTE FILLING

HAZELNUT FILLING

FRANGIPANE

PASTRY CREAM

LEMON CREAM

LIME CREAM

LIGHT CHOCOLATE SAUCE

SEMISWEET CHOCOLATE GLAZE

GANACHE

CARAMEL SAUCE

VANILLA SAUCE

PRALINE SAUCE

LIGHT LEMON SAUCE

BOURBON SAUCE

RASPBERRY SAUCE

ORANGE SAUCE

STRAWBERRY SAUCE

CHUNKY STRAWBERRY SAUCE

MELBA SAUCE

VANILLA GLAZE

LEMON GLAZE

RUM GLAZE

RASPBERRY JELLY GLAZE

CRANBERRY JELLY GLAZE

SWEETENED WHIPPED CREAM

CINNAMON SUGAR

Makes 2 cups

2 cups sugar   2 tablespoons ground cinnamon

Combine the cinnamon and sugar in a bowl and mix thoroughly. Transfer to an airtight container and store at room temperature for up to 6 months.

VANILLA SUGAR

Makes 1 cup

1 cup sugar   used for another purpose), rinsed
1 whole fresh vanilla bean, or 3 split   and dried
   and seeded vanilla beans (seeds

Combine the sugar and the vanilla bean or beans in a blender and pulverize. Store in an airtight container at room temperature for up to 6 months.

NOUGAT

Makes 3 cups

1½ cups plus 2 tablespoons sugar   ½ vanilla bean, split lengthwise
                                      3 cups sliced almonds

1. Line a rimmed baking sheet with aluminum foil. Place the sugar in a heavy saucepan. Use a sharp paring knife to scrape the seeds from the vanilla bean into the pan. (Reserve the bean for another use.) Cook on medium-high heat, stirring constantly, until the sugar melts and becomes a uniformly amber color, 5 to 7 minutes.
2. Stir in the sliced almonds, and pour the Nougat onto the prepared baking sheet. Let it cool completely, and then crush it with a rolling pin. Crushed Nougat will keep in an airtight container at room temperature for up to 1 month.

CARAMELIZED ALMONDS

Makes about ¾ cup

¾ cup sliced almonds	½ vanilla bean, split lengthwise
½ cup confectioners' sugar	

1. Combine the almonds and confectioners' sugar in a heavy saucepan. With a sharp paring knife, scrape the seeds from the vanilla bean into the pot. (Reserve the bean for another use.) Cook over medium-high heat, stirring constantly, until the sugar is completely dissolved and light amber in color, 5 to 7 minutes.
2. Pour the coated nuts onto an ungreased sheet pan and allow to cool. Caramelized Almonds will keep in an airtight container at room temperature for up to 1 month.

CARAMELIZED PECANS

Makes about 1⅓ cups

1 cup pecan halves	½ vanilla bean, split lengthwise
½ cup confectioners' sugar	

1. Combine the pecan halves and confectioners' sugar in a heavy saucepan. With a sharp paring knife, scrape the seeds from the vanilla bean into the pan. Cook over medium-high heat, stirring constantly, until the sugar is completely dissolved and light amber in color, 5 to 7 minutes.
2. Pour the coated nuts onto an ungreased sheet pan and allow to cool completely. When they have hardened, chop them coarsely. Caramelized Pecans will keep in an airtight container at room temperature for up to 1 month.

CARAMELIZED PUMPKIN SEEDS

Makes about 1 cup

1 cup unsalted pumpkin seeds
½ cup confectioners' sugar

½ vanilla bean, split lengthwise

1. Combine the pumpkin seeds and confectioners' sugar in a heavy saucepan. With a sharp paring knife, scrape the seeds from the vanilla bean into the pan. Cook over medium-high heat, stirring constantly, until the sugar is completely dissolved and light amber in color, 5 to 7 minutes.
2. Pour the coated seeds onto an ungreased sheet pan and allow to cool. Caramelized Pumpkin Seeds will keep in an airtight container at room temperature for up to 1 month.

CANDIED CITRUS ZEST

Makes ¾ cup

4 or 5 oranges, lemons, or limes	1 tablespoon light corn syrup
1 cup water	Red, yellow, or green food coloring
¾ cup sugar	

1. Use a citrus zester to remove the zest from the fruit in narrow strips. (Reserve the fruit for another use.) Place the zest in a saucepan and add cold water to cover. Bring to a boil and boil for 1 minute.
2. Drain the zest, and rinse it under cold water to wash away the bitterness.
3. Combine the 1 cup water with the sugar and corn syrup in a small saucepan and bring to a boil. Add the zest and a few drops of food coloring: red for oranges, yellow for lemons, or green for limes.
4. Cook slowly over low heat until the mixture reaches the thread stage (220 to 225 degrees on a candy thermometer), 10 to 15 minutes. Remove the pan from the heat and allow the zest to cool in the syrup. Store in an airtight container in the refrigerator for up to 2 months. Lift the zest from the syrup before using.

LIGHT SYRUP

Makes 1 quart

1 quart water   2 cups sugar

Combine the water and sugar in a medium saucepan and bring to a boil. Remove from the heat and allow to cool to room temperature. Use immediately, or refrigerate in an airtight container for up to 2 weeks.

HEAVY SYRUP

Makes 2 cups

1 cup water   1 tablespoon corn syrup
1½ cups sugar

Combine the water, sugar, and corn syrup in a small saucepan and bring to a boil. Remove from the heat and allow to cool to room temperature. Use immediately, or refrigerate in an airtight container for up to 1 month.

ALMOND PASTE FILLING

Makes about 1 cup

1 cup almond paste (available in
    specialty stores and some super-
    markets; see headnote, page 322)

1 teaspoon ground cinnamon
1 teaspoon grated lemon zest
3 to 4 tablespoons water

Combine the almond paste, cinnamon, lemon zest, and 3 tablespoons water in
the bowl of an electric mixer fitted with the paddle attachment. Mix until
smooth. The mixture should be soft enough to spread onto dough without tearing the dough. If it is too stiff, add more water, 1 teaspoon at a time, until it
reaches the desired consistency.

HAZELNUT FILLING

Makes about 1¼ cups

1 cup almond paste
3 tablespoons unsweetened hazelnut
    paste (available in specialty stores
    and some supermarkets)

3 to 4 tablespoons water

Combine the almond paste, hazelnut paste, and 3 tablespoons water in the
bowl of an electric mixer fitted with the paddle attachment. Mix until smooth.
The mixture should be soft enough to spread onto dough without tearing the
dough. If it is too stiff, add more water, 1 teaspoon at a time, until it reaches
the desired consistency.

FRANGIPANE

Makes about 1 quart

1 cup (2 sticks) unsalted butter,
  softened
1 cup sugar
2 cups almond flour
  (see Note, page 272)
5 large eggs, at room temperature

½ tablespoon pure vanilla extract
1 teaspoon grated lemon zest
2 tablespoons dark rum
¼ cup plus ½ tablespoon all-purpose
  flour

Combine the butter, sugar, and almond flour in the bowl of an electric mixer and beat until smooth. Do not overbeat. Add the eggs, one at a time, scraping down the sides of the bowl after each addition. Stir in the vanilla, lemon zest, and rum. Stir in the all-purpose flour until just combined. Use immediately, or store in an airtight container in the refrigerator for up to 1 week or in the freezer for up to 2 months.

PASTRY CREAM

Makes 5 cups

Whole eggs are fine here, but if you have extra egg yolks sitting around, perhaps left over from making a meringue, you can use them instead.

¾ cup plus 2 tablespoons sugar
½ cup plus 2 tablespoons cornstarch
5 large eggs, or 8 large egg yolks
1 quart whole milk

1 tablespoon pure vanilla extract
Pinch salt
4 tablespoons unsalted butter, chilled
  (optional)

1. Whisk the sugar and cornstarch together in a medium bowl. Whisk in the eggs or egg yolks.
2. Bring the milk to a boil in a large saucepan. Slowly dribble ½ cup of the hot milk into the egg mixture, whisking constantly. Dribble another ½ cup of the milk into the egg mixture, again whisking constantly.
3. Whisk the egg mixture back into the milk and return the pan to the heat. Bring to a full boil, whisking constantly. Remove the pan from the heat and pour the mixture into a bowl. Stir in the vanilla, salt, and butter if desired. Allow to cool completely. Then cover with plastic wrap and refrigerate for up to 2 days. Push Pastry Cream through a fine-mesh strainer before using.

LEMON CREAM

Makes about 2 cups

5 large lemons
1½ cups sugar
4 large eggs

1 cup (2 sticks) unsalted butter, cut
   into cubes

1. Remove the zest from the lemons with a grater, and set it aside. Cut each lemon in half and squeeze the juice into a small bowl.
2. Combine the zest, juice, sugar, eggs, and butter in a heavy-bottomed saucepan, and bring to a boil over medium-high heat. Boil for 30 seconds, whisking constantly and making sure that the mixture is not sticking to the bottom of the pan.
3. Remove the pan from the heat and pour the mixture through a fine-mesh strainer into a nonreactive bowl. Cool to room temperature. Refrigerate Lemon Cream in an airtight container for up to 1 week, or freeze it for up to 2 months.

LIME CREAM

Makes about 2 cups

5 large, juicy limes
Juice of 1 lemon
1½ cups sugar
4 large eggs

1 cup (2 sticks) unsalted butter, cut
into cubes
Green food coloring (optional)

1. Remove the zest from the limes with a grater, and set it aside. Cut each lime in half and squeeze the juice into a small bowl.
2. Combine the zest, lime juice, lemon juice, sugar, eggs, and butter in a heavy-bottomed saucepan, and bring to a boil over medium-high heat. Boil for 30 seconds, whisking constantly and making sure that the mixture is not sticking to the bottom of the pan.
3. Remove the pan from the heat and pour the mixture through a fine-mesh strainer into a nonreactive bowl. Stir in a very small amount of green food coloring if you'd like your Lime Cream to be pale green. Cool to room temperature. Refrigerate Lime Cream in an airtight container for up to 1 week, or freeze it for up to 2 months.

LIGHT CHOCOLATE SAUCE

Makes 2 cups

8 ounces semisweet chocolate,
chopped, or semisweet chocolate
chips

1½ cups water
¼ cup sugar

Place the chocolate in a heatproof bowl. Bring the water and sugar to a boil in a small saucepan. Pour the boiling water mixture over the chocolate, and whisk until smooth. Use warm, or refrigerate for up to 1 month and rewarm on top of the stove or in the microwave before using.

SEMISWEET CHOCOLATE GLAZE

Makes about 2½ cups

One 12-ounce bag semisweet
chocolate chips

1 cup plus 6 tablespoons heavy cream

Place the chocolate in a heatproof bowl. Bring the cream to a near boil in a small saucepan. Pour the hot cream over the chocolate and whisk until smooth. Cool to room temperature. Refrigerate for up to 1 month and rewarm on top of the stove or in the microwave before using.

GANACHE

About 2 cups

12 ounces bittersweet or semisweet chocolate, chopped, or semisweet chocolate chips

1 cup heavy cream

1. Place the chocolate in a heatproof bowl. Bring the cream to a near boil in a small saucepan. Pour the hot cream over the chocolate and whisk until smooth. Cool to room temperature. Use immediately, or refrigerate for up to 2 weeks and then warm in a microwave until soft before using.
2. To whip Ganache, transfer the mixture to the bowl of an electric mixer fitted with the whisk attachment, and whip until light and fluffy. When done, it should resemble very light chocolate buttercream.

CARAMEL SAUCE

Makes 2 cups

1 cup plus 2 tablespoons sugar
1 vanilla bean, split lengthwise
1½ cups heavy cream

8 tablespoons (1 stick) unsalted butter, cut into cubes

1. Place the sugar in a heavy saucepan. Use a sharp paring knife to scrape the seeds from the vanilla bean into the pan. (Reserve the bean for another use.) Cook on medium-high heat, stirring constantly, until the sugar melts and becomes a uniformly amber color, 5 to 7 minutes.
2. While the sugar is cooking, bring the cream to a boil in a small saucepan. When the sugar is amber, carefully pour the hot cream into the sugar, about ½ cup at a time. Be careful, as the mixture will bubble up. Remove the pan from the heat and stir in the butter. Allow to cool until tepid and use immediately, or store the sauce in an airtight container and refrigerate it for up to 2 months. Bring the sauce to room temperature before using.

VANILLA SAUCE

Makes 3 cups

½ cup sugar

5 large egg yolks

2 cups whole milk

2 vanilla beans, split lengthwise

1. Whisk the sugar and egg yolks together in a medium bowl.
2. Combine the milk and vanilla beans in a heavy saucepan and bring to a boil.
3. Slowly dribble ¼ cup of the hot milk into the egg yolk mixture, whisking constantly. Dribble another ¼ cup of the milk into the egg yolk mixture, again whisking constantly.
4. Whisk the egg yolk mixture back into the milk and return the pan to the heat. Cook on low heat, stirring constantly with a wooden spoon or rubber spatula, until the mixture shows the first sign of coming to a boil. Quickly strain the sauce into a bowl, and allow it to cool to room temperature. Use immediately, or refrigerate in an airtight container for up to 3 days.

PRALINE SAUCE

Makes 3 cups

¼ cup sugar
5 large egg yolks
2 cups whole milk

½ cup praline paste (see headnote, page 459)

1. Whisk the sugar and egg yolks together in a medium bowl.
2. Bring the milk to a boil in a heavy saucepan.
3. Slowly dribble ¼ cup of the hot milk into the egg yolk mixture, whisking constantly. Dribble another ¼ cup of the milk into the egg yolk mixture, again whisking constantly.
4. Whisk the egg yolk mixture back into the hot milk and return the pan to the heat. Cook on low heat, stirring constantly with a wooden spoon or rubber spatula, until the mixture shows the first sign of coming to a boil. Quickly strain the sauce into a bowl, and whisk in the praline paste. Cool to room temperature. Use immediately, or refrigerate in an airtight container for up to 3 days.

LIGHT LEMON SAUCE

Makes 1½ cups

1 tablespoon cornstarch
½ cup sugar
1 cup boiling water

3 tablespoons fresh lemon juice
1 teaspoon grated lemon zest
2 tablespoons unsalted butter

Mix the cornstarch and sugar together in a small saucepan. Whisk in the boiling water. Place the pan on the stove and bring to a boil over high heat. Boil until thickened, 2 to 3 minutes. Stir in the lemon juice, lemon zest, and butter. Transfer the sauce to a bowl, and cool to room temperature. Keep covered at room temperature for up to 8 hours.

BOURBON SAUCE

Makes 1 ½ cups

1½ tablespoons cornstarch
½ cup sugar
1 cup boiling water
3 tablespoons fresh lemon juice

1 teaspoon grated lemon zest
2 tablespoons unsalted butter
¼ cup bourbon

Mix the cornstarch and sugar together in a small saucepan. Whisk in the boiling water. Place the pan on the stove and bring to a boil over high heat. Boil until thickened, 2 to 3 minutes. Stir in the lemon juice, lemon zest, and butter. Then stir in the bourbon. Transfer the sauce to a bowl and cool to room temperature. Keep covered at room temperature for up to 8 hours.

RASPBERRY SAUCE

Makes 2 ¼ cups

1½ pounds fresh raspberries, or two
   12-ounce bags frozen unsweetened
   raspberries, thawed

½ cup sugar

Combine the raspberries and sugar in a blender and blend until smooth. Push the mixture through a fine-mesh strainer into a bowl. Use immediately, refrigerate in an airtight container for 2 days, or freeze for up to 3 weeks.

ORANGE SAUCE

Makes 1 cup

½ cup strained apricot jam
2 tablespoons Grand Marnier
2 tablespoons water

1 navel orange, peeled, all pith
removed, flesh cut into small
cubes

Stir the jam, Grand Marnier, and water together in a medium bowl. Stir in the orange pieces and their juices. Use immediately, or refrigerate in an airtight container for up to 1 week.

STRAWBERRY SAUCE

Makes 3 cups

2 pints fresh strawberries, washed,
stemmed, and halved

½ cup sugar
1 tablespoon fresh lemon juice

Combine the strawberries, sugar, and lemon juice in a blender and blend until smooth. Use immediately, refrigerate in an airtight container for up to 3 days, or freeze for up to 2 weeks.

CHUNKY STRAWBERRY SAUCE

Makes 1½ cups

1 pint fresh strawberries, washed and
    stemmed
½ cup confectioners' sugar

1 tablespoon Cointreau or other
    orange-flavored liqueur
½ tablespoon fresh lemon juice

Combine the strawberries, confectioners' sugar, Cointreau, and lemon juice in a medium bowl and mash with a potato masher until some of the berries release their juices; there should still be many large pieces of berries. Use immediately, or refrigerate in an airtight container for up to 2 days. Do not freeze.

MELBA SAUCE

Makes 1½ cups

½ cup strained red currant preserves
½ cup Raspberry Sauce (page 516)

½ cup Strawberry Sauce (page 517)

Mix the red currant preserves, Raspberry Sauce, and Strawberry Sauce together in a medium bowl, and push the mixture through a fine-mesh strainer into another bowl. Use immediately, refrigerate in an airtight container for up to 2 weeks, or freeze for up to 2 months.

VANILLA GLAZE

Makes about ½ cup

1 cup confectioners' sugar
1 tablespoon water

1 tablespoon pure vanilla extract

Whisk the confectioners' sugar, water, and vanilla together in a small bowl until smooth. Use immediately, or cover with plastic wrap and refrigerate for up to 1 week.

LEMON GLAZE

Makes about ½ cup

1 cup confectioners' sugar
2 tablespoons fresh lemon juice

1 teaspoon grated lemon zest

Whisk the confectioners' sugar, lemon juice, and zest together in a small bowl until smooth. Use immediately, or cover with plastic wrap and refrigerate for up to 1 week.

RUM GLAZE

Makes about ½ cup

1 cup confectioners' sugar
1 tablespoon water

1 tablespoon rum

Whisk the confectioners' sugar, water, and rum together in a small bowl until smooth. Use immediately, or cover with plastic wrap and refrigerate for up to 1 week.

RASPBERRY JELLY GLAZE

Makes 2 cups

½ cup cold water
½ envelope unflavored gelatin
(or 3 sheets; see page 119)

1½ cups Raspberry Sauce (page 516),
or room temperature

Pour 1 inch of water into a small saucepan and bring to a bare simmer. Place the cold water in a small heatproof bowl and sprinkle the gelatin on top. Let stand to dissolve. Place the bowl on top of the simmering water and heat, whisking constantly, just until the gelatin melts, 30 seconds to 1 minute. Whisk the melted gelatin into the Raspberry Sauce. Let thicken slightly, 30 minutes, before using as a glaze. Don't let it become too thick to pour. Raspberry Jelly will keep in an airtight container in the refrigerator for 2 to 3 days. Rewarm it in a double boiler until it is just pourable (but not hot) before using.

CRANBERRY JELLY GLAZE

Makes 2 cups

½ cup water
¾ envelope unflavored gelatin
   (or 4 sheets; see page 119)

1½ cups Cranberry Puree (page 43)

1. Place the cold water in a small bowl and sprinkle the gelatin on top. Let stand to dissolve.
2. Bring the Cranberry Puree to a boil in a small saucepan. Whisk in the dissolved gelatin. Let cool to room temperature, and use immediately.

SWEETENED WHIPPED CREAM

Makes enough for 8 topping portions

1 cup heavy cream, chilled
1½ tablespoons confectioners' sugar

½ teaspoon pure vanilla extract

Place the cream in the bowl of an electric mixer fitted with the whisk attachment, and whip on high speed until soft peaks appear. Add the confectioners' sugar and vanilla, and continue to whip until the cream just holds stiff peaks. Do not overwhip. Use immediately, or cover with plastic wrap and refrigerate for up to 2 hours. Hand-whip refrigerated whipped cream for a few seconds before using.

Mail-Order Resources

The Baker's Catalogue
P.O. Box 876
Norwich, VT 05055-0876
800-827-6836
kingarthurflour.com

Bakeware; baking ingredients, including specialty and nut flours, chestnut puree, chestnut spread, chocolate, dried fruit, and nuts; cake- and cookie-decorating supplies; parchment paper; sheet gelatin; sanding sugar; paste food coloring; glazed red cherries; candied lemon and orange peel

Bridge Kitchenware Corporation
214 East 52nd Street
New York, NY 10022
800-274-3435; 212-838-6746
bridgekitchenware.com

Enormous supply of bakeware and pastry items, including rolling pins, cooling racks, pastry bags, cookie cutters, Silpat pads, chocolate molds

Easy Leaf Products
6001 Santa Monica Boulevard
Los Angeles, CA 90038
800-569-5323; 213-469-0856
easyleaf.com

Edible gold foil

New York Cake and Baking Distributors
56 West 22nd Street
New York, NY 10010
800-94-CAKE-9; 212-675-CAKE
nycake.com

Bakeware and candy-making supplies; including dipping forks and marzipan sculpting tools; chocolate; glucose; nut pastes; food coloring; candied violets; sheet gelatin; icing fondant; cocoa butter; coloring oil for chocolate

J.B. Prince Company
36 East 31st Street, 11th Floor
New York, NY 10016
212-683-3553
jbprince.com

Professional-grade bakeware and pastry supplies for professionals and home cooks

Sur la Table
Pike Place Farmers Market
84 Pine Street
Seattle, WA 98101
800-243-0852
surlatable.com

High-end bakeware

Sweet Celebrations
7009 Washington Avenue South
Edina, MN 55439
800-328-6722
sweetc.com

Bakeware and cake-decorating equipment; cardboard cake rounds and cake boxes

Williams-Sonoma
100 North Point Street
San Francisco, CA 94133
800-541-2233
williams-sonoma.com

Reliable source for high-quality bakeware

Wilton Industries
2240 West 75th Street
Woodridge, IL 60517-0750
800-994-5866
wilton.com

Cake-decorating supplies, including pastry bags and tips; candy-making supplies, including dipping forks; paste food coloring

METRIC EQUIVALENCIES

LIQUID EQUIVALENCIES

CUSTOMARY	METRIC
¼ teaspoon	1.25 milliliters
½ teaspoon	2.5 milliliters
1 teaspoon	5 milliliters
1 tablespoon	15 milliliters
1 fluid ounce	30 milliliters
¼ cup	60 milliliters
⅓ cup	80 milliliters
½ cup	120 milliliters
1 cup	240 milliliters
1 pint (2 cups)	480 milliliters
1 quart (4 cups)	960 milliliters (.96 liter)
1 gallon (4 quarts)	3.84 liters

DRY MEASURE EQUIVALENCIES

CUSTOMARY	METRIC
1 ounce (by weight)	28 grams
¼ pound (4 ounces)	114 grams
1 pound (16 ounces)	454 grams
2.2 pounds	1 kilogram (1,000 grams)

OVEN-TEMPERATURE EQUIVALENCIES

DESCRIPTION	°FAHRENHEIT	°CELSIUS
Cool	200	90
Very slow	250	120
Slow	300–325	150–160
Moderately slow	325–350	160–180
Moderate	350–375	180–190
Moderately hot	375–400	190–200
Hot	400–450	200–230
Very hot	450–500	230–260

INDEX